D0056341

The
Prosecution
Responds

The
Prosecution
Responds

An O.J. Simpson Trial Prosecutor
Reveals What Really Happened

Hank M. Goldberg

A Birch Lane Press Book
Published by Carol Publishing Group

A Birch Lane Press Book
Published by Carol Publishing Group
Birch Lane Press is a registered trademark of Carol Communications, Inc.
Editorial, sales and distribution, and rights and permissions inquiries should be addressed to Carol Publishing Group, 120 Enterprise Avenue, Secaucus, N.J. 07094

In Canada: Canadian Manda Group, One Atlantic Avenue, Suite 105, Toronto, Ontario M6K 3E7

Carol Publishing Group books may be purchased in bulk at special discounts for sales promotion, fund-raising, or educational purposes. Special editions can be created to specifications. For details, contact Special Sales Department, Carol Publishing Group, 120 Enterprise Avenue, Secaucus, N.J. 07094.

Manufactured in the United States of America
10 9 8 7 6 5 4 3 2 1

Library of Congress Cataloging-in-Publication Data

Goldberg, Hank M.
　The prosecution responds : an O. J. Simpson trial prosecutor reveals what really happened / Hank M. Goldberg.
　　p.　　cm.
　ISBN 1-55972-361-0 (hc)
　1. Simpson, O. J., 1947–　　—Trials, litigation, etc.　2. Trials (Murder)—California—Los Angeles.　3. Prosecution—California—Los Angeles.　I. Title.
KF224.S485G65　1996
345.73′02523′0979494—dc20
[347.30525230979494]　　　　　　　　　　　　　　　　　96-31299
　　　　　　　　　　　　　　　　　　　　　　　　　　　　　CIP

"This is a search for the truth." Lawyers on both sides used this phrase repeatedly throughout the Simpson trial. Yet there is no agreement about what the truth was in this case: whether Simpson was really guilty, what the evidence really showed, why the jury acquitted him, and what social implications the case raises.

I suppose it would be overly ambitious to dedicate this book to finding the truth of this case. Therefore, I dedicate it to beginning a meaningful dialogue about this trial and what it really means.

Contents

Author to Reader

The case of *The People of the State of California v. Orenthal James Simpson* was a bizarre, almost dreamlike occurrence, of the kind that seems to have a particular affinity for Los Angeles. It also constituted perhaps one of the most extraordinary events in legal history.

Since the time I was assigned to the case as a member of the prosecution team, hundreds of people have approached me and written to me with questions. The case obviously struck an emotional chord across the nation and throughout the world. There is a hunger for knowledge and understanding of what happened and why. The extensive media coverage seems not to have illuminated but rather to have clouded the real issues and the actual evidence presented. For a long time to come people will want to know what really happened.

During the trial, and in its aftermath, a virtual cottage industry evolved of "expert analysts" who attempted to explain the trial and critique the prosecution. Virtually all of the major criticisms were regurgitated recently in Vincent Bugliosi's book entitled *Outrage*. As the title implies, like other works, it is full of vitriol and accusations and is lacking a dispassionate, thoughtful discussion of the case.

Criticism of the prosecution includes the argument that we relied too much on evidence that O. J. Simpson had abused his wife, Nicole Brown Simpson, in order to establish a motive for murder. Bugliosi takes the opposite view: the prosecution should have presented even *more* domestic-violence evidence. Some have argued that the prosecution erred by calling Detective Mark Fuhrman and not sufficiently distancing itself from him. Again, Bugliosi disagrees, arguing that the prosecution should have *embraced* Fuhrman and should have stood behind him.

By comprehensively revealing the behind-the-scenes strategy and tactics of the prosecution, I will show that in virtually every major tactical decision, the prosecution chose the best available option. In each instance, I will provide enough information regarding the key decisions to allow readers to form their own opinions on such issues. But more important, readers will see how such decisions fit within the overall case strategy and made sense in the context of the trial as a whole. The failure to do this is the principal weakness of the outside "analyses" from commentators such as Vincent Bugliosi.

For example, Bugliosi confesses that he did not watch the entire trial because he found it boring. While writing his book, Bugliosi called me several times to ask specific questions about what happened during the trial. When I asked him why he did not consult the trial transcript, he replied that it was too expensive to obtain a copy. He admitted that he did not read most of the transcript: he just reviewed specific portions such as the closing arguments.

Even though I participated in the trial, it was necessary for me to reread the transcript in order to write this book. Failure to do so would undoubtedly have resulted in significant distortions, misrecollections, and failures of analysis. There are a number of examples of such mistakes in Vince's book. For instance, he accuses DNA prosecutor Woody Clarke of failing to elicit that a laboratory that did DNA testing for the prosecution had failed certain proficiency tests years earlier. Not so. Woody Clarke addressed this issue in detail during his direct examination. Had Vince reviewed the trial transcript, he would have avoided making this and other unfounded criticisms.

Similarly, Vince argues that the prosecution should have introduced O. J. Simpson's statement to the police in which he proclaimed his innocence. On its face, this is an astounding recommendation. The jury would have been allowed to hear the defendant's self-serving denial during the tape-recorded police interview, and the prosecution would have been unable to cross-examine Simpson. Vince's position is even more astounding when considered in the context of all of the evidence the prosecution presented against Simpson. Why does Vince argue that the prosecution should have used Simpson's statement? Because in the statement Simpson admitted to bleeding in his Bronco and at his estate on the night of the murders—an incriminating admission. Vince, unlike millions of Americans, did not watch much of the trial. Because he also failed to thoroughly review the trial transcript, he apparently was ignorant of the fact that the defense was not contesting that Simpson bled in the Bronco and at his home the night of the murders. Why would we introduce a self-serving statement

simply to prove something that was not in dispute? An expert commentator who comprehensively reviewed the evidence and relative
positions of both the defense and prosecution would not have made
such an egregious mistake.

Finally, many of the commentators, including Bugliosi, fail to
consider the sociopolitical forces that were at work in the Simpson
case. In this book we will see that the jury in this case was predisposed to accept the idea that Simpson was an African-American
victim of the white establishment. Vince's failure to place the case
into its overall social framework results in serious faults in his analysis.

For example, Vince actually makes an argument so astounding
that I must quote it. He suggests that the prosecution should have
called former football player Jim Brown to testify that " 'there was
no evidence of O. J. in the black community.' " Further, according
to Vince, Brown could have established that " 'O. J. is the modern
representation of the house Negro,' who . . . dressed well and
lived much better than the plantation workers."

Forget, for a moment, that such an irrelevant, outrageous, and
offensive attack would have been inadmissible. Vince's strategy
would have played right into the hands of those willing to believe the
prosecution and police were out to get a successful African American who had "made it" as a celebrity in white society. It is impossible
to conceive of anything that would have alienated this jury, or any
jury, faster than Vince's proposed strategy. In a case that presents
conclusive physical evidence proving guilt, you don't distract, anger,
and alienate the jury by calling the defendant a "house Negro."

Yet buried within his diatribe against the prosecution, Bugliosi
concedes that the not guilty verdict is traceable to dynamics other
than the merits of the case presented against Simpson. Quoting
himself in an earlier interview, Vince says that external social factors
that influenced the verdict "could be things like 'race, celebrity, and
bogus allegations of police misconduct.' " Yet nowhere does he actually analyze the effects of such social and political forces on the
verdict. These are only a few of the many examples of errors of fact
and analysis that Vince makes in *Outrage*.

No book can entirely document a trial that took over nine
months to present. Nor can one thoroughly present all aspects of a
trial that produced over forty thousand pages of transcript and was
reported on in thousands of hours of television coverage and mil-

lions of pages of print media accounts. However, my book presents in-depth coverage, from inside the prosecution, of the five key aspects of the case: the domestic-violence evidence, Mark Fuhrman, the scientific and physical evidence, defense expert Henry Lee, and the closing arguments. I was involved in all of these aspects.

The Prosecution Responds is not intended to be merely an overview of the Simpson trial. Rather, it *explains* the trial by quoting portions of the trial transcript itself and through actual exhibits, rather than relying on the author's arguably biased recollection. It will take you inside the prosecutors' offices, where Marcia Clark, Chris Darden, Rock Harmon, Woody Clarke, Brian Kelberg, Bill Hodgman, other team members, and I made key strategy decisions.

There is a common theme in each chapter. The prosecution presented overwhelming evidence of guilt. Each issue the defense raised was convincingly shown to be spurious. Therefore, the answer to the question so many are asking—why was the verdict "not guilty"?—cannot be found in the evidence, the jury instructions, or the courtroom tactics of the prosecution or defense. We must look to factors external to the courtroom itself to understand the verdict.

Having shown that the explanation for the trial's outcome cannot be discovered within the four walls of the courtroom, the book will address in its conclusion some of the external factors that played a role in the case. The trial and its outcome have polarized the nation. The case raises larger issues about racism, sexism, the problem of domestic violence, the nature of celebrity status in our society, the proper role of community police departments, and the impact of media coverage on criminal trials. The Simpson trial is also likely to be an impetus for changes in our legal system.

I hope that this book will allow interested members of the public to truly understand the entirety of the case. The Simpson trial focused attention on some of the most challenging problems of our time. Issues arose that the criminal justice system and criminal trials were not intended to handle, let alone resolve. While I believe the outcome represents a travesty of justice, it is my sincerest hope that out of this tragedy can come some good. For too long we have tried to deal with painful problems in our society by ignoring them. We hoped that if we didn't look at them, perhaps they would go away. Confronting the truth is the first step toward change. I hope this book will, at least in some small measure, contribute to discovering the truths inherent in this case.

Acknowledgments

There are so many people I need to acknowledge regarding this book, it is hard to know where to end. But the beginning is easy. My father, Mel Goldberg, has been a professional television and motion picture writer for forty-six years. He must be at the top of my list. He tirelessly edited, cajoled, and coached me through this book. Without him, I would never have started, let alone finished. The loving support of my family, my mother, Orpha, and my siblings, David, Dru, and Luke, was another necessary ingredient.

Another group of very important people are all those who committed a year or more of their lives to seeking justice for the Goldmans and Browns. I was honored to work alongside these exceptionally talented people. Of course, they include Marcia, Chris, and Bill as well as Natalie Agajanian, Kathy Behfarin, Lydia Bodin, Margie Budden, Melissa Decker, Susan Dozier, Mathew Gibbs, Dana Escobar, Patti Jo Fairbanks, Lisa Fox, Gil Garcetti, Scott Gordon, Brian Kelberg, Cheri Lewis, Ken Lynch, Darrell Mavis, Tracy Miller, Leticia Minjares, Kathy Ozawa, Michael Price, Tom Ratanavaraha, Steve Oppler, Michael Runyon, David Wooden, and Alan Yochelson. Our investigators were: Wil Abram, Mike Armstrong, Ken Godinez, George Mueller, Gary Schram, Mike Stevens, and Dana Thompson.

Of course, the Brown and the Goldman families were a source of strength and support throughout the trial.

I also appreciated working with our outstanding investigating officers, Tom Lange and Phillip Vannatter.

I specially have to thank those who taught me almost everything I know about forensic science. Prosecutor Lisa Kahn helped bring me up to speed after I joined the prosecution team and was a continual source of support. Woody Clarke's expertise and consistent good humor made working with him a pleasure. Rock Harmon was another tremendous resource in understanding the forensic portion of the case.

Bill Bodziak, of the FBI laboratory, is one of the best expert witnesses with whom I have ever worked. Douglas Deedrick, of the FBI lab, and Gary Sims, of the Department of Justice lab, are also world-class experts and deserve recognition. Greg Matheson and Collin Yamauchi of the LAPD crime lab were both exceptionally generous with their time in teaching me about the science of serology. Notwithstanding the brutally unfair attack Dennis Fung underwent, he always came up smiling and ready to move forward. And I can't forget Andrea Mazzola, "Rookie of the Year." Working together with these people was one of the high points of my career.

Two members of the prosecution team deserve special mention. Diana Martinez, the junior lawyer assigned to me, worked side by side with me throughout the trial and helped get me through one of the most difficult trial experiences of my career. Jonathan Fairtlough, also a talented new prosecutor, did exceptional work coordinating our graphics and computer support. He and Diana were always there, sometimes at 6 A.M., to go over the exhibits I needed for the coming court day. I will never forget their extraordinary efforts.

The people at Decision Quest, who donated their services in providing the graphics used during the trial, did exceptional work during a very stressful and hectic trial. Also, the people at Cognitech donated their services and time in performing photographic enhancements.

I need to thank all my friends and colleagues from the Santa Monica Branch Office who constantly called, took me out to lunch and dinner, and sometimes just plain nagged to make sure I didn't lose any more weight during the trial: Lori Aiu, Randy Baron, Steve Barshop, Monica Blodget, Beverly Campbell, Mike Carroll, Lydia Delgadillo, Yvonne Dodd, Helen Gordon, Mary Hanlon, Christine Johnston, Farrel Lebenzon, Darren Levine, Elizabeth Lippitt, John Lynch, Katherine Mader, Danette Meyers, Lael Rubin, Jeff Semow, Stephanie Sparagna, Phil Stirling, Richard Stone, and Wendy Widlus.

Finally, I would like to thank my agent, Mike Hamilburg, and my editor, Hillel Black, of Carol Publishing, for patiently guiding me through my first writing project of this kind. I also appreciated Frank Lavena's sharp and concise editing.

1

My Landscaping Project Would Have to Wait

I WAS COMING FROM the hardware store where I had purchased hinges to repair the windows on my house. As I drove my 1985 Toyota Corolla north on Bundy Drive, I couldn't help but notice the day. Had I turned on the radio, undoubtedly I would have heard someone announce, "It's a beautiful day in sunny southern California." It was the kind of day you see on L.A. postcards, the ones that make residents wonder, Where is that place? On such a day, I just couldn't help but marvel at the much-touted, imported palm trees, normally inapparent to those of us born and raised here. When my eyes dropped back to ground level, a word popped into my mind. Murder.

On that day, June 13, when I passed what I later learned was Nicole Brown's condominium, there were several police cars parked outside. I saw homicide detective Brian Carr, one of my friends, getting out of an unmarked car. Obviously, someone had been murdered. I thought the case would probably be tried in the Santa Monica courthouse, where I worked as a deputy district attorney. I wondered whether I would be assigned to it.

I had been a deputy district attorney for the county of Los Angeles for nine years and had developed a reputation as an experienced prosecutor. I was known in the office as a legal strategist and researcher. I had prosecuted a number of homicide cases, including several that attracted significant media attention.

1

At the time, I was involved in my own major case. Together with another prosecutor, Katherine Mader, I was preparing a case against a Los Angeles city police officer, Douglas Iversen. Shortly after the L.A. riots, Iversen, a white officer, had shot and killed John Daniels, an African-American tow-truck driver. Prior to the media frenzy that accompanied the Simpson case, the Iversen case was extensively covered.

Later that evening, I heard on the news that one victim was O. J. Simpson's ex-wife. The other victim was a young man named Ron Goldman. On the afternoon of the thirteenth, I learned that Simpson had returned from a trip to Chicago and given a statement to police downtown. It seemed as if Simpson was a key suspect. Although I knew who Simpson was, I did not regard him as a major celebrity. To me, Simpson was a former football player and grade-B movie actor. I assumed that the case wouldn't get the media attention that the child-molestation investigation involving Michael Jackson had generated. At the same time, it was apparent that the media was devoting more than a normal amount of space and time to the story.

This meant the Special Trials Unit of the district attorney's office, located downtown, would handle the case. I would have nothing to do with it. So much the better. I had just purchased a "fixer-upper," as they are known in the real estate trade. Built in 1929, the house needed extensive repairs. Between that and the Iversen case, my plate was full.

On the afternoon of June 17, 1994, at around 2 P.M., five days after Nicole and Ron were murdered, I poked my head into one of the Santa Monica D.A.'s offices. A few of my coworkers were looking at the Simpson coverage on TV. By now, blood testing of drops left at the crime scene had linked Simpson to the murders. I heard the news that Simpson had escaped and his whereabouts were unknown. He had been at the home of a friend, Robert Kardashian, in Encino, a suburb of Los Angeles. Simpson had earlier been informed that a warrant had been issued for his arrest. His attorney, Robert Shapiro, had told the police that Simpson would turn himself in at police headquarters.

But Simpson had missed two different deadlines set for his surrender, the first at 11:00 A.M. A police car had been dispatched to the Encino location. According to Shapiro, when the two officers arrived, they discovered that Simpson and his friend, Al Cowlings, had disappeared from the home without being detected.

Later that afternoon, as Simpson's "suicide" note was read, one of the senior lawyers opined: "I think the defense set this up. I think they did this to gain sympathy for him." Some other prosecutors voiced agreement.

That was unlikely, I thought. At the time, I felt that Simpson's fleeing would help the prosecution. Flight from justice would constitute evidence of Simpson's guilty conscience and help prove culpability. It seemed as if in a few short moments everyone had gone from thinking he was innocent to assuming he must be guilty. By about 6:30 P.M. we heard another report that a motorist had just informed the police that he had spotted the white Bronco—the suspected get-away vehicle the police were looking for. The infamous Bronco chase had begun.

That evening, at around 7:30 P.M., I was at my parents' condo in West Los Angeles watching the coverage of the chase on television. I was on the phone when the police and news helicopters following the chase flew over my parents' condo. I was talking to the man who was installing my central air-conditioning.

As I spoke to the air-conditioning man, I witnessed a truly shocking incident. By now the so-called Bronco chase was nearing its end. Among the thousands who dotted the freeways, most of whom were white, and watched in homes, bars, and other public places, sympathy was with Simpson. Many shouted, "Go, O.J., go!" Others, many of whom were friends of Simpson's, reaffirmed their faith in his innocence and begged him on radio and television not to commit suicide.

I was amazed. Less than two hours earlier it seemed as though everyone assumed he was guilty. Now there was an outpouring of public sympathy for a man who stood accused of slaughtering two people.

The air-conditioning man had bad news. The contract did not cover the actual cost of hooking up the air-conditioning to the electrical system. That would cost an additional six hundred dollars at least! I was upset. But I was more disturbed by the spectacle on television.

The chase ended when the Bronco returned to Simpson's Rockingham estate in Brentwood shortly before 8 P.M. The Bronco was parked in the driveway and Simpson was sitting in it with a gun. I watched the LAPD SWAT team members standing outside the Bronco pleading with Simpson, trying to get him safely out of the car and into his home. They violated standard police-officer safety tactics. They were in the vehicle's "kill zone," presenting easy targets if Simpson suddenly turned the gun on them. These tactics would not have been used for any ordinary armed assailant suspected of a double murder.

When Simpson eventually turned himself over to the police at 8:45 P.M., many sighed with relief. Simpson was saved. Could we now convict him, jail him for life, or worse yet, impose the death penalty? This state of mind is epitomized in an interview by Mary Melton with a USC student quoted in the *L.A. Weekly*. Mike, a sophomore engineering student, said he still believed in "the Juice."

> The boys of Sig EP are not yet ready to forsake U.S.C.'s conquering hero. It's really weird. It's made me reexamine my morals. I was a really big fan of O.J.'s. And then I found out he did it. I mean, when I considered the evidence, it probably pointed out the fact that he did it. But I find myself pulling for him. I hope he gets off—which, when I think about it, is really bad.

The next day, I discussed the case, as everyone in Los Angeles probably did, with some friends and colleagues. Of course, other than from the sketchy media reports, we didn't know what evidence existed. But it didn't seem to matter. Based on what happened during the Bronco chase, we felt that unless they had this guy on videotape or the equivalent, we would never win this case. I thought, I'm glad I'm not prosecuting it.

Looking back on the events of that day, I find it remarkable that some commentators think the Bronco chase should have been introduced. The issue would have been whether Simpson was trying to commit suicide or flee from justice. I can't imagine how introducing this equivocal evidence, this emotional powder keg, could possibly have convinced this jury of Simpson's guilt when nothing else would.

After Simpson was taken into custody and jailed, pending the case's resolution, I was immersed in the Iversen trial. By early October 1994, it came to a close. Emotionally, it was by far the most difficult trial experience of my career. Prosecutions against police officers for on-duty shootings are notoriously difficult. Jurors simply do not want to convict a police officer for "making a mistake," even if that mistake amounts to a homicide.

Katherine Mader and I charged Iversen with second-degree murder. Iversen was investigating the tow-truck driver for an expired registration. The homicide occurred in South Central Los Angeles, a predominantly African-American neighborhood. When the tow-truck driver became angry and pulled out of a gas-station lot, Iversen shot him from behind. Iversen claimed that the tow-truck driver posed a threat to pedestrians who were in the tow truck's path. Numerous witnesses, most of whom were African Americans, vehemently disputed this assertion. Our hard-line stand against Iversen didn't win us any friends in the Los Angeles Police Department. Our only support came from the local leadership within the African-American community.

At this time, it would have been impossible for me to have predicted that only months later the Simpson prosecution, of which I would become a member, would be accused of conspiring with the police to frame Simpson.

When the Iversen jury returned in early October, all the jurors agreed that Iversen was guilty. However, they could not agree on what crime he had committed. Three thought he was guilty of second-degree murder. Nine thought he was guilty of involuntary manslaughter. As I recall, two African-American jurors and one white thought he was guilty of second-degree murder (fifteen years to life). Eight whites and one African American thought he was guilty of the lesser charge, involuntary manslaughter (four-year maximum). Hence, the case had to be retried. The district attorney, Gil Garcetti, and his senior administrators considered the hung jury a major victory. Given the difficulty of prosecuting police officers, few thought a jury would unanimously agree that Iversen had committed a homicide. But they did, and they differed only in degree.

Intellectually, I also realized that the outcome represented a moral victory. However, I felt bitterly disappointed. I was tired and looked forward to taking my first vacation in five years. Before doing so, I returned to my regular assignment at the Santa Monica courthouse.

I was shocked to see that the courthouse still looked like something out of *Blade Runner*. It had not recovered from the January 1994 Los Angeles earthquake. The acoustic ceilings were removed, and none of the interior walls extended to the roof. The carpets were gone, revealing the cement floors. The noise was unbelievable.

When I went into one of the courtrooms, I saw a colleague of mine, a former deputy district attorney who was now a successful defense attorney, Paul Takakjian. Katherine Mader and I had tried a murder case against Takakjian's client in 1992. His client was sentenced to death. Takakjian warmly greeted me. "Hank," he asked, "when are you going to be on the Simpson case?"

I asked him what he was talking about.

He replied, "You're the best legal researcher and writer in the D.A.'s office. It figures they'll put you on the case."

"I'm not going to be on that case," I said. "The jury selection has already started."

The following day, October 7, on the Friday of the week the Iversen jury returned, I visited a neighborhood nursery and ordered several large bushes so I could begin landscaping the front of my house. I find gardening very relaxing and thought I would finally have time to finish many of the projects I had begun at my new home. The phone rang at about the time I had dug a hole big enough to accommodate a large azalea.

It was my friend and colleague Katherine Mader. She said that Gil Garcetti, the district attorney, asked her if I would be available to work on Simpson until Iversen was retried. She told him I would. She told me she wanted to give me advance warning. But of what?

I returned to the azalea. Luckily, it was in the hole and planted by the time the phone rang again. It was Bill Hodgman. Bill is a top administrator in the district attorney's office and an outstanding trial lawyer who has prosecuted many high-profile cases, including that of Charles Keating. Several months earlier, Gil Garcetti had appointed Bill to coprosecute the case with Marcia Clark. At this point, it was anticipated that Bill and Marcia would be the only trial lawyers in court. In the coming months, regardless of the press of the case, Bill was consistently warm, compassionate, and never lost his cool. Most important, he was never too busy to ask me how I was feeling and how my house was coming along.

During this conversation, Bill told me, "The defense is trying to bury us with paper. We have been caught up responding to these motions and need to take a more aggressive posture. I've heard your skills as a legal researcher and writer are second to none."

I didn't respond. I didn't know Bill well at the time and thought he was simply buttering me up to get me to agree to work as a glorified law clerk. But before I could begin to feel sorry for myself, Bill added, "I also want someone behind the scenes to coordinate the continuing investigation and map out strategy, a kind of 'case manager.' " Bill explained that the only other senior lawyer we had on the case was Cheri Lewis, and she was totally bogged down handling the legal motions. "How would you feel about being on the case?"

I interpreted this district attorney lingo to mean "You're on the case. When can you report?"

"Bill," I said, "I just finished Iversen. I'm beat. I had planned to take a vacation. I have not had a vacation in almost six years."

I heard no reaction at the other end of the line. "Bill, I work for the D.A.'s office," I added, "and I will go where I'm assigned."

"That's my philosophy, too," Bill said.

"Incidentally," I asked, "what state of the case are you in?"

"Starting jury selection," Bill replied.

"What kind of a jury can we get?" I inquired hopefully.

"I don't know, Hank." He paused and repeated, "I don't know."

My landscaping project would have to wait. In my wildest nightmare, I didn't imagine that it would have to wait for over a year.

2

The War Room

ON THE MORNING OF October 10, 1994, unable to eat any breakfast, I drove toward downtown Los Angeles, to the sound of National Public Radio's news hour, interrupted by my stomach's occasional growls. I arrived early at the Criminal Courts Building (CCB), where I hurriedly purchased a coffee and doughnut before heading upstairs to the eighteenth-floor D.A.'s office.

The CCB is a 1970s-vintage large, square structure of approximately nineteen floors, surrounded by a concrete grid that makes the building look like a massive, square beehive. For the Simpson case, scores of cables connected the twelfth floor, where the media was housed, down to dozens of satellite trucks parked outside. From a distance, this arrangement gave the building the appearance of being connected to a thick umbilical cord. The Simpson trial was on the ninth floor.

No one seems to know the exact number of floors, for as the building's oral history has it, the contractor saved money by building fewer floors than the plans required. The contractor compensated by skipping several numbers when assigning them for each floor. The stairs that should have led to the "grand" entrance lobby were never completed. What was originally intended to be the front of the building is now the rear entrance and can be accessed through two "temporary" staircases that have been there forever.

The inside of each court, hallway, and lobby is dimly lit—a brilliant county cost-saving measure. One day, toward the end of the Simpson case, I was returning to my office after a grueling day in court. I opened the door to what I thought was the eighteenth-floor corridor. Suddenly, I realized I must be in the wrong place. That was strange. I confirmed that I was indeed on the eighteenth floor. So I opened the door again and entered the corridor. Soon I realized that I was in the right place but didn't recognize it at first because it looked so different. I said to the first person I saw, "What happened here? Did they paint?"

My colleague answered, "They just turned the lights up. They're having an open house here tomorrow for the Domestic Violence Unit."

After the open house, the lights were dimmed again, and things returned to normal.

The morning I first reported for the case, I went to Bill Hodgman's office. That morning was extremely hectic. The lawyers were in the middle of selecting the jury and litigating various motions. Bill said, "Hank, we're so glad to see you. I'm sorry I don't have time to introduce you to everyone."

"Don't worry about it. What do you need me to do?"

Bill handed me three motions the defense had filed about a week earlier."We need to respond to these."

I looked at the motions and saw that there were only a few days before the judge would consider them. Bill could probably see from the look on my face that I didn't think we had much time.

Bill said, "There's only one I'm concerned about." He pointed to a motion dealing with the leak of the 911 tape of Nicole reporting domestic violence. "Just take a look at the others and do the best you can."

"No problem," I responded. Bill was already halfway out the door, heading to court.

Bill said, "Your office will be in the 'War Room.'"

The War Room? In all my years in the D.A.'s office I had never heard of it. This sounded interesting. As I wandered around looking for the War Room, I imagined a sparkling clean white room with private offices adjoining a common lobby and a bank of television sets monitoring each station covering the case. I envisioned several high-tech computer work stations. Of course, I knew better.

Finally, I located the entrance to the War Room, one of the hundreds of nondescript doors off the labyrinth of corridors winding their way through the eighteenth floor. When I opened the door, I was struck by the shocking-green carpet. I imagined that the carpet had been selected by a fictional county employee called the county colorist, the same person who selected the ugly brown color used on school-building exteriors.

I entered the War Room, a windowless, dingy room, approximately forty feet square, which was subdivided into cubicles. The dividers did not reach the ceiling. My office was one of the cubicles. In the days to come, the number and energy of the people working in that room would raise the noise level to a low roar. Prosecutor Cheri Lewis, five paid law clerks, about half a dozen volunteer law clerks, and I would occupy cubicles there. Only Marcia and Bill had their own office, outside the War Room. In the days to come, DNA prosecutors Rockne Harmon and Woody Clarke would be assigned a cubicle in the room. For a period of time, prosecutor Christopher Darden, who later joined the team, was also assigned a cubicle. Well into the case, Chris was given his own windowless office. When I spoke to people on the phone, they would ask, "Are you at a party?"

Fortunately, in the D.A.'s office I had worked under similar conditions for years and developed the ability to block out noise in order to concentrate on my work. However, this skill was honed to brand-new levels while I was working on *Simpson*. Occasionally, the law clerks and young lawyers on the case would test the phenomenon by loudly talking about me behind my back, only feet away. They wanted to see how long it would take before I realized they were there.

In this time frame, between October 1994 and the opening statements in January 1995, I was studying the voluminous investigatory reports so as to come up to speed on the case. I was also assisting with the ongoing investigation and handling legal motions.

As I began learning about the murders of Ron and Nicole, the case struck home. Literally. I grew up on Los Angeles's west side. For several years, my family lived in a Brentwood condominium complex next door to the apartment that Ron rented years later. Ron often had coffee, as I did, at Starbucks, on San Vicente, adjacent to his apartment. Across from Starbucks is a restaurant where my family and I often ate years before it was called Mezzaluna, the restaurant where Ron waited tables.

Although he worked as a waiter and occasional model, like so many in Los Angeles, Ron's dreams were much bigger. Someday he would own a major restaurant-nightclub, become a star, raise a family.

I might have run into Nicole and Ron many times; I would never know. Young and athletic, they were the type of people who dot the Brentwood streets.

After their murders, I came to know them: Ron, through Fred Goldman's passion to find justice for his murdered son; through his sister's, Kim Goldman's, inconsolable sorrow at the loss of a beloved brother; and through his stepmother, Patti, who courageously held her family together in the face of tragedy. Few can forget Patti pulling Fred away from the cameras when he was overcome with grief and anger. Their presence throughout the trial was a source of inspiration for me and the other members of the team. They personified the victims for whom we were fighting.

I came to know Nicole on a deeper level. On the surface, we saw Nicole's zest for life, her beauty, and her love for her children. Ron was at the wrong place at the wrong time. But with Nicole we had to document a motive for murder. In the months to come I pored over endless news articles, tips, transcripts, and police reports revealing Nicole's tragic history.

As I dug deeper into the case, the endless legal battles continued. The first motion I argued was only a week after joining the team. Until then, I had no idea that I would be making appearances in court.

When I went down to Judge Ito's court for the first time, I noticed it was considerably smaller than it appeared on television. Because the counsel tables were not large enough to accommodate the multitude of lawyers on both sides, Judge Ito set up a second row of narrow counsel tables. The walking space between the two rows was difficult to negotiate. What little space remained was crammed with sophisticated projection equipment called the Elmo, which we had never used before in court. The courtroom sometimes made us feel as if we were litigating the case on a postage stamp.

On television, the audience section appeared rather large. In reality, it contained only four rows of bench seating. The Goldmans were assigned seats in the front row, behind the prosecution's counsel table. Simpson's supporters had a section of seating on the court's opposite side, behind the defense lawyers. Regular members of the news media also had assigned seats. The writer Dominick Dunne, who himself had lost a child through murder, was preeminent among this group. A few members of the public were able to attend the trial, pursuant to a lottery system. But there was always room for the celebrity spectators who often attended. (Apparently, the court allowed celebrities to attend without having to go through the lottery system.) The courtroom was always packed.

To make matters worse, the large number of people in Judge Ito's courtroom created its own independent atmosphere. It produced rapid dehydration unless one constantly drank bottles of water. Apparently, the Evian company noticed the phenomenon and sent boxes filled with bottled water to us. Once, they stopped sending for a week or two, so we switched to Crystal Geyser, which prompted Evian to send more.

When I first entered the courtroom to argue one of the endless legal motions, I was nervous. I knew that millions of television viewers were watching me and that legal pundits would dissect my argument. However, Marcia and Bill were more than pleased with my presentation, and Judge Ito ruled in our favor.

By November, Chris Darden joined the prosecution team. He temporarily became the "case manager" and coordinated the investigatory efforts. Shortly thereafter, the defense filed a motion to kick Chris off the case. The motion was based on the fact that Chris conducted a grand-jury investigation to determine whether charges could be filed against Al Cowlings, Simpson's friend who drove the Bronco during the chase. The defense alleged, without any legal support, that Chris could not utilize knowledge gleaned from the Cowlings grand-jury investigation against Simpson.

While I was working on this motion and others, investigative efforts continued. One day, I was asked to fly to New Mexico to interview a potential domestic-violence witness. I arrived at the airport about forty-five minutes early and met the investigator who would be conducting the interview with me. Since I was early, I sat down about forty feet from the boarding gate, facing it. I used the time to prepare the response to the motion to remove Chris from the case. I pulled out my legal materials and began to read. My newly improved ability to block noise worked its magic. Somehow, in the forty-five minutes that followed, I failed to notice several hundred passengers boarding the plane in front of me or to hear the boarding calls over the loudspeaker. I lost track of time until a minute after the plane left the gate. For the duration of the case, I made a mental note not to get hit by a bus.

The following week, I argued the motion to remove Chris, and Judge Ito rejected the defense claims. We had no way of knowing how important this victory was to become. Weeks later, during opening statements, when Bill Hodgman suffered what at first appeared to be a heart attack, Chris became Marcia's cocounsel.

An equally important legal battle during this time frame was waged over the admissibility of the domestic-violence evidence, which showed the motive for Nicole's murder. This evidence would be the foundation on which the prosecution's case rested. Its admissibility would determine the scope and course of the trial.

3

Presenting the Motive

WE WOULD BE TELLING the jury and the world that smiling, affable O. J. Simpson took a knife and carved two people to death with it. Only through the domestic-violence evidence could we explain why.

When I first joined the prosecution team, one of the most daunting challenges we faced related to the domestic-violence evidence. Substantial progress had already been made in investigating Nicole's relationship with Simpson. Trying to present an accurate portrait of a relationship in a domestic-violence case always constitutes a challenge, since the abuse typically occurs behind closed doors. In domestic-violence murder cases the only witness to most of the history of abuse, other than the defendant, is dead.

However, we were flooded with tips from news sources and from people calling or writing to us with information. We conducted interviews of family members, friends, Simpson's acquaintances, his golf buddies, neighbors, and possible witnesses to alleged incidents at hotels, restaurants, and a variety of other places. Slowly, we were able to find enough pieces of the puzzle to see the true nature of the relationship.

For example, we made significant efforts to locate Simpson's first wife, Marguerite Thomas. LAPD officer Terry Schauer, in a report dated November 20, 1994, informed us:

> Approximately 20 years ago, I was assigned to West Los Angeles Division as a patrol officer, as I still am today. I recall responding to a Domestic Violence Radio Call at the home of O.J. Simpson. . . . [Marguerite Simpson] was there with

two small children. She told us that she had been hit by her husband O.J. Simpson, who left the location.

On several occasions in December, Chris told me that every effort we made to interview Mrs. Thomas was thwarted. "She's obviously not going to give us an interview."

On December 27, 1994, Chris, Marcia, and the investigators went to Marguerite's home in Fullerton to serve a subpoena and attempt to talk to her. Mrs. Thomas opened the door. When she saw Marcia and Chris, she slammed the door shut.

Now we faced a dead end. We could not call Mrs. Thomas as a witness without first interviewing her, since we did not know exactly what she would say or whether it would be admissible. And she would not be interviewed. Thus, our efforts to seek potentially relevant information from her came to naught.

We were similarly frustrated in our attempts to interview Simpson's girlfriend, Paula Barbieri. At around the same time, I mentioned to Chris, who was spearheading the domestic-violence investigation, that we should interview her. I wanted to determine the nature of her relationship with Simpson and whether she had broken up with him just before the murders. Of course, Chris agreed.

Later, I asked Chris whether Barbieri would be interviewed. He informed me, "Paula is telling us to pound sand."

In California criminal cases there is no procedure to force a witness such as Barbieri to grant the prosecution a pretrial interview. Thus, it would be unwise to call her as a witness without knowing what she would say.

The Simpson civil trial is another matter. Barbieri was simply given a subpoena, which forced her to testify at a deposition, a relatively informal procedure, with a court reporter but not a judge present. According to news reports of the deposition, Barbieri testified that she had broken up with Simpson shortly before the murders.

In California there are no depositions in criminal cases. The reasoning seems to be that allowing depositions would lengthen the pretrial proceedings, thereby compromising the defendant's right to a speedy trial. The lack of depositions severely handicaps efforts by law enforcement to gather relevant information from reluctant witnesses.

In addition to finding witnesses to incidents of domestic violence, an equally tremendous challenge confronted us. We needed to show that the evidence was legally admissible. It is an often quoted maxim of Anglo-American jurisprudence that "a defendant must be tried for what he did, not for who he is." This means that a defendant's prior criminal background and instances of misconduct are generally inadmissible.

However, there are exceptions to this rule. We needed to show that the evidence was admissible under one or more of these exceptions. One that I believed applied to our case was that evidence of prior misconduct may be admissible to prove motive.

Our first strategy session occurred one Saturday in December 1994, while jury selection was still under way, and about six weeks before opening statements. We all met in the law library of the district attorney's office, on the seventeenth floor of the CCB. When I arrived, Scott Gordon and Lydia Bodin were sitting at a table surrounded by piles of open law books. They had already begun typing notes into their own personal laptops. Scott is in his forties, with graying salt-and-pepper hair and a bearing that reflects his background as a former police officer. Later, members of the press corps said Scott looked like a handsome version of Newt Gingrich.

I had not met Lydia previously. Lydia, also in her forties, is an attractive woman with a gentle manner. She spoke quietly but with an authority that made me want to hang on to her every word. Scott and Lydia are two of the district attorney's top experts in prosecuting domestic-violence cases. I had a lot to learn, but between Scott and Lydia, I had great teachers.

During this meeting I recall expressing my strong feelings about the importance of this evidence. In murder cases the prosecution is not legally required to prove motive. However, it is difficult to present a case to a jury without giving them some rational explanation as to why the murder occurred.

I said, "The jury is not going to believe that Simpson, a beloved sports hero, suddenly woke up one morning and out of the blue brutally murdered two people. We need motive evidence. Otherwise, when the question is posed to the jurors 'Why would O. J. Simpson do this?' we would look silly shrugging our shoulders and saying, 'Gee I don't know, but we don't have to prove motive.' "

Scott and Lydia had already reached the same conclusion. Scott noted that "the public believes that Simpson was a friendly, affable, peace-loving guy. Not the type of guy that's going to commit murder. If we can't get in motive evidence, that erroneous perception of his character will win the day."

"But how," I asked, "do we best articulate to the judge, and ultimately to the jury, how the domestic violence shows this motive?"

Scott started to lay out in broad brush strokes our theory of the domestic-violence evidence. "These kinds of abusive behaviors are all about control. When you understand that the ultimate goal that the batterer is trying to accomplish is control of the victim, then a variety of otherwise seemingly unconnected events become understandable as part of an overall strategy to maintain that control. Things like telling her who she can be friends with, how much money she can spend, what kind of clothes she can wear, belittling her, demeaning her—all of these things accomplish the end objective: control."

Lydia continued, "What I find so significant here are the events shortly before the murders. Shortly before the murders, Nicole gave back a bracelet Simpson gave her. That has great symbolic value. It's ending the relationship. On the night of the murders, she rebuffed him at the dance recital involving their daughter Sydney. She didn't invite him to sit with her and didn't invite him to dinner afterward. And Simpson's comments to Kato later that evening clearly conveyed that in Simpson's mind the relationship had come to an end."

Scott picked up where Lydia left off. "It was over. And Simpson had lost control. What is the ultimate act of control after you have tried everything else and it doesn't work? Murder."

I could see that both Scott and Lydia were somewhat excited by the degree to which the evidence fit the classic pattern they were so used to seeing in their cases. At this point, I asked whether we could present expert psychological testimony explaining the dynamics of abusive relationships. Jurors typically find such testimony very helpful in domestic-violence cases. I felt it would be useful to have an expert explain the connection between domestic violence and murder.

Scott and Lydia pondered this question for a few seconds as I continued. "I know the case law which says you can introduce expert testimony to refute certain myths and misconceptions the defense sometimes raises about battered women."

Often the defense argues: Why didn't she just leave if she was really battered? Why does she want to drop charges if she's really a victim? Why is she recanting? How could an intelligent, educated woman put up with such abuse? I knew that the prosecution can often introduce expert testimony to refute those misconceptions. Experts can explain the traumatization these women suffer, called battered woman's syndrome, a form of traumatic stress disorder. This helps explain why it may be difficult for them to leave. "But what I want to know," I asked, "is, can we introduce expert testimony to explain Simpson's conduct and his state of mind?"

"No," Lydia replied. She searched through the layers of open law books in front of her and read a provision of Evidence Code section 1107(a). Then she summarized: "So we can introduce the evidence to refute certain myths and misconceptions if the defense raises them. But we can't introduce the evidence to show that Simpson fits a batterer's profile. The reason for this law is that we don't want an expert coming into court and saying the defendant is in fact a batterer."

Scott had a slightly different take. "I'm not so sure. That's one area we all need to take a closer look at. Maybe we can use expert testimony to some extent."

"And if we can't?" I asked.

No one answered. I guess we were all wondering whether the jury would understand the evidence without an expert to explain how it all fits together.

Later that day we divided up the task of preparing the brief. Lydia would review and present all the facts relating to the instances of domestic violence. I would handle the legal arguments regarding the admissibility of the evidence. Scott would tackle the thorny issue of whether, and to what extent, we could present expert testimony.

For my section of the brief, a preliminary draft had been prepared by Darrell Mavis, a young prosecutor in his mid-twenties, with a few years of experience. It was good. But I wanted to draft a brief which would definitively demonstrate why evidence of prior acts of domestic violence had to be admitted in a case such as ours.

This type of work has always fascinated me. It may be difficult to understand why it was necessary to do extensive research and to construct an elaborate brief regarding the law relating to the admissibility of the domestic-violence evidence. To comprehend why this was necessary, it is helpful to know a little about the American legal system. Every state in the United States, with the exception of Louisiana, follows the "common law." The common law is a system of law that we, along with other former British colonies, inherited from England. Louisiana, a former French colony, follows the civil system of law.

Several things make the common law unique. Unlike the civil system, where only the legislature has the power to make law, common-law courts are authorized to actually make law. For example, before 1965, the California legislature had never created any rules of evidence. Therefore, the courts created their own, based on the common law. This is done through a system known as stare decisis, or "to abide by decided cases." Once an appellate court decides a case, the opinion can be published. The legal rulings articulated in that opinion become binding law on any lower court forever unless or until the case is overruled by a higher court or the legislature steps in and changes the law. The legislature is always free to change laws the courts create unless the law is based on the court's interpretation of the Constitution. The legislature can only change constitutional interpretations by amending the Constitution.

To determine how the law is related to an issue, such as the admissibility of domestic-violence evidence in a murder case, it is often not possible to look it up in any one law book. The Evidence Code does not provide the rule as to whether domestic-violence evidence is admissible in a murder case. Therefore, it was necessary to carefully trace a line of appellate-court cases, which we researched back to 1909, involving murders by people in such relationships as husband and wife or boyfriend and girlfriend. The holdings of these cases are law. However, the proposition of law for which the cases stand is open to interpretation.

For example, if I found a particular appellate-court case that let in the domestic-violence evidence, I could argue to Judge Ito that the case was "on all fours" with our case, or "on point." That would mean that there were no material distinctions between what happened in that case and what happened in ours. If Judge Ito agreed, he would have to follow that case.

However, the defense would argue that the case was "distinguishable"; that is, there existed material differences between the facts of that case and ours. The defense could also argue that those portions of the case I cited to the court were "dicta," an extraneous comment in a judicial opinion not necessary for the decision of the case. For example, I cited a case called *People v. Zack,* which clearly stated that evidence of the nature of a relationship should be admissible in cases like ours. However, the defense stated that this language was dicta. Whether something can be defined as dicta is, of course, subject to interpretation.

In trying to piece together how the law stands on a given point, a lawyer in a common-law jurisdiction can rely on two types of authority. One type is "binding authority"—a case from a higher court or statute that directly answers the question at hand. If the case is "distinguishable" or the ruling in question is, in fact, "dicta," it is not binding.

The second type of authority is "persuasive authority." Persuasive authority includes rulings from a court of equal jurisdiction, a sister state, another common-law country, or dicta. Another form of persuasive authority is published articles, treatises, and commentaries by law professors, lawyers, and law students. For example, since I have written several law-review articles reviewing particular legal issues, I was allowed to cite myself to Judge Ito, on certain points of law, as "persuasive authority." Judges may, but are not required to, consider persuasive authority.

There is something which, to a lawyer, is almost magical about this seemingly byzantine legal system. Because often the law cannot be readily determined, it is subject to research, interpretation, debate, and argument. It is an alluring notion that the law is what "I persuasively maintain it to be." It is this feature that, through the ages, has caused many young law students to fall in love with common law, as some men fall for a mistress.

Like many young law students, the law bug bit me sometime in my first year. But a love for the law was not why I went to law school. I didn't know that I would love the law. Perhaps the decision was in the making much earlier.

One of my earliest memories is sitting in the backseat of my parents' Mercedes after they picked me up from Henrietta's Nursery School in Brentwood. As I sat in the backseat, there was only one topic of conversation: Vietnam.

Once I exclaimed, "Vietnam, Vietnam, all I ever hear about is

Vietnam!" My parents burst out laughing. But it was not the last time I was exposed to this topic or to scores of other sociopolitical issues throughout my life.

At the age of four, and throughout my childhood, I remember the endless meetings and fund-raisers my mother held in the pool house of our Westwood home on warm summer nights. It was usually my function to hold our giant white German shepherd, Frisky, whose name described her personality. Frisky was the sweetest dog I ever knew but looked like a white wolf. I would assist with the food and beverages, and since Ron Kovic and the rest of the Vietnam Veterans Against the War were voracious eaters, my most important job was to find something to eat for Jane Fonda, who often arrived late. I would listen for hours to the lectures, discussions, and often rancorous arguments that my older brother and sister found too boring and managed to escape.

I fondly remember those years. My family sat around the kitchen table eating dinner—my parents, my older brother, David; my older sister, Dru; and later, my younger brother, Luke. We discussed and argued the important issues of the day—Vietnam, of course, integration, affirmative action, homelessness, crime, welfare reform, whether Tito's Tacos is more widely known in Los Angeles than Taco Tah, why African-American basketball players seem to be able to jump higher than whites.

Voices raised, and tempers flared. It was not the Waltons, but I loved it. And sixteen years after my lament "Vietnam, Vietnam, all I ever hear about is Vietnam," I had the opportunity to go to law school and pursue a profession that allowed me to learn, discuss, absorb, and yes, to *argue*.

As a young child, I once asked my father, "Why is Mom always going to meetings and marches and all that stuff. Sometimes I hardly ever see her. Why does she do that?"

"Because she has to," my father answered simply.

I guess that's why I went to law school and became a prosecutor. Because I had to.

I graduated from UCLA at age nineteen, with a degree in political science. I finished law school in 1985, at age twenty-two, and was hired by the D.A.'s office, the youngest deputy D.A.

Immediately, I fueled my search for social justice by joining the D.A.'s office. I was making thirty-three thousand dollars a year.

While my friends were working in private firms and driving BMWs, I chugged along in my little Toyota. Well, I thought, let them buy their Wilshire Boulevard condos. But after less than three years in the D.A.'s office, I succumbed and joined Pettit and Martin, a major Los Angeles law firm, at almost twice my D.A.'s salary. I was pushing around papers and arguing for our client, a multibillion-dollar company, against the enemy, another multibillion-dollar company, and I really did not care. So hat in hand I returned to the D.A.'s office in 1989, and I have been there ever since.

Tragically and ironically, a few years after I left the firm, a madman, armed with an automatic weapon, burst into the firm's main office in San Francisco, spraying it with dozens of rounds, killing a number of lawyers.

So when I set out to write my portion of one of the most important briefs in the "trial of the century," I relished the opportunity. In my section of the brief I was able to show an entire body of case authority for admitting evidence of quarrels, enmity, or hostility in relationships predating murders. From this body of case authority, I decided to argue to Judge Ito that there is a special rule of evidence favoring the admissibility of domestic-violence evidence in cases like ours.

While we were preparing the domestic-violence brief, we consulted extensively with Dr. Donald Dutton, a psychologist, a professor at the University of British Columbia, and one of the world's leading experts in the field of domestic violence. Don worked with us closely in developing the theoretical framework for the domestic-violence portion of our case. The following represents a condensed version of several conversations Scott, other prosecutors, and I had with Don in the War Room.

Don was describing the three phases of battering, known as the "cycle of violence." There's the battering phase itself; the contrition, or honeymoon, phase; and finally, the tension-building phase.

I asked, "Do you believe that women can actually experience traumatic bonding as a result of this relationship which can make it difficult to leave?"

"We get attached to people who intermittently treat us well, then badly, well, then badly," Don said. "One of the effects of traumatic bonding is that with time a woman can forget the negative stuff and remember what was good about the relationship."

I asked Don to describe how emotional abuse relates to physical abuse in an abusive relationship.

He replied that violence is not the only means of control in such relationships. "I had a male client once, who beat up his wife in 1985," Don said. "This client told his wife, 'Next time it is going to be worse.' She told me that when he beat her his physiognomy changed, his nostrils flared, he had a very different expression on his face. For the next six years he never hit her again, but whenever she saw that expression on his face, she immediately toed the line. So there was a continuing control that went on even though there was a seven-year gap between that 1985 incidence of physical abuse and the next incidence of physical abuse. So there's an interaction between emotional abuse and physical abuse."

"Don," I asked, "how can we say that something relatively minor, like Nicole rebuffing Simpson at the dance recital, could be significant in precipitating a murder?"

Don paused for a moment. "There are two main things that come out of the studies regarding what precipitates the murder. First, and most importantly, is estrangement. Then jealousy and a history of physical abuse."

"Exactly what constitutes 'estrangement'?"

"In his mind the relationship is finally lost," Don replied. "That totally changes his psychology at that point. It goes from controlling her to destroying her, and there is considerable psychiatric literature on that."

I paused to consider this. "But can a relatively minor event be the trigger?"

"Yes. Let's say, for example, a woman has always answered his phone calls even though they have been divorced. And suddenly she stops answering his calls. That might seem like a trivial thing. But to him that might have major symbolic significance. It tells him this relationship now is lost."

"I've heard that when estrangement occurs the woman is facing unprecedented danger."

"Right," Don said. "The risk ratio magnifies her chances of being killed by a factor of six."

Scott said, "Don, one of the features we have in our case that's very difficult for us is this public persona of O. J. Simpson, this kind, affable, all-American guy. How do you answer the question 'How could this guy be a batterer?' "

Don answered, "In the last book I wrote on this, the principal dancer of the New York City Ballet had just been arrested for wife assault. I put it in the book to show that there really are two person-alities at work here and you simply can't draw conclusions about the intimate personality from what goes on in transactions outside the home. The idea that you can draw conclusions or inferences about what the man is like with his wife based on his interactions with men in the public world is erroneous. It's one of the myths that the research in this area is trying to dispel."

"Is there any psychological diagnosis in the *Diagnostic and Statistical Manual of the American Psychiatric Association* that applies to batterers?" I asked.

Don looked at me quizzically. "That's a good question. Actually, there isn't any one diagnosis. One of the common public per-sonalities is a narcissistic personality who has an exaggerated or a grandiose view of their own appearance, who needs constant rein-forcement, who overreacts to any kind of slight criticisms and is incapable of developing empathy with other people."

"Is that a diagnosis, or are you just describing Simpson?" This drew a smile from Scott and Don.

As I listened to Don, I thought his testimony would be pure gold if we could present it to the jury. But it seemed clear that the Evi-dence Code barred testimony explaining the batterer's motivations.

During these meetings with Don Dutton and his colleague Mary Dutton, no relation, I became very impressed with their insight and expertise. One comment they made struck me as strange. I do not have a clear recollection of the context in which it arose, but one, or both, of the Duttons predicted that Marcia and Chris were going to have an affair by the end of the trial. I paid little attention to this comment. I thought it was ridiculous. Marcia also dismissed the comment as being groundless. How did they conclude that they would have an affair?

In mid-December, several weeks after my first meeting with Scott and Lydia, we met again to bring our three sections of the brief together. We were going to meet in the single conference room that is available to the almost one thousand lawyers in our office. How-ever, it was occupied. So we were allowed to work in D.A. Gil

Garcetti's conference room, filled with large, comfortable leather chairs and a big granite conference table that was apparently donated to the office. This is one of the few pleasant work spaces in the entire office. Ordinarily, this space was off limits to trial prosecutors. But in the Simpson case we were the captains of the ship. We berthed wherever it was feasible. With Gil's permission.

During this meeting I told Scott and Lydia that although I had prosecuted domestic-violence cases for some time, I had learned much more about the psychology of such relationships because of the Simpson case.

I continued my thought. "But we can't assume that just because Judge Ito is a former prosecutor and experienced trial judge that he necessarily completely understands these things. Maybe we should include the 'power and control wheel' in the brief. It kind of ties together all the various mechanisms that batterers use to control the victim—emotional abuse, isolation, economic abuse, et cetera—virtually all of which we have in this case."

"Good idea," Scott said.

After painstakingly assembling the brief, by late in the evening we completed the final touches. By the end of the evening the entire eighty-page document was on computer disk and properly formatted for court.

"Done!" Scott exclaimed. "Let's print this puppy tomorrow and file it." We were exhausted, but at the same time elated. We were too tired to anticipate the D.A. office's patchwork quilt of antiquated, incompatible computers.

The next morning, I started to print out the brief. After about the first ten pages, the printer malfunctioned. I called our computer maven, Jonathan Fairtlough, an extremely talented young prosecutor. He worked on the printer for about an hour.

Scott poked his head in to check on the document, "How are we doing?"

"Not too well. The computer printer is malfunctioning, and I can't find a single other compatible printer in the D.A.'s office!"

"No problem. Let's transfer the document to my computer and print it out in my office," Scott said.

And we did that. However, when we switched the document to Scott's computer to continue printing, it reformatted the document and threw off all the spacing. It was a mess.

By now Lydia Bodin was also working with us and checking each page to make sure that the formatting looked right as it came off Scott's computer.

It took the three of us working together the entire morning and most of the afternoon just to print this one document, which we presented to the court hours before the deadline. I figure this little episode cost the taxpayer about eight hundred dollars in wasted attorney time, about twice the cost of buying a new printer!

4

Prelude to Murder

THE BRIEF COMPLETED, we were now prepared to lay bare before the court the ugly story of one man's brutality to one woman. As presented in the brief we submitted to Judge Ito, here is some of what we learned about Nicole and Simpson's relationship:

Simpson and Nicole first met in 1977, when Simpson was a running back for professional football's Buffalo Bills. Nicole was seventeen years old; Simpson, twenty-eight. At the time, Simpson was married to Marguerite. An intimate relationship ensued between Simpson and Nicole. Soon Nicole was spending much of her time in Buffalo with Simpson, who divorced Marguerite in 1978 and began living with Nicole.

Simpson began physically abusing Nicole almost immediately. In a diary Nicole prepared and later gave her lawyer, she wrote:

> Early in first year 1977 in San Francisco after his baby died [Simpson's child by his first wife drowned in a swimming pool] I found an earring in my apartment bed on Bedford. I accused O.J. of sleeping with someone named Terri. He threw a fit, chased me, grabbed me, threw me into walls. Threw all my clothes out of the window into the street three floors down. Bruised me. Al Cowlings calmed him down.

In the diary, Nicole wrote that while in New York, Simpson threw her to the ground on a street corner after they left a friend's anniversary party. The beating continued after they arrived at their hotel. Nicole wrote, "He continued to beat me for hours as I kept

27

crawling for the door." He "called my mother a whore and pre-
tended to call her and tell her that." She also wrote that Simpson
"hit me while he fucked me."

On another occasion, Nicole wrote that, while at their Rockingham home, Simpson beat her badly and locked her in the wine
closet. In her notes, Nicole described how he beat and kicked her
for a period of time, watched television while she begged to be
released from the wine closet, and subsequently beat and kicked her
again. Nicole later recounted this incident to her attorney, her sister
Denise, and her friend Faye Resnick.

Maria Baur, who worked as a maid for Simpson, told us that in
1984 or 1985 she entered Simpson's Rockingham estate and saw
Nicole crying outside. When she entered the house, she saw twenty
to thirty framed photographs of the Brown family smashed and scat-
tered on the floor. Baur was too scared to ask Simpson what happened. She also recalled Nicole wearing dark sunglasses indoors on
a number of occasions.

In a December 17, 1994, tape-recorded interview, Albert Aguilera told a D.A. investigator, Michael Stevens, about an incident that
occurred on or around the Fourth of July, in 1986 or 1987, at
Laguna Beach. It was a sunny day, and he was strolling in the water,
about waist-deep, just cooling off. Mr. Aguilera was with a friend
named Art. A local, Aguilera knew that Simpson lived in the area
and had seen him a few times on the beach.

Suddenly, Art said, "Oh, look. There's O.J. and his wife."

Aguilera said that "it looked like they . . . weren't very far
from the shore. . . . They looked like they were having a conversation. . . . She was facing him and looked like she was teasing him.
. . . It didn't look like he was in a good mood, though. . . . And
before I knew it, he hit her with one hand. It was like a slap, but it
was strong enough that it knocked her down. And then when she
went down, he cowered over her . . . like he was trying to say, I'm
sorry, at first. Then, when she kept crying, he was trying to tell her
to stop. He was getting upset because she wouldn't stop crying. And
then he was like starting to almost yell at her for making a scene."

Nicole described an incident that took place in 1986 in which
Simpson, Nicole, and their neighbors, the Von Watts, were drinking
and listening to music at a club. She wrote in her journal that Simpson beat her up when they got home and completely ripped off her
sweater and slacks. Nicole suffered a large bruise on her head. We

found photographs of the torn clothing Nicole described in her journal. Simpson took Nicole to a hospital where she told the doctor she suffered the injury as a result of a bicycle accident.

The treating physician, Dr. Martin Alpert, said he did not believe Nicole's explanation. Typically, bike-fall victims sustain injuries to many areas of their bodies. She had an abrasion to the back of her head about the size of a quarter. He also said that Nicole was very upset. She obviously suffered the injuries by some other means.

In 1986, Simpson smashed her white Mercedes with a baseball bat because she arrived home late after visiting a friend. Both Westec Security Services and the LAPD responded to Nicole's telephone call for help.

Detective Mark Fuhrman was one of the patrol officers that responded to the call. In a memorandum regarding the incident, Fuhrman indicated that when he arrived at Rockingham he saw Nicole and Simpson. Nicole was seated on a white Mercedes-Benz, crying. Simpson was pacing back and forth. The vehicle windshield was broken. Fuhrman asked, "Who broke the windshield?"

Nicole responded, "He did," pointing to Simpson. "He hit the windshield with a baseball bat."

Simpson exclaimed, "I broke the windshield. It's mine. . . . There's no trouble here."

Nicole refused to make a report.

Sgt. Mark Day, who worked for Westec in 1986, corroborated this account. Day recalled responding to the Rockingham house and contacting Nicole.

> She was crying, her face was puffy and she was very upset. She stated that she had a fight with O.J. and when she tried to leave he took a baseball bat to her car. . . . Simpson walked out and met me at the front door. He stated he had lost his temper but that everything was okay now.

After this brief was written, we continued to receive new leads. In a January 3, 1995, tape-recorded interview, Connie Good informed D.A. investigator Stevens about incidents in 1977 or 1978. They occurred when Nicole lived next door to Ms. Good's boyfriend, on Ashton Street in Brentwood.

Ms. Good told Stevens that "on one particular evening, I believe I was visiting [my boyfiend]. . . . And all of a sudden, he said, 'Shh. Shh. Listen.' And we both became very quiet, and we did hear O.J.

and Nicole having a major, violent argument. . . . He was screaming, yelling, shouting. She was crying, wailing. We heard thuds, you
know, loud noises like thuds. . . . Sounded like it was either on the
floor or against the wall. . . . The tone of his voice was very violent.
. . . Four letter words. . . . 'Fucking bitch,' you know. 'Motherfucker. . . .' It sounded like he was beating her. . . . I think it
sounded to me like she was like crying. . . . I did not call the police—because he was a celebrity. . . . I saw both of them together
either one or two days later."

Stevens asked, "Did you notice anything unusual?"

"Yes," she replied. "We were in an elevator with O.J. and Nicole.
. . . And she had black eyes."

Later, Mike asked, "You knew who O.J. Simpson was, just basically from television?"

She responded, "I loved him. I absolutely loved him. I mean, I
loved the image he portrayed on television. . . . He was very
charming. . . . And I realized at that point that he leads a completely different life in reality."

The brief continued documenting Simpson's reign of terror.

In her diary, Nicole described a beating she suffered in 1988
after a gay man kissed her son, Justin. "O.J. threw me against the
walls in our hotel and on the floor. Put bruises on my arms and
back. The window scared me. Thought he'd throw me out."

A January 1, 1988, journal entry contains a graphic description
of the physical and mental abuse Nicole suffered. Nicole, her daughter, Sydney, her mother, Juditha, and a sister, Minnie, had gone to
see *Disney on Ice*. Simpson was invited to join them but refused,
stating that to attend such an event would "cramp his style." When
Nicole and the family returned home, Simpson and Al Cowlings
were drunk. Simpson complained that he had been left out and
loudly began calling Nicole a "fat liar." At the time, Nicole was two
months pregnant.

Simpson shouted repeatedly, "You're a fat pig. You're disgust-
ing." He continued ranting, "You're a slob . . . I want you out of
my fucking house."

Nicole tried to escape his verbal abuse by going upstairs. She
could hear her husband berate her in front of Cowlings, who remained downstairs.

Simpson screamed, calling Nicole a fat liar. "I stopped fucking
her, and now I jack off, the fat ass." He then locked his wife out of

the bedroom. When Nicole tried to enter the bedroom, Simpson stated, "Get out of my fucking house, you fat-ass liar. I want you to have an abortion with the baby."

Nicole pleaded with her husband, "Do I have to go tonight? Sydney's sleeping. It's late."

Simpson yelled, "Let me tell you how serious I am! I have a gun in my hand right now! Get the fuck out of here!"

Nicole grabbed Sydney and a few items of clothing and fled the house.

Alfred Acosta, a former limousine chauffeur, recalled an incident that occurred during 1988 or 1989 when he picked up Simpson and Nicole at a charitable fund-raiser. Simpson and Nicole were seated in the rear of the limousine. While en route to the Rockingham estate, Acosta saw Simpson "backhand" Nicole, striking her in the face. Apparently afraid that Simpson might beat her, Nicole invited Acosta into the house. Once inside, Nicole ascended the stairway. Simpson followed her. Mr. Acosta saw Simpson lunge and swing at Nicole but was not able to see if the blow actually struck her.

The brief then discussed another incident that was not introduced, since we were not convinced that the witness to the incident, who had sold his story to the tabloids, was telling the truth.

In May 1991, Eddie Reynoza, an actor on the set of *The Naked Gun 2½* had a conversation with Simpson about cars and women. Reynoza claimed that Simpson said that if he ever caught any of his wife's boyfriends driving any of his cars, he would "cut their fucking heads off!"

I participated in discussions involving witnesses with credibility problems similar to Reynoza's. For example, a witness named Jill Shively claimed that she saw an agitated Simpson, driving his Bronco, run a red light and swerve to avoid her car. This incident took place at the corner of San Vicente and Bundy Drive, a minute's drive from the Bundy crime scene and within minutes of the probable time of the murders.

In November 1994, shortly after I joined the prosecution team, Marcia Clark and I had a discussion one evening in her office in which she reviewed the key evidence against Simpson to help bring me up to speed. She had a window office that was jam-packed with boxes, videotapes, notebooks, and a television set. A large, almost life-size, framed picture of Jim Morrison was hanging on the wall behind her desk, apparently held there by magnets. Throughout the trial, I kept looking at the picture, waiting for it to come crashing down. On her desk was a smokeless ashtray and almost always an open bag of pretzels. (By the end of the trial, we had probably eaten several hundred dollars' worth in her office. I would occasionally tell Marcia I would chip in for the pretzels, but she refused. I felt guilty about it until after the trial, when I learned about her book advance.)

This was one of the first lengthy face-to-face meetings I had with Marcia. I had never met her before. I was surprised how warm, sweet, and down-to-earth she was, something I hadn't picked up from the little I had seen of the television coverage.

During the meeting I asked, "What about the women who saw Simpson in the Bronco near the time of the murders?"

Marcia answered, "Hank, you know, witnesses are coming out of the woodwork who are interested in money and publicity."

"Right," I said. "I never interviewed this witness, but her account seemed plausible to me."

"Think about it, Hank. I talked to this witness. And if we don't know whether someone's telling the truth, how in hell can we present that witness and tell the jury they should believe her?"

I came away from this meeting impressed. I liked Marcia's take-charge attitude and her command of the facts of the case. I knew she would tell me exactly what she thought without holding back. But most important, her unwillingness to present evidence she distrusted demonstrated high ethical standards. Obviously, these same standards were applied in deciding not to call witnesses like Eddie Reynoza.

Months after this meeting with Marcia we discovered evidence of another incident of abuse. Gioconda Redfern baby-sat for Nicole's children in 1992. She told us that Simpson would call the residence almost every weekend asking about Nicole's whereabouts. He would complain about Nicole's behavior and manner of dress. One weekend he called approximately fifty times in a two-hour period. She could hear Nicole answer the phone and tell Simpson over and over again: "Leave me alone . . . leave me alone . . . leave me alone."

On many occasions, according to Ms. Redfern, Simpson would

suddenly show up when she would take the children to the park or for lunch. On another occasion, Simpson followed Nicole in his car.

The brief continued recounting the details of Nicole's relationship with Simpson. Nicole divorced Simpson in October 1992. Simpson did not handle the divorce very well. He called Nicole's mother, Juditha, repeatedly. He often told her, "People say I should stay away from her, but I can't. I love her. I love her. People tell me to let her go, and I can't let her go."

Nicole agreed to attempt to get back together with Simpson. In May 1993, Simpson and Nicole dined at California Beach Sushi with Faye Resnick and her fiancé, Christian Reichardt. During a conversation with Resnick, Nicole mentioned a man she had dated after she and Simpson divorced. When Simpson heard this, he became enraged. He turned to Resnick and exclaimed, "What the fuck is she doing, Faye? Why does she have to go and ruin everything by saying that name? Just when everything's fucking going good. Why does she do me like that, Faye? Goddamn! That bitch."

Ms. Resnick ran into the ladies' room and locked the door behind her. According to Faye, moments later, Simpson broke through the door. "Goddamn her, Faye! Why does she do this to me . . . ? She fucks with me all the time, that bitch! Why does she do this to me?"

Eventually, they left the restaurant. As they approached the sidewalk, Simpson screamed at Nicole, "Get in the car, you fucking bitch! I'm taking you home!"

As Simpson continued to yell at Nicole, a police car pulled up beside them. An officer asked Nicole and Resnick if they were all right. Simpson began to charm the officer. It worked.

The officer advised Simpson, "Look, O.J., you've had a lot to drink. . . . [J]ust go home and simmer down." Once again, Simpson's fame and positive public image evidently caused the police to avoid any further investigation.

The brief discussed a number of instances of stalking. In 1993, Simpson hid in the bushes late one night and peered through Nicole's window and watched her making love with Keith Zlomsowitch. At the time, Nicole and Simpson were divorced and were not attempting reconciliation. In June or July 1993, Nicole told a friend, "Everywhere I go . . . he shows up. I really think he's going to kill me."

He once appeared at the Mezzaluna restaurant and told her

dinner companion, Keith Zlomsowitch, "She's still my wife." In another incident, he suddenly appeared at the Tryst restaurant in West Hollywood and stared at Nicole and male members of her dinner party. The brief recounted a number of other occasions when Simpson just happened to appear at locations where he ran into Nicole.

For example, Jefferey Keller, one of Ron Goldman's friends, described an incident in 1994 when Simpson suddenly appeared at Starbucks while he, Ron Goldman, and Nicole were having coffee. Simpson was visibly angry and called to Nicole. When she walked over to Simpson's car, Keller listened as Simpson shouted at her.

In this same time frame, Nicole told her mother, Juditha Brown, that Simpson was "following me again, Mommy. I'm scared. I go to the gas station. He's there. I go to the Payless shoe store. He's there. I'm driving and he's behind me."

Simpson told Nicole's mother about how he obsessed over Nicole. During a phone conversation a few months before the murders, he said, "The only woman I want in my life and I can't have is your daughter."

Elizabeth Holmes was the personal trainer for Simpson's next-door neighbors the Salingers. She told us that in January 1994 she saw Nicole Brown pull into Simpson's driveway in a Ferrari. Then she saw Simpson yelling and screaming at Nicole. He was ranting about photographs taken of Nicole in Aspen.

Then Simpson shoved Nicole against his Bentley. Ms. Holmes heard a loud "thud" as Nicole struck the vehicle.

After playing golf one day in March 1994, Simpson and a friend, Bill Thibodeau, drove through a side alley while en route to Nicole's house. Simpson said that it was the "secret way" or "back way into her house." He added, "Sometimes she doesn't even know I'm here."

In May 1994, Simpson and Thibodeau were playing golf. Thibodeau asked Simpson why Nicole's birthday party had been canceled. Nicole's birthday was May 19, 1994. He described Simpson's reaction. "[He] stopped and started explaining to me how [Nicole] is just ripping him up inside. . . . He . . . clenched his fist and described how she was tearing him up and that . . . she wasn't worth the trouble. . . ."

In the following months Nicole and Simpson attempted to reconcile, with little success. He ordered Nicole not to see any other man until August, when he moved to New York to do commentary for NBC. Nicole refused to go along with Simpson's demand. Simpson warned Nicole's close friend Faye Resnick that unless Nicole agreed not to see any other man, he would kill her. During a telephone conversation, Faye asked, "Did you mean it when you said you'd kill her? I mean, really mean it?"

"You heard me," he roared. "If she's with another man, I'll kill her. You tell her she'd better play her role and look like my wife. . . . You tell her that, Faye."

Later, Simpson told Faye Resnick, "She's not my wife, and she's not going to be my wife. She's made that quite clear to me. So I want her to face all the pain she's made me face."

When Resnick asked Simpson why he insisted on threatening Nicole, he replied, "It's because she doesn't want to be with me anymore. And I just can't be her friend anymore. I want her to be in as much pain as possible. Without me, she's nothing. Let her live in reality for a while so she'll appreciate how good she had it with me."

According to Faye Resnick, who had been staying at Nicole's condo at the time, approximately two weeks prior to Nicole's death, a set of house keys to Nicole's home was stolen. Not surprisingly, at the time of his arrest, the police located two sets of keys to Nicole's home on Simpson's person.

After the brief was filed, we learned that five days before the murders a woman named Nicole from West Los Angeles phoned a battered women's hot line called Sojourn. She complained that her ex-husband was stalking her and that she was afraid of him.

At Nicole's funeral, witnesses saw Simpson approach Nicole's casket. They heard him say, "I'm sorry . . . I'm sorry. I loved you too much."

They heard Juditha Brown ask her former son-in-law, "Did you kill my daughter?"

Simpson replied, "I loved her . . . I loved her . . . I loved her." Sometime later, Simpson returned to the casket and again said, "I loved you too much . . . That was my problem . . . I loved you too much."

The evidence showing the pattern of abuse was overwhelming. Even now I can hear Nicole's plaintive voice crying for help. "He's O. J. Simpson, I think you know his record. . . . He's following me again, Mommy. . . . I'm scared. He's fucking going nuts. . . . He's gonna beat the shit out of me. . . . He's going to kill me."

The evidence shows that he did.

5

Could We Tell the Jury About Domestic Violence?

How could a man with everything be guilty of these crimes? This question was foremost in the minds of many people. The question Scott, Lydia, and I asked ourselves was, how much evidence would we need to alter this mind-set?

On the morning of January 11, 1995, after the jury was selected and almost two weeks before the opening statements, the hearing to determine the admissibility of the domestic-violence evidence commenced. Scott, Lydia, and I met in the eighteenth-floor elevator lobby to go down to Ito's court. Scott was adjusting the collar of his shirt. We did not say much to each other.

"My throat's kind of dry," I said.

"So is mine," Scott said.

"Mine, too," Lydia chimed in.

I am sure we were all thinking the same thing. This evidence was key—the motive for murder. We had a mountain of evidence. Would Judge Ito reduce it to a molehill? Most of the legal pundits seemed to conclude that the evidence was inadmissible. That the hearing was televised and widely watched didn't calm our nerves.

Dean Gerald Uelmen, a stocky, scholarly-looking man with gray hair who appeared to be in his mid-sixties, rose to present the defense position. He had been my evidence professor at Loyola Law School. I remembered him as a first-rate professor with a sharp, analytic mind, a clear understanding of the rules of evidence, and an ability to share that understanding with his students.

Uelmen argued, before Judge Ito, that there is no relationship between domestic violence and murder because of the total number of domestic-violence incidents, less than 1 percent resulted in a homicide.

When I heard this, I thought, how asinine. Scott whispered to me, "That's like saying that there's no connection between sex and pregnancy because most of the time women have sex they don't get pregnant."

Uelmen painstakingly demonstrated that for each incident the prosecution presented, the defense would offer a dramatically different interpretation of it. For example, he presented the defense spin on Simpson's having spied on Nicole and Keith Zlomsowitch making love. He said, if the prosecution's theory is that jealousy was the motive of the murders, "then this incident in 1992 really undercuts that theory. In effect, it shows that Mr. Simpson, even observing his wife engaging in sexual activity with another man, did not become ballistic, did not interrupt them, did not physically assault anyone."

Gerald Uelmen's argument gave new force to my fear that on an incident-by-incident basis, people who were predisposed to reject such evidence could find a way to do so. Uelmen's comments reinforced my opinion that we had to introduce a substantial amount of domestic-violence evidence. However, it was not clear just how much evidence we would present. Introducing certain incidents might result in directing the jury's attention toward that which was equivocal or arguable and away from the seemingly indisputable physical and forensic evidence.

After Uelmen concluded his remarks at the January 11, 1995, hearing, Scott Gordon passionately and persuasively addressed the court. He refuted the defense argument that there is no connection between domestic violence and murder. He argued that in cases where a woman was killed by a boyfriend or husband, 90 percent of the women reported prior acts of abuse. In 45 percent of the cases studied, the leading motive for murder in such relationships was recent estrangement. The second leading motive, in an additional 15 percent of the cases, was the killer's suspicion that some other man was involved with the woman. Scott argued that both jealousy and estrangement characterized Simpson's relationship with Nicole.

Scott then summarized studies which showed that the Simpson

case bore the classic characteristics of a domestic-violence murder. In such cases, the killers inflicted harm much greater than was necessary to kill the victim. More than half the stabbings involved multiple wounds over the entire body. Most of the offenders studied attacked their victims within close physical proximity. In almost 60 percent of the cases the killer bludgeoned, strangled, stabbed, or slashed his victim's throat. As I listened to Scott, I thought of the horrific autopsy photographs showing the multiple wounds to Ron and Nicole.

Scott then turned to a discussion of the dynamics of an abusive relationship. He listed the behaviors a batterer employs to control his victim. They included intimidation, emotionally abusing a woman by insulting her, telling her she's crazy, mitigating what occurs within the home, unpredictable behavior, cutting a woman off from her support systems, limiting her friends, telling her what clothes she can wear, controlling the finances.

"[J]ust the kind of things that were done in this case," Scott added. "And that last terminal mechanism of control, the way to make sure that the batterer can have her and no one else will, is to kill her." Scott said, "The defense is right; this is a murder case. . . . [T]his murder took seventeen years to commit."

When I began my argument at the hearing, I reminded the court that Gerald Uelmen had claimed that the prosecution was labeling the case as one of domestic violence and that we did so to prejudice Simpson by calling him a wife batterer.

I told Judge Ito, "The prosecution has not *labeled* this case. The prosecution did not tell the defendant in this case to engage in a pattern of abuse against Nicole Brown Simpson over a period of seventeen years. The prosecution did not tell the defendant to commit a domestic-violence homicide. He did those things by himself."

I told Judge Ito that for the jury to understand the brutality of the murders, they had to understand Simpson's jealousy and possessiveness. Why would he kill Ron Goldman, whom he had probably only seen on one occasion before, at Starbucks? Ron was in the wrong place at the wrong time. Simpson did not know that Ron was returning Juditha Brown's glasses. In his paranoid jealousy, Ron was a potential suitor. That may explain "why he killed him, the brutality of it."

I summarized the defense position. They wanted to sanitize the relationship with neutral historical facts. "They got married on a certain date, they separated on a certain date, they divorced on a certain date, they tried to reconcile and that didn't work. They broke up."

That is what the defense wants the jury to hear, but it is a misleading scenario. The terms "husband and wife" are not neutral. "They imply love, they imply fidelity, they imply that this man at least at one time took an oath that he would honor, that he would protect, Nicole Brown Simpson. . . . That is the exact opposite of what we know the truth to be." The defense position would "perpetrate a fraud on the jury, and the California case law does not permit that."

During my argument, Judge Ito interrupted and posed a very insightful question. He asked whether presenting our theory of the murder to a jury would "make any sense unless you can put it into the battered woman's syndrome context" by calling an expert witness on domestic violence.

I responded that expert testimony would be very helpful but that the jury could use common sense to see the connection between the evidence of abuse and Nicole's murder. "[H]e had tried everything else. . . . He tried to take away her sense of personal dignity through the belittlement, through the name-calling. . . . He took away her sense of physical security through the abuse and the violence. And then, when there wasn't anything else that he could think of to take away from her, he took away her life."

We all felt good about our presentation. We were confident that Judge Ito would allow into evidence a significant number of the domestic-violence incidents. Paradoxically, we also felt depressed. Based on Judge Ito's questions to me about the law not allowing experts, we knew we would not be allowed to present such testimony, without which many of the domestic-abuse incidents might be rendered meaningless.

Six days after we argued the motion, Judge Ito handed down his ruling. In a meticulous and well-reasoned order, he held that all the statements Nicole made to other people and in her diary were inadmissible hearsay. Hearsay is any statement made outside the court that is being offered in court as true. For example, the statements Nicole made in her diary that she was beaten would be hearsay if we offered them to prove she was, in fact, beaten.

Judge Ito ruled that most of the evidence of assaults against Nicole was admissible. He excluded the 1977 incident in which Connie Good overheard Simpson beating Nicole and the 1986 incident in which Dr. Alpert treated Nicole for what she claimed to be a bicycle accident.

He also excluded the incident in the mid-1980s when Maria Baur saw Nicole outside Rockingham crying and also noted the broken pictures. The incident that Faye Resnick witnessed at California Beach Sushi in Hermosa beach, when Simpson exploded after Nicole mentioned a former boyfriend, was disallowed.

Although Judge Ito excluded some important evidence, overall we were very pleased with the ruling. The ruling left Chris Darden with sufficient latitude to accurately and meaningfully characterize the nature of the relationship to the jury.

But would this jury buy it?

6

Why the Jury Frightened Us

AFTER THE DOMESTIC-VIOLENCE hearing concluded, I spent most of my time with Marcia working on her opening statement. Opening statements are the most crucial part of the trial. Research on jurors indicates that they often make up their minds about a case early, after the opening statement is presented. Therefore, it is critical to present a powerful opening.

Chris and Marcia did just that. Chris reviewed the "cycle of violence" that characterized Simpson's relationship with Nicole. Marcia meticulously reviewed the physical evidence connecting Simpson to the murders, showing the jury that each piece "matches the defendant."

The first day of the opening statements, January 24, was the first time I got a good look at the jury. After court recessed, I talked briefly with DNA prosecutor Rock Harmon. In the elevator, on our way back to our offices, both of us were relatively quiet. "So what did you think of the jurors?" I asked.

Rock hesitated. "Did you see the way they were dressed?"

"They were dressed to the nines," I answered. "I don't like it."

Rock said, "You know, I've been in this business a long time. And whenever something happens to make the jurors believe that it's a special case or that they have to act differently, we are screwed. We count on jurors just acting the way they normally act. Because when they do what they normally do, what they normally do is to

41

convict. When they start treating the case specially, then strange things happen.''

Trial lawyers use many subtle clues to assess jurors. We look at the way they are dressed, their body language, whether they seem receptive to us, and whether they have a conservative versus a liberal appearance. Of course, these kinds of assessments have a limited degree of reliability. I did not like this jury, and I sensed that they did not like us.

Later, I mentioned to Bill Hodgman what I thought about the jurors. ''That's the worst-looking jury I've ever seen in my entire life. It has nothing to do with the racial composition of the jury. They just don't look like prosecution jurors, not one of them. They seem to be responding more favorably to Cochran than to Marcia or Chris. I have tried cases downtown before. I never had a jury that looked like that. What happened?''

''Hank, it was the most incredible thing. At first, Judge Ito excused many potential jurors who admitted even minimal accidental exposure to media coverage after he ordered them to avoid coverage about the case. That's how you end up with a juror who only reads the racing forms. By the time we were done, the panel we had left was really skewed. We were boxed in.'' Bill explained why he and Marcia did not exercise more of the twenty peremptory challenges. Bill was referring to the fact that both sides are given the same number of peremptory challenges, which generally permit an attorney to excuse prospective jurors without cause. The exception is that under a U.S. Supreme Court ruling, an attorney must be able to state sound reasons for excusing members of a minority group. Bill explained that he and Marcia had carefully analyzed all the jurors' questionnaires. So when they kicked off jurors they knew who the replacements would be. ''The jurors who would be replacing them were even worse than the ones we considered kicking.''

In an opening statement that took several days, Johnnie Cochran, in the style of a Sunday sermon, went on the offensive. He railed about a ''cesspool of contamination'' at the LAPD lab. He described the prosecution's evidence as corrupted, contaminated, and compromised. Stunningly, contrary to Chris's statement that a ''cycle of violence'' characterized Simpson and Nicole's relationship, Cochran said that Simpson's conduct, in truth, showed a "cycle of *benevolence*."

Most notably, he outlined the expected testimony of a number of witnesses who never testified, the most significant being Rosa Lopez. Lopez claimed that she saw Simpson's Bronco parked all night long outside Rockingham the night of the murders. Later, because she wanted to return to El Salvador, she testified in a conditional examination, a procedure during which a witness testifies outside the jury's presence so that the transcript can be presented later during the trial. Chris thoroughly annihilated her credibility on the witness stand, exposing her story as a lie. Most memorable was the tragicomic vision of this woman testifying before the entire world as to what she supposedly saw and responding to Chris's questions over and over again with: "I don't remember." The defense chose never to present her transcript testimony to the jury.

Cochran promised to deliver witness Mary Anne Gerchas, who would testify to seeing four Latinos and a white man hurriedly leaving the vicinity of Nicole's condo about thirty minutes after the probable time of the murders. Unfortunately for the defense, Gerchas was revealed as a con artist, with many lawsuits pending for fraud. Later, she pled guilty to fraud charges.

During Cochran's opening statement I went to the LAPD crime laboratory, after court adjourned, to begin my interviews of the laboratory people. I returned to court around 7 P.M. As I was walking down the hall toward the War Room, I bumped into Gil Garcetti. "Hank, did you hear what happened?" he asked.

"No," I replied.

"Bill had to go to the hospital. It may be a heart attack."

"Oh, my God!" I couldn't believe it. It brought home the cliché we have all heard. The guys who always seem to be in control suffer the worst stress; they keep it inside because they do not want to burden others. "Is he going to be okay?"

"I think so," Gil replied. "It's the stress. It's not worth losing your health over this case. Any case."

Thank God, Bill recovered quickly and was able to resume his place as a major player in the trial, but was no longer Marcia's cocounsel, the position Chris had assumed.

Later that night, when I was leaving for home, I walked out of the office with Chris and Marcia to the elevator lobby. Chris said, "Hank, can you do the coroner?"

"No way," I said. "Dennis Fung and the crime scene is taking more time than I ever thought possible."

Marcia chimed in, "Chris, he can't do the coroner. He can't do it! He has Dennis."

"Can you do shoes?" Chris shot back, smiling.

"Yes, I can do the shoes. But no other accessories."

Marcia said to me, "I want to get Brian Kelberg to do the coroner. Do you know him?"

Brian Kelberg is a wiry-bearded prosecutor in his early forties. He is a true genius, with a photographic memory. As head of the medicolegal section of the DA's office, he specializes in cases involving medical issues. Brian works out of an office which can only be entered through a narrow passage to his desk, a canyon between the boxes and piles of papers that fill the office. At this desk, every day, Brian eats his lunch, a candy bar and a liter bottle of diet soda.

I told Marcia, "I've talked to him several times. I know he's brilliant. Let's get him aboard."

7

"I've Had a Lot of Dreams About Killing Her"

WE OPENED OUR CASE with the dramatic, heartbreaking sounds of Nicole screaming in fear. On January 31, 1995, Sharyn Gilbert, our first witness, testified that she was the 911 operator who received an emergency call for assistance from the Rockingham estate in the early-morning hours of January 1, 1989. Under Chris's questioning, Gilbert testified that she "heard a female screaming and . . . heard someone being hit."

The tape was played before the jury. No intelligible conversation from Nicole could be heard on the tape. But it clearly conveyed that a frightening assault was in progress.

Cochran conducted the cross-examination. It was clear that Cochran wanted the 911 operator to testify it could be a "mutual fight" and that Nicole might have started it. Simpson often publicly stated that Nicole was a strong woman who sometimes got hurt when he was trying to restrain her. But Sharyn Gilbert refused to budge. She did not hear a man screaming; she heard a woman screaming.

Next Chris called Det. John Edwards. He testified that on January 1, 1989, he was a patrol officer in West Los Angeles. At 3:30 A.M. he received a radio call regarding the 911 call at Rockingham. He told the jury that when he "went into the hills on Rockingham, it was . . . dark, it was misty, it had been raining earlier in the evening." He got out of the car and pressed the call button near the gate.

A female voice came over the speaker and identified herself as Michelle, the housekeeper. The officer told her he needed to speak to the woman who made the 911 call.

The housekeeper said that no problem existed there.

Edwards replied that he wasn't leaving until he saw the person who had made the 911 call.

Then, according to Edwards, "a woman came running out of the bushes to my left. . . . She was a female Caucasian, blond hair. She was wearing a bra only as an upper garment, and she had on dark—I believe it was dark, lightweight sweatpants or night pajama bottom, and she ran across and collapsed on the speaker—the identical kind of a speaker post on the inside of the gate. She collapsed on it and started yelling, 'He's going to kill me. He's going to kill me.' "

Edwards continued, "Then she pressed the button, which allowed the gate to open, and then she ran out again yelling, 'He's going to kill me. . . .' She was hysterical."

"And she ran out to me. . . . She collapsed on me. . . . She was wet. She was—she was shivering, she was cold. . . . I could feel her . . . her bones and she was real cold and she was beat up."

Edwards's graphic description silenced the courtroom. Chris stared at Edwards for a long moment. He had heard this story a number of times, but it seemed to leave him no less shaken. Finally, Chris, in his quiet, understated tone, summarized the testimony and drove home the prosecution's theory of the case with one seemingly innocuous question. "What, if anything, did she say to you after she collapsed?"

Officer Edwards replied, "She said, 'He's going to—he's going to kill me.'

"I said, 'Well, who is going to kill you?'

"She said, 'O.J.' "

Chris paused again, allowing the jury to consider this evidence before continuing. Then he asked Edwards to describe Nicole's injuries. "She had a cut approximately one inch, I believe, on her left upper lip. She had a swollen right forehead. . . . I believe her left eye or right eye was starting to blacken, it was swollen, and she had some sort of an imprint or some sort of a swollen mark that you could see on her cheek. . . . And she had a hand imprint on her throat, on the left side of her throat." Nicole told him "that O.J. had slapped her, hit her with his fist, and kicked her . . . I think, pulled her by the hair."

He testified that his partner put a jacket on Nicole to stop her from shivering and sat her down in the patrol car to take a crime report. Edwards told the jury that Nicole stated, " 'You never do anything about him. You come out. You have been out here eight times. You never do anything about him.' "

After Nicole signed the crime report, Officer Edwards "saw Mr. Simpson walking towards me from the house wearing a bathrobe." He shouted, " 'I don't want that woman in my bed anymore. I got other women. I don't want that woman in my bed anymore.' "

The officer then told Simpson "that Nicole had obvious physical injuries . . . and that she wanted him arrested and I was going to have to place him under arrest for spousal battery."

According to Edwards, Simpson's temperament flared up to "a very loud, furious, angry mode again." He said, " 'I didn't beat her. Just pushed her out of the bed and nothing more.' " Then he said, " 'You've been out here eight times before and now you're going to arrest me for this?' And I remember he emphasized 'this.' Then he said, 'This is a family matter.' "

Edwards told Simpson to get dressed, and Simpson disappeared inside his house.

Finally, Edwards's supervisor arrived at the scene so that Simpson and Nicole could be transported in different cars. Edwards testified that as he was talking to his supervisor, Simpson fled the scene in his Bentley.

The officers returned to their vehicles and pursued, but Simpson got away.

On cross, Cochran asked questions that raised the implication that maybe the eight previous occasions on which the police went to Simpson's house were social calls.

On redirect, Chris laid this ghost to rest. "When the defendant told you that the police had been out to the house eight times before, did he tell you that they had been there on social calls?"

"No. As a matter of fact, I believe it was the same sort of thing," Detective Edwards replied.

The next day, the morning of February 1, I arrived at work by 8:00 A.M. Shortly afterward, Marcia and Chris approached me. One of them asked, "Are you familiar with the issue regarding the Ron Shipp statements?"

I was basically familiar with the issue, but I nevertheless said, "Clue me in."

Chris read from his trial notebook. "Simpson told Shipp: 'I was interviewed by detectives and they asked me to take a lie detector test' and [Shipp] replied, 'Well, what did you say?' And he kind of chuckled, and he says, 'Hey, to be truthful, Ron, man, I've had a lot of dreams about killing her.' And he says, 'I really don't know about taking that thing.' He did not say he wouldn't take it. He says, 'I really don't know about taking it.' "

Marcia said, "Hank, if you can get this in, I'll buy you dinner."

I asked, "Why me?"

"Ito likes you," Marcia replied.

This opinion was shared by others in the office. Around this time, one of our office's high-level administrators, Frank Sundstedt, said to me, "Judge Ito obviously has a lot of respect for you." This assessment would soon change dramatically.

After Marcia made the assignment, I quickly walked back to my office to write out an argument. I had plenty of time, about thirty minutes, before I had to present it. As soon as my argument came off the computer printer, I ran to the elevator lobby to go to court. I bumped into Chris and Marcia. The elevator door opened, and we entered. Marcia asked, "Ready?"

"We'll soon find out," I replied.

I argued to Judge Ito that the dream evidence, like the domestic-violence evidence, shows "that the defendant had an obsession with Nicole Simpson and that it was an obsession that led to her murder. I guess we could term it a fatal obsession. Isn't that precisely what the statement to Mr. Shipp is saying? 'I have been dreaming about killing my wife.' Isn't that powerful, powerful evidence of that fatal obsession?"

During my argument Judge Ito observed, "I agree that it is an interesting statement, and were I in your shoes, I would probably want to get it to the jury."

Defense attorney Carl Douglas argued the motion for the defense. I always felt a little sorry for Carl; his designated function on the defense team appeared to be to take the rap for any defense transgressions. In fact, someone sent us a cartoon showing Carl falling on a sword. Carl argued that just because Simpson supposedly dreamed about killing Nicole didn't mean he killed her.

After Carl's argument, Judge Ito said to me, "I'm interested, Mr.

Goldberg, in Mr. Douglas's argument of what is the significance of dreams?''

As I stood at the podium and began to answer Judge Ito's question, Marcia passed me a note. '' 'A dream is a wish your heart makes'—Walt Disney.'' I had to make a conscious effort not to laugh.

I answered Carl's argument that dreams are irrelevant. "Well, I was also very interested by that argument, too, because it seems to be so preposterous," I responded. "I mean, let's imagine, for example, Your Honor, that he simply had said, 'I have been dreaming about Nicole every day of my life . . .' not that he was going to kill her, just that he had been dreaming about Nicole. Wouldn't that in and of itself be relevant to show the issue of this obsession, this fixation on this woman, that he has not let go of it—let go of her? The fact that he is dreaming about killing her simply magnifies several hundredfold the relevance of the statement that he has been dreaming about Nicole.''

Finally, Ito ruled: "The statement regarding the dreams about killing will be admitted.''

After the arguments, Ron Shipp, a former LAPD officer, testified that he had known the defendant for twenty-six years. He left the force in 1989. Ron's brother Mike played football against Simpson in high school. Through this connection, Ron first met Simpson when Ron was about sixteen years old. Eventually, they developed a close relationship, although the defense argued that Shipp was simply a Simpson groupie.

One afternoon, months after his testimony, I saw Shipp sitting in the waiting area of the War Room. I introduced myself. We got to talking about our feelings about the case. Ron told me that a large segment of the African-American community now saw him as "being a traitor for testifying against O.J.''

"After everything, do you wish you hadn't done it?" I asked.

"No," Ron said. "I had to do it. I know in my heart I did the right thing.''

Ron impressed me as much as any other person I met during the trial. Here was a kind, moral, true gentleman.

Under Chris's questioning, Shipp testified that from 1978 to 1982 he was assigned to the West Los Angeles Division of the LAPD and would often visit Simpson at his home. He testified: "If I was on patrol, sometimes I would take [police officers] over there. I used to get a kick out of not telling them where I was going and ringing the doorbell and have O.J. come out and greet them."

Chris asked a seemingly insignificant, casual question. But it undermined the defense contention that the LAPD was out to get Simpson. "Did the defendant agree to appear at the LAPD's annual Christmas party?"

"Yes, he did," Shipp replied.

Was this the same police department whose officers would risk prison to frame Simpson?

Shipp testified that a few days after the January 1, 1989, incident, at Nicole's request, he went to the Rockingham estate to talk to Simpson about domestic violence. In this time frame, Shipp lectured police at the academy about the psychological profiles of domestic-violence victims and their batterers. According to Shipp, when he and Simpson discussed the January 1, 1989, incident, at first Simpson claimed that "Nicole was the aggressor and came after him and that he was acting in self-defense. . . . Then I told him what Nicole said had happened."

Next, Shipp showed Simpson the psychological profiles of batterers. "After we went over all the profiles, he denied that any of those were him except for maybe one." Shipp explained that when he showed Simpson the "pathologically jealous profile," Simpson admitted, " 'Maybe I might be a little jealous.' "

Shipp related that at a later date Simpson asked him to help him out on the domestic-violence charge; " 'Hey, Ron, can you get this taken care of?' " Ron, with candor and a degree of shame, admitted that he tried, unsuccessfully, to get Nicole to "sign off" on the police report, saying she didn't want to prosecute.

Later, Nicole did ask to drop the charges. However, in California a victim does not have this right. It is up to the prosecutor. Simpson eventually pled no contest to the charge and was given probation and a small fine and was ordered to undergo counseling sessions, some of which were completed over the phone.

Next, Chris asked Shipp about his having gone to the Rockingham estate after learning of Nicole's murder. Shipp told the jury about the conversation he had with the defendant the day after the murder at the Rockingham estate in the TV room. Shipp asked Simpson how he got the cut on his finger. "He said he did it in Chicago."

Later that evening, Simpson asked him to come upstairs to talk.

Shipp testified that after they went upstairs to Simpson's bedroom, Simpson made the statement about having dreams of killing Nicole.

During Chris's direct, Shipp admitted that at first he did not tell the detectives or the prosecutors about this statement. "I didn't want to tell the detectives at the time. . . . I just wanted everything to go away." Later, during cross, he explained further: "I didn't want to be going down as a person to nail O.J."

Carl Douglas conducted the cross-examination. Douglas attacked Ron Shipp in a sharp, accusatorial style. "Isn't it true, sir, that by being the witness who has a conversation with Mr. Simpson, that is going to possibly enhance your profile around the world?"

Shipp answered painfully but with conviction, "Mr. Douglas, there's no way, shape, or form that I would sit here and go through all this, put my family through this, for an acting career. I couldn't care less if I do any acting." Later, he added, "I'm doing this for my conscience and my peace of mind. I will not have the blood of Nicole on Ron Shipp. I can sleep at night, unlike a lot of others."

Then Carl Douglas asked a question which, like previous questions, was apparently based on statements from Simpson himself that Shipp felt were lies. "Didn't you take Mr. Simpson out to behind the garage to show him the area where the glove was supposedly found?"

In his reply Shipp addressed Simpson directly. "This is sad, O.J., but no. This is really sad."

Later, during a side-bar conference, Shipp mouthed "Tell the truth" to Simpson.

Through his cross-examination Carl repeatedly implied that Ron Shipp had a problem with alcohol. Shipp testified that his drinking problem had ended in 1989.

On Chris's redirect, he asked Shipp, "Have you obtained any monetary gain at all as a result of the information and knowledge you have relative to this case?"

"Not so ever."

Chris turned to the 1989 beating incident. After first denying any problem, Simpson finally agreed that he was a batterer. Shipp testified that he told Simpson to go public with his problem and "explained to him that a lot of times if you come forth with women's groups and admit you have a problem, that people will welcome you more." However, Shipp testified that Simpson changed his mind the next day because he had received advice—he wouldn't say from whom—that it was not a good idea to admit being a batterer.

On Carl's recross, rather than trying to directly attack the points Chris had made, he returned to the irrelevant alcohol issue. He accused Shipp of having been drunk at Simpson's wedding reception. He even accused him of drunk driving.

Until recently rereading the transcript, I didn't get a sense of how extensively the defense was allowed to attack Ron Shipp about irrelevant matters such as whether he had a past problem with alcohol and whether he was ever in a Jacuzzi with a woman other than his wife at Simpson's estate. Chris's objections to these lines of questioning were overruled. Most courts would not have allowed this type of attack on a witness. It was a harbinger of things to come.

On February 2, 1995, Michael Stevens testified. He had conducted a search of Nicole's safe-deposit box at Union Bank in Brentwood. In the box he removed photographs of Nicole showing bruises and injuries, a will, and three letters from Simpson apologizing for the 1989 incident. In one he stated: "Let me start by expressing to you how wrong I was for hurting you. There is no exceptible [sic] excuse for what I did. . . . I'm not going to blame being drunk thats [sic] no excuse. . . . Love Me."

In another letter, Simpson wrote

Nicole:
  Well, it seems that the worst part is behind us. I want you to know that whatever you might think to the contrary I'v [sic] taken full responcibility [sic] for this. . . . I love our time last weekend. I know to you it may not have been much, but it showed we can get along. *I love you and losing you is the only thing that madder* [sic] *to me.* So lets not forget the past. Lets work *together* (for the first time) to improve the futurr [sic] live [sic] together. Know [sic] manner [sic] what I love you. O.J. (emphasis added):

I always found the line that losing Nicole was the only thing that mattered to Simpson highly significant. That single sentence summarized the prosecution's entire theory of the motive for the murder.

Here were love letters from Simpson, swearing that he would change, that the beatings were over, avowing endless love. And then there was another 911 call. Witness Terri Moore took the call on October 25, 1993, at 9:54 P.M. from Nicole's home on Gretna Green. The following are excerpts from an official district attorney transcript of the call. (Three asterisks means unintelligible.)

OPERATOR: 911 Emergency

NICOLE: Yeah, can you send someone to my house?

OPERATOR: What's the problem there?

NICOLE: Well, my ex-husband or my husband just broke into my house and he's ranting and raving. . . . [H]e's crazy. . . . Could you get someone over here now to 325 Gretna Green, he's back? Please.

OPERATOR: Okay. What does he look like?

NICOLE: He's O. J. Simpson, I think you know his record. Could you just send somebody over here . . . ? He's in a white Bronco. . . . He's fucking going nuts. . . .

OPERATOR: Okay, just stay on the line.

NICOLE: I don't want to stay on the line. He's gonna beat the shit out of me. . . . [The court ordered this statement to be cut out of the tape, so the jury never heard it.]

NICOLE: He's screaming. . . .

OPERATOR: Okay. Okay. What is he saying?

NICOLE: Oh, something about some guy I know and hookers and * * * and I started this shit before and. . . . [i]t's all my fault, I started this before. I just don't want my kids exposed to this. . . . He broke my door. He broke the whole back door in. . . .

OPERATOR: Is he inside right now?

NICOLE: Yes. Yeah. . . .

NICOLE: O.J., the kids are sleeping . . . !

SIMPSON: You didn't give a shit about the kids *** fucking *** in the living room, they were here. You didn't care about the kids then . . . ! [referring to when Simpson saw Nicole making love to Keith Zlomsowitch]

OPERATOR: Just stay on the line, okay . . . ? Is he upset with something you did?

NICOLE: A long time ago, it always comes back. . . . No one can talk, listen to him. . . .

SIMPSON: * * * I don't give a shit anymore * * * motherfucker * * *

NICOLE: O.J., O.J, could you please leave. Please! Please leave!

SIMPSON: I'm not leaving * * * fucking * * * when I'm leaving
* * *. . . .

NICOLE: O.J., please, the kids * * *

SIMPSON: * * *

NICOLE: The kids are asleep * * * Please.

SIMPSON: * * *

OPERATOR: Is he leaving?

NICOLE: No. . . .

OPERATOR: Are you the only one in there with him?

NICOLE: Right now, yeah. . . .

OPERATOR: Has this happened before or no?

NICOLE: Many times. . . .

SIMPSON: * * * goddamn * * *

UNIDENTIFIED VOICE: * * * regarding Gretna Green Way, the suspect
is still there and yelling very loudly. . . .

SIMPSON: * * * and I try my goddamn best. I ain't putting up with
no * * * fucking * * *

OPERATOR: Do you see the police, Nicole?

NICOLE: No, but I will go out there right now. . . . I'm gonna
hang up.

Next, Sgt. Robert Lerner testified that he responded to this 911
call. He noticed Simpson's Bronco haphazardly parked in the middle of the street, about four to six feet away from the curb. He saw
the door Simpson broke to enter the location. As usual, the police
did nothing.

8

"And We Kissed Each Other Good-bye"

WE HAD DOCUMENTED years of pain Nicole had suffered at Simpson's hands. Through Denise Brown, Nicole's older sister, we hoped to bring that pain home to the jury. Except for her brown hair, Denise bore a striking resemblance to Nicole. She represented her sister in this trial in a physical as well as emotional way. If her testimony could reach the jurors, maybe we would have a chance.

On February 3, Denise, who shared Nicole's beautiful looks and at times the violence visited upon her younger sister, took the stand and was made to revisit the tragedy that ended in her sister's death. Denise testified that she and her parents, Louis and Juditha, lived in Dana Point, California. She is the oldest of the four Brown sisters, then Nicole, then Dominique, then Tanya.

She described an incident in 1987 when Denise, Nicole, Simpson, and another friend went to a bar, the Red Onion, in Laguna Beach. Denise said that they were drinking, goofing around, and being very loud. "And then at one point, O.J. grabbed Nicole's crotch and said, 'This is where babies come from and this belongs to me.'

"And Nicole just sort of wrote it off as if it was nothing like . . . she was used to that kind of treatment."

Next, Denise related an incident in the early 1980s when she and Ed McCabe, her boyfriend, went out to dinner with Simpson and Nicole. After dinner they went to Simpson's house on Rockingham.

55

Denise told Simpson that "he took Nicole for granted."

Simpson "blew up." He started ranting and threw pictures off the walls. He ran upstairs and threw clothes down the stairs. Then he "grabbed Nicole, told her to get out of his house, wanted us all out of his house, picked her up, threw her against the wall, picked her up, threw her out of the house." Denise continued: "Then he grabbed me and threw me out of the house."

This was at the end of Denise's testimony for that day. She was crying as she sat on the witness stand. At a side-bar conference shortly before court adjourned for the weekend, Cochran, at length, objected that Denise was crying so close to the jury.

When court reconvened on Monday, Denise described that during the incident where they were thrown out of the house Simpson's "whole facial structure changed. Everything about him changed. . . . His eyes got real angry. It was as—his whole jaw, everything started, you know—his whole face just changed completely when he got upset. . . . [I]t wasn't as if it was O.J. anymore. He looked like a different person."

When I heard this testimony, it reminded me of the story Dutton had told us about the woman describing her husband when he beat her: "His face changed, his physiognomy changed, his nostrils flared, he had a very different expression on his face."

Denise testified that after this incident they spent the night at the Beverly Hills Hotel. In the morning, Nicole decided to return to Simpson.

When I heard this testimony, I thought about how returning to the batterer is so characteristic of abused women. I lamented the fact that we would not be able to call an expert witness to explain this phenomenon.

Continuing with her testimony, Denise related that Sydney was born in 1985 and Justin in 1988 and that Nicole gained weight when she was pregnant. While she was pregnant, Denise heard Simpson call her a fat pig.

Then, when Nicole would lose weight, Simpson "loved it. 'Look at her. She looks great, doesn't she? She's mine.' "

Denise also testified to the events the day of the murders, June 12, 1994. She drove up from Laguna Beach to attend Sydney's dance recital with her sisters and her father and mother. The recital was at Paul Revere School in Brentwood. She testified that when Simpson arrived, he briefly greeted the Browns.

"Did he greet Nicole?" Chris asked.

"No, he did not." Denise described Simpson as having "a very bizarre look in his eyes. It was a very faraway look. . . . It was actually really kind of spooky. It was a frightening look. . . . He just had a very different look about him. . . . It just didn't look like the O.J. that we knew."

After greeting them, "he got a chair and put it in the corner by one of the back doors and he stuck the chair in the corner away from all the auditorium seats. . . . Every time I turned around, he was staring at Nicole."

After the recital was over, Denise and the family were planning to go to dinner. However, Nicole did not invite Simpson.

I felt that this was the final act of estrangement. It said to Simpson, irrevocably, It's over. Nicole is gone.

Toward the end of her direct examination Chris Darden asked, "What did you do after dinner was over?"

Denise, her voice quavering, replied, "We got up and—we got up and we walked out, and Nicole was going to go get some ice cream with the kids. And we kissed each other goodbye. The last thing I told her was that I loved her." She broke down sobbing and apologized to the court. "I'm sorry."

Robert Shapiro conducted a brief and mild cross-examination. The only matter of note he raised was a home videotape showing the defendant saying goodbye to the Brown family after the recital. This tape also showed Justin jumping up and being lifted by his father. Simpson appeared to be smiling at that time.

On redirect, Chris decided to use the videotape to refute Cochran's claim during his opening statement that Simpson had been suffering from acute arthritis on the day of the murder. "Mr. Simpson didn't appear to have any difficulty lifting his seventy-five-pound son, did he?"

"No," Denise replied.

Chris called Candace Garvey, a friend of Nicole's, to buttress Denise's testimony about Simpson's strange, out-of-character behavior the evening of the dance recital. She testified: "It was almost like he was simmering. . . . [W]hen he stared at me, I felt like he was looking right through me, and it scared me a little bit."

Next, Cynthia Shahian testified that she was a close friend of Nicole's. Nicole showed her a letter Simpson had written to her only six days before the murders. The cold, legalistic letter said, "*Because of the change in our circumstances,* I am compelled to put you on writ-ten notice that you do not have my permission or authority" to use Rockingham for your mailing address.

The part about the change in their circumstances was extremely important. It was additional evidence of estrangement.

Cynthia Shahian was the last witness during the domestic-vio-lence portion of the case. Later that day, I poked my head into Marcia's office to ask her how we were doing. Primarily, I wanted to know how much time I had left to prepare my section of the case.

Marcia said, "I think Chris put on a solid case demonstrating the nature of the relationship and the domestic violence. All of our strongest, least debatable evidence is in. I want to move on to the time-line evidence." She was referring to the evidence showing that Simpson had no alibi for the time frame of the murder. She contin-ued, "Then we'll swing into the forensic evidence. At the end of the case, we'll turn back to domestic-violence, bracketing the case with the domestic violence evidence."

What every trial lawyer learns is that no matter how carefully the case may be planned, one must be flexible. Complex case litigation can be compared to a high-level game of chess. An attorney must project, If I make this move, what will my opponent do to counter it, and how will I counter his response? It may be necessary to project twenty moves into the trial and calculate all of the possible permuta-tions. Except that in trial advocacy, unlike chess, you have more than your opponent with which to be concerned. One must not only consider the opposition but also the judge and, most important, the jury. Therefore, reasonable, experienced attorneys can and often do differ about the many complex tactical issues involved in a trial.

Later, as we will see, it became apparent to Marcia, and eventu-ally to all of us, that the jury had turned off. Months later, the plan to put on more domestic-violence and stalking evidence was scrapped.

But it seemed Chris had done it. With the evidence he had presented, he had put the knife in Simpson's hand—through Simp-son's own angry, explosive voice on the 911 tape. Nicole, from the grave, had also spoken to this jury: "He's going to kill me." We prayed that the jury would listen.

9

The Hole-in-the-Doughnut Defense

A WEEK AFTER we called our first witness, the domestic-violence portion of the case came to a close. Now Marcia would provide the answer to the previously hotly debated question of whether Simpson had the opportunity to commit the murders in time to meet the limousine driver who took him to the airport.

Marcia, through the testimony of a number of Ron Goldman's coemployees at the Mezzaluna restaurant, established the crucial time-line evidence culminating in the discovery of the murders. She demonstrated that Simpson had no alibi during this crucial period of time.

Nicole, her mother, father, and two sisters, and Nicole's two children, Sydney and Justin, left Mezzaluna at around 8:30 P.M., on the evening of June 12. Nicole and the children crossed the street and purchased ice cream at Ben & Jerry's.

Nicole's mother, Juditha, phoned the restaurant at 9:37 P.M. and stated that she had left a pair of prescription glasses in the vicinity of the restaurant. The glasses were recovered in the gutter where the Brown's car had been parked. At about 9:43 P.M., Nicole called the restaurant and spoke to Ron Goldman.

Ron offered to return the glasses to Nicole at her Bundy condo, a half a mile from the restaurant. Ron left the restaurant at about 9:50 P.M. Marcia established that Ron had plenty of time to walk to his apartment about half a block from the Mezzaluna, change his clothes, and drive the short distance to Bundy in time to arrive by 10:15 P.M., the approximate time of the murders.

With another series of witnesses, Nicole's Bundy neighbors, Marcia pieced together the parts of the puzzle establishing that the murders probably occurred around 10:15 P.M.

Pablo Fenjves testified that he lived behind Nicole's condominium. He was in his apartment that night and, at approximately 10:15 to 10:20 P.M., heard the insistent barking of a dog. He described it as a "plaintive wail." He determined the time based on the TV program he was watching.

Eva Stein testified that she and her boyfriend, Louis Karpf, lived next door to Nicole and that she was awakened by loud, persistent barking, which was unusual, in the vicinity of Nicole's condo. She awoke at approximately 10:15 P.M. Louis Karpf testified that he arrived home at around 10:45 P.M. He also heard loud barking. He saw Nicole's Akita, Kato, in the street on Bundy, running and walking aimlessly and barking very loudly.

Mark Storfer lived just south of Nicole's condo. He was putting his son to bed when he heard the barking. He was concerned that the noise would wake his son. About three minutes after the barking started, he looked at his clock. It was 10:20 to 10:21 P.M.

Steven Schwab, another neighbor, testified that he walked his dog every night between 10:30 and 11:00 P.M. on weekends. He saw the dog at the corner of Dorothy and Bundy at around 10:55 P.M. and noticed blood on its back paw. Kato followed Mr. Schwab as he continued walking. As Kato passed houses, he would look up the pathways and howl. Kato followed Schwab home. Schwab arrived there at around 11:05 P.M. and met a neighbor, Sukru Boztepe. Mr. Boztepe agreed to take care of Kato for the night.

Subsequently, Mr. Boztepe decided to try to find Kato's owner. The dog became more and more agitated as it literally pulled Mr. Boztepe back to the crime scene. When they arrived at Nicole's condo, Kato looked up the walk. This caused Mr. Boztepe also to look and discover Nicole's body lying in a pool of blood streaming down the walkway. Ron's body was not visible at first view. Mr. Boztepe began to knock on neighbors' doors to summon the police.

After two days of testimony by time-line witnesses, the first officer to arrive at the crime scene took the stand. Robert Riske arrived at Bundy at 12:13 A.M. on Monday, June 13. He found Ron's body a few feet north of Nicole's, in a small area of Nicole's garden, which was surrounded by a tall wrought-iron fence. This enclosure created a virtual cage that made Ron a standing target for the savage, multiple knife wounds.

Officer Riske checked the victims to determine whether they were dead. Marcia elicited that Officer Riske and his partner, Miguel Terrazas, carefully inspected the crime scene, using a flashlight. He saw one glove. The door to Nicole's condo was open. When he entered, he saw no sign of ransacking or forced entry. While inspecting for evidence, Riske's partner pointed out blood on the rear gate. Riske's testimony about one glove and blood on the rear gate dismantled the defense conspiracy theory. It rendered stillborn their theory that originally there were two gloves at Bundy and that Detective Fuhrman later moved one to Rockingham. It also disproved the defense theory that the blood on the rear gate had been planted after June 13.

Marcia established that before Fuhrman arrived at the scene, Riske took a number of officers through the crime scene and pointed out evidence to them. Marcia established that six officers only saw one glove before Fuhrman ever set foot on Bundy.

Johnnie Cochran had not concluded his cross-examination when court recessed for the weekend. I was eager to see what would happen when court reconvened. It would provide some insight as to the direction of the defense attack and the shape of the trial to come.

That weekend, the prosecution suffered a major blow. Months before the opening statements, Marcia told me that during Riske's testimony she wanted the jury to see Bundy. Jury views are uncommon in Los Angeles County. Judges are loath to conduct them because of the time and expense. However, we felt that it was important for the jury to see the extremely confined space where Ron and Nicole were killed. Knowing that Ron had been trapped in a confined space when he was murdered would enable the jury to understand why maneuvering to defend himself or to flee would have been very difficult.

The defense wanted the jury to also view Rockingham, which we opposed. We felt that doing so would create sympathy for Simpson by reinforcing his celebrity-hero status. Moreover, since the crime was not committed inside the Rockingham estate, viewing the home's interior would be irrelevant. However, Judge Ito agreed to allow a viewing of both locations.

I felt strongly that photographs of the evidence and the bodies at Bundy should be posted at locations throughout Bundy so that the jury could mentally reconstruct how the scene appeared on June 13. Days before the visit, in Judge Ito's chambers, I argued that not using this procedure would render viewing the crime scene meaningless. Without photos, the jury would not be able to figure out exactly where the bodies and evidence had been discovered. I had used the same method during a previous murder trial, and the jury had later told me that it had been invaluable to them in mentally reconstructing the crime scene. For unknown reasons, Judge Ito denied my request.

I told Marcia that what little benefit we might receive from the Bundy viewing would be negated by the Rockingham tour. She said, "Forget it, Hank. It's a moot point. Ito is hung up on this tour. He's looking forward to it." Marcia asked me to attend the viewing. I told her I didn't want to go, since I was still preparing my end of the case. Marcia replied, "You're going to present a major part of the case. It relates to the crime scene. It's important for the jury to see you there and begin to associate you with the case."

That Sunday, January 12, 1995, the grand tour began. We started out in the morning. Members of the prosecution team, including Marcia Clark, Scott Gordon, and I, rode in a minivan. We joined a procession consisting of a large sheriff's bus for the jury and a number of minivans. LAPD Metro Division, which conducts presidential motorcades, whisked us to the crime scene. LAPD's SWAT team provided security. We traveled west on the Santa Monica Freeway, one of the city's most important arteries. It had been shut down for the motorcade.

We got off the freeway in West Los Angeles and drove west toward Brentwood. As we passed the Veterans Administration Hospital, which is on the border of Westwood and Brentwood, I saw a large LAPD staging area. There were at least a hundred police officers there in case something happened. All that was missing was a brass band, bikinied cheerleaders, and Simpson, dressed in his football uniform, waving to the crowds from a bubble-top limousine.

Finally, we reached the Bundy location. We waited on the sidewalk in front of Bundy as groups of jurors walked through the location. The street was shut down, and Judge Ito restricted the airspace above. I stood in front of the location and talked briefly with Ito. He looked like a boy who had just opened his Christmas presents and discovered he got everything he wanted and more. Referring to the massive nature of the operation, he said, "Isn't this great." Like a general, he seemed all at once awed and pleased that he had the power to command such an operation.

I was appalled. Speechless. All I could think of was the cost and inconvenience of this little adventure, still another Simpson-trial sideshow.

In the movies, after a murder is committed, the crime scene is cordoned off with tape and an armed guard is stationed at the location until after the trial. If this procedure were used in Los Angeles, half the city would be covered with crime-scene tape. The police released both the Bundy and Rockingham locations on the evening of June 13. Since then, Simpson's daughter, Arnelle, had been living at Rockingham.

After the Bundy viewing, the motorcade proceeded to Rockingham. It was the second time I had been there. The first had occurred weeks earlier, when the defense allowed members of the prosecution to see the location. Before the jury entered, someone from the prosecution team brought some issues to my attention. Changes that had been made inside the residence after our first visit were immediately noticeable. A fire was burning in the fireplace, a Bible was strategically placed on a table in the living room, pictures of Simpson with his family were hung on the wall of the staircase to the second floor and in Simpson's bedroom. Marcia objected to these crass attempts to influence the jury. Judge Ito ordered that one picture be taken down and the fire extinguished. No other alterations were required.

When I walked through the residence with a group of jurors, I noticed other changes. When I had visited weeks earlier, the carpet in the guest room had been flooded by a leaking roof during the recent rains, and there had been a pungent odor of mildew. Now the room was filled with the smell of a brand-new carpet. The place was immaculately clean. As the jurors walked through the living-room area, they passed what I referred to as the Simpson shrine, a trophy room packed to the rafters with awards and memorabilia paying homage to the man we were trying for murder. The room contained the Heisman Trophy, the most coveted award a football player can obtain.

When I walked upstairs, I noticed that the pictures I had seen during my last visit, of Simpson with his white golfing buddies, were gone. They were replaced with pictures of Simpson with African Americans. When I entered Simpson's large bedroom, the French doors leading to the balcony were flung wide open. As I walked toward the open doors, the soothing sound of flowing water was clearly discernible. I looked down. The defense had turned on an artificial waterfall that spilled into the pool below.

I was angry and dejected. How could Ito have allowed such a tour of Simpson's estate? What a shameful attempt to distract the jury and evoke sympathy for Simpson.

And it worked. It became a major theme that resonated with the jurors: How could a man with all this wealth and comfort commit two brutal murders?

When court next convened, Johnnie Cochran engaged in a painstaking cross-examination of Officer Riske's actions at the Bundy crime scene.

A common line of attack by defense attorneys is to compile a list of things the police did not do in investigating a crime. They then go through the list to try to make the investigation appear incompetent. Every defense attorney can always think of something which arguably might have been done. This line of attack is intended to distract the jury away from the real issues and the actual evidence. In criminal cases, the real issue is the strength of the evidence the prosecution produces, not speculation about what evidence has not been produced but could have been. As one judge before whom I have tried many cases often tells a jury: "As you travel through life, friends, whatever may be your goal, keep your eye on the doughnut, and not on the hole." In the Simpson case, the tactic of concentrating on the hole was employed to ludicrous extremes.

For example, Johnnie Cochran attacked Riske's competence for not having documented the extent to which some ice cream in a cup on a banister inside Nicole's condo had melted. Cochran's hard-hitting cross on the ice-cream issue penetrated even deeper. "Could you tell from the condition of that melting ice cream, as you have described it, what was the flavor of the ice-cream?"

"I have no idea," Riske was forced to concede.

Cochran was making important gains on the ice cream front.

"Can you tell whether it was one scoop or two scoops or whatever?" Cochran demanded.

Again, Riske, who appeared to be melting under Cochran's ice-cream cross, did not know.

Cochran continued to strike blow after blow. He established that Riske failed to lift the cup to see "whether it left a ring or anything."

Similar lines of cross-examination were exhaustively explored. Riske failed to photograph the burning candles to document the degree to which they melted, test the bathwater in the tub to see how warm it was, or examine the dog's teeth to determine if it had bitten anyone. The defense did not bother to establish how a dog's tooth that bit someone hours earlier might look any different. This cross took over two court days to complete.

On redirect, Marcia defused the explosive ice-cream issue. She established that the ice cream was melted around the outside and still frozen in the middle. Marcia established that neither the melting rate of ice cream and candles nor bathwater temperatures would be an accurate means of determining the time of the murders. This was especially true, since the disagreement between the defense and prosecution as to the probable time of the murders was only about fifteen minutes.

The doughnut-hole defense was employed again against the next witness to testify, Sgt. David Rossi. He was called to corroborate certain key facts that Officer Riske had established. Rossi had also seen only one glove at Bundy and blood on the rear gate. He had made both discoveries before Detective Fuhrman had arrived.

As this testimony continued, I was busily working to prepare my section of the case. However, I was also trying to monitor what was happening in court by watching the TV coverage and reading the transcripts at night. The conclusion I drew was that the testimony of Officer Riske and Sergeant Rossi struck deep into the heart of the defense conspiracy theory. They established that there was only one glove before Fuhrman arrived, and they saw the blood on the rear gate.

On cross, there was no suggestion that they were part of a conspiracy or were lying. The extensive, often humorous questions went to the issue of competence. The conspiracy theory did not flower in full bloom until weeks later, when the defense hoped that the jury had forgotten their testimony.

Next, Det. Ron Phillips took the stand. He testified that he and

Detective Fuhrman had arrived at Bundy at 2:10 A.M. As did the other witnesses before him, Ron corroborated that when he and Mark Fuhrman walked through the crime scene for the first time, there was only one glove. Ron also noticed the blood on the rear gate.

At 2:39 A.M., Ron Phillips learned that Robbery/Homicide, an elite unit within the LAPD operating out of downtown, was going to take over the investigation. He waited at the crime scene until Robbery/Homicide detectives Tom Lange and Philip Vannatter arrived. Before Robbery/Homicide took over the case, Ron testified, Comdr. Keith Bushey had ordered him to notify O. J. Simpson in person and to extend him "VIP" treatment.

Later that morning, at 6:05 A.M., he eventually located Simpson in Chicago and spoke to him over the phone. Ron informed Simpson that his ex-wife had been killed. The first words out of Simpson's mouth were " 'She's been killed? What do you mean she's been killed? Oh, my God, Nicole is dead.' " Then he got very upset.

Ron said to Simpson, "Mr. Simpson, please try to get ahold of yourself. I have your children at the West Los Angeles police station. I need to talk to you about that."

Simpson asked, " 'What do you mean you have my children at the police station? Why are my kids at the police station?' "

Ron replied, "Because we had noplace else to take them. They are there for safekeeping. I need to know what to do with your children."

Simpson said, " 'Well, I'm going to be leaving out of Chicago on the first available flight. I will come back to Los Angeles. Is Arnelle there . . . ? Let me talk to Arnelle.' "

He did not ask how Nicole had been killed, when it happened, how it happened, who killed her, or any other question concerning the circumstances of his ex-wife's death.

The morning before Cochran commenced his cross-examination of Ron Phillips, I went to Emil's, a local bakery and coffee shop near my house. I live in Westwood, a residential area in Los Angeles. At 7:00 A.M. before heading downtown, I often stopped there. The customers in the early mornings are mainly retired senior citizens, mostly Jewish. Particularly endearing to me are the Yiddish accents many of them have, as did my paternal grandparents. When I was a child, Grandma Hattie lived with us for a time. When talking to me or my older brother and sister, her dialogue was peppered with Yiddishisms. I had thought for some time that my name was Bubela.

I would hear those same inflections several times each week during the trial as I was given advice: "Hank, this Mr. Cochran, he's a shrewd cookie. He has the jury eating out of his hands." I found them to be more knowledgeable about the trial than the so-called media experts. They had a warm affection for me; they were my "fans." The mornings I spent with them were comforting to me.

Once, they put a leather glove on one of the outside tables near the entrance. When I entered, they chorused "Look, Hank, it's the missing glove from the crime scene!"

The morning of Ron Phillips's cross, I spoke to one of my friends from Emil's, Mary, a Beverly Hills schoolteacher in her fifties. She told me she thought Ron Phillips's testimony that Simpson failed to ask questions about the circumstances of Nicole's death was devastating. She herself had wanted to know everything when she was informed that her husband had been killed.

Whether or not one had ever lost a family member, the general reaction to Phillips's testimony was that Simpson's failure to ask appropriate questions seemed suspicious. I was curious to see what Cochran would do with this evidence during cross.

Johnnie Cochran skillfully elicited that Simpson appeared to be stunned and upset when he heard the news of Nicole's death. He had Ron Phillips explain that different people react to shocking situations variously.

I knew that Cochran's very simple but effective cross would be more than sufficient to negate this testimony in the jury's eyes. Based on jury questionnaires, we believed that the Simpson jury, like much of the public, wanted to believe that this sports icon could not have murdered anyone. I made a mental note to analyze how effectively the defense would be able to defuse other similar, equivocal testimony about Simpson's state of mind, such as the Bronco chase and the self-serving statement Simpson gave to Detectives Lange and Vannatter on June 13.

Detective Tom Lange, who, together with Detective Vannatter, was in charge of the investigation, was the next witness Marcia called. Lange, a seasoned veteran, is in his late forties, balding, and mustached. He wears wire-rimmed glasses. He comes across as a no-nonsense, model police officer. It would be typecasting for him to play *Dragnet*'s Sgt. Joe Friday: "Just the facts, ma'am, just the facts."

Tom was precise and crisp in answering Marcia's questions. His testimony essentially corroborated areas covered through other witnesses. Of note, he testified that Ron Phillips showed him the blood drops on the rear gate, seemingly striking another nail into the coffin of the defense theory that those drops were planted weeks later.

On cross, Cochran continued with the doughnut-hole defense, attacking the quality of the police work. Adding to those topics raised with the other officers, Cochran established that Lange had failed to determine precisely what type of music was playing on Nicole's sound system when he entered the condo. Lange could only say that it seemed "to be New Wave, modern-type music, instrumentals." Cochran asked Detective Lange if he had determined "whether this was an FM [station] or a CD or a tape or whatever?"

"No," Detective Lange was forced to admit.

Cochran elicited that the blood on the rear gate at Nicole Simpson's house was not collected until weeks after the murders. Later, this fact would become the basis for the defense theory that the blood had been planted. Although Tom and a number of officers had seen the blood on June 13, the crime-lab personnel had overlooked it. It was not collected until July 3, when Tom noticed it was still there while revisiting the crime scene with Marcia Clark and Bill Hodgman.

Cochran also returned to all the standard issues, such as not checking the dog's teeth. During Cochran's cross, "chilling" new information was elicited about the ice cream. Tom had conducted a follow-up investigation and had determined that the flavor was Chocolate Chip Cookie Dough. Stung by the revelation, Cochran quickly recovered. He established that although Lange attempted to determine the average melting rate of Chocolate Chip Cookie Dough, he entirely failed to investigate Rain Forest Crunch.

Cochran also alluded to a defense theory, which was never fully presented to the jury, that the murders could be a Colombian drug-lord "hit." This fantasy was manufactured out of thin air. The theory was that hit men could have been targeting Nicole's friend Faye Resnick, who had lived at Bundy for a period of time. The suggestion was that maybe Faye Resnick, who had a drug problem, owed money to the drug lords. The hit men mistook Nicole for Resnick, murdered her, and were forced to "hit" Goldman when he arrived.

On redirect, Lange testified that the crime did not appear to be drug-related or a drug hit. Lange pointed out that the murderer employed "overkill," inflicting many more wounds than necessary to kill the victims. "It appeared to be motivated by rage and not narcotics related."

On his final cross, Cochran continued to pursue the drug-related-killing theory. This allowed Detective Lange to explain, "The fact that the victim may have a friend who uses drugs—in light of no other evidence in that regard—has very little consequence to me. The fact that every bit of that evidence that I have in this case points toward the defendant has a lot more to do with this."

On Wednesday, March 8, after eight days on the stand, Tom Lange was finally excused. But the crime-scene portion of the people's case was not over. In a sense, it had just begun.

10

The Mark Fuhrman We Thought
We Knew

WHAT SHOULD HAVE BEEN a relatively mundane event, calling another witness to testify about the crime scene, was to become the most pivotal moment in the trial. After Tom Lange's testimony, Marcia Clark called Det. Mark Fuhrman to the stand.

I first met Fuhrman around 1987. At the time, I was a relatively new deputy district attorney, assigned to the West Los Angeles Municipal Court, where I would conduct preliminary hearings in which a judge decides whether there is sufficient evidence for a case to go to trial. A small number of more productive police officers were regulars at the courthouse. They handled greater caseloads and made more arrests than most of their colleagues. Mark was one of those regulars.

Mark was a muscular officer, about six feet two inches, in his mid-thirties, with a military bearing and clipped manner of speech that reflected his marine background. He looked and acted like a prototypical marine; in fact, he had served in Vietnam. I always had the impression that he was in combat and had seen and experienced things he didn't want to talk about. During the Simpson trial I learned that he served his tour of duty on a transport ship.

As a young man, Mark had wanted to become an artist. This surprised me because I thought he was too rigid in his thinking and too narrow minded to possess any artistic ability.

He was born in a small town in Washington in 1952. There was only one black family in the town. As a child, Mark would sometimes tease the two boys in that family and call them the "N" word.

Mark's father was a truck driver. Mark later told a psychiatrist that he hated his father, seeing him as irresponsible and unkind. His parents were divorced when he was seven. He described his mother as a "mean drunk."

I never heard Mark say anything to me or in my presence that indicated racist beliefs. Nor did anyone ever tell me anything about Mark that indicated racial bias. Moreover, Mark was always very friendly to me, and I did not sense any anti-Semitism. Nor did I see any signs of a personality disorder. However, I had heard that he had a collection of World War II memorabilia, including Nazi medals.

Mark graduated from the police academy second in his class. During his early career he received mediocre performance evaluations, but this can only become apparent, however, if one knows how to read LAPD evaluations. Excellent means good; good, competent; competent, a dismal failure. It takes a while to catch on. Words like "immaturity" or "arrogance" on an otherwise good evaluation, as on Mark's early ones, signal a real problem.

When I first met Mark, I thought he was a true believer, which, in the criminal justice system, is what new professionals are often called. Frequently, new public defenders believe that most of their clients are innocent; new prosecutors, that all defendants deserve the maximum sentence; new police officers, that every person who commits any criminal violation is a "scumbag" who deserves to be severely punished.

I saw in Mark an anger, arrogance, and lack of perspective. To Mark, there were no shades of gray. He didn't have the maturity and perspective that I have seen in many more experienced officers.

However, in a positive sense, Mark was one of the few officers who could consistently be counted on to show up in court on time and would make the extra effort to locate witnesses and conduct follow-up investigations. By late 1988, I was reassigned to the South Central Los Angeles Juvenile Court and would no longer see him.

I didn't see him again until 1990. By then, I was working in the Santa Monica Judicial District, which includes West Los Angeles. By this time, Mark had become a detective in the West Los Angeles Division. He had changed over the years. He seemed to have mellowed and to have gained more perspective and maturity. In my experience, that often happens when police officers move through the ranks. I thought that perhaps the change in Mark was due to his becoming a detective. Being a good detective requires one to be fairly open-minded.

And Mark was a good detective who enjoyed doing his job. He started working the robbery table and later moved to homicide. Danette Meyers prosecuted many of Mark's cases. She is an excellent, hard-charging African-American deputy district attorney, colleague, and friend of mine. Danette and Mark got along marvelously. They worked well as a team and often socialized together. Before Mark took the stand, Danette told Chris Darden that in her opinion Mark was not a racist.

During that same time frame, I gave my unsolicited opinion to Chris and other members of the prosecution team. In his book *In Contempt,* Chris mistakenly writes that I had prosecuted a murder case in which Mark was one of the lead investigators and that I had heard that he was called Fuhrer-man and Fuhrman the German and was a racist. In fact, when asked what I thought about Fuhrman, I said, "I think he's a fascist." I told Chris that my opinion was based on intuition, Fuhrman's conservatism, and the fact that he collected Nazi memorabilia. I used the word *fascist,* even though it was probably groundless, because I wanted to make it clear that Fuhrman could be a problem. I did not want to lure Chris into a false sense of security.

I recall using the same terminology in discussions with prosecutors Scott Gordon and Cheri Lewis, who was responsible for handling the Fuhrman legal issues. I also disagree with Chris' perception that Scott and other members of the team were confident Fuhrman would not present a problem as a witness. Scott, Cheri, and team members were well aware of the potential dangers. However, many people on the team, Chris included, believed that hiding him was no option because the defense would surely "discover" him and ram him down our throats.

The first time I spoke to Mark regarding the Simpson case was sometime in November 1994, shortly after I was assigned to the prosecution team. By then, the defense had publicly said that Mark was a racist and claimed that he planted evidence.

Mark told me, "These allegations about planting evidence and me being a racist are unbelievable. They are not just difficult for me personally—that wouldn't be so bad—but I'm concerned about my wife and children. It's been really hard on them. The idea that I'm going to plant evidence is ludicrous. I can't believe that they don't even need any evidence to make these allegations."

In addition to talking to deputy district attorneys and officers who knew Mark, it was necessary to dig deep into his background for any indication of racism.

Mark's record revealed three incidents the defense could use to suggest that Mark was a racist. We made a motion to exclude each of them on the grounds that they were irrelevant to the issues in the case. Moreover, introducing the evidence and allegations of racism would be highly inflammatory and could throw the jurors off track in their efforts to rationally discover the truth.

The first incident involved a claim for disability that Mark made against the city. In 1981, thirteen years before the murder, Mark claimed that his job as a policeman had put him under so much stress that he was no longer able to work as a cop. Several psychiatrists had evaluated him. Mark told them that after his divorce in 1980 he became more aware of the problems he was facing at work.

The psychiatric report concluded that there was

> some suggestion here that the patient was trying to feign the presence of severe psychopathology. This suggests a conscious attempt to look bad and an exaggeration of problems which could be a cry for help and/or overdramatization by a narcissistic, self-indulgent, emotionally unstable person who expects immediate attention and pity. However, from behavioral observations and from an overall pattern in the tests, the presence of severe psychopathology is doubtful to say the least.

In addition to indicating that Mark was faking his claimed emotional problems, the report contained several other shocking references to things Mark said. Mark told the psychiatrist that "[h]e was in the Marines from 1970 to 1975. During his last 6 months, he 'got tired of having a bunch of Mexicans and niggers that should be in prison, telling (him) they weren't going to do something.' "

The report also contained explicit, detailed references to violent thoughts and deeds Mark had claimed to have. It indicated that Mark joined the LAPD in 1975. Shortly thereafter, he was working a gang detail in East Los Angeles. The report continued:

He was in a fight "at least every other day . . . ." He recalls choking, kicking, and punching a man after he was unconscious. In another incident, a man was on PCP [phencyclidine] and the patient kicked his legs out from under him. Then, he broke the man's elbows. He says that the other policemen were standing around watching him. Afterward, he wondered what he was doing.

However, the experts evaluating Mark concluded that he was lying about or exaggerating such incidents. The report concluded that sometimes police officers fake violent thoughts and actions to get retirement benefits.

Further suggestion that the patient's subjective complaints are self-serving are seen in his description of his response to Internal Affairs Investigations, his MMPI [Minnesota Multiphasic Personality Inventory] profile and his lack of emotion in describing violent thought content.

In May 1983, Mark's suit was dismissed on the grounds that he had not been truthful regarding his violent behavior.

The next incident occurred in 1985 or 1986. In that time frame Mark was accused of making racist statements at a Marine Corps recruiting office in Redondo Beach. Kathleen Bell worked as a real estate agent in an office above the recruiting center. In a letter written to Johnnie Cochran she said that she occasionally stopped in to the office to talk with the marines working there. Mark occasionally visited the recruiting office because he was interested in the reserves. In her letter to Cochran, Kathleen Bell claimed that Mark made racist statements to the effect of wanting to burn all of the "niggers." He supposedly made this comment to her in the presence of two marines. Months later, Kathleen Bell testified to the incident in detail.

Our office and the LAPD interviewed the marines who worked at the recruiting center when Fuhrman visited there. One of the recruiters, who was supposedly present during the incident, Joseph Foss, completely contradicted Bell's claim. He remembered introducing Bell to Fuhrman. He stated that Bell was interested in Mark but Mark "graciously" made it clear that he was not interested in her. She simply walked away. There was no discussion about African Americans, and no racist comments were made.

The other two marines who worked at the office during the time frame in question also denied witnessing the Bell incident.

Cheri, Chris, and LAPD detective Pietrantoni reinterviewed one of the marines, Maximo Cordoba, on January 20 at the D.A.'s office. He stated that he never saw Mark and Bell together. However, he recalled that either Mark or Ron Roher, another marine that Mark sometimes spoke to about reserves, used the word "boy." Then he changed his statement and claimed that Mark used the word boy. Although the exact context is unclear, Cordoba claimed that he said to Ron Roher, "I was just trying to help your boy," referring to Fuhrman.

Fuhrman supposedly responded, "You can't help me, boy," or, "You're the boy."

However, a week later Cheri and Detective Pietrantoni interviewed Ron Roher, who was supposedly present during the "boy" incident. He denied that it ever occurred and did not remember Fuhrman using the word.

The third incident occurred in 1988. In that year, Mark was involved in a case that resulted in the shooting of an armed robber named Joseph Britton. Britton sued the police department. He claimed that an LAPD officer had approached him and demanded, "Why did you run . . . You stupid nigger, why did you run?" There were contradictory statements as to whether this officer was Fuhrman. For example, during a deposition, Mr. Britton described the police officer that shot him as "a white male with red hair, red mustache." This was not Mark Fuhrman.

On October 12, 1994, on the *CBS Evening News,* Britton was asked whether Mark had said anything racial.

He replied, "At this point—no, I can't say that he did."

What did I make of these incidents when I learned about them for the first time in late 1994? I was not totally surprised about Mark's statements in his disability suit. They were made in the early eighties and were not inconsistent with the more rigid Mark Fuhrman I knew in 1987. However, they were inconsistent with the Mark Fuhrman I knew after 1990.

My own belief was that Mark was probably not currently a racist. This was based on the changes I saw in him after 1990 and his interaction with African Americans, both socially and in the workplace. For example, at this time, we had several African-American crime victims who were willing to come forward and testify to Mark's good character and compassionate treatment. African-American colleagues of Mark's, with whom he played basketball, also vouched for his character.

Therefore, I believed Mark was what I referred to as a "recovered racist." I thought something must have happened in his life to change his attitudes about minorities. I wondered whether such a change could have been associated, for example, with a religious conversion. Since I knew Mark and assumed that he would not be offended by my asking, I inquired whether he was religious and regularly went to church. He said he did not.

I shared this incident, my view of Mark, and my theory that he was a recovered racist with the other prosecutors on the team, including Cheri Lewis. Cheri, who was responsible for much of the behind-the-scenes work preparing for Mark's testimony, is a feisty blond lawyer in her mid-thirties, a top-notch legal researcher and writer, with a tenacity that cuts to the heart of the matter. One afternoon I told Cheri of my recovered-racist theory. I added, "If I'm right, this would be a good way of presenting the matter to the jury. Being reborn is such an American concept. Like in the song 'Amazing Grace': 'I once was lost but now I'm found, / I was blind, but now I see.' " I said jokingly, "Maybe we can play the song with full choral accompaniment as Mark marches to the stand."

Cheri smiled and then said seriously, "I know what you're talking about. But Mark won't cop out [admit] to that."

Even though it might have been nice to present Mark as "a recovered racist," we simply can't tell a witness what to say. Therefore, if Mark would not admit that at one time he was a racist and then changed, we could not tell him to testify that way simply because it would play well with the jury.

I remember one brief conversation I had with Marcia in the War Room in which we discussed the issue of calling Mark as a witness.

After relating my recovered-racist theory to Marcia, I summarized our options: "One, we could simply not call him; two, we could call him and only have him on the stand for minutes, just to testify about the glove; or three, we could call him and question him the way you would any other witness."

"We can't hide him," Marcia responded. "Not calling him isn't an option. If we don't call him, the defense will. If the judge gives them the opportunity to cross-examine Fuhrman about racism and using the 'N' word, that may be their best and perhaps only opportunity to inject that into the case. They're not going to forgo that opportunity just because we didn't call him. They will call him themselves. Then it would look like we were scared of him or that we tried to hide him from the jury."

Marcia's logic seemed clear. However, I like to play devil's advocate to test whether there is some flaw in an analysis.

"What if we decide not to call Fuhrman?" I posed. "We can still introduce the glove he found at Rockingham because Fuhrman didn't collect that glove; Dennis Fung did. Then, if we convince the judge that there is no evidence that the glove was planted, the defense should be precluded from asking Fuhrman, 'Did you plant the glove,' because they have no good-faith belief that he did plant it. Therefore, the question is improper."

"And where does that get us?" Marcia asked.

"If they can't question Fuhrman about planting the glove, then can't we prevent them from calling him at all? Can't we say, 'Judge, they're setting up a straw man. They only want to call Fuhrman because they want to impeach him by asking him about racism.' They're not really interested in anything he can add to the case. They're just calling him as an opportunity to inject race.' "

From Marcia's quick response it was obvious she had already run through every possible permutation, including this one. "Fuhrman has so many other things to which he could testify. He was the first to discover blood on the Bronco, he walked on the crime scene at Bundy, he climbed over the wall. Let's say that Ito were to rule that the defense can't call Fuhrman for the sole purpose of asking him whether he planted the glove."

Marcia then asked rhetorically, "Do you really think Ito is going to preclude the defense from calling Fuhrman to question him about whether he contaminated the crime scene, whether the Bronco was locked when he found the blood, any other host of things? If Ito rules that they can question Fuhrman about racism, we're going to see him on the witness stand. It's just a question of who calls him, us or them."

"So then the only real question," I said, "is how extensively are we going to question Fuhrman on direct?"

"Right," Marcia said. "What do you think?"

"Our position is that Mark is not an important part of our case. There isn't a single piece of relevant evidence in this case that rests on Mark Fuhrman—including the glove. I would put him on and off. 'Oh, you found a glove? You didn't collect it, someone else did? You didn't collect any evidence? You didn't do anything else? Thank you, goodbye.' I'd do about a fifteen-minute direct. That way we emphasize that he's not a key witness. His credibility is irrelevant."

"I agree," Marcia said.

As I look back on this conversation, I still can't fault the logic. If we had known then what we know now, we would still probably have had to call him; otherwise, the defense surely would. The only difference would be that had we known then that months later tapes of Mark making racist comments would be discovered, we could have prepared the jury during the opening statement. Although the tapes revealed racist attitudes, they had no relevance because Mark Fuhrman could not have planted any evidence.

The week before the opening statements, Cheri and Chris argued the prosecution's motion to prevent Mark from being cross-examined about racism. During this motion, Chris passionately argued that the "N" word should be excluded from the trial.

Outside the jury's presence, Chris told Judge Ito, "It will do one thing. It will upset the black jurors, it will issue a test, it will give them the test and the test will be whose side are you on? The side of the white prosecutors and the white policemen or on the side of the black defendant and his very prominent black lawyer? That is what it is going to do. Either you are with the man or you are with the brothers."

He argued that introducing evidence that Mark used the "N" word would taint the entire prosecution case, not just Mark Fuhrman. "[T]he next white police officer takes the witness stand, the jury is going to paint that white police officer with the same brush."

Chris argued that if Judge Ito allowed Cochran to "play this race card," it would change the focus of the case. "It is a race case then. It is white versus black . . . us versus them." He argued that introducing race would cause the jury to forget about the evidence. If Fuhrman used the "N" word, then in the jurors' minds the case is over: "he must have planted the glove."

I saw the tail end of Chris's argument, on TV, as I was walking through the reception area of the War Room. Several prosecutors were watching. All seemed visibly moved. Some applauded. Norm Shapiro, a senior-level administrator, beamed: "Brilliant, absolutely brilliant!"

And it was. Chris powerfully addressed himself to the legal prejudice that would result from the use of this word. But he did more than that. His comments were heartfelt. Nevertheless, I was concerned with how Johnnie Cochran would twist Chris's argument. In my mind, I could see Cochran, the consummate actor-lawyer, waiting in the wings.

Cochran began: "[Mr. Darden's] remarks this morning are perhaps the most incredible remarks I've heard in a court of law in the thirty-two years I have been practicing law. His remarks are demeaning to African Americans as a group. I want . . . to apologize to African Americans across this country. . . . It is demeaning to our jurors to say that African Americans who have lived under oppression for two-hundred-plus years in this country cannot work within the mainstream, cannot hear these offensive words. . . . I am ashamed that Mr. Darden would allow himself to become an apologist for this man."

This was vintage Cochran at his very best, and worst. Listening to his argument was personally painful to me, a body blow. I have never seen an attorney make such an argument. His remarks had nothing to do with the relevance of the evidence or its prejudicial effect. He was not making any legal or factual argument. His comments did not sound calculated to persuade Judge Ito. It seemed they were entirely directed toward damaging Chris's standing in the eyes of African Americans watching the trial and in the eyes of any African-American jurors who, contrary to Judge Ito's orders, may have learned of the exchange.

I saw Chris soon after this argument, when he returned from court. He was sitting at his desk in his cubicle in the War Room. He was resting his head in his hands. I did not know what to say. I'm sorry, Cochran shouldn't have said those things? Finally, I blurted, "Chris, what Cochran did was inexcusable—totally wrong—unfair."

Chris, deeply hurt, looked up at me. "I don't want to go back down to court this afternoon."

"Chris, don't you think you have to go back down?"

He paused, looking down. "Yeah."

I was saddened to see such an attack against this honorable and decent man. I first met Chris when I was assigned the Iversen case. Chris did the initial investigative work. Certain segments of the office were opposed to the Iversen prosecution. However, Chris championed this cause. I knew that Chris suffered significant personal grief within the office as a result of his strong beliefs about filing Iversen.

Chris played an instrumental role in getting me assigned to the case. After the Iversen case was assigned to Katherine Mader and me, perhaps because Chris felt I was championing his position, he would often refer to me as "my lawyer," as in "Hank is my lawyer." Later, during the Simpson case, Marcia also adopted this practice.

Chris also prosecuted the infamous Thirty-ninth and Dalton Street case, where a number of LAPD officers were charged with trashing an apartment in an African-American area of town during a search for narcotics. Such prosecutions made him unpopular in certain circles within the LAPD. But Chris was willing to stick his neck out to fight against racism and injustice, even if it meant going after a cop. It was ironic that this man, who—perhaps more than any other person in our office—had dedicated a large part of his career to prosecuting such cases, was now being wrongfully accused of being an apologist for a white racist cop. I knew, without question, that Chris's argument was not a cynical attempt to protect Fuhrman or the LAPD; it was motivated by the sincerest desire to see the truth prevail in this case.

Months after the verdict, I heard that Simpson, in an interview, said Chris seemed like an unhappy man. That is very far from the truth. He has an excellent sense of humor and enjoys life. Of all Chris's strengths as an investigator and trial lawyer, there is one that clearly sets him apart. More than any man I have ever met, Chris has the capacity to feel the pain of the victims he fights for in his cases. Obviously, that is something that Mr. Simpson cannot understand.

Of course, Chris did return to court later that afternoon. During the afternoon session, Gerald Uelmen made a comment during his argument on the Mark Fuhrman issue that I found interesting.

Uelmen made it absolutely clear that if the prosecution did not call Fuhrman, the defense would. He told Judge Ito that if the prosecution attempted to avoid presenting Mark Fuhrman's testimony, "he will make another appearance in this case, *being called as a hostile witness by the defense,* because he has a lot of relevant testimony to offer with respect to the Bronco automobile . . . [and] lots of questions that are going to come up with respect to how evidence was contaminated in terms of the parade of officers who went from one scene to the other." (emphasis added)

* * *

After the trial, defense attorney Alan Dershowitz, in his book, on television, in newspapers, and in every venue that would hear him, trumpeted that the prosecution lost the case when they introduced the race card by calling Mark Fuhrman. Dershowitz must not have heard or read the words of his cocounsel Uelmen: If they don't call him, we will. Apparently, Uelmen himself forgot about making this comment. Now, over eight months after the trial, after writing his book and appearing on TV talk shows, Uelmen has joined Dershowitz in claiming that the prosecution erred in calling Fuhrman to the stand.

On January 20, 1995, Judge Ito handed down his ruling regarding the Fuhrman issue. Mark's disability suit was excluded from evidence, since it had happened thirteen years earlier.

Judge Ito agreed with Cheri Lewis's argument that the Britton incident, in which Mark allegedly shot the suspect and called him the "N" word, should be excluded, since there was no credible evidence that Mark was involved.

However, the court's ruling as to the Kathleen Bell incident was more complex. Judge Ito found that Mark's alleged comment about pulling over vehicles just because they carried an interracial couple could be relevant, since Simpson is African American and Nicole was white. Judge Ito ruled that if the defense could produce evidence that Mark planted the glove, the incident would be admissible.

As to the issue of the use of the "N" word, the court ruled:

> The racial divisions that exist in this country remain the last great challenge to us as a nation. How we evolve and hopefully solve this problem will be our memorial in history. . . .
> If the challenged racial epithet was used in a relevant incident, it will be heard in court.

We interpreted this ruling as a complete victory. The defense would be allowed inquiry into the Kathleen Bell incident only if they could produce some evidence that the glove had been planted. We knew they could never do that, because it never happened.

Only three days later, without producing any evidence that the glove had been planted, the defense was allowed to reargue Judge

Ito's clearly reasoned, well-defined ruling. Judge Ito's practice of allowing the same issue to be reargued several times is very unusual. Most judges do not allow an issue to be relitigated unless there is a change in the law or the facts that materially alters the circumstances.

Seeking to expand the scope of permissible cross-examination of Mark Fuhrman, defense attorney F. Lee Bailey said: "I think once Fuhrman hits the stand without any warning to anybody as to what we're up to, we're able to ask him, 'Don't you hate black people and haven't you said so on many occasions.' "

This argument was preposterous. If accepted, it would allow cross-examination about the "N" word of any witness in any case. In every case, from this day forth, any officer could be asked about the "N" word even if the officer played a minor role in the overall case and even if there was no evidence to prove that the officer did anything inappropriate. There would be no limitation on the ability of attorneys to throw a case into disarray by using this one simple term. Later, dismissed juror Jeanette Harris said in a far-ranging television interview that she believed that a man who is a racist would plant evidence.

However, remarkably, during this hearing, Judge Ito agreed with the defense position and reversed his earlier ruling requiring the defense to show that the glove was planted before they could ask Mark about racism. In a striking U-turn, he held: "I find the issue of racial animosity to be something that they're entitled to cross-examine on."

This ruling also explains why later, during Mark's cross-examination, Marcia did not continually object when the defense asked Mark about whether he used the "N" word. The court had ruled that such inquiry was proper.

On a Sunday in February 1995, Mark underwent a mock cross-examination. It took place in the Grand Jury Hearing Room, a large room with tiered seating. During this session Mark was questioned by Chris Darden, Alan Yochelson, and Terry White. Alan Yochelson and Terry White were the prosecutors on the Rodney King case.

I was preparing for the testimony of other witnesses at the time and did not participate in the session with Mark. After the session, however, I could see that the prosecutors involved, especially Chris, were visibly upset.

Subsequently, *Newsweek* published a false story that Mark made racist statements during the session. However, immediately after the mock cross-examination I spoke to Chris. He seemed dejected and spoke frankly to me in a quiet tone of voice. "What happened?" I asked.

Chris said, "I think this guy is going to come across as a racist."

I peppered Chris with questions: "What did he say, Chris? How bad was it? Did he admit he's a racist?"

"No. It wasn't what he said. It's how he said it. It's his attitude." Chris paced his office floor and spoke as if he were thinking out loud. "It's like he just doesn't care about what people think. I'm afraid he may fight back on the stand in a way that may sink us."

"He did well at the prelim," I said. "But the only issue regarding Fuhrman is whether he planted the glove, right?"

"Yeah," Chris answered.

I continued: "And there's no evidence, not even a shred, that he planted it."

Chris continued pacing. "Well, of course. That's not the point. The point is the effect that introducing this issue into the trial is going to have and how it's going to play."

I knew what Chris was talking about. Introducing this issue into the trial could distract the jury from the real issues and evidence. The issue of racism is very difficult for prosecutors to handle. We cannot frankly discuss the issue as a society, and there is no effective way for prosecutors to discuss it before a jury. For this reason, most prosecutors actually breathe a sigh of relief when the defendant is white.

In fact, I had a conversation about these difficulties with Marcia shortly after the Fuhrman mock cross. One evening in her office we were talking briefly about the Fuhrman issue. I observed that the issue of racism is a very perplexing problem when it's introduced into a criminal trial.

"Tell me about it," Marcia agreed.

I continued: "I find it interesting that we as prosecutors have standard ways of handling most issues that reoccur in criminal cases. We have blueprints as to how you prosecute a drunk-driving case— what you say in the opening statement, how you handle the defense expert, how you structure your closing argument. We have blue-prints for gang cases. But we don't have a blueprint as to how you deal with the issue of racism. We've never had any seminars discussing this. Quite frankly, I don't know the best way to deal with it."

"Any ideas?" Marcia asked

"I think it would be useful if we, as an office, had a brainstorming session where a number of experienced white and African-American prosecutors got together for a day and just kicked around different approaches to handling this issue. Do you say something about it in your opening statement? Do you ignore it? What do you say? What can you say as a white prosecutor that's appropriate and not insulting? I don't feel that we have any generally accepted answers to these questions. I know I don't. Of course, this should have been done long before our case."

"I've dealt with this issue before," Marcia said, "and I feel pretty comfortable talking about it. But I think your suggestion about getting lots of input is a good one."

Shortly after the *Newsweek* article broke about Fuhrman's mock cross-examination, a meeting was called of all the members of the Simpson team. It took place one afternoon in Garcetti's conference room. Gil Garcetti sat at the head of the granite table. Marcia and Chris sat on either side of him. The rest of us, about fifteen all told, sat around the table.

Gil, in a mild tone of voice, expressed consternation about the leak that there had been a mock cross-examination of Mark Fuhrman, expecially considering that parts of the story were false. He reminded us of our ethical obligations as attorneys to maintain the confidentiality of sensitive information.

As Gil spoke, Chris sat there fuming.

After Gil left, Chris cut loose in a seething, angry tone I had never before heard from him. "I can't believe this! Whoever did this is the lowest scumbag! We will find out who is responsible. If you think you can get away with it, you're dead wrong! You should just come forward. There is no way you can keep it a secret. There's going to be an Internal Affairs Investigation." Stressing each word and picking up a head of steam toward the end of the sentence, he said, "We—are—going—to—find—out—who—you—are!"

Chris's angry tirade went on for several minutes. During this, Marcia sat there uncomfortably silent, as did I. I understood how

Chris felt. Someone he trusted had betrayed us. But during this time I kept thinking that many of the people who were directly involved in the mock cross-examination were not present. It was very possible that Chris's outburst was misdirected.

Later that night Marcia said to me, as if apologizing for the episode, "We have to be extra careful about sensitive information. From now on we'll have to keep a lot of this stuff among the three of us." However, for several weeks some members of the prosecution team and I felt as if we didn't want to know anything about sensitive issues outside our area of the case.

We never did find out who was responsible for the *Newsweek* story.

In this time period, while I was trying to make a conscious effort not to become involved in any discussions regarding Fuhrman, I stopped by Marcia's office to say good night. Marcia and Chris were having a discussion. Chris turned to me. "Hank, how would you feel about putting Fuhrman on?"

Marcia turned in my direction, waiting for my answer.

Marcia had previously told me that Chris was having second thoughts about conducting Mark's direct examination. But Chris's question took me entirely by surprise. As I stood in the doorway, Marcia and Chris kept looking at me, waiting for my response. I couldn't believe this. I had been assigned one of the case's toughest witnesses, Dennis Fung. Now they wanted me to do Fuhrman!

Finally, my mouth opened, and words started tumbling out. "I know that Fuhrman is a big issue for us—big issue—but I'm completely—completely—bogged down with preparing for the scientific evidence. I'm spending a lot of time with the people at the crime lab. Dennis Fung, you know. And Dennis—Dennis is going to be a big problem for us, as you know."

"Yeah, I know," Marcia said.

At the time, I felt that the evidence-collection issues were as much of a potential problem for our case as Mark Fuhrman was. The issues constituted a time-consuming process of damage mitigation. Although a similar effort was required in the case of Fuhrman, I simply did not have the time to do both before Fuhrman was called.

Marcia glanced at Chris, "It might look bad if a special prosecutor were called in to handle Mark Fuhrman."

"I agree," I said. "It would look like you guys are avoiding a hot potato. It would seem like we were so afraid of him that we needed to distance both of you from him."

Chris nodded his head.

After a few moments of silence, Marcia decided that she would present Mark herself.

11

Never Used the "N" Word in Ten Years

AFTER ALL THE HAND WRINGING, Marcia's direct of Fuhrman seemed uneventful. On direct, Fuhrman appeared to be an experienced homicide detective routinely doing a job he had done numerous times before. It was Bailey's much-anticipated cross that we were worried about.

Before getting into Mark's participation in the homicide investigation, Marcia asked him about the incident in 1985 in which Simpson smashed the windshield of Nicole's car with a baseball bat.

This incident showed that, far from desiring to get Simpson, Mark took little interest in the episode. He testified that he made no effort to further investigate the incident, to encourage Simpson's prosecution, or to embarrass Simpson by contacting the media. The point being, if he was out to get African-American men who have relationships with white women, why did he treat Simpson with kid gloves? Even if Mark was, in fact, a racist at this time, it certainly did not extend to O. J. Simpson.

Marcia then turned to the heart of the matter. Mark and his partner, Ron Phillips, arrived at Bundy at 2:10 A.M. The location had already been secured with crime-scene tape and cordoned off. Marcia established that Mark had known that other officers had already searched the Bundy scene before his arrival and would have noticed a second glove if it had been there. So in order for Mark to have moved a second glove to Rockingham, he would have had to involve all the other officers in a conspiracy.

Officers Riske, Phillips, and Fuhrman proceeded down the walkway, westbound, toward the alley, and through a rear gate. After this walk-through, Mark wrote in his notes that he saw "two blood spots at bottom inside of gate." This was compelling evidence that Mark and others had seen the drops long before anyone could have dreamed of planting Simpson's blood and long before Simpson's blood was drawn.

Mark gave a briefing to Detective Roberts and showed him the single glove. Mark also showed him the rear-gate blood drops. According to the defense theory, this officer would also have had to join Mark's instant conspiracy. At around 2:40 A.M., about thirty minutes after Mark first arrived at the scene, Detective Phillips told Mark that Robbery/Homicide was going to take over. Shortly thereafter, Mark waited in the street until Detectives Vannatter and Lange, of Robbery/Homicide, arrived.

After their arrival, Ron Phillips asked Mark, "Can you take us up to the . . . Rockingham house?"

Mark replied, "I went there on a radio call a long time ago. I think so."

Detectives Fuhrman and Phillips then drove to Rockingham, with Detectives Lange and Vannatter following.

In the car, Phillips told Mark that he had talked to Commander Bushey and that Bushey wanted a police officer to personally notify Simpson of the murder. At 5:10 A.M. they arrived at Rockingham, a lavish estate of about one acre, surrounded by a fence. The detectives rang the buzzer at the gate.

While the others were waiting at the gate buzzer, still unable to rouse anyone inside, Mark noticed that the Bronco was parked askew, the front wheels hugging the curb and the back ones jutting out almost two feet into the street. It looked as if the car had been parked in a frightful hurry.

Fuhrman walked up to the Bronco and noticed a spot of blood on the driver's door handle.

Mark returned to join the other detectives. "I think I saw something on the Bronco," he said. Then Detectives Fuhrman, Vannatter, and Lange walked to the Bronco, where Mark showed them what he had discovered. They ran a Department of Motor Vehicle check on the Bronco and discovered that it was Simpson's. According to Mark, both he and Detective Vannatter expressed their concern about the blood on the Bronco, since they had just come from the scene of a double murder.

Mark called Westec, a private security patrol, and asked, "Is there anybody that's supposed to be at home now?"

The Westec operator responded, "Well, there's a live-in maid that's supposed to be there twenty-four hours a day."

By now it was around 5:45 A.M., almost forty-five minutes after they had arrived at Rockingham. Mark told the jury, "We had some small pieces of evidence that would indicate that quite possibly somebody had left the Bundy scene and come to the Rockingham location. . . . We had previously discussed our concerns about another possible victim or a kidnap-type robbery/ murder-suicide. We had no idea exactly what we were confronted with at that point."

Mark testified that Detective Vannatter concluded that they would have to find a way into the Rockingham estate. Mark asked, "You want me to go over the wall?" Mark Fuhrman was the logical choice because he was the youngest and in the best physical shape of the four men there.

Mark climbed over the wall and opened the gate for the others. They knocked at the front door and received no response. The detectives then walked around a path to the rear of the residence to the guesthouse, a good-sized room attached to the main house but with a separate entrance from the backyard. There they knocked on the door and roused a sleepy, befuddled Kato Kaelin. Ron Phillips told Kato, "There might be some sort of an emergency." When questioned about Simpson's whereabouts, Kato pointed the detectives in the direction of Arnelle's room, a room adjacent to Kato's that also has a separate entrance to the backyard. (Arnelle is Simpson's adult daughter from his first marriage.)

Mark remained with Kato as the other detectives walked to Arnelle's room. Kato told Mark that at about 10:45 P.M. he was talking on the phone to a girlfriend when he heard a crash or thump on his wall. He asked her if there had been an earthquake. She said no. Kato described how he went out to investigate. While investigating the noise, he saw a limo. Kato did not explain why the limo was there. Mark wanted to investigate the source of the thumps.

Mark and Kato then went into the main house. Fuhrman asked Kato to wait and give a statement to Detective Vannatter.

It was approximately 6:10 A.M. or 6:15 A.M. when Mark walked down the narrow pathway to investigate. When he got to the area that appeared to be outside Kato's room, Mark testified, he "continued walking down the path, and when I got approximately fifteen or twenty feet away, I saw a dark object and I continued to walk towards that object." He saw that the object was a glove.

It could be simply surmised that whoever used the narrow pathway may have bumped into a large air conditioner overhanging the pathway, accounting for the thumps that Kato heard. This hurried race along the narrow path may have dislodged the glove. Whatever the theories of how the glove got there, the facts are unimpeachable.

Marcia elicited that it was not until *after* Mark discovered the Rockingham glove and showed it to the other detectives that he learned that Simpson was in Chicago on the night of the murders. This established that at the time Mark discovered the glove, which is when the defense alleged it was planted, he had no way of knowing whether Simpson had an ironclad alibi. Why would Mark Fuhrman plant a glove if, for all he knew, Simpson may have been out of town or even out of the country at the time of the murders?

After Marcia concluded her direct, defense attorney Lee Bailey conducted the cross-examination. Bailey, a nationally famous trial lawyer, was reputed to have had excellent cross-examination skills. The much-ballyhooed bout between Bailey and Mark had been fueled by Bailey's bombastic boast that he would do the most "annihilating, character-assassinating" cross-examination ever. Bailey was, in many eyes, the image of an over-the-hill ex-champ desperately trying to make a comeback.

Bailey always had a thermos in court from which he periodically sipped. On one occasion, I joked with Bailey as to what was in the thermos. He just smiled.

Bailey started his cross by asking Fuhrman about his qualifications to investigate a crime scene. This seemed like a barren area for cross, since it had already been established that Fuhrman and Phillips were only responsible for the crime scene for a scant forty-five minutes before they were relieved.

Eventually, Bailey asked about the Kathleen Bell incident. It appeared that Bailey was attempting to get Mark to say categorically that he had never met Kathleen Bell. On cross-examination, lawyers try to get witnesses to make unqualified statements that they can disprove. At first, he had some success. He boxed Mark into stating,

"What I'm certain is . . . that I didn't meet Kathleen Bell" at the recruiting station.

With this seemingly categorical denial, Bailey should have moved to another topic. One of the "rules" of cross-examination is: "Know when to stop asking questions." However, even the most experienced lawyers sometimes fail to quit when they are ahead.

Bailey then let Mark off the hook. He got Mark to state that he recalled seeing a female at the recruiting station. When asked if the woman could have been Miss Bell, Mark replied, "I don't know. . . . I didn't pay much attention to whoever came in there."

Undeterred, Bailey continued this line of questioning. Mark's answers were getting progressively worse for Bailey. Under Bailey's questioning, Mark testified that he probably did meet Kathleen Bell but did not remember doing so.

Bailey asked Mark whether he could have met Bell and not "even know that you met her?"

"That would be correct, sir, yes."

Thus, Mark resisted Bailey's trap by refusing to testify categorically that he never met Ms. Bell. Obviously, meeting her almost ten years earlier was not all that memorable.

If the jury—and the world—couldn't buy a racial bigot committing perjury and planting evidence, Bailey would try another theory. In an accusatory style, Bailey asked a series of questions: "Weren't you a little bit angry that you were being shoved out of a murder [investigation] . . . ? Didn't bother you a bit . . . ? Weren't you a fellow that had spent a good part of his career waiting for an opportunity to make, quote, 'the big arrest' . . . ? Did you realize, when you hurdled the wall, that you were inexorably a part of this case for as long as it might last?"

Mark's simple answer to these accusations: "I don't think I was thinking any of those things, sir."

At the beginning of the second day of Bailey's cross, new allegations against Mark were made. Bailey claimed that Maximo Cordoba, who worked at the marine recruiting station, would testify that Mark said, "Let's get something straight. The only boy here is you, nigger. And then Cordoba leaves the building, and Fuhrman follows him out into the parking lot and repeats the same epithet."

Marcia Clark angrily responded, "These allegations get more outrageous by the minute, and I'm stricken again by the preposterousness of the claims of the defense." Marcia questioned whether

Cordoba really said this, "because according to the statements he has given us, he never said anything like that."

Bailey shot back, "Your Honor, I have spoken with him on the phone personally, marine to marine. I haven't the slightest doubt that he will march up to that witness stand and tell the world what Fuhrman called him on no provocation whatsoever."

That night, Cordoba appeared on *Dateline NBC* and said that he had never spoken to Bailey. He repeated his recent allegation and said that he never mentioned it before because he just recently remembered the event during a dream.

On his third day of cross-examination, Bailey sought to use a glove and plastic bag, presumably to demonstrate how Mark could have concealed a glove and transported it to Rockingham. The glove, however, was a size small. Marcia objected. "I can't even tell if it is a man's or woman's glove. Size small. I guess it is Mr. Bailey's."

After an extensive cross-examination that established almost nothing, Bailey finally asked a question that ultimately shifted the focus of the case from Simpson to Mark Fuhrman.

Bailey asked, "Do you use the word nigger in describing people?"

Marcia's objection was overruled.

Mark replied, "No, sir."

MR. BAILEY: Have you used that word in the past ten years?

MARK: Not that I recall, no.

BAILEY: You mean if you called someone a nigger you have forgotten it?

MARK: I'm not sure I can answer the question the way you phrased it, sir.

BAILEY: You have difficulty understanding the question?

MARK: Yes.

BAILEY: I will rephrase it. I want you to assume that perhaps at some time, since 1985 or 6, you addressed a member of the African-American race as a nigger. Is it possible that you have forgotten that act on your part?

MARK: No, it is not possible.

BAILEY: *Are you therefore saying that you have not used that word in the past ten years, Detective Fuhrman?*

MARK: *Yes, that is what I'm saying.* (emphasis added)

BAILEY: And you say under oath that you have not addressed any black person as a nigger or spoken about black people as niggers in the past ten years, Detective Fuhrman?

MARK: That's what I'm saying, sir.

BAILEY: So that anyone who comes to this court and quotes you as using that word in dealing with African Americans would be a liar, would they not, Detective Fuhrman.

MARK: Yes, they would.

BAILEY: All of them, correct?

MARK: All of them.

Marcia's redirect examination was effective and to the point. She established that at the time Mark Fuhrman walked down the pathway where he discovered the glove, he did not have any of the information that would have been necessary to frame Simpson.

He did not know the time of death of Ron and Nicole, whether Simpson had an alibi for the time of the murders or could have been in another state at the time, whether there were any eyewitnesses to the murders, whether there were any earwitnesses, or whether Kato had already checked the pathway before Mark did.

He claimed never to have used the "N" word in ten years. I found this assertion highly suspect. In the halls of Congress, in presidential tapes, in locker rooms of the Yankees, Dodgers, and Lakers, throughout, that word is used. Sometimes it is used in a hateful, pejorative way. It is also used in friendly byplay between African Americans and whites, such as on neighborhood basketball courts.

Maybe Mark meant that he had not used the word in the last ten years as an ugly insult hurled against an African American. Weeks after this testimony, Cheri Lewis and I went over this portion of the transcript with a fine-toothed comb. We were alarmed by the possibility that witnesses other than Kathleen Bell might come forward to say that Fuhrman used that word within the last ten years. Cheri said, "If you carefully look at the context, he seems to be saying that he didn't use the 'N' word as an insult directed against someone—like, he never arrested someone and called them an 'N.' He's not necessarily saying that he never used it at all."

"I don't know," I said, "it seems to be a flat-out denial to me."

Cheri shook her head while glancing over the transcript one more time. "I'm afraid you might be right."

When Cheri said this, I wondered, Why couldn't Mark have been less arrogant? It was as though each time Bailey flung the "N" word in Mark Fuhrman's face, Mark dug in like a marine under siege. You're not going to make Mark Fuhrman back down, little man.

After Mark's testimony, we felt that we came out relatively unscathed. The theory floated by the defense, that Mark planted the glove by carrying it in a plastic bag to Rockingham in his sock, bordered on the absurd. Mark was calm, reasoned, and professional. The defense witnesses who could impeach him (contradict his testimony) on the use of the "N" word—Kathleen Bell, Maximo Cordoba, and Joseph Britton—all had significant credibility problems. But there was no way to know what new witnesses would come forward. So by the end of Fuhrman's six days on the witness stand, his testimony denying using the "N" word stood there like a volatile bomb, waiting to explode.

12

Lied About and Libeled

When Det. Phillip Vannatter rose to take the oath to tell the truth—
something he had done probably hundreds of times in his distinguished career of over twenty-six years—he probably could not have
imagined that months later the defense would brand him, together
with Fuhrman, a "twin demon of evil." When I first met Phil in
October 1994, it struck me that his physically imposing appearance
contrasted with his warmth, wit, and gentlemanly demeanor. I only
wished that the jury had seen more of that side of him.

His direct was straightforward, brief, and basically uneventful.
Under Chris's direct, Phil testified that on June 13 he also saw blood,
which the defense claimed was planted later, on the rear gate at
Bundy.

He explained the events leading to the entry into Simpson's
Rockingham estate. He told the jury that since he didn't know his
way up to Rockingham, he asked Fuhrman to direct him to that
location. An additional reason all four detectives went was that
Detectives Vannatter and Lange wanted to interview Simpson. They
thought that Fuhrman and Phillips could aid in collecting Simpson's children, who had been brought from Nicole's condo to the
police station to await a parent or guardian. Phil arrived at Rockingham at 5:10 A.M.

He corroborated Mark Fuhrman's testimony as to why they decided to go over the Rockingham wall. Phil told the jury why he
became concerned after blood was discovered on the Bronco. He
"had just left a very brutal murder scene. . . . It appeared there

should be people at the [Rockingham] home there, and we were
getting no response—we had also learned that there was supposed
to be a live-in maid. . . . I became concerned that this could be
another crime scene. . . . This could be an extension of the Bundy
crime scene where someone could have been killed or injured."

I never understood the public controversy over Vannatter's decision to enter the Rockingham estate without a warrant. The "exi-
gency exception" to the requirement of a warrant is well
recognized. If a police officer has a strong suspicion that an emergency may exist, he is entitled to enter a location without a warrant.
When people ask me about Phil's decision, I ask them to put themselves in Phil's shoes. You arrive at Rockingham after viewing the
Bundy crime scene. Although you have been a detective for many
years, you are horrified by the brutality of the murders of two young
people. You see their knife-slashed bodies, the blood-drenched
ground. As you walk down the Bundy trail, you note the trail of
blood leading away from the bodies toward the alleyway, to the left
of a trail of bloody shoe prints. You conclude that your suspect has
been cut. You learn that Nicole was Simpson's ex-wife.

When you arrive at Rockingham, you try repeatedly to summon
someone inside the residence. You learn from the security company
that the maid is supposed to be home. There are cars parked inside
the compound gate, and there's a Bronco at the curb. You repeatedly buzz at the gate and hear the phone ringing inside. But no one
answers. Then you see a drop of blood on the handle of the Bronco,
parked haphazardly outside.

Would you have a strong suspicion that there could be an emergency inside the compound? Would you want to take the risk that
someone lay inside dying as you spent at least an hour getting a
search warrant by telephone?

Later, under Chris's questioning, Vannatter testified that the day
after the murders, after interviewing Simpson at Parker Center, the
LAPD's downtown headquarters, a nurse at the LAPD's jail dispensary drew blood from Simpson. Vannatter took the sample to Rockingham to give it to Dennis Fung, of the LAPD crime laboratory.
Asked why he did not book (check the property into evidence in the

Property Room) the blood after receiving it at Parker Center, Vannatter explained, "I couldn't book it at that point. I didn't have an item number, I didn't have a DR [Division of Records] number. I knew that the criminalist was at Rockingham and as soon as the criminalist takes custody of the evidence item, essentially I consider that booked. I knew he was there. I hand-carried it to him for the chain of custody and to protect that piece of evidence." So he took the sample to Dennis Fung, at Rockingham, so that Dennis could book the blood together with the other evidence.

The cross of Detective Vannatter was left to Robert Shapiro. Shapiro originally headed the defense team. But when Cochran arrived on the scene, after the preliminary hearing, he was relegated to the position of benchwarmer.

As I monitored Vannatter's testimony, I continued to attempt to determine where the defense was going, conspiracy or contamination? It appeared to be the latter. Shapiro exhaustively continued to pursue the doughnut-hole defense. Stunningly, he even revisited the ice-cream issue.

By contrast, there was little during the cross to indicate that the defense was actively pursuing their conspiracy theory. Shapiro did attack Vannatter's credibility as to why the four detectives decided to go to Rockingham in the early-morning hours of June 13. Vannatter explained that Fuhrman and Phillips accompanied them to Rockingham so that "they could direct us to the location because Fuhrman had been there before." He repeated that Fuhrman and Phillips could aid in transporting the children. He continued: "I had concerns for the children. . . . I was informed that a commander of the police department had ordered an in-person notification, and I knew it was going to be a newsworthy case, and I thought it best that we make notification before the press did."

What I found most striking about the cross-examination was what was absent. On direct Detective Vannatter had described obtaining Simpson's blood sample on the afternoon of June 13, after Simpson's interview at Parker Center. He described taking the vial back to Rockingham and giving it to Dennis Fung.

Interestingly, Shapiro, during his cross-examination, did not accuse Vannatter of doing anything untoward with the vial. He did ask him numerous questions as to whether he could have booked the vial at Parker Center. But Shapiro did not accuse the detective of lying about giving the vial to Dennis Fung at Rockingham or keeping it overnight.

Detective Vannatter's decision to bring the vial to Rockingham to deliver it to Dennis Fung is now considered highly controversial. In fact, he could not have booked the vial into evidence at Parker Center. For evidence to be booked, it is necessary to have a DR number. Since Dennis Fung was in possession of virtually all the evidence collected to that point, a DR number would be assigned when Fung booked his evidence. There was no DR number when Vannatter obtained Simpson's blood. He did what most detectives would have done under the same circumstances.

At around this time, I spoke to Marcia in her office to verify my assessment of what was happening in court, since I would imminently be presenting my evidence. I said to Marcia, "I don't see much of the conspiracy defense. It's all the police didn't do this or shouldn't have done that. Contamination. Incompetence. But the blood was definitely on the rear gate on the thirteenth. They didn't dispute that. There was only one glove at Bundy. They didn't dispute that. Phil [Vannatter] definitely gave the blood vial to Dennis [Fung] to take to the lab. Shapiro didn't lay a glove on that, either. Where's the conspiracy?"

Marcia replied, "I think it's just going to drop out of the case altogether by the end."

"Actually, it would be nice if we could keep them going in the direction of conspiracy," I mused aloud. "They can bury the contamination defense in mind-numbing technobabble. But conspiracy just can't hold up when examined with even a modicum of common sense."

As I continued working with my witnesses, I began to focus on the contamination-incompetence line of attack. This seemed to be where they were headed.

We could not have been more wrong. Already, in the media, the trial was beginning to assume elements of a drama-fantasy that had to be fueled daily by cliffhangers, such as "Detective keeps blood vial overnight? Stay tuned for news at eleven."

The media's legal analysts seemed ready to buy any theory the defense raised: deceit and deception, contamination and conspiracy. It seemed as though the sound bites continued to live even after being disproved by the facts. If the legal analysts were trumpeting the unreasonable, could the jury be far behind?

13

America's Most Famous Houseguest

KATO KAELIN, THE MAN LATER BILLED as "America's most famous houseguest," followed Detective Vannatter's four-day stint on the stand. I had first met Kato one evening about a month earlier, when Marcia interviewed him in her office. Marcia asked me to sit in on the interview to double-team Kato in an effort to pry more information out of him.

When Marcia greeted Kato, a blond mop-haired surfer type, I saw a side of Marcia I had not been aware existed. "Hey, guy, how's it going?" Marcia said. Marcia's fluent "dudespeak" caught me completely off guard. She was trying to make a fidgeting, hesitant Kato more comfortable.

Both Marcia and I use the interview technique of first asking broad, open-ended questions related to a topic, designed to draw out as much information as possible, and then asking narrower questions to clarify the answers and fill in the details. We asked Kato to characterize Nicole and Simpson's relationship. "Any arguments? Fights? What can you tell us about the relationship in general?"

While continually reconfiguring himself in his seat, Kato answered such questions in a way that would provide as little information as possible. He only gave two specifics. One was a bland, colorless description of the 911 incident in 1993, when Simpson broke down Nicole's backdoor. "It was—like—basically a loud argument. The door was—like—it was already—like—partially busted."

He also mentioned an "argument" between Nicole and Simpson at a party at the home of Bruce Jenner, a former Olympic Decathlon medalist. According to Kato's hazy description, Simpson became upset when Nicole made reference to a former boyfriend.

By the end of the approximately three-hour interview, Kato had said nothing about Nicole's telling him that she thought Simpson would kill her. Nor had he characterized the thumping as sounding as if someone had first bumped into the air conditioner, then the wall, and then the air conditioner again. That description was made by Kato in March 1996, six months after the trial ended, on the *Geraldo* show, after Kato's popularity was in decline.

When we finished Kato's interview, after he left Marcia's office, I looked at Marcia and chuckled as I shook my head. "Wow!"

"Look," Marcia said caustically as she rapidly lit another cigarette and took several quick puffs, "we're lucky he told us as much as he did. He wouldn't even be telling us about the thumps and that Simpson's whereabouts were unaccounted for during the murders except that he was already locked in, 'cause he told Fuhrman and Vannatter the story early that morning, before he knew the significance of what he was saying."

I thought about what Marcia was saying for a moment. "Well, I think you should explain that to the jury. Tell them, 'Ladies and gentlemen, this guy's not a happy camper. Therefore, to the extent he is saying anything against Simpson and helpful to the prosecution, it's twice as reliable. Because if he had it his way, he wouldn't tell us anything.' "

"Believe me, I intend to," Marcia said.

It was common during these late-night sessions with Marcia that our intense, sometimes heated conversations were interrupted. The phone rang. As if hitting a button, Marcia's personality changed. The office, the case, and I disappeared. She spoke functional broken Spanish. I understood enough. She was talking to her housekeeper-nanny. Then, in the most gentle, loving tone, she spoke to her youngest son: "Mommy's coming home, Mommy's coming home, *sweetie,* Mommy's coming home. *Honey,* if you let Mommy off the phone, then I can finish here so I can come home."

Then more Spanish before she hung up. A moment passed.

Marcia and I would quickly resolve whatever issues could not wait so that she could get back to her sons.

As much as I admired Marcia's extraordinary talent as a prosecutor, it was witnessing these phone conversations with her children that impressed me the most.

On March 21, 1995, Kato Kaelin took the stand. When Nicole was living at Gretna Green in 1993, Kato had rented out the guesthouse there. When Nicole moved to Bundy in 1994, Kato was going to move into a room there with its own entrance. However, Simpson asked him not to do so. Kato got the feeling that Simpson felt "it wasn't right for me to be in the same house, a man in that same house with Nicole and the children. . . . [I]t could possibly have been that he was thinking that I might be with Nicole [sexually]." Simpson allowed Kato to live in an attached guest room at Rockingham rent-free. Kato, showing the jury his ability as a stand-up comic who could also be funny while sitting in the witness chair, got a laugh when he was asked whether living with O. J. Simpson would enhance his ability to get work as an actor. Kato replied, "I don't think we were going for the same parts."

On June 12, 1994, Kato first saw Simpson at around 2:00 or 2:30 P.M. in the kitchen area. They had a casual conversation about Simpson's golf game earlier that day. Simpson planned to go to Sydney's recital at 5:00 P.M. During this conversation, Simpson spoke of his relationship with Nicole, saying that it was over. Simpson also told Kato that he wasn't sure whether his girlfriend, Paula Barbieri, was the one for him. That afternoon, Simpson spoke to a young woman, Tracy Adele, Kato's friend. Simpson may have discussed setting up a date, but Kato was not sure.

Kato saw Simpson in the breakfast nook in the house again between 6:30 or 7:00 P.M., after Simpson returned from the recital. Simpson told Kato, referring to the tight dress Nicole wore, "Oh . . . wearing those tight outfits . . . What are they going to do when they're grandmas?"

At around 9:00 P.M., Simpson came to Kato's room. Simpson said he only had a hundred-dollar bill and needed five for the skycap. He asked Kato for some money, and Kato gave him a twenty-dollar bill. Simpson said he was going to go and get a hamburger.

"Mind if I come with you?" Kato asked.

Marcia inquired, "Did he seem real excited to have you come?"
"Wouldn't you?" Kato replied.

That got Kato his biggest laugh of the day. He grinned impishly at Marcia, as though thanking her for giving him the straight line.

They took the Bentley to McDonald's. Kato testified that Simpson was wearing a dark-colored sweat outfit at the time.

After returning from McDonald's, Kato saw Simpson for the last time that night standing by the Bentley at 9:35 P.M. The time was established through phone records showing that Kato made a phone call at 9:37 P.M., about two minutes after leaving Simpson.

Later that night, Kato called a friend, Rachel Ferrara. While on the phone, he heard a loud thumping noise from the south pathway, near the air-conditioning unit. Kato asked Rachel if there had just been an earthquake. Later, through other witnesses, Marcia would establish that the thumps had occurred between 10:51 and 10:52 P.M. At that time, Kato left his room to investigate. While outside, he saw a limousine parked behind the Ashford gate. He paid no attention to it, figuring Simpson would buzz the gate open.

Kato continued to check on the noise, but, more afraid than curious, he stopped mid-route.

After the limousine was inside the compound and Kato had returned to the driveway area, he observed a little black bag in the driveway near the Bentley. A few seconds later, when he saw Simpson, Kato informed him about the noise. They went to the kitchen to find a flashlight, to explore the area from which the thumps came. Suddenly, Simpson changed his mind. He told Kato that it was late and he was liable to miss his flight.

After they left the house, Kato offered to pick up the small black bag, but Simpson said, "No, I'll get it." No one ever saw that bag again. For the first time ever, Simpson asked Kato to turn on the alarm system. Kato said that he did not want the responsibility and did not know the code, that Simpson would have to do it himself.

In describing these events—the thumps, Simpson's sudden appearance at Rockingham minutes later, Simpson's concern for the black bag, his lack of concern for the source of the thumps, and his unusual request that Kato set the alarm—Kato testified with all the enthusiasm of an accountant reading out loud a profit-and-loss statement. But the bland words belied the picture of a befuddled, agitated man. Thumps behind the wall? Let's get a flashlight and investigate. No, never mind, got to catch a flight. Set the alarm? No, I'll do it myself.

The limo left at about 11:15 P.M. At 11:40 P.M., Kato received a call from Simpson. He had forgotten to turn on the alarm. Simpson gave Kato the code to arm the system.

The remainder of Marcia's direct was unimpeached corroboration of Detectives Vannatter, Lange, Phillips, and Fuhrman. Kato testified that after the detectives woke him up, Mark Fuhrman noticed that Kato's eyes were red and checked them, asked whether he had been drinking or taking drugs, and inspected Kato's clothes and shoes, presumably for blood. This established that far from zeroing in on Simpson as a suspect, Mark Fuhrman seemed to be focusing more on Kato.

Kato also corroborated that he did not tell Fuhrman what time Simpson left the house for the plane trip. This testimony established that before Fuhrman discovered the Rockingham glove, as far as he knew, Simpson was in Timbuktu at the time of the murders. The point: If Simpson might have an airtight alibi, why plant the glove?

Another important piece of corroboration was Kato's testimony that Detective Vannatter wanted to know where the Bronco keys were. Kato did not know, and the keys were not found. The point: the police did not have access to the Bronco and could not have planted evidence inside.

Most important, while walking out of the house after he agreed to accompany the police to the station to give a statement, Kato saw some blood in the foyer area. The point: It was not planted after the police got Simpson's blood hours later. It was already there.

Kato told the jury that the first time he saw Simpson back at Rockingham, Simpson and his minions were huddled around the television. The program was discussing the time frame during which Simpson's whereabouts were unknown. According to Kato, Simpson said, "Kato, you know I was in the house."

Marcia waited a moment to let the import of this statement sink in: Simpson was asking Kato to give him an alibi. Kato could not do it. As if discussing something no more significant than the weather, Kato testified that he informed Simpson that he did not see him go into the house.

Marcia summarized Kato's testimony by driving home the point that Simpson had no alibi from 9:35 P.M., when Kato last saw him by the Bentley, to 10:51 P.M., when Kato heard the thumping noises.

This was Simpson's window of opportunity to commit the murders: between 9:35 P.M. and 10:51 P.M. No matter how hard Kato may have dreaded incriminating his friend, his testimony left this window wide open.

Under Shapiro's cross, Kato's demeanor seemed to change. He was forthcoming, and Shapiro cross-examined him as a friendly witness. He testified that he did not see anything strange about Simpson's mood the evening of the murders. Simpson was not depressed, angry, agitated, or distracted. There was nothing unusual about the way he looked that day or the way he acted. He also minimized the extent of any friction in Nicole's relationship with Simpson. He testified that there were only two incidents in which he had heard them yelling at each other. One was the 1993 incident at Gretna Green. As for Simpson kicking the door down, no big deal. The door was already broken. The other argument was over an ex-boyfriend of Nicole's at Bruce Jenner's Christmas party. No big deal. Overall, according to Kato's best psychological evaluation, Simpson was not jealous, and Nicole and Simpson seemed to get along well.

However, at the end of Shapiro's cross, Kato's testimony corroborating the officers and establishing the crucial window of opportunity to commit the murders remained unchallenged.

On redirect, Marcia adopted an aggressive stance, in effect, cross-examining Kato. She forced him to admit that he failed to disclose the Christmas Eve incident when asked about arguments during his testimony before the grand jury. She forced Kato to concede that Simpson was upset when he commented about Nicole's tight dresses. "But that was not your testimony before, was it, Mr. Kaelin?" Marcia demanded.

"No."

"Earlier, you testified that he was relaxed and nonchalant when he spoke about Sydney at the recital; isn't that true?"

"Yes."

Marcia also asked, "You don't have any book proposals out?"

Kato replied unequivocally, "No, I don't want to do a book."

Shortly after Kato's testimony, the prosecution received a copy of Kato's tape-recorded book proposal, created in December 1994. In February 1986, almost six months after the trial, there were widespread discussions in the media concerning inconsistencies between

Kato's book, coauthored by Marc Eliot, and his testimony. Many have wondered why the prosecution did not recall Kato as a witness to confront him with these inconsistencies.

One of the problems with the book is separating out truth from literary license. For example, in the book proposal Eliot wrote that on the day of the murders "Kato observes O.J.'s darkening mood as the afternoon wears on." The phrase "darkening mood" is entirely inconsistent with Kato's description of Simpson when he testified. However, Kato did not use the phrase "darkening mood" in his interview with Marc Eliot on which the book proposal was based. For instance, on the tape Kato says of Simpson's mood after the dance recital, "You know, he seemed a little quiet." So although I agreed with Marc Eliot's interpretation of Kato's comments, our jury might not have.

There is a striking example of Kato Kaelin's use of literary license. In a December 27, 1994, interview with Eliot, Kato described an incident at Nicole's wake. According to Kato, Nicole's friend Cora Fishman pounded on Simpson's chest and demanded, "Why did you do this, why did you do this?" Simpson responded, "I'm sorry. I'm sorry."

If true, Simpson's response would constitute a confession. It would be legally admissible in court. If Simpson had told Fishman that he did not kill Nicole, the incident would have been inadmissible, because Fishman's opinion that Simpson killed Nicole is not evidence. Therefore, Simpson's response, if any, to Fishman's accusation was critical. Fishman herself later had a change of heart and landed squarely in Simpson's camp.

In a February 1, 1995, interview with Eliot, Kato revisited this incident. Conspicuously absent this time around was the comment attributed to Simpson: "I'm sorry." Apparently struck by this obvious discrepancy, Marc Eliot asked Kato, "Did he tell her, 'I'm sorry,' or something?"

"I didn't hear that," Kato replied. Therefore, on this critical material point, Kato gave two versions. Which is why the prosecution could not impeach Kato by asking him about the statements he made to Marc Eliot. It may be difficult to tell whether those statements were embellished.

* * *

Two months after Kato's testimony, his friend Grant Cramer gave a far-ranging interview on *20/20*. He said that Kato spent countless hours with the defense team preparing for his testimony. Cramer related that as a result Kato became almost paranoid. At times, he was afraid to start his car for fear it might blow up. Kato also gave Cramer a different picture of Simpson's demeanor on the night of the murders, at variance with Kato's account on the witness stand. Kato told Cramer that when Simpson was putting his bags into the limousine, his actions and his looks were bizarre. There was a glazed look in Simpson's eyes. He would open his eyes wide and contort his face spastically.

Cramer also gave an interview to the police. According to Cramer, Kato said that when he arrived at Rockingham on June 13 at around 6:00 P.M., Simpson hugged him and said, "Thank God you were here and you can say I was at home when this thing happened." Grant Cramer told the police that when he viewed Kato's testimony on television, Kato "responded to questions very cautiously and would say something without really saying anything." Cramer believed that the manner in which Kato testified about the events was very different from the way he related them to him. For example, Cramer said that Kato underplayed the thumping noises and Simpson's demeanor the evening of the murders. There was another problem with impeaching Kato by calling Cramer and/or Eliot as witnesses. If we impeached Kato on relatively minor points, such as his subjective evaluation of Simpson's demeanor on June 13 and how loud the thumping sounds were, we would run the risk that the jury might throw the baby out with the bathwater. They might disregard all of Kato's testimony, which overwhelmingly favored the prosecution.

However, considering his testimony on the stand, his talks with Eliot and Cramer, and his interviews given after the trial, many are left with the clear impression that Kato knows more than was contained in his testimony. We are still left wondering, What did Kato really know, and when did he know it?

14

A Large Six-Foot Figure Mysteriously Enters the House

THE WEEKEND BEFORE LIMOUSINE DRIVER Allan Park took the stand, Johnnie Cochran escorted the Reverend Jesse Jackson to visit Simpson in jail. After the visit, before a battery of television cameras and print and radio reporters, Reverend Jackson uttered two damning words to describe Simpson's mental state: "remorse and contrition."

There can be no argument about those two words and what they mean: deep and painful sense of guilt for wrongdoing.

When limousine driver Allan Park drove into Brentwood to pick up his famous passenger, he could not have conceived that he was literally driving into history. Although Park took the stand following Kato Kaelin, the two men were polar opposites. Kato was coy and waggish, Park, stolid and sincere. Allan Park told the jury, under Marcia's questioning, that since he had never been to Brentwood before, he started out early. Simpson's flight was at 11:45 P.M. Park arrived at Rockingham at around 10:22 P.M. He looked at the curb number to verify that he was at 360 North Rockingham. This was the area of the curb where the detectives saw the Bronco early the next morning. But at 10:22 P.M., the night of the murders, it was not there. Since the pickup time was not until 10:45 P.M., he waited outside the Ashford gate of Simpson's estate.

At 10:40 P.M., he pushed the buzzer to the gate. No answer. He tried two or three times. No answer.

Based on cell-phone records, at 10:43 P.M., Allan Park called his boss to ask him what to do, since Simpson was not home. After placing the call, he buzzed again. No answer. He called his boss again at 10:49 and left a message. He tried the buzzer yet again. No answer.

At 10:52 P.M., Allan Park's boss called him back and told him to continue waiting. During this conversation, Park saw Kato. This was when Kato was investigating the thumping noises. Almost simultaneously, Park saw a six-foot-tall African-American person of approximately two hundred pounds wearing all dark clothes "come into the entranceway of the house just about where . . . the driveway starts." Based on cell-phone records, the time was 10:54 P.M.

Park buzzed again. This time, Simpson answered and said he had overslept and had just got out of the shower and would be down in a few minutes.

Park also saw the black duffel bag that Kato had described. When Allan tried to put it in the limousine, Simpson protested, "No, no, that is okay. I'll get it." They left for the airport between 11:10 and 11:15 P.M. On the ride, Simpson repeatedly said, "You know, man, it's hot." Simpson turned on the air-conditioning and opened his window. A couple of times Simpson repeated, "It doesn't pay to get dressed in a hurry," and, "I know I forgot something." Yet, as Allan Park described it, "it was mild, [we were] having our normal June gloom, foggy nights." Mr. Park was not hot. Also, during the trip Park saw Simpson "bent down, looking; seemed like he was just checking his bags to see if he had everything." When they got to the airport, Park noticed beads of sweat on Simpson's forehead.

Cochran's cross did not play on reasonable doubt but rather to those on the jury who would cling to unreasonable doubt no matter how far-fetched. He asked questions seemingly intended to support various explanations he gave in his opening statement to account for Simpson's presence in the yard late at night. For example, Cochran asked whether the figure Allan Park saw could have had a robe on.

"Could have," Park admitted.

Therefore, maybe, as suggested in the opening statement, Simpson had been outside chipping golf balls or had been in the house all along and just stepped out for fresh air. Cochran also elicited that Allan Park could not be positive the person he saw going into the house was Simpson. (Simpson admitted on an interview show shortly after the trial that it was he.)

Seizing upon Allan Park's admission that he was not wearing his prescription glasses, Cochran offered questions about Mr. Park's nearsightedness. The implication was that if Park was nearsighted, the figure might not have been Simpson or could have been him in a bathrobe, chipping golf balls, or getting fresh air. However, Mr. Park used the opportunity to say, by way of clarification: "I don't wear them very often at all. . . . I think they make my eyes worse."

But by the end of Cochran's lengthy cross and recross, which produced 175 pages of transcript and took two days, Allan Park's testimony established the last link of the prosecution's time line: Simpson was not home at the time of the murders.

Allan Park's testimony was my two-minute warning. It signified that the crime-scene/time-line phase of the case was drawing to a close and that I would soon have to take the field. On Friday, March 31, 1995, about two months after the opening statements, court recessed for the weekend. I would be up next.

15

The Center of the Storm

FOR TWO MONTHS after joining the prosecution team, I was certain that I would have no role in presenting the case before the jury. This was before I learned that just as the defense theories could change from day to day, so could the roles of the prosecutors.

In December 1994, a short time before opening statements, I was assigned the task of doing the behind-the-scenes preparation of the "chain of custody" evidence in the case. Chain of custody is legal shorthand for the requirement that whenever an attorney attempts to offer certain physical objects into evidence, he or she must establish that the object being introduced is the same one that the police originally seized. For example, when an undercover police officer purchases rock cocaine from a suspect, the prosecution must establish that the rock that was tested is the very same one that was purchased.

Often chain of custody is a completely insignificant, though necessary, feature of a trial. The defense will frequently enter into a stipulation (an agreement between both sides in a lawsuit to certain facts) to the chain of custody. Not so in the Simpson case.

In late November 1994, before I was assigned the chain-of-custody portion of the case, I discussed with Bill Hodgman the central role it would play in our case. Hodgman was, at this time, still Marcia's cocounsel. In substance, I said to him that the LAPD had collected all the significant evidence in our case. Almost all of the biological evidence had passed through the LAPD's laboratory before it was sent to outside labs—the California Department of Justice (DOJ) and Cellmark—for DNA testing.

Bill nodded his head as I spoke. "Both labs are excellent, they're not easy targets. So we have three sets of results on key pieces of evidence: from the LAPD lab, DOJ, and Cellmark."

"Right," I said. "So, arguing that the laboratories made a mistake isn't a viable option for Simpson. The defense will focus their attack on the evidence at a point *before* it was sent out for testing. SID [Scientific Investigations Division] will be the focus of that attack."

Bill appreciated the fact that the SID was "where the battle would be fought."

We expected that in early January 1995, before opening statements, the defense would exercise their right to conduct a hearing to determine whether DNA evidence should be admitted. Until a new scientific technique has been approved by an appellate court, the defense is entitled to conduct a full-scale hearing to determine whether the technique has gained "general acceptance" in the scientific community. Otherwise, the new technique is inadmissible. This hearing is called a Kelly-Frye hearing, named after the appellate-court cases establishing the legal requirement. The defense strategy was clear. They were going to try to bury us in a blizzard of pretrial legal motions to keep key evidence from the jury. The Kelly-Frye hearing spearheaded this effort. If we lost, a crucial part of our case, the DNA evidence, could not be presented to the jury.

In most cases the size and complexity of *Simpson*, there is a pretrial period of many months or even a couple of years. Most defendants request numerous continuances to give their attorneys more preparation time. However, Simpson exercised his statutory right to a speedy trial. The defense probably employed this unusual tactic hoping to catch the prosecution unprepared. Consequently, jury selection commenced on September 26, 1994, just over three months after Simpson's June 20, 1994, arraignment.

This short period was our only pretrial opportunity to prepare the complex case. Throughout the trial, information poured in from the public and from press sources that needed to be investigated. The volume of police reports, interviews, tapes, transcripts, and laboratory reports was simply staggering. This material now fills over one hundred boxes. The number of legal written briefs filed occupies about ten three-ring notebooks. (About one or two briefs, of five to fifteen pages each, are filed in an average murder case.) The number of witnesses and the hours we spent interviewing them vastly exceeds anything I have ever previously seen. I spent about fifty hours interviewing witness Dennis Fung of the LAPD crime laboratory. In the typical case, a prosecutor would interview such a witness for about twenty minutes in the hallway just before his testimony.

We did not have the many months, and sometimes years, that most lawyers in complex cases are given to prepare their cases. As a result, lawyers and resources were added in stages. Prosecutors Cheri Lewis and Darrell Mavis joined the team to assist Marcia and Bill. Five law clerks were also working on the case full-time. Before the case concluded, they passed the bar and were hired as new deputy district attorneys.

After I joined the team, prosecutors Rock Harmon and Woody Clarke came aboard, followed by Chris Darden, Brian Kelberg, and Alan Yochelson. Subsequently, about half a dozen part-time law clerks volunteered. The defense had even more lawyers who made appearances in court: Johnnie Cochran, Barry Scheck, Peter Neufeld, Robert Blasier, Robert Shapiro, Carl Douglas, Gerald Uelmen, DNA expert William Thompson, appellate lawyer Alan Dershowitz, and a couple of others who appeared briefly.

Toward the end of December 1994, Judge Ito recessed the court for the holiday. After the holiday, we anticipated that the Kelly-Frye hearing would take a minimum of a month. While DNA lawyers Rock Harmon and Woody Clarke were occupied with the Kelly-Frye hearing, in court, outside the jury's presence, Marcia, Bill, and Chris, who were going to present the case before the jury, could continue their preparation. Among other things, they needed to interview witnesses, prepare exhibits, and make numerous strategy decisions. We were looking forward to the month-long additional preparation time provided by the Kelly-Frye hearing, although with a sense of trepidation in the event that some or all of the DNA evidence would be excluded.

After the holiday break, at the beginning of January and before the opening statements, the defense made a surprise announcement. They were waiving the Kelly-Frye hearing. When I heard the news on the TV in the reception area of the War Room, it was as though a battle alarm had sounded. *We were going to trial now,* a month earlier than expected. I quickly walked to my cubicle. I've got to start working, fast. I turned on the computer. But where should I start? I looked at the rows of color-coded notebooks filled with witness interviews, briefs, police reports, laboratory reports, and scientific articles that seemed to grow by the day. I couldn't remember whether "chain of custody" was blue, red, or green. One of the younger lawyers poked his head into my cubicle and asked, "What do you think about them waiving the Kelly-Frye?"

I turned and must have looked as if he had just asked me to explain Einstein's theory of relativity. I cleared my throat. "We won." The defense also won, I thought. They distracted us with the threat of the hearing and got us into court at least a month sooner than we had anticipated.

Moments later, Marcia came into the War Room, where she saw a flurry of activity. The lawyers and law clerks were busy working, lining up witnesses, summarizing reports, and organizing materials for trial. Marcia marched toward me with the energy and determination of a general marshaling her troops for battle. In a calm, firm voice she said, "Hank, will you put on the chain-of-custody evidence?" Although posed as a question, to me it sounded like a command.

It took a few seconds for what she was saying to register. I was unprepared. No one had previously discussed with me the possibility of presenting evidence before the jury. I realized that this would be an incredible challenge. I stuttered in an effort to respond. Although I can't remember exactly what I said, I agreed to present the evidence.

I walked back to my cubicle and slowly sat down. Whatever I was feeling, Bill and Marcia had to be under even more pressure.

So later, when Marcia passed through the War Room, I apologized "for my fumbling answer when you asked me to do the 'chain of custody.' I don't want you to worry about me. You have enough on your mind."

"Hank, I was worried about this part of our case," Marcia said. "I picked you so I won't have to worry. I know you will do the best that can be done with it."

I returned to my cubicle, took down volume one of the blue chain-of-custody notebooks, sat at the computer, opened the document containing my notes on the witnesses, and started to work. Late that night, after my mind had turned to mush, I put the notebooks away and turned off the computer, then sat immobilized for a few minutes before leaving for home. I'm really screwed, I thought. I've only been on the case for a little over two months. I have no case history. I don't know everything that's transpired up to this point. How do I get up to speed?

My new status as one of the trial lawyers became even more problematic, for there was no way I could prepare my section of the case and be in court at the same time. Therefore, I would have to keep tabs on what was happening in court by selectively watching TV and by reading the transcripts at night.

It is unheard of for an attorney to present a significant portion of a major trial and not be physically present during substantial portions of the testimony. Yet attorneys on both the defense and prosecution were faced with this dilemma. I felt as if I were being parachuted into the middle of an ongoing battle.

I thought about what Bill Hodgman had said earlier that day during a team meeting in the War Room. He had explained that since we were going to trial sooner than expected, we would use more of a team approach in presenting the evidence. He gave a pep talk delivered in a calm, modulated tone of voice.

One thing Bill said made a particular impression on me. "We haven't had the time to prepare the way we would have liked. Perhaps it won't be as smooth as we would like. There may be some missteps. But we have a strong case and a lot of evidence, and somehow we have to just make sure we get the evidence up there."

As he spoke, Bill seemed remarkably relaxed. Only weeks later when Bill suffered what appeared to be a heart attack did I realize what he was going through.

At the tail end of this meeting, Chris, employing his dry sense of humor, said something I clearly remember. "Every lawyer for himself."

The next day, at work, I spoke to Kathy Mader, hoping for some sympathy. I explained to her what had happened the previous day. "They put *you* in charge of forensic evidence?" Kathy asked incredulously. I knew what was coming. I love Kathy dearly as a friend and colleague. We shared what I still consider my most important case, the Iversen trial. Kathy has one major flaw. She always tells the truth. "Hank, you're good. Hell, you're great at the legal stuff and in court. But when it comes to science, you can't even hang a picture."

I thought, What in hell did hanging a picture have to do with it?

But I bit my tongue. She was telling the truth. The fact is I did have to hire someone to hang a picture in my house.

"Hankster, I hate to say it, but you have no aptitude for science. I'm sorry," she said, patting me on the back, "but it's the last thing in the world you should be responsible for."

"Gee, thanks, Kathy," I said. "Thanks for the vote of confidence." I added defensively, "Anyway, I do like science. I've always found it fascinating." Lamely, I had to admit, "It's just not my greatest strength."

She patted me on the back again, "Well, if there's anything I can do to help, I'm here."

That night, I drove home and thought about what Kathy had said: "You have no aptitude for science . . . it's the last thing you should be responsible for."

I recalled the first time words like that were spoken to me. Mrs. Fisher, my elementary school principle, a heavyset, grandmotherly woman with a tone of voice that was at once gentle, yet removed, was talking to me on the playground under the flagpole. As she put her hand on my cheek, she told me she thought it would be best if I didn't go on to junior high school the following year.

She was saying I should be left back. It was true that I hated school. I was not interested in formal learning. In the third grade I was tested to see if I had a learning disability. That's odd, the testers concluded. I was a "near genius."

Near genius, I thought. Almost a genius. Close enough to genius to get me off the hook. Why should the teachers worry if I was having trouble learning. After all, I was a "near genius."

So when Mrs. Fisher asked me if I wanted to stay in elementary school another year, I looked up at her, squinting, for the sun was in my eyes. The flag was flapping in the breeze far above her head. It was like the gunfight at the O.K. Corral, just Mrs. Fisher and me.

"Are you asking me whether I want to be left back?" I asked politely. "No, thank you."

That afternoon in the schoolyard, something clicked. I decided to succeed, to get good grades. I began to study and started the laborious process of compensating for six years of academic neglect. Literally overnight, I was transformed into a good student.

I pulled the car up to my house and looked up at the darkened windows. Startled, my mind occupied by my early years, I realized that I had no recollection of my fourteen-mile drive, between getting on the Harbor Freeway near the Criminal Courts Building, and this moment. I sat in the car for a few minutes still thinking about Kathy's comments, "no aptitude for science." If I could go from being left back to being a good student overnight, what was I worried about? Emotionally exhausted, but—strangely—exhilarated, I was looking forward to the challenge ahead.

Later that week, on a Saturday morning, I decided to take a long walk through Sunset Canyon, a rustic, upscale residential community that winds its way down to the Pacific Coast Highway and one of the world's most beautiful beaches. I often took these walks during the trial to relieve tension. I stopped briefly near a bluff overlooking a stream of joggers wending their way through the canyons. One of the joggers veered off in my direction. It was Harvey Giss, a well-known, seasoned prosecutor in our office. Harvey asked, "So, Hank, what do they have you doing on the case?"

"Chain of custody."

Harvey shook his head. "Oh, that's great. LAPD's handling of the evidence—that's where the entire defense attack is going to be focused. They're going to claim LAPD screwed up the evidence before it was tested by contaminating or planting it. You're going to be at the center of the storm."

I was impressed that Harvey, who was not involved in the case, immediately understood the implications of my assignment. As I watched Harvey jog away, I kept thinking about what he had said. "The center of the storm."

16

Preparing for Dennis Fung

EVEN BEFORE BEGINNING MY PREPARATORY WORK, I realized that I would face insurmountable problems. Most of my witnesses were criminalists from the LAPD Scientific Investigations Division (SID). (A criminalist is a scientist who collects and analyzes physical evidence and testifies to his findings in court.)

Andrea Mazzola, the criminalist who did most of the physical-evidence collection, was brand-new and had little crime-scene experience, as opposed to the experienced senior criminalist, Dennis Fung. However, Marcia had warned me that, based on his testimony at the grand jury hearing, Fung was going to be a very difficult witness.

Dennis, I soon learned, was a young, mild-mannered scientist, a competent member of his profession, in his early thirties but appearing much younger, who felt far more comfortable with a microscope or at a crime scene than on a witness stand.

The duties Dennis and Andrea performed were relatively simple—collecting evidence and packaging it for later testing. However, Rock Harmon and Woody Clarke warned me that Barry Scheck would make their task appear about as simple as crossing Niagara Falls on a tightrope.

Finally, I was aware that the SID could be attacked as an institution. It was seriously underfunded. The criminalists were underpaid. Many experienced and talented scientists had left to join other law-enforcement crime labs, such as that of the Los Angeles County

Sheriff's Department. None of these problems could be corrected in our case.

Also, I needed to essentially train myself as to how a criminalist conducts crime-scene investigations. I figured that Rock and Woody would have expertise in the area of evidence collection, so I started with them. Rock is a prosecutor with the D.A.'s office in Alameda County, near San Francisco; Woody is a prosecutor with the San Diego D.A.'s office. Both were on loan to us for the duration of the trial, to handle the DNA aspects of the case.

Rock is a scrappy middleweight with a biting sense of humor who epitomizes the saying "He says what he means and he means what he says." In many ways Woody is the polar opposite. Woody, who could be described as a button-down type of guy, often peppered his conversations with corny puns. And he knew they were corny. Whereas Rock has more of an in-your-face style, Woody is more professorial. Both are excellent prosecutors and world-class attorney-experts on DNA. One of the high points for me on the case was working with people like Rock and Woody.

Naturally, the first order of business in preparing the portion of the case dealing with how the evidence was collected would be to consult with both Rock and Woody. I asked them, "What can you guys tell me about this aspect of the case?"

Rock said, "We know very little about this shit. Because it never comes up. No one's ever cared before."

"Because it doesn't make any difference how it's collected," Woody added. "Basically, certain problems in the collection could cause you to get no result. But they aren't going to give you the wrong result."

Thus, I was essentially covering new territory, in that evidence collection had previously not been a major factor in criminal trials. It would be necessary to gain expertise in this relatively unexplored area by training myself. Eventually, I read every leading textbook discussing crime-scene investigation and articles that criminalists sent me from the LAPD and the Sheriff's Department. It was also necessary to get up to speed in conventional serology, the traditional blood-testing techniques that were developed before DNA testing. I had some background in serology from previous cases in the D.A.'s office. But I needed to learn more.

One of the things that fascinates me as a prosecutor is the opportunity to study in-depth fields outside the legal profession. I use a four-step procedure in learning about new technical areas. First, I talk to lawyers who have developed expertise in the area and ask for suggestions. There is no point in reinventing the wheel. Second, I read the relevant scientific literature even if I only slightly understand it. I try to develop some basic understanding of the scientific concepts involved. Third, I talk to experts and have them explain the area to me. For example, the LAPD's chief forensic chemist, Greg Matheson, gave me private lectures at the crime lab about electrophoresis and ABO-blood-group typing. Greg showed me where various steps in the testing process took place and the instrumentation used. This ability to visualize the testing process makes comprehension infinitely easier. Finally, I reread the literature, which at that point, made sense.

As I continued working on the preparation for the chain-of-custody portion of the case, I began to appreciate, even further, the enormity of the task. The Simpson case involved a tremendous amount of biological evidence. On June 13, 1994, the day after the murders, Dennis Fung and Andrea Mazzola collected six bloodstains from the "Rockingham trail"—the trail of blood that commenced with the blood drop on the Bronco handle and ended at the front door of Rockingham. They removed two additional samples from the interior of the house: one in the foyer (consisting of three closely spaced blood drops) and one in the master bathroom. They collected a sock, which was eventually found to contain blood, from a rug in Simpson's bedroom. They collected the glove from the narrow service walkway at the rear of the residence, behind Kato Kaelin's guesthouse.

That same day, at Bundy, Dennis and Andrea collected eight stains from the area around the victims' bodies. They also collected five blood drops on the "Bundy trail," a trail of blood drops to the left of bloody shoe prints leading from the victim's bodies, down a pathway to the rear of the residence, and to an alley. Two blood samples were removed from a set of bloody shoe prints that led down the trail toward the alley. Also, a left glove, the mate to the one at Rockingham, was recovered between Ron's and Nicole's bodies. Near the glove was a knit cap and an envelope, in which Judith Brown's eyeglasses had been placed and on which there was a partial bloody shoe print and blood spatter. Twenty days later, on July 3, an additional three bloodstains were collected on the rear gate of the Bundy residence.

Two days after the murder, on July 14, 1994, Dennis and Andrea collected eleven bloodstains from the interior of the Bronco. This evidence included bloodstains in the well of the interior driver's door handle, several stains on the center console, between the driver's and passenger's seat, and a stain on the steering wheel. In addition, Dennis removed a portion of a bloodstain on the Bronco's carpet, consistent with a shoe print.

In the typical case involving biological evidence, there are one or two stains. Here there were fifty-one stains of significance.

There were approximately one thousand pages of handwritten laboratory notes tracing the history of these items from the time of collection. The SID has no computer tracking system to store this information. Sorting through the paperwork to determine the history of each item took Diana Martinez, my assistant, and me over two full weeks of work to complete.

I spent about 150 hours interviewing the SID criminalists necessary to prove chain of custody. I went to the SID facility about thirty times for this purpose. For example, Dennis Fung and I discussed every possible aspect of his testimony. During one interview session with Dennis, I asked, "What does DNA stand for?"

Dennis stared at me blankly, then smiled broadly. "Does not apply."

I smiled at this joke. "No, seriously." I waited for an answer. Silence. "Dennis, you have a degree in chemistry, a degree in criminalistics, you took organic chemistry, you're a smart guy. You know this." More silence. "Does deoxyribonucleic acid ring a bell?"

"Yes, yes."

"Dennis, do me a favor, just memorize this one thing for me."

"I'll write it on my hand," Dennis said, laughing.

Later, during that conversation, Dennis had to call one of the units within the SID, *where he worked*. He could not remember the telephone number. I quickly rattled it off.

He laughed. "Gee, Hank, you know everything I know plus everything you know."

Nevertheless, interviewing the witnesses was really a learning experience for me. I had to understand the scientific theory and the SID practices relating to evidence collection and testing.

There were more problems. Both Dennis Fung and Andrea Mazzola testified at a number of pretrial hearings. When I read the transcripts of these hearings, I noticed that a number of their statements were inconsistent with the actual facts. This is a common occurrence. When people orally relate the facts of a given incident, they will state them a little differently each time. This phenomenon is well known to trial lawyers. Judges always caution juries, as did Judge Ito, about placing too much emphasis on inconsistent statements because "failure of recollection is a common experience; and innocent misrecollection is not uncommon."

Dennis Fung made one inconsistent statement worth mentioning. The first time Dennis testified in this case was at a grand jury hearing on June 22, 1994. He was not interviewed before he testified and had not prepared for his testimony. He was questioned about the collection of evidence at Bundy and Rockingham for no more than ten to twenty minutes.

During this hearing, Dennis answered certain questions in a way that could make it appear that he had personally collected certain evidence which, in fact, Andrea Mazzola had physically gathered. He did not do so intentionally. He simply thought the question was directed toward inquiring *what* was collected, not *who* collected it. So he used the pronoun "I" instead of "we."

I had to make a tactical decision regarding whether to ask Dennis about this inconsistency when I questioned him on direct examination. There are two schools of thought about how to handle this type of problem. The clear majority of trial lawyers believe that such issues should be brought out on direct examination to "take the sting" out of them. This majority view is based on old-time trial lore passed down through the years from one generation of trial lawyers to the next. I, however, subscribe to a minority view that if the issue in question is not a legitimate criticism, it should not be brought out during direct examination. This view is based on research showing that jurors basically view lawyers the way they view used-car salesmen.

If a used-car salesman tells you that the cherry-red Mustang you are looking at "purrs like a kitten," you tend to be skeptical. But, if he tells you that the engine needs to be overhauled, you believe him. He would not tell you something negative about the car unless it was true.

Now, imagine that you leave this car dealership and go across the street, to a competitor. The competitor tells you, "That cherry-red Mustang you were looking at, its transmission needs overhauling." You would tend to distrust the negative things this salesman has to say about his competitor's car.

Research on jurors shows that the same approach holds true for trial lawyers. If you say something bad about your own case, the jury will automatically believe you. But if the opposition criticizes your case, the jury may not believe it.

Therefore, I generally will not bring out negative points about my case unless I genuinely feel that the jury should consider them because they are legitimate criticisms. I believed that impugning Dennis Fung's integrity was not a legitimate approach for the defense to take. If I allowed them to raise this point on cross-examination, then we could argue: "Look at how unfair the defense is by calling Dennis a liar based on ambiguous testimony he gave at prior hearings. Look how easily and recklessly they accuse people of perjury."

If the defense did suggest that Dennis Fung was lying, as painful as this would be for Dennis and for me, it would result in a tactical advantage to the prosecution. For the defense to paint these mild-mannered scientists as evil coconspirators would help our case. We could point out: "Ladies and gentlemen, not only do you have to believe Fuhrman was involved but Dennis Fung would also have to be involved, and Andrea Mazzola, and many others." It is easier for a jury to believe that one rogue cop somehow lied or even planted evidence than to believe a broad-based, massive police conspiracy to frame an innocent man. I thought that if the defense theory required the jury to believe that Dennis and Andrea were involved in a massive conspiracy, we should win.

Another difficult problem for attorneys is to decide how to handle a witness whose testimony presents many issues. In preparing for Dennis's testimony, I completed a laundry list of about thirty issues about which the defense might question him. But the defense never even asked about many of the most troubling issues on my list.

For example, after Dennis and Andrea did their work on the defendant's Bronco, fingerprint experts thoroughly dusted the vehicle for prints. They found an identifiable print on the driver's-side doorjamb. This print was so close to some blood drops and blood smears that for a while we thought the print itself was in blood. This fingerprint turned out to be Al Cowlings's. I sought out Chris to talk to him about the print. Chris, punctuating his response by jabbing his finger in the air after each word, said, "If that print's in blood, we're going to get an arrest warrant for Al Cowlings as an accessory to murder!"

After interviewing the print people, we determined that the print probably was not in blood. But it left many intriguing questions unanswered. Why was Al Cowlings's print on the doorjamb of Simpson's Bronco so close to the blood? How did it get there? Any answers we could come up with to these questions were pure speculation. The defense chose never to present any evidence regarding Cowlings's print, so the jury never learned about it.

I could not foreclose the inherent problems in Dennis's testimony. In such cases, the goal is damage control. Therefore, my objective with the LAPD criminalists was simple. They did not do anything to alter the test results. My definition of success was simply to prove that whatever else might be said about the criminalists, they did not contaminate the evidence.

Days prior to Dennis's testimony, I spoke to Peter Neufeld one afternoon after court recessed about scheduling. Neufeld, an attorney from New York, specializes in DNA evidence and often works with Barry Scheck. He is a loud and aggressive advocate with a pronounced Brooklyn accent. Whatever one may think about his style as a lawyer, he is highly competent and prepared. Neufeld wanted me to give him a complete rundown of the order of my witnesses.

"Peter," I said, "we only have to give you three days' notice."

Neufeld replied, "Dennis Fung and Andrea Mazzola will only take a week."

"Are you kidding?" I replied. "Bob [Shapiro] said they're going to take a month."

Neufeld made the internationally recognized puffing sound that signifies contempt. "Bob? What does he know?"

The Sunday before Dennis was called, I was working downtown. That evening, my parents and older brother were going to a play at the Music Center, about a half a mile from the courthouse. I walked over to have dinner with them before the play. We sat outside and ate sandwiches on the Music Center's concourse. I was apprehensive about presenting my first witness during the Simpson trial. I knew Dennis would not fare well. Despite all my preparation, I didn't know whether I would be able to control the damage. It was akin to putting my finger in a leaky dike.

As I watched people stroll along the concourse and the fountain in its center, I thought about what my grandmother used to say in her Yiddish accent. "Time takes care of everything."

My family looked worried. I turned to them. "With any luck, by this time next week, I'll be finished with my part of the case."

"I hope so," my mother said with a smile, which unsuccessfully masked her tearing eyes.

17

A Faltering Prosecution Witness

WHEN DENNIS FUNG TOOK THE STAND on April 3, I had no idea that we were commencing a marathon examination that would stretch over nine court days.

My direct examination lasted only two days. I gently guided Dennis through his credentials, which actually sounded impressive. He was a senior criminalist with the SID and had over ten years of experience. He had investigated hundreds of crime scenes.

The centerpiece of the direct examination related to a strategy I had worked out with coprosecutors Rock Harmon and Woody Clarke, who would be presenting the actual DNA evidence. We concluded that the key to reaching our goal—demonstrating that the criminalist did not contaminate the evidence—could be accomplished with a simple but thorough explanation of how blood evidence is collected. There was no way to present this evidence without calling the two people who collected it. Demonstrating how the evidence was gathered was also a legal prerequisite to introducing the test results on the evidence.

The most important point to be made relating to the evidence collection involved something called the *substrate controls*. Dennis Fung and Andrea Mazzola used a blood-collection technique involving cloth swatches. It involved applying moistened cloth squares, averaging about a quarter of an inch square, to the bloodstain. However, before any swatches are applied to a particular stain, a cloth swatch is moistened and applied to a nonbloody area as close to the bloodstain as possible. This blank swatch is called a substrate control.

When a substrate control is tested and no biological material (such as DNA) is detected, it shows that there was no contamination during the collection and processing. In our case, *all of the substrate controls of the blood drops tested negative.* This powerfully demonstrated that the evidence had not been contaminated.

Dennis Fung demonstrated the collection procedures to the jury. I passed out swatches to the jurors to inspect. Using a series of boards with step-by-step photographs illustrating the process, Dennis Fung showed how the swatches were used to soak up the blood, placed into small test tubes for drying at the lab, and finally, packaged after they were dry.

We also introduced evidence, through Dennis Fung, that seemed to put a major dent in one of the defense's key arguments regarding planting. The defense claimed that the three stains on the rear gate at the crime scene—stains 115, 116, and 117—were planted because they were not collected until July 3, almost three weeks after the murders. Neither Dennis nor Andrea could remember seeing them on June 13, the day they collected the evidence. However, Marcia had already established that half a dozen police officers saw them on June 13.

Fortunately, weeks before Dennis took the stand, after a painstaking examination of the photographs with a magnifying glass, Woody found something. Late one night he shouted to me to come to his cubicle, in much the same manner that Alexander Graham Bell must have shouted, "Watson come here," when he invented the telephone.

Woody had pulled out a perspective shot photographed on June 13 and taken from about fifteen feet away that showed the bottom half of the rear gate. With a magnifying glass called a loop—our constant companion when examining the photographs in the Simpson case—Woody pointed out the spot to me.

"We got them!" I exclaimed.

One of the bloodstains on the rear gate was clearly visible. This drove a stake through the heart of the defense theory that the blood was planted weeks later.

During my direct examination of Dennis, when I attempted to introduce a blowup of this photograph, defense attorney Barry Scheck went ballistic. Scheck is a feisty little guy with a broken nose and, at times, a manic brilliance that has gained him many doting fans and more than a few enemies. Scheck is the only man I know who can both whine and yell simultaneously. Employing this unique vocal gift at a side bar, Scheck fought tooth and nail to keep the photograph out of evidence. "Your Honor . . . we have a small version of that photograph, but we never had a blownup version."

This was a spurious objection. The defense had been provided with first-generation photographs from the crime scene. They could have found the stain in question, just as Woody had, with a magnifying glass. Judge Ito overruled the objection and allowed the photograph. Tragically, the jury apparently never considered this evidence during deliberations in determining whether the blood was planted. In post-trial interviews, numerous jurors continue to raise questions about the possible planting of blood on the rear gate, apparently ignoring or forgetting about the clear photographic proof to the contrary.

Toward the tail end of my first day on direct, I turned to an issue that the defense emphasized during its opening statement: that Simpson's blood vial was originally numbered 18 and then was changed to 17. Over the Elmo—the court's computerized projection system—I showed Dennis Fung and the jury a "property report," an official police form that constitutes a laundry list of the evidence the police had collected.

The reason for the reassignment of the numbers on the vial was so that items would be numbered in the order in which they were received. Dennis explained that this renumbering made the reports less confusing and was done to comply with bureaucratic rules relating to how property reports should be completed. In fact, a major advantage of Detective Vannatter's decision to deliver the blood vial to Dennis at Rockingham was to keep the item numbers in proper chronological order. Keeping the numbers in order may seem like a trivial detail. It is not. In cases with numerous items, such as this one, it is extremely confusing to the lawyers, and ultimately the jury, when the item numbers are not maintained chronologically. This was another reasonable explanation for Detective Vannatter's decision. The unreasonable explanation, which the jury still seems to believe to this day, is that Detective Vannatter, one of Johnnie Cochran's "twin demons of evil," kept the blood vial overnight to plant evidence.

On direct, I questioned Dennis to show that the change of the number on the blood vial was readily explained as a reasonable attempt to comply with sensible bureaucratic rules. However, the property report I showed over the Elmo also contained a reference to two items that were irrelevant to the case: an airline ticket and a baggage claim. These items did not relate to Simpson's flight to Chicago. Before I joined the prosecution team, the defense had made a motion to suppress all evidence found at Rockingham, claiming the search warrant had been invalid. Because the airline ticket and baggage claim were irrelevant to both sides, the people and the defense agreed not to present this evidence to avoid the necessity of consuming court time litigating whether they were admissible.

This was where my concern about my incomplete "case history" cost me. I did not read the transcript of the suppression motion because it had seemed irrelevant to my part of the case; and no one told me of the agreement not to introduce these irrelevant items. Scheck was apparently also unaware of this agreement: I showed him my copy of the property report just before I presented it to the jury on the overhead projector, and he did not object.

At the end of the court session, at a side bar, Cochran pointed out that we had agreed not to present the baggage claim and airline ticket. He treated it as if it were no big deal. It wasn't.

I was feeling very good about the way the direct was going. My colleagues were, perhaps prematurely, congratulating me. At one point that day, I passed the television set in the reception area. It was tuned to the trial. Local-television expert-commentator Al De Blanc was asked why such an important part of the case was not done by Marcia Clark, the lead prosecutor. I recall De Blanc saying that no one could have done a better job than I was doing. Later, former district attorney Bob Philobosian, another commentator, told me he publicly stated that it was the best direct examination he had ever seen. I was about to be taught an important lesson about paying attention to television commentators.

The sense of well-being was short-lived. To my surprise, the next day, in court, Gerald Uelmen gave an inappropriately impassioned argument asking for a jury instruction to sanction the prosecution because of my failure to redact, that is, cut out, the reference to the airline ticket and baggage claim in the document I showed the jury the previous day. Uelmen called it "egregious" and "deliberate." The tone of the argument caught me off guard considering how Cochran had addressed the issue the previous day. To my surprise, Judge Ito agreed to instruct the jury about the mistake I had made.

Toward the end of my direct, I mistakenly put another document on the projector that also contained a laundry list of items seized, including the airline ticket and baggage claim. I showed this document to Scheck before placing it on the Elmo. He did not tell me that the document included those items. I cannot say whether he saw them and wanted me to make the mistake of displaying them or simply overlooked them. The entire purpose of showing opposing counsel a document before you display it is for them to raise any objections before the jury sees it.

However, after the document was displayed, the defense objected. Scheck played the mistake for all it was worth. Judge Ito dramatically walked off the bench and looked at the overhead projection to see if it was possible to see the reference to questioned items. It was possible. Judge Ito ordered the jury into the deliberation room.

After the jury left the room, both the defense and I made arguments to the judge about the issue. I explained to Judge Ito that the prosecution did not gain anything from my mistake.

Judge Ito cut me off. "Well, Mr. Goldberg, were I in your shoes I would be thinking about adopting an attitude that the court would be receptive to hearing."

As I heard these words, I thought, What is he talking about? An attitude he would be receptive to hearing? I thought he would be receptive to hearing the facts.

He continued: "I would be contemplating how best to salvage my credibility before the court, and I would be thinking about that I couldn't say mea culpa too many times in this situation were I in your shoes."

"Your Honor, I did," I said calmly and respectfully. "I said it the first time, I will say it again, and I said it during my argument." I told Judge Ito that it wasn't the first time a mistake was made by the prosecution, by me, or by defense counsel, and it wouldn't be the last. "I just didn't know how soon it was going to occur," I added ironically.

This drew some chuckles from the audience. I have found that

As a young child, when my parents would have meetings and fund-raisers in our Westwood home, my function was to take care of our German shepherd, Frisky.

This photograph of me was taken around the time I completed my undergraduate studies at UCLA, at age nineteen.

In 1985, at age twenty-two, I graduated from Loyola Law School and commenced my career in the D.A.'s office.

I'm standing at the podium next to Marcia Clark while Dennis Fung is on the witness stand. Shortly after this, Marcia changed her hairstyle. For several days, this was the leading news story, and it detracted some attention away from Dennis, a fact for which I was very grateful. Also depicted here are *(from left to right)* Johnnie Cochran, Carl Douglas, and Robert Shapiro. *(Globe Photos)*

Marcia, Chris Darden, and I are seated at counsel table.
As they consult, I look at some notes. (*Globe Photos*)

Mark Furhman is pointing to photographs of the Bronco to
illustrate his testimony. Furhman was polished, articulate,
and professional. From the standpoint of his performance on
the stand, he was one of the better police officer witnesses.
However, as the public learned, there is much more to evaluating
a witness's credibility than his demeanor. (*Globe Photos*)

During his cross-examination of Dennis Fung, Barry Scheck is pointing to a prosecution exhibit, a map of Rockingham. Chris and Marcia are in the background. (*Globe Photos*)

Judge
Lance Ito
(*Lisa Rose,
Globe Photos*)

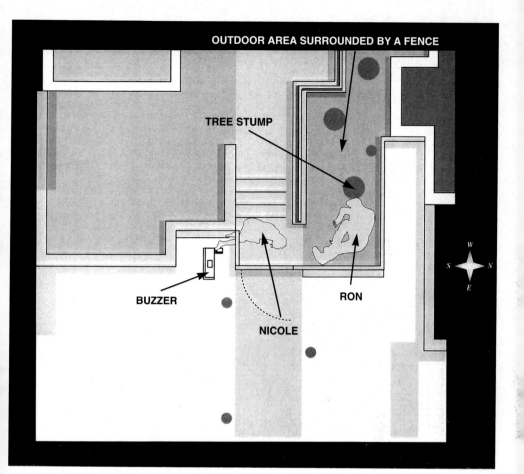

OUTDOOR AREA SURROUNDED BY A FENCE

TREE STUMP

BUZZER

RON

NICOLE

W

S — N

E

This close-up map of Bundy shows the outlines of Ron Goldman's and Nicole Brown Simpson's bodies. Ron was attacked in an outdoor area surrounded by a tall wrought-iron fence. His head came to rest against a tree stump, which must have further limited his maneuverability. Compare this map with photo A (in the color insert) showing the Bundy glove. The glove, knit cap, and envelope containing the eyeglasses were found just south of Ron's foot, in the opening to the caged-off area. (*Trial exhibit supplied by Decision Quest*)

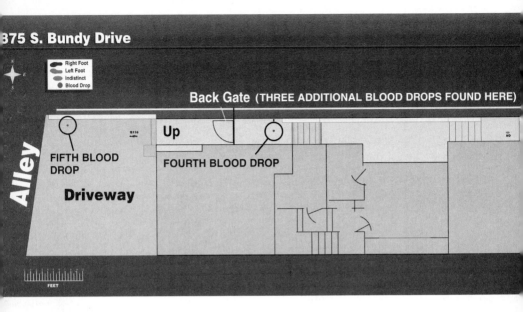

Right Foot
Left Foot
Indistinct
Blood Drop

N
E
S

Back Gate (THREE ADDITIONAL BLOOD DROPS FOUND HERE)

Alley

Q116

Up

AO

FIFTH BLOOD DROP

FOURTH BLOOD DROP

Driveway

FEET

This diagram shows the walkway outside Nicole's Bundy condo. Look for the easternmost footprint, Q68. (This heel impression can also be seen in photo A of the color insert). Note the strange configuration of footprints L, M, N, and O (*see blowup below*). This was the pattern I referred to as "the O.J. Shuffle." The diagram also shows the five blood drops of the Bundy trail. The first drop is to the left of footprint H, indicating that the perpetrator was cut on the left side, as was Simpson. The back gate contained three other drops, also linked to Simpson, which the defense claimed were planted. (*Trial exhibit supplied by Decision Quest*)

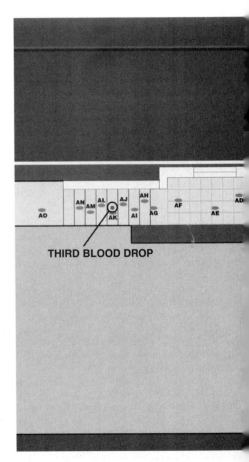

AN AL AJ AH
AM
AO AK AI AG AF AE AD

THIRD BLOOD DROP

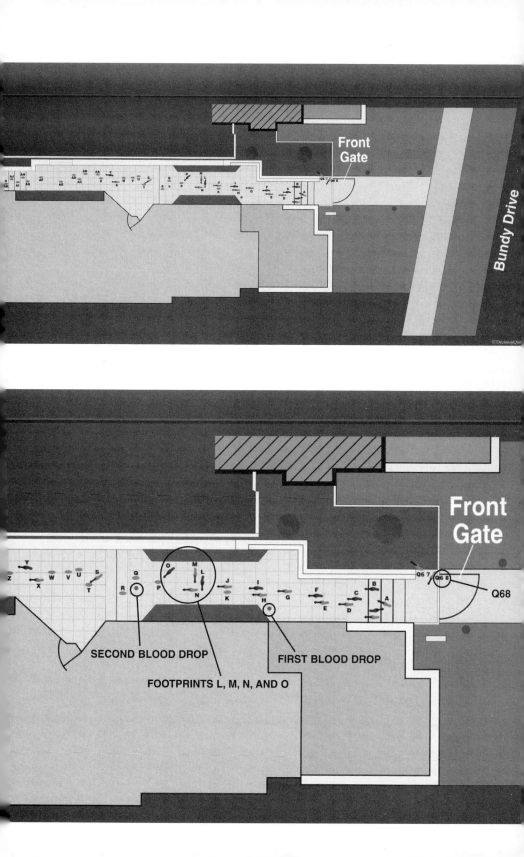

360 N. Rockingham Avenue

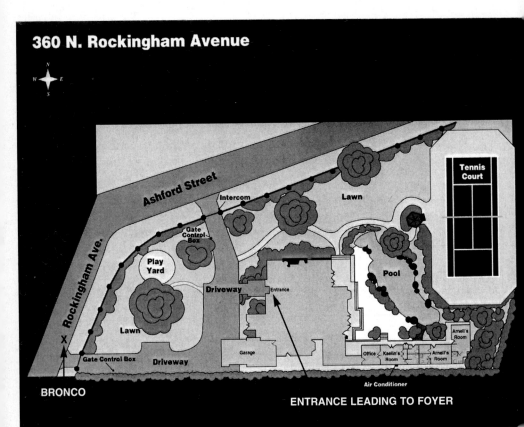

This is a diagram of Simpson's Rockingham estate. After the murders, the Bronco was found parked outside the Rockingham Avenue gate, just north of the driveway. A trail of blood drops led from the exterior driver's handle up the south driveway to the entrance. Just inside the entrance is the foyer, where an additional three drops were recovered. The defense claimed that Simpson left this trail after he cut himself retrieving the cell phone from the Bronco the night of the murders. Note the air conditioner on the narrow south pathway behind Kato's room. This is where the Rockingham glove was recovered. (*Trial exhibit supplied by Decision Quest*)

some sense of humor is vital to seeing things in their proper perspective. This was blown way out of proportion.

Judge Ito did not appreciate my little joke. He glared at me. So I continued to explain my position in a lawyerlike way. My error did not harm the defense. In short, no harm, no foul. I apologized.

However, the judge cut me off, and not too gently. "Somehow I get the feeling [your apology] is not heartfelt."

I thought I heard the audience in the courtroom gasp slightly at this, as if to say to the judge, "Give him a break."

I replied, "I would still ask Your Honor to think about whether or not—Your Honor has questioned . . . my integrity."

He interrupted me, but this time more gently, "I didn't say that." A few moments later, he added, "Mr. Goldberg, before we go too much further, *please accept my apologies to you* if I seem irritated, but this day has not gone well. It started off with many different arguments over many contentious items, and it has been a bad day today." (emphasis added)

I smiled. "I agree with that, Your Honor."

Now Judge Ito was apologizing to me, and I truly accepted and appreciated it.

But later, in the office, when I painfully watched the incident on television, I was angered. Out of all the times that attorneys either accidentally or intentionally ignored his orders, this seemed like the least appropriate time to excoriate an attorney both in front of the jury and on national television. Interestingly, just days later, Barry Scheck asked me to agree to introduce the airline ticket and baggage claim. Incredible! He had raised such a scene when I accidentally showed the jury the documents referencing these items, and now he wanted to introduce them himself! Finally, I agreed.

The difficulties I was having in court during my direct with Dennis were almost overshadowed by the news I received as soon as I stepped into the hallway to return to my office. An investigator with my office told me he wanted to speak to me. Upstairs in my cubicle, in the War Room, he said, "Hank, a little while ago we received a bomb threat at your house. We sent the LAPD out there to check it out."

It had been a really great day. Judge Ito had chewed me out in front of a couple of million people as if I were a schoolboy caught cheating on a quiz. Now some maniac was threatening to bomb my house.

That evening, I was accompanied home with an armed D.A. investigator. My mother, my father, my brother David, and I had dinner at Da Pasavale, a first-rate Italian restaurant in Beverly Hills. The gun-toting investigator accompanied us.

My family was concerned about the bomb threat. I was worried that Dennis might collapse under Barry's cross. "Hank, try not to be so distracted and enjoy your dinner," my mother said. "Who's distracted?" I said as I stared at the normally delicious-looking lasagna sitting in front of me, trying to work up an appetite. "Really, I'm not distracted." Unable to eat much of the lasagna, I said to my mother, "Would the court please pass the bread?"

Probably no forensic witness has ever before had to endure the blistering cross-examination and unfounded attacks launched against him. Curiously, Lee Bailey treated Mark Fuhrman in a professional and comparatively courteous manner during cross-examination. No such treatment for the evil Dennis Fung. His marathon cross-examination, lasting seven court days stretching over two weeks, was the longest of any witness in the trial.

In truth, however, Dennis was a faltering, hesitant witness. Time and time again, he became flustered, unable to adequately address himself to issues we had discussed many times during our more than fifty hours of interviews together. Over and over, Dennis answered elaborate, often ridiculous hypothetical questions by agreeing that the scenario contained in the hypothetical was "possible." He realized that he was doing this but was unable to answer differently the next time a far-fetched hypothetical was presented.

When questioning an expert witness, it is permissible to pose hypothetical questions to them. A hypothetical question assumes a certain set of facts to be true and asks the expert to interpret them. Most judges require that the assumed facts be based on evidence that has or will be introduced at trial. Judge Ito did not apply this rule.

For example, Scheck asked a series of questions about a blanket Detective Lange brought from Nicole's condominium and used to shield her body from public view. Scheck asked Dennis whether it was possible that the blanket from Nicole's condominium could have contaminated other evidence at the crime scene if the blanket contained hairs from Simpson. Dennis could have said, "If you mean to suggest that could explain why over a dozen hairs from Simpson were found in the knit cap near Ron's feet, my answer is no."

But when Scheck asked these hypothetical questions, such as about the blanket, and demanded to know whether his hypothetical was possible, Marcia, Chris, and I would glance at each other as Dennis leaned forward, turned toward Scheck, and blinked. We would watch as his chest began to draw in air and his mouth opened. As the sounds started to gurgle forth from his windpipe, we would hope against hope and pray that he would not say, "It's possible." Then we would hear the beginning of the first word, "It's . . ." No, no, Dennis, don't say it, tell Scheck he's a putz, tell him it's a dumb question, tell him it's almost *impossible.* But then: "Possible."

This quiet, mild-mannered scientist, a decent and honest man, could not effectively defend himself against wild accusations of participating as a key player in a conspiracy to frame Simpson.

The so-called legal commentators were all over Dennis Fung. Initially, they were all over me, too. Some questioned whether Dennis had been adequately "prepared." Others flatly stated that I had blown it by not adequately preparing him.

Dennis was not "prepared." To me, that notion suggests that a lawyer tells a witness what to say or a better way to say it. Prosecutors must not "prepare" witnesses. We interview witnesses. We find out what they are going to say, and we can even tell them the questions they will be asked. But we do not "prepare" them.

Moreover, I do not believe it is possible to change an expert witness overnight. The ability to perform in a laboratory or at a crime scene versus the ability to perform in court are two very different things. I could not change Dennis Fung's inherent difficulties as an expert witness any more than I could alter the fact that Andrea Mazzola had little crime-scene experience. Being an outstanding expert witness is a function of both innate talent and extensive practice.

One night, toward the end of Scheck's cross, I joined my parents and brothers for dinner at Junior's, a bustling Jewish delicatessen in West Los Angeles. My family and I had been going to Junior's since they moved to Los Angeles in 1961. My father is a writer for television and motion pictures. When the early days of live television ended, my family picked up and moved west to join the Hollywood film community. I was born in L.A.'s Good Samaritan Hospital in

1962. By age three, I had come to believe that Junior's matzo ball soup, sometimes touted as Jewish penicillin, could cure all ailments.

As we sat at a booth, over a bowl of matzo ball soup, I said, perhaps melodramatically, "My career is over. Between Ito's public tongue-lashing and being raked over the coals because I didn't prepare Dennis, this is the worst thing that's ever happened to me."

My brother David insisted that Judge Ito's bashing made Ito look bad, me look good. I said, "You're my family, and maybe you saw it that way, but to other people I came off terribly." All I wanted was to enjoy some of my soup.

When I was halfway through a large matzo ball, one of the waitresses, who has known me since I was a child, said, "You're doing such a beautiful, beautiful job. I liked the way you stood up to that Judge Ito." Before I could continue eating, a number of people came over and expressed similar sentiments.

Throughout the trial literally hundreds of people offered similar words of support and encouragement. The honking horns and thumbs up from people at coffee shops and in the streets, and the supportive letters—all of these things meant so much coming from the people who pay my salary.

The legal commentators advised that after Scheck's devastating cross-examination I should do as little redirect on Dennis as possible. I knew otherwise. The defense had gone too far. The rational trial-lawyer side of me realized that the defense's overreaching cross-examination and reckless accusations against Dennis should have the effect of calling into question other arguably more legitimate points raised during cross.

Days before Dennis's redirect examination, Marcia and I met in her office to go over the laundry list of potential items I could deal with on redirect. There were many on the list. Marcia and I both understood that if I asked Dennis about certain issues, it might give Barry another opportunity on recross and inflict even more damage against a vulnerable witness.

"You've got to keep it to the essentials," Marcia cautioned. "If we don't have to ask him about a certain topic, let's not do it." Marcia and I carefully worked out a strategy designed to rehabilitate Dennis on all the key points without exposing new vulnerabilities. It was like walking on a tightrope, but intellectually I knew the strategy should work.

On an emotional level, I was not so confident. The night before my redirect, I went into Marcia's office, where she was talking with Chris. "I just want you to know that I'm sorry. I feel personally responsible for every ridiculous answer Dennis gave on cross."

"No," Marcia responded. "Hank, you did everything with him that anyone could do. I had trouble with him as a witness when I called him at the grand jury, and there was no cross-examination, and he was only on the stand for about an hour! Hank, no one, no one, could have done any better with him."

Chris agreed. I appreciated Marcia's warm remarks, and I appreciated how supportive she was.

However, the morning of my redirect, I still felt terrible. Early that morning, while walking through the empty, darkened corridors leading to the War Room, Gil Garcetti rounded the corner. "How do you feel?" Gil asked.

"Apprehensive," I replied.

"That's to be expected," Gil offered.

As I continued my way to the War Room, I wondered what Gil, my boss, was really thinking. I wished we had explained to him the problems we were facing with Dennis in advance, to soften the blow. However, I never had strategy discussions with Gil regarding my witnesses. I couldn't quite figure out where the suggestion that he "micromanaged" the case, something I had often heard in the press, originated.

By the time I let myself into the deserted, still War Room, my mind turned back to Dennis. All trial lawyers, I reminded myself, have had the experience of things happening in court that, at the time, feel like disasters. But we believe that we can "fix" anything: with further examination, by calling another witness, or in argument to the jury. It's manageable. All trial lawyers have experienced a judge yelling at them.

But my mental pep talk wasn't working. Let's face it, Hank, few lawyers, if any, have had the experience of this type of publicly televised embarrassment. I returned to Judge Ito's excoriation, the commentators' harsh criticisms of me and Dennis, and the pain of watching him testify day after day during cross. I felt something that I have never experienced before in my ten years as a trial lawyer. I couldn't go forward.

18

A Smoking Gun

SHORTLY BEFORE I BEGAN redirect examination, there was an off-the-record side-bar conference. During this conversation Robert Shapiro spoke to me briefly. I had known Bob since I joined the D.A.'s office ten years earlier. He regularly appeared in Beverly Hills court defending small drug cases.

Interestingly, one of Bob's specialties had been questioning the chain of custody of the narcotics. Invariably, Bob would raise small discrepancies between how much the narcotics weighed when the officer weighed them as opposed to when the lab weighed them. These discrepancies were explainable given the extremely small quantities of the drugs involved, whether the packaging was included in the weight, and that the police used less accurate scales than the chemists.

His favorite trick was to ask the officer to describe what the narcotics looked like before the officer opened the sealed narcotics-evidence envelope on the witness stand. The officers would provide the description "It's two rocks, each about the size of a pencil eraser." Then the officer would open the package and find that the chemist had broken one of the rocks into several pieces. Bob would play up the discrepancy for all it was worth. I can't remember such tactics ever working.

But essentially the defense strategy in the Simpson case involved a much more elaborate variation on the same theme. Throughout the trial, Bob was courteous and professional in his dealings with us.

But he always looked uncomfortable, as if he wanted to be someplace else.

During the side bar in Judge Ito's court, before I began the redirect examination of Dennis, Bob said to me, "*I* sure wouldn't look forward to having to do the redirect examination." I still do not know whether this was just an offhanded comment or some effort to "psych me out." I just smiled politely. A challenge, I thought. God, how I wanted to obliterate Scheck's cross in the first five minutes of my redirect. But I didn't have the ammunition.

Just before beginning redirect, we discovered something: a smoking gun. I knew I could wipe out the last point Scheck had made during cross-examination, his grand finale. Scheck had brazenly accused Dennis of intentionally destroying a missing page from his notebook to cover up a conspiracy to frame Simpson.

Scheck's bravura finish was good but risky. Scheck is a detail man. In the hours he had spent preparing for his coup de grâce of Dennis, he thought he had found something. The originals of the form that Dennis and Andrea Mazzola had filled out during the crime-scene processing had been turned over to the defense for inspection. Page 4 of this form was not filled out. One could tell that page 4 was a photocopy, not the original, because there were no staple holes in it, just marks corresponding to the locations where the staple holes would have been on the original.

During cross-examination, Scheck asked about page 4. Scheck attempted to prove that Dennis Fung was lying about receiving the blood vial from Detective Vannatter at 5:20 P.M. at Rockingham. Scheck was claiming that if page 4 showed that Dennis left Rockingham at 5:15 P.M., that would have been before Vannatter arrived with the blood vial at 5:20 P.M.. Therefore, he could not have received the blood vial from Detective Vannatter. The implication was that Detective Vannatter kept the vial overnight. In a series of questions, Scheck asked, hypothetically, "If page 4 indicated that you actually left Rockingham at 5:15 P.M., wouldn't that prove that you were lying when you stated you received the blood vial at 5:20 P.M. from Detective Vannatter?"

Over my objection, Dennis answered, "If there was that time there, yes, it would."

Scheck's question was like asking, "If the world were flat, would you be afraid to take trains." One could say, "It's not flat. I can't answer." However, Dennis's answer allowed Scheck to ask more groundless, accusatorial questions:

"And that is why you destroyed the original page four, Mr. Fung . . . ? That is because you got rid of the original page four, isn't that true?" He pressed, "That is because it had the wrong time on it. Isn't that true?"

With even greater fanfare, lacking only blaring trumpets, the defense passed out the form, including page 4, to the jurors. The jury carefully inspected the documents, looking at the absence of staple holes on page 4. Eight court days after the cross-examination commenced, Scheck was finished. He triumphantly sat down, as if fully expecting the jurors to rush forward shouting, "Not guilty."

I watched the jurors inspecting the documents as if someone had just handed them the Holy Grail. I whispered to Marcia, "Why are they looking at this so carefully? This is bullshit!"

We broke for a recess.

Moments before commencing my redirect examination, it occurred to me that when Dennis was photocopying the crime-scene form, he could have accidentally replaced a photocopy of page 4 for the original. "Dennis," I said, "let's take a look through your notebook that contains your copy of the crime-scene forms." We found it! As if by God's hand, the original page 4 was there. Never in my life have I been so excited at seeing a blank, otherwise meaningless bureaucratic form.

I started by having Dennis Fung explain that he kept his own copy of reports relating to the case in a binder. I had him explain how he searched through the binder. "During the recess, sir, did you have an opportunity to look in your notebook and find the original of page four?"

"Yes."

I asked Dennis a series of questions to establish that he was an expert tool-mark examiner, which qualified him to express an opinion as to whether the several staple holes on page 4 matched the holes on the rest of the document. "Sir, can you please visually compare the staple holes on page four to the staple holes on the succeeding page. . . . And can you form any conclusion about that comparison?

Dennis responded, "I can form a preliminary conclusion. . . . [T]his appears to be the document that was missing from this set of originals."

I asked Dennis why he only expressed a "preliminary" conclusion.

He explained, "I would have to go back to the lab and look at it under controlled—a controlled situation with a microscope and other tools."

Later, matching the fanfare of Scheck's original display of the documents, I passed the documents around to the jury after showing them on the giant overhead projector. The jurors examined them carefully, but with less interest than they showed during Scheck's display of the documents.

I felt this served as a perfect example of the irrationality and unfairness of defense attempts to show that there was a mass conspiracy to frame the defendant. Scheck's line of questioning went to the very heart of the defense: that Vannatter had the blood vial overnight and that Dennis Fung allowed him to have it and was lying to cover up these facts. Without any basis whatsoever, they accused Dennis Fung of destroying this page because it would show that he left Rockingham at 5:15 P.M., five minutes before Vannatter arrived.

I thought that this single little exchange said volumes about the case and the depths to which the defense sank in making totally groundless, irresponsible allegations against good people. It showed that their theories were predicated on trivia: melting ice cream, bathwater, and staple holes. They were willing to predicate a conspiracy theory based on the absence of staple holes in a meaningless bureaucratic form.

But that little exchange also said something about Dennis Fung. I can only imagine how I would have felt if allegation after groundless allegation was fired against me on the witness stand. Everyone in the courtroom knew that the original page 4 had been found.

However, Dennis Fung was the consummate scientist. After eight days of character assassination, eight days of humiliation, nitpicking, and baseless allegations of the worst sort, any other witness would have taken that page 4 and rammed it down Scheck's throat. But Dennis Fung wanted to take that page, put it under his microscope, and examine it more carefully.

After addressing the page 4 issue, I moved to another key area Scheck had raised during his cross. Scheck had implied that it seemed suspicious that Dennis Fung could not specifically recall which witnesses saw Vannatter give him the blood vial.

For many criminalists, receiving a blood vial is inconsequential and occurs several times a day. It is not a memorable event, such as one's first kiss. Dennis could not have imagined that eight months later someone would accuse him of involvement in a conspiracy because he could not recall who witnessed him receiving the blood vial. I questioned Dennis about the precise moment when Detective Vannatter gave him the vial. Employing the tone of voice of a carnival barker summoning the crowds to view one of the world's great wonders, I asked, "Did you make it a point to call out to people, 'Hey, everyone, I'm getting the vial! Can everyone gather around so I can have some witnesses?' " Naturally, Dennis explained that it would have been unprofessional to have done so.

Another area of my redirect also dealt with Scheck's contention on cross that Dennis did not really receive the blood vial from Detective Vannatter. Before they testify, I always tell witnesses that if they are not positive about something, make it clear by saying, "I believe," or, "I think," or, "I don't remember," I don't know why this concept is so difficult for people to follow. In my experience, even officers who have been testifying for years have trouble doing this. On cross-examination, Scheck had asked Dennis to describe the packaging that contained the gray envelope that held the vial when it was taken from Simpson's house and brought to the crime-scene truck parked outside.

During his cross-examination Scheck had asked Dennis what the blood vial was in when he took it to the crime-scene truck. Dennis had said it may have been in a paper bag, but he didn't really recall, or maybe it had been in a posse box (a little metal box under a notepad), or maybe he had just carried it in his hand.

I thought, Dennis, why didn't you just say you can't remember? When Scheck asked the question again, he got Dennis to commit to an answer. "So it would be one of those three ways . . . either . . . in your hand, in a paper bag, or in a posse box?"

"Yes."

I thought, Oh, no! Now Dennis has testified that the blood vial was definitely carried out in one of those three ways, even though moments earlier he said he wasn't sure.

Scheck thought he had set Dennis up for impeachment. He showed Dennis a series of different videotapes from news coverage. They showed Andrea Mazzola and Dennis walking out of the Rockingham residence and putting various bags into the crime-scene truck. Upon seeing these tapes, it became clear to Dennis that the vial was not in one of the three types of receptacles he had mentioned. In fact, Andrea was carrying the envelope containing the blood vial in a plastic garbage bag. Scheck charged that these tapes showed that Dennis Fung was lying about having received the blood vial from Detective Vannatter at Rockingham on June 13.

The accusations were flying: "Mr Fung, are you having some trouble keeping this story straight about getting the blood vial, blood sample, from Detective Vannatter from Rockingham?" Again, Scheck asked, "And when you saw these series of tapes, Mr. Fung, you realized that you had been caught in a lie, didn't you?"

This is where having talented lawyers working behind the scenes comes in handy. While I was in court with Dennis, attorneys Bill Hodgman and Alan Yochelson, and Jonathan Fairtlough, were feverishly working to obtain a complete, unedited copy of the news footage shot outside Rockingham on June 13. Usually, the media will not turn over outtakes. Outtakes are footage not aired on television. Under California law, the media is entitled to maintain the confidentiality of certain materials in order to protect them in their news-gathering efforts.

After concluding with the page 4 issue, at the point in my redirect examination where I was about to finish asking questions regarding the receipt of the blood vial, I kept looking at the clock and at the door. It was clear that Bill wasn't going to come bursting through the door carrying the footage. I stalled by asking a few additional questions before we broke for the weekend. Saved by the bell.

By Sunday, the unedited news-footage videotape shot outside Rockingham had arrived. Later that morning, over cream cheese, lox, and bagels, Dennis Fung and I watched the videotape on the VCR in the War Room. The camera had a time counter that was accurate to within thirty to forty seconds. The footage showed detective Phil Vannatter pulling up at 5:17 P.M. As he walked up the driveway to Rockingham, he was carrying a leather attaché case, the way a schoolboy would carry a notebook against the side of his body. A gray piece of paper sat on top of the attaché case. A gust of wind blew back the top of the paper, allowing us to see the reverse side. We could clearly observe the flap and metal clasp, showing that it was the back of an envelope. When I saw this, my heart started pounding. But it got even better.

Then, as Phil continued to walk to within a few feet of the camera, the wind blew the envelope back so that the front could be seen. We could see a form printed on the face of the envelope. It was the gray evidence envelope containing the blood vial! Dennis quickly jumped out of his chair, placing his face within about two feet of the television set. I also stood. We had clear photographic proof that Vannatter, just as he had testified, had brought the envelope into Rockingham for the purpose of turning the vial over to Dennis. How could we get any luckier?

Then, as we continued to watch the tape, the counter showed the time as 5:19 P.M., the time Dennis had recorded having received the blood vial. We could see a long shot of the front door at Rockingham. Just inside the foyer, we could see Dennis. In one hand he had the plastic garbage bag. In the other, he had what could only have been the evidence envelope containing the vial.

When we saw this, Dennis jumped up and screamed, "Yes! Yes! Yes!" as though Magic Johnson had hit a three-pointer to win the seventh game of the championship series. There was more.

At 5:42 P.M., a shot showed Dennis Fung and Andrea Mazzola leaving the residence. Andrea was carrying the trash bag. As she passed the camera, one could see a square outline, the approximate dimensions of an evidence envelope, as the wind caught the plastic bag.

We both began laughing. The defense conspiracy theory was demolished. They'd have to throw in the towel, I thought, and switch to contamination. There was no way to say that the blood vial hadn't been turned over to Dennis just as Dennis and Phil had testified. Now the jury couldn't possibly believe the centerpiece of the defense conspiracy theory—their scenario about the blood vial. In fact, I wondered how they could believe anything that the defense had told them.

After Dennis left, I walked to the little kitchen on the eighteenth floor of the D.A.'s office. The kitchen, an otherwise worn and unremarkable little room, has one saving grace: a large picture window with a magnificent view overlooking the older sections of downtown. I gazed out the window, as I often did, to rest my eyes after hours sitting behind the computer. It had stopped raining. The cloud-filtered late-afternoon light cast a gray pallor over the buildings and numerous railroad tracks, creating the unreal appearance of a sprawling miniature train set. The two largest buildings on the horizon were the state-of-the-art twin towers of the County Men's Central

Jail. Because of lack of financing and notwithstanding massive over-crowding in the jail's older section, the towers have been standing empty for several years, silent sentinels to L.A.'s future.

I wondered what the jury would make of the tape when we played it the next day. I watched the changing shapes and directions of the thick plumes of water vapor, which rose from the roofs of the larger buildings, until they evaporated into nothing. Isn't it interesting, I thought, that something so substantial looking can so easily fade away.

19

"Where Isss Ittt, Misterrr Fung?"

ON MONDAY, OUR FIRST ORDER of business was to play the videotape to the jury. While the tape was being played, I looked over at the jury several times. Their stone faces occasionally looked back at me.

After the tape had concluded, seemingly disposing of the defense conspiracy theory, I turned to the remaining issues relating to evidence collection and contamination.

During my redirect of Dennis, I was less concerned about covering these substantive areas. Rock Harmon, Woody Clarke, and I had developed what we called a "cleanup" strategy to undo some of the inevitable damage and confusion that would occur during the testimony of both Dennis and Andrea. Rock and Woody had attended several of my interview sessions with Dennis and Andrea before I called them as witnesses. Rock often commented that he thought my witness interviews were "extremely meticulous and detailed."

"You mean boring," I would say. Rock referred to our marathon interview sessions as a "Hankeroo."

After our initial interview with Dennis, Rock, Woody, and I met in the War Room. We agreed that part of our cleanup strategy would involve calling witnesses to address some of the issues raised on the cross-examinations of Dennis and Andrea. These witnesses included the top experts in serology, the science of testing blood and other body fluids. Polished and articulate, they had the qualifications to explain in detail how the blood evidence that was collected could not have made the test results erroneously point toward Simpson.

Employing this strategy, during my redirect of Dennis, I did not have to ask him detailed questions about contamination. Dennis simply testified that his collection was done in accordance with his laboratory's specifications.

The only other notable issue raised about the evidence collection was whether it was a "mistake" for Detective Lange to have placed a clean blanket, taken from the Bundy residence, over Nicole's body in order to shield it from public view. Similarly, the defense contended that Dennis had made a "mistake" when he brought the packaged Rockingham glove into the caged-off area where Ron's body lay. Detective Lange wanted to see if the two gloves matched. Presumably, the defense was trying to imply that the hair and fiber evidence that connected Simpson to the crime could have come from the blanket.

With Dennis, I established that the blanket never came into contact with the items on which hair and trace evidence was found—the knit cap, Ron's shirt, and the Rockingham glove. Any contamination of the Rockingham glove would have been impossible, since it never left its package. It was ludicrous to believe that hair from the blanket could have flown inside the knit cap, where hair consistent with Simpson's was found. Perhaps for this reason, the defense never used the blanket theory during closing arguments.

I wanted to conclude my redirect of Dennis by showing how easy it was to Monday-morning-quarterback a criminalist's work at a crime scene. I read to the jury a passage from one of defense expert Dr. Henry Lee's books, *Forensic Science—An Introduction to Criminalistics,* on which Dennis had relied. Using defense expert Dr. Lee's own words would force Lee into corroborating Dennis when he testified on this point. And he did. In the book, Lee said, "Of course perfection in this or any other human endeavor is never achieved. It is probable that no crime scene has ever been processed in such a way that hindsight would not allow someone else to criticize the work at a later date."

I was using the words of the defense's expert to soften some of the blows Scheck had struck. The message: Nitpicking was easy—

and unfair. Moreover, if the ability to criticize a crime-scene investigation were deemed to raise a reasonable doubt, then every defendant would have to be let free. Legitimate criticism is *always* possible. "Mistakes" are always made.

Toward the end of Dennis's testimony, I decided to attempt to humorously summarize Scheck's entire attack on Dennis Fung. Earlier, in attempting to defuse the June thirteenth rear-gate photo, which clearly showed one of the red stains that was collected on July 3, Barry Scheck had asked Dennis Fung to point to the location of a second stain that was not in the camera's view. He did it using a loud, accusatorial tone that sounded like a schoolyard challenge or taunt: "Where isss ittt, Misterrr Fung?"

I posed my last question with a sneer, which, I have been told, was a pretty decent imitation of Scheck. I asked Dennis whether he recalled Scheck's asking him, "Where isss ittt, Misterrr Fung?"

As we were leaving court that day, I passed Cochran. I whispered to him. "Johnnie, can you please let Barry do all of the cross-examinations?" Johnnie, who almost always had a quick comeback, just smiled.

That night, literally every analyst discussing Fung's testimony said I had done a great job of rehabilitating a witness who had earlier seemed beyond repair. However, the only piece of my redirect shown on every channel news program again and again was my imitation of Barry Scheck's cross-examination technique: "Where isss ittt, Misterrr Fung?

On April 19, UCLA law professor and commentator Peter Arenella, in a column in the *Los Angeles Times* entitled "What a Difference a Day Makes," also agreed that the redirect had rehabilitated Dennis Fung. Indeed, for me this was another reminder of one of life's lessons. Barry Scheck had gone from a lawyer who had done a devastating job of cross-examination, a textbook for defense attorneys, to a lawyer who had stayed too long at the ball and turned from a prince into a frog.

What happened to Dennis Fung? After the lengthiest ordeal of any witness on the stand in this case, the judge finally told him matter-of-factly, "Mr Fung, I'm going to excuse you from further testimony in this case at this time."

From the expression on Dennis's face, one would have thought

that Judge Ito had just announced that he had won the Irish Sweep-
stakes. He almost leaped from the stand and bolted for the exit. But
his path was blocked by a smiling Johnnie Cochran, Robert Shapiro,
and other members of the defense team—and a smiling Orenthal
James Simpson. The team that had tried to assassinate his character
by branding him a coconspirator and bungler was now extending its
hands outward toward Dennis. My mouth open, I witnessed Dennis,
with a warm grin, accept their handshake and Shapiro's hug.

I cannot understand how Dennis—after being dragged through
the mud in a public character assassination viewed by countless millions, portrayed as an incompetent buffoon at best and a lying, per-
juring coconspirator at worst—could have accepted the handshakes
and embraces of those who had demeaned him.

The next day, Bill asked me about the handshaking incident.
Raising my arms in mock surrender, I said, "Okay, I admit it. I
forgot to tell Dennis not to shake their hands and hug the defense
attorneys on the way out." Bill laughed.

"Really," I continued, "I think it's great. It shows just how insin-
cere they are. If they really believed half the allegations about Dennis Fung, if they believed their attacks were warranted, how could
they have embraced him when he left the stand?"

Bill smiled, "I agree."

Months later, Dennis and I returned to the scene of the crime—
to Bundy—to prepare a chart of the footprints for shoe-print expert
Bill Bodziak's testimony. En route, we stopped for lunch at the Apple Pan, an old-fashioned, local hamburger joint, reputed to be one
of L.A.'s best. I have been going there for the past thirty years. Two
of the countermen have known me for almost that long.

Dennis and I were seated on bar stools at the counter. Over
hamburgers and fries, Dennis raised the issue. "I bet you were wondering why I shook the hands of the defense team on my way out." I
shrugged. "Well, it crossed my mind." But I basically knew why. He
was so eager to get off the stand, he would have run into anyone's
arms.

He said, "I was in somewhat of a daze after leaving the stand. I
really wasn't aware of what was happening."

After swallowing a bite of hamburger, I turned to him and
smiled. "You're okay, Dennis."

20

Rookie of the Year

JUST BEFORE COMMENCING Andrea Mazzola's direct, I participated in an unreported side-bar conference. I asked Judge Ito, in a very friendly manner, "How are you doing today?"

"How are *you* doing?" he asked. Perhaps referring to my roller-coaster ride with Dennis and anticipated difficulties with Andrea, he added, "There's a lot of pressure on you right now."

Andrea Mazzola was the next witness after Dennis. Andrea is in her early thirties, with curly graying hair and the bookish demeanor of a librarian. When pushed, she can dig her heels in and take a stand. I knew that Andrea had more natural ability as an expert witness than Dennis. However, she also presented potential problems that troubled me.

For example, Andrea did most of the physical-evidence collection of the blood in Simpson's bathroom. While there, she observed something in the dirty-clothes hamper. It could also be seen in some photographs taken in the bathroom.

I first noticed this object when Marcia and I were going over the photographs in her office shortly after I joined the prosecution team. As we flipped through the photo books of the numerous crime-scene photos, we came to the pictures of Simpson's bathroom. Marcia pointed to the dirty-clothes hamper. "See that. Can you see that?"

"Oh, my God, I can't believe it. Was it collected?" I asked.

"No." Marcia shook her head.

What I could see in the photographs were men's garments that matched Kato Kaelin's description of the clothing Simpson was wearing on the night of the murder. Equally important, the clothes in the hamper appeared consistent with black cotton fibers found on the Rockingham glove and on Ron's shirt.

Later, during one of my interviews with Andrea before she was called as a witness, I asked her, "What about the clothing in the hamper? Did you see it?"

Andrea said, "I didn't examine it."

"Why?"

"Because no one asked me. That wasn't my job."

Of course, as the least senior person on the scene, Andrea was basically doing the grunt work. She was supposed to collect the items that she was specifically told to collect.

But since Andrea was aware that the clothing was present, I thought it was possible that the defense would try to make the LAPD out to be incompetent Keystone Kops. The murderer's clothing was possibly right under their nose, and they left it there!

I had to consider whether to elicit the evidence about the clothing testimony on my direct in order to "take the sting out of it." However, similar to the issues with Dennis Fung, such as when he said, in his grand-jury testimony, "I" collected the evidence rather than "we," presenting this testimony would seem to place undue emphasis on it.

Perhaps it was in the mutual interest of both sides not to elicit information about the clothing. The defense would not want to imply that the police had reason to believe the clothes were worn during the murders and would not want to furnish an explanation as to why the prosecution was unable to present evidence of bloody clothing. Nor was it in the prosecution's interest to highlight such an obvious oversight. It would be one more red herring to divert the jury's attention from evidence relating to Simpson's guilt and to focus their attention on what the LAPD did or did not do and what the clothing might or might not have shown. Again, it would be concentrating on the hole rather than the doughnut. I concluded that the defense would not ask about the clothing. I was right.

During my interviews with her, Andrea told me another interesting story. She said, "Dennis couldn't believe that O.J. Simpson could possibly be guilty. On the day we collected the evidence and into the next day he kept saying over and over, 'Not O.J., not O.J., it can't be O.J.' Finally, I said, 'Enough already.' I didn't even know who O.J. was until Dennis told me."

Later, I asked Dennis about this. He told me, "O.J. was one of my idols."

"When did you decide he was guilty, Dennis?"

Dennis replied, "Not till after the test results."

I was perplexed. I was talking to a rational, intelligent forensic scientist. How could he be overcome with the same feelings of support for Simpson that affected other people? "After collecting the Rockingham glove, the blood in the foyer, and the blood drop in his master bathroom, didn't you think he was guilty?"

"No," Dennis answered.

I related the story that Andrea and Dennis had told me to Marcia and asked whether we should introduce it to show that Dennis and Andrea were not likely conspirators. Marcia said what I was thinking. "The part about Andrea not knowing Simpson is very believable. I didn't know him when I first got the case."

I interrupted: "I barely knew him. I just knew him from the Hertz commercials. Before the murder, I'm not sure I would have recognized him if I saw him on the street."

Marcia continued: "But the part about Dennis not knowing Simpson was guilty is confusing. I wouldn't use it."

During my direct, I wanted to illustrate simply and graphically that Andrea was more than qualified to employ simple collection techniques. I elicited her educational background. She had a four-year degree in criminalistics from Cal State. She took courses in general chemistry, organic chemistry, qualitative analysis, biochemistry, microbiology, and trace analysis (dealing with hair and fiber evidence). I elicited the various criminalistics seminars she had attended as a student and after graduating.

After joining the LAPD in January 1994, she went through the Scientific Investigations Division (SID) Academy, which offered hands-on experience in evidence collection and processing techniques. By the time I had finished this line of questioning, she no longer sounded like a "trainee," as the defense had painted her. During the opening statement, the defense had made a big deal about whether she was qualified to collect key evidence, such as the knit cap and glove.

I asked Andrea to demonstrate to the jury how she had collected the items. She gingerly picked up the glove by grasping it between the thumb and forefinger of her gloved hand and carefully placed it into its packaging. It was so simple, I chuckled slightly and asked: "That's all there is to it?"

She replied, "That's all there is to it."

I paused for a moment. "And did you feel qualified to do that after being involved in the forensic-science community for about six years?"

"Yes," she said matter-of-factly.

Both Andrea's and Dennis's assignment to the crime scene was sheer happenstance, as was Lange's and Vannatter's involvement. They all just happened to be on call that night. Neither Fuhrman nor anyone else thought to themselves, I know, let's get Dennis and Andrea here. They'll be as eager as we are to frame O.J. Since most of these people did not know each other and were at the scene through happenstance, how could they all instantly have come together to frame Simpson?

Andrea was able to corroborate Dennis's testimony that he received the blood vial from Vannatter. Later, back at the lab, she saw the vial. Now the defense was forced to place the bookish Andrea Mazzola on their growing list of conspirators and perjurers. Dennis clearly did not fit the part of scientific adviser to a grand conspiracy to convict a beloved sports star. Andrea fit the part even less.

My examination clipped along at a fast pace and lasted just slightly more than one complete morning court session. Peter Neufeld, the loud, pugnacious defense attorney with the Brooklyn accent, conducted a four-day-long cross-examination. One morning before court convened, Peter was sitting at counsel table reading a profile that was written about him in the *Daily Journal,* the major newspaper for lawyers. As I stood over his shoulder, he read out loud. The article described him as being an effective but mild-mannered attorney. I wondered, but restrained myself from asking, whether they were describing Peter Neufeld or Mr. Rogers. Obviously, Peter was thinking the same thing. Repeating the passage containing the mild-mannered description, he turned to me and asked, "Are they sure they're describing the right guy?"

His cross was extremely detailed and very accusatorial in tone. So much so, in fact, that during the first day of his cross, I couldn't restrain myself from smiling. I thought that the jury would hate

Neufeld for questioning Andrea as though she were Lizzie Borden, the infamous ax murderess. She seemed an even less apt target for such venom than Dennis had.

The centerpiece of Neufeld's cross-examination came in support of the defense's conspiracy theory. Neufeld suggested that someone threw away all of the blood evidence Dennis and Andrea had collected, including its packaging, and replaced it with new planted evidence. The basis for this accusation was that during a pretrial hearing Andrea mistakenly testified that she initialed all of the bindles and coin envelopes into which the swatches were placed. In fact, Dennis Fung initialed most of them.

Neufeld advanced the position that if Andrea initialed the envelopes, the envelopes should still show her initials. Since they did not, "that would mean these envelopes were not the original envelopes." So according to the defense's planting theory, the person doing the planting had to have thrown away the whole enchilada—the original swatches, bindles, and coin envelopes—and started all over again. To vote not guilty, the jury would have to buy this.

We knew that what Neufeld was suggesting absolutely, positively, did not happen. Andrea testified that she was sure all the bindles were, in fact, the originals because she recognized either her handwriting or Dennis's on them. Moreover, I showed that the coin envelopes were the originals because the criminalists took pictures of them before the packaging took place.

During her direct, Andrea utilized the same series of demonstration boards that Dennis had employed during his testimony to illustrate, step by step, the evidence-collection and processing procedures. I had also created a videotape of the same procedure.

Neufeld chose to show the tape during Andrea's cross-examination. The defense tried to nitpick various things that were done during the collection—Andrea Mazzola touched the ground with her gloved hand, and when she removed a clean swatch from its receptacle, some other clean swatches fell on the ground. Neufeld implied that doing these little things were errors.

The overall effect of the tape, however, was to show how simple the procedure was and how the substrate controls functioned as a guarantee against contamination.

On redirect, Andrea explained that none of the types of alleged mistakes could change the results.

On recross, Neufeld asked, "So as you sit here today, having seen this videotape . . . it is your opinion that there were no mistakes made by you?"

Andrea answered matter-of-factly. "None that I can really see, no."

Neufeld said, "Thank you."

Peter Neufeld paused, seeming to collect his thoughts, and then moved on to another area. No other witness ever contradicted or questioned Andrea's testimony that she did not make mistakes while collecting the blood. After this, the defense's attack on the blood-evidence collection seemed to fade out of their case. Much later, during closing arguments, Scheck admitted that the evidence was not contaminated during the collection phase.

Having nowhere to go on the contamination issue, on recross Neufeld asked, in feigned horror, about the adequacy of the security procedures for the evidence. He questioned in detail about the size of the opening of the roll-up door that Dennis and Andrea walked through to get inside the crime lab's Evidence Processing Room, the room where the evidence swatches were dried and packaged.

He went on: "And if once inside, someone opened that roll-up door, then other people could come and go from the Evidence Processing Unit through that large door, which is big enough for a car or truck; is that right?" He was suggesting that someone may have sneaked into the relatively small room without Dennis and Andrea knowing.

In re-redirect, I asked ironically, "Is it possible that maybe some person ran in there and snuck into the Evidence Processing Room and then hid until you and Mr. Fung left?"

NEUFELD: Objection, leading and speculative.

JUDGE ITO: Sustained.

GOLDBERG: Well, did you see anyone scurry into the room and hide, waiting for you and Mr. Fung to leave?

MAZZOLA: No.

GOLDBERG: All right. And when you left the Evidence Processing Room, were the doors closed?

MAZZOLA: The door was closed.

GOLDBERG: And locked?

MAZZOLA: And locked, yes.

By the end of her four days on the stand, we had convincingly shown that no "mistakes" were made that would cast doubt on the blood results. Her testimony shattered the concept that she and

Dennis were part of a conspiracy to frame Simpson. In the final analysis, Neufeld's tour de force predicating a conspiracy theory on whose initials were on the envelopes and bindles was as ludicrous as Scheck's staple-hole theory.

Andrea surprised me. She performed much better than I had thought possible given her relative lack of experience on the witness stand. During cross-examination, when Neufeld was trying to get Andrea to say she was a rookie, Judge Ito observed that she could be "rookie of the year." The next time I went to the crime lab, after Andrea's testimony, I saw a handmade sign: Andrea Mazzola, Rookie of the Year. I guess she was.

21

Inside the Secret LAPD Lab

THE TESTIMONY OF BOTH Andrea and Dennis consumed almost the entire month of April. After Andrea left the stand, on April 27, and we recessed for the weekend, I was exhausted. I thought about how, a month earlier, I had sat with my family on the Music Center's concourse, hoping that my part of the case would be concluded in a week. However, I still had one major witness to go, Greg Matheson.

When I began preparing for the chain-of-custody portion of the case, Matheson was the first witness I talked to. Greg is a chief forensic chemist, one of the three top administrators at the SID. A man in his forties, he looks more like a former linebacker than a scientist, but he has a calm and gentle demeanor.

My first meeting with Greg took place at the main SID facility. It is in a building known as Piper Tech, located in a section of downtown Los Angeles about a mile from the courthouse. Piper Tech is an extremely large, brutal-appearing structure that looks like a post-apocalyptic police station. The LAPD flies its helicopters from the structure's roof, giving the entire building the feel of a beached, concrete aircraft carrier.

The SID is a large, windowless facility occupying what would be one of the aircraft carrier's lower decks. Inside, the facility appears clean and modern. It consists of several different, separate laboratories connected by a U-shaped hallway. Each laboratory has large glass windows that allow people to see into the lab from the hallway. Near each window is a button that, when pressed, activates a recording that describes the work being performed inside the lab. This arrangement is designed for public tours of the facility. I discovered this one day when I was interviewing Dennis at the lab before his testimony. As we walked down the corridor, Dennis blithely pushed every button along the way, producing a cacophony of electronic voices that chattered at us as we walked. "Dennis," I said, "remind me not to get on an elevator with you. You'll push every button."

During my first meeting with Greg, it was clear he would make an exceptional witness. Scrupulously honest and unbiased, he is highly qualified in the area of his expertise: conventional blood testing. Greg's credentials are impeccable. He was one of the past presidents of the California Association of Criminalists. Greg is certified by the American Board of Criminalistics, has thirteen years of experience in serology, and has extensive "bench experience," that is, hands-on experience conducting forensic testing.

Most important, Greg also has extensive experience in the field, processing crime scenes. As an expert both in crime-scene processing and blood testing, Greg was the perfect witness to convincingly assault the defense's contamination theory. Greg would be the first witness in our "cleanup" strategy. I recall one commentator suggesting that perhaps Greg should have been called before Dennis Fung. This strategy would have been insane. After we saw exactly where Dennis and Andrea needed shoring up, Greg was the perfect witness to help us accomplish just that.

During one of my first meetings, months before Dennis took the witness stand, Greg took me on a tour of the SID Piper Tech facility. One might wonder what I, or any attorney, would be looking for during this tour. The answer is, I didn't know. Greg showed me the various locations through which the evidence in this case passed in the same chronological order as the path the evidence actually took.

First, we saw the Evidence Processing Room. It looked like a small warehouse, with two large tables in the center of the room and large drying hoods on the back wall of the room that could be used to dry bloody garments. It had a roll-up door leading to the outside and a key-card-monitored entry door into a storeroom of the laboratory. Greg showed me a cabinet where most of the biological evidence in our case had been dried before being packaged. It was a regular kitchen-type cabinet. I noticed that it could not be locked. "While the evidence was being dried in this room, was the door locked?" I asked hopefully.

"Yes," Greg said.

I made a mental note to ask more detailed questions about this later.

"After the evidence is dried and packaged, it can be booked into the Evidence Control Unit," Greg explained as we walked out of the Evidence Processing Room. "We'll see that next."

Greg used his key card to enter a vast room stuffed with manila evidence packages and boxes of evidence. The room must be 30 feet wide and 140 feet deep. Along one wall of the room were Rotomat refrigerators. The refrigerator door is about twelve feet long and one and a half feet wide and swings down. Greg pulled the door open. Inside were numerous plastic cartons all filled with sealed gray envelopes. Greg pushed a button, and the shelf rotated downward and was replaced by another. I could see that the contraption was like a giant refrigerated vending machine of the kind that sells apples and sandwiches.

"Greg, I had no idea what a huge operation this is."

Greg said, "That's right, you have no idea. The Simpson case was not the only murder we handled in 1994. Last year, SID handled about 856 homicides. We have thirty evidence rooms like this one throughout the city. We analyzed evidence in about twenty-eight thousand cases last year."

I looked around the vast room trying to visualize what thirty rooms stacked side by side would look like. It would be several football fields filled with evidence. "Greg. Say someone somehow broke into this room and wanted to find Simpson's blood vial. Could they do it?"

"You see all of these envelopes?" Greg gestured to the long row of sealed envelopes on the shelf of the Rotomat refrigerator. None of these are in any alphabetical or numerical order. Trying to find Simpson's blood vial would be like trying to find a needle in a haystack."

"So someone breaking in couldn't find it. But how do *you* find it?" I asked.

"Well, each envelope is bar coded. When the envelope is placed at a certain location, we scan it into our evidence-tracking computer, which tells us where we can find the envelope. But you can't access the computer when the lab's not open. And cops don't know how to use that computer. Not even I always know. And when the lab is open, cops, and even criminalists, don't have access to this room. As a supervisor, I do have access. The only way to get evidence out is to check it out.''

We then left the Evidence Control Unit and started walking toward the serology lab, where the evidence was brought for testing. Greg used a key card to open the door. Serology looked like a clean, efficient laboratory, with a walk-in freezer at the rear. We walked into the freezer. Greg pulled down a standard-size cardboard box. "See this box?" I peeked inside. I could see various packages and envelopes in the box. Greg said, "That's the biological evidence in the Simpson case.''

Holy shit, I thought. All the evidence that I had heard so much about for months—the gloves, the cotton swatches used to collect the blood trail, the socks—it was all here. Even though I was in a freezer, I felt a sudden rush of heat, and I was almost afraid to ask my next question: "Why isn't that box sealed?''

Greg stammered slightly. "I—I thought we don't have to prove chain of custody in the lab. I mean, the lab's—the lab's a secure facility, Hank.''

"Greg," I said, "that box should have been sealed. When you need to do testing, you break the seals, take out the evidence, test it, and when you're done, you slap another seal on it.''

Greg quickly responded, "But we've been going into that box repeatedly for testing and to send evidence out for testing. *This is in a secure facility,*" Greg said with emphasis. "Only criminalists can get in here, and a permanent record is made of entries through the key-card system. We've never had a problem before. *Never.*''

"We've never had a Simpson case before.''

I knew that the defense had just gone on a tour of the facility days before. "Well, when the defense took their tour of the facility, what did they say when they saw the box?''

"Nothing," Greg replied.

As I drove back to work in the early evening, I couldn't stop thinking about the box. I thought that the defense would make this open box the centerpiece of their conspiracy theory.

When I returned to the office, I checked the voluminous hand-written records from the SID to determine that the box was brought into the serology lab and unsealed about a week after the murders. I needed to figure out a way to show that any planting would have to have occurred before then.

* * *

"Now it's time for revenge," I said to Matheson as we headed to Judge Ito's courtroom. "Greg Matheson strikes back."

"Would you stop." Greg laughed, perhaps embarrassed by my confidence in him.

On this morning, May 1, I would finally be presenting a witness who was fully capable of defending himself under the most rigorous cross-examination. For almost a month I had been presenting evidence in court while listening to the defense float a ludicrous theory that several uniformed police officers, four detectives, and two criminalists were involved in a massive, intricate conspiracy and cover-up to frame O. J. Simpson. When Greg Matheson took the stand, my first question, after he stated his name and title, was: "And sir, in that capacity or in any other, are you part of any conspiracy in this case to frame the defendant?"

"No, I am not."

I asked some questions about the physical layout of the SID. This presentation was made with a large board that contained a map of the facility with photographs of the SID. This emphasized the points about security that Greg had made during my tour and showed that the SID did not look like the "cesspool of contamination" the defense had described during the opening statement.

With the computerized security-system records, I was able to demonstrate the impossibility of tampering with the evidence. Andrea Mazzola and Dennis Fung testified that at around 7:00 P.M. on the evening of June 13, they left the evidence locked and secured in the Evidence Processing Room. Greg testified that the computer records showed that no one had entered the room between the time Dennis and Andrea left on the evening of June 13 and 6:03 A.M. the morning of June 14, when he entered the room and assessed the evidence. No one was in the room overnight, unless, as Peter Neufeld had implied during Andrea's cross, someone had sneaked in when Dennis and Andrea entered and hid in the cabinets until they left.

The computer records showed that criminalist Collin Yamauchi was in the Evidence Processing Room on the morning of June 14 at 10:00 A.M.. That is when Collin started testing the evidence. Hence, by 10:00 A.M. on June 14 it was too late to do any planting. The testing was already under way. Any planting would have to have occurred between the time that Greg first entered, at 6:03 A.M., and the time the testing process was under way at 10:00 A.M.. During that time frame, Andrea, Dennis, Greg, and Collin were continuously in and out of that room. If anyone had been tampering with the evidence, they would have been caught.

To demonstrate this, I asked Greg whether there was any location in the Evidence Processing Room where a person could secrete themselves so that they could go unobserved by someone who walked into the room.

"No, there is not."

I wanted to make sure the jurors understood the point. "Is there any kind of mechanical device or other device in the Evidence Processing Room that would warn someone in the Evidence Processing Room that someone was approaching and about to enter, maybe a device that might yell out, 'Warning, someone is about to enter the Evidence Processing Room. All evidence tampering must cease.' "

The question drew both a laugh and an objection, since my question was argumentative. So I rephrased the question and then continued. "Now, with respect to the people that entered this room between the two time frames that we've been focusing on, are all of those trusted employees of the Scientific Investigations Division?"

"Yes," Greg said emphatically.

So unless this was a massive conspiracy involving Dennis Fung, Andrea Mazzola, Greg Matheson, Collin Yamauchi, and other trusted criminalists who were in and out of that room on the morning of June 14, tampering with the evidence simply could not have occurred.

Greg's testimony also placed a dent in the defense claim that blood was planted on the sock. In his opening statement, Cochran had claimed that during a June 29 inventory of all the evidence Greg had determined that there was no blood on the sock and had documented this finding on an inventory form. Later, blood was found. Cochran had claimed that this proved it was planted.

Greg's testimony proved that Cochran was wrong. Greg had not searched for blood on June 29. The inventory form that Cochran had referred to did not state that a search for blood was conducted. Rather, it stated that a search *needed* to be conducted in the future. In a normal trial these types of misstatements of fact would undermine an attorney's credibility with the jury.

Another defense canard was the claim that if there was blood on the socks, one should be able to see it. So I asked Greg, "Well, shouldn't you be able to see blood if there was blood on there?"

He answered, "It depends on the color and the type of material it's on." He explained that it's "very difficult to see blood on black denim, Levi's, that type of thing, difficult to see blood on any black material." Only by using high-intensity light under laboratory conditions could Greg actually see a stained area. In fact, blood could not be seen on the socks under the lighting of the courtroom or in high-quality photographs taken of the socks.

Another pillar of the defense planting theory was cut from under them. The defense claimed during their opening argument that 1.5 millileters of blood was missing from the blood vial. The blood vials are not calibrated; they do not have little hash marks on them, as does a measuring cup, indicating amounts. In a vial, 1.5 milliliters of blood would fill up about one-half inch of the vial. That's all. It's a small amount.

The nurse who drew the blood did not measure it He had no reason to. My thought: If Greg, who had been working with those vials for over thirteen years, could not accurately visualize how much blood was in a vial, then how could the nurse? Therefore, we had no way to determine precisely how much blood was in the vial from the start. I elicited that when Greg inventoried the blood vial, he underestimated the amount of blood in the vial by almost 2 milliliters.

When I asked Greg how accurate he was in estimating how much blood was in one of those vials, he replied, "Obviously not very. I was far off."

Matheson made clear that even if one is trying to measure, it's hard to be exact. It's impossible to account for every drop of blood. Unaccounted for drops are lost each time the vial is opened for testing.

Even after we proved the inability to account for each drop of blood or to accurately measure such small amounts, the defense persisted. During cross-examination, defense attorney Robert Blasier's crowning glory was a giant graphic of a blood vial used to demonstrate the theory that blood was missing.

With the assistance of our graphics whiz, Jonathan Fairtlough, we created red patches representing blood. During Greg's testimony on redirect, for each time the vial was opened for testing, Greg placed a patch on the defense's blood-vial exhibit. Adding all of these amounts, including the amount of blood used during each testing transaction, no blood was missing from the vial. After Greg's testimony, I thought the missing-blood theory should have about as much currency as Scheck's staple-hole theory and Neufeld's initials-on-the-bindle theory.

Greg also landed several solid blows against the contamination defense. I asked him a series of hypothetical questions involving outrageous collection procedures to illustrate that the collection technique cannot turn the suspect's blood into Simpson's blood. I inquired what would happen if someone collected the blood with their bare hands. "It's not going to change [the blood] in any way." Greg explained to the jury. "You may be adding . . . your own biological material, *but it wouldn't change what's already there.*" (emphasis added)

I wanted to be certain that the jury clearly understood the importance of Greg Matheson's testimony. To drive the point home, I wanted to show that a cat could literally collect the evidence. Whimsical? Perhaps. But in one question I felt we could deflate a month of nitpicking with Dennis and Andrea and the idea that evidence-collection techniques could have caused the perpetrator's blood to appear to be Simpson's.

GOLDBERG: Let's say you had a situation at a crime scene where a cat walked into the crime scene and collected some of the blood by stepping in it with its paw. Could you collect the evidence off the cat's paw and still test that?

MATHESON: Yes, we could. I would want a control collected from a clean paw to see if the cat contributed anything to it, but you could test it.

GOLDBERG: Okay. So if evidence at a crime scene could be collected by a house cat, do you think that the criminalists Andrea Mazzola and Dennis Fung were qualified to collect the evidence in this case?

This question drew an objection, but the point was made. Of course, a house cat did not collect the evidence in our case, nor did someone using his or her bare hands. In viewing the videotape of Andrea Mazzola's collection procedure, Greg testified that the collection procedure was proper. No defense witness ever contradicted this testimony. The point was that even the preposterously poor collection techniques I asked about could not have contaminated the evidence and turned the suspect's blood into Simpson's.

Another key component of Greg's testimony related to his test results. He performed conventional blood tests on some of the key evidence in the case. These tests are much older than DNA technology. His conventional blood testing involved both ABO testing and electrophoresis. The ABO system was invented at the turn of the century and classifies people's blood into four types: A, B, AB, and O. Analogous to the ABO system, electrophoresis examines enzymes in body fluids, such as blood, where different people have different enzyme types. But before getting into some of the highly probative tests Greg performed, I needed Greg to address the results from his tests of the blood found under Nicole's fingernails.

During opening statements, Cochran dropped another bomb that failed to explode. He said that there was blood under Nicole's fingernails that could not have come from Nicole, Simpson, or Ron Goldman, suggesting it belonged to the "real killer." The media were ablaze with this statement. "Blood Under Nicole's Nails May Point to Real Killer." In a case in which it was necessary to have a breaking headline every day, the media could not wait to hear the full story.

Cochran told the jury, during his opening, that according to Greg's laboratory report the blood under Nicole's nails could not have come from Simpson or the victims. Another misstatement. In fact, Matheson's report read that Nicole Brown could "not be excluded as a source of the stain."

Greg testified that the blood under Nicole's fingernails was probably her own. Later, prosecution witness Gary Sims supported Greg Matheson's opinion. Moreover, DNA testing of the fingernail scrapings also showed that they contained Nicole's blood. Defense witness Dr. Henry Lee, also an expert serologist, did not testify about this issue. However, he implicitly agreed with Greg's testimony by endorsing Greg as a "good scientist."

Greg's most powerful testimony concerned his own test results on some of the evidence. Greg did tests on one of the bloodstains from Bundy. Based on this conventional testing, Greg found that this blood drop was Simpson's and would match only .5 percent of the population, or one out of every two hundred people.

This means that if someone else committed the murder, the chance that that person just coincidentally matched Simpson is half of 1 percent. In a normal case, if there was other significant evidence connecting the suspect to the crime, such as proof of motive and opportunity, this test result would be enough to prove guilt beyond a reasonable doubt.

Greg Matheson's testimony concluded on Friday, May 5, five weeks after Dennis first hit the stand. I was done. Woody Clarke and I gleefully packed all my trial notebooks, science texts, science articles, policy and procedural manuals, laboratory notes, charts and diagrams, and court transcripts in the small shopping cart we used to wheel the materials into court every day.

Happily navigating the cart through the narrow strait between both counsel tables and the auxiliary row of counsel tables, we hit a sandbar. Peter Neufeld was standing in front of us. He snipped, "I didn't know *you* would ask a *sleazy* question like that; it must have been someone else's idea."

A sudden rush of adrenaline, and five weeks of bad memories swept over me. Sleazy? In my ten years in court, I had never seen such sleaze, I thought. Barry and Peter had continually asked improper questions to suggest I had coached the witnesses and suborned perjury. Judge Ito had found that they were asked in bad faith and sometimes cautioned them, but not in front of the jury.

For example, Scheck had asked Dennis whether, in my interview sessions with him, he had tried "to work out testimony that the prosecutors would find satisfactory." On one occasion, Neufeld had asked Andrea if the prosecutors told her "they wanted you to testify at this trial that your [prior testimony about initialing the bindles] was false."

Judge Ito sustained the objection and sternly said, "Counsel, without the court reporter, please." At side bar, Judge Ito found that Neufeld's question was asked in bad faith and admonished him not to persist.

But he did persist. Shortly after, he implied that we told Andrea to lie about not initialing the bindles because "if the prosecutors could not produce the original bindles that you claimed you had initialed, that could be devastating." Implying that these mild-mannered criminalists were perjurers and had been told to commit perjury was totally improper.

I angrily objected. Judge sustained the objection and mildly said, "The jury is to disregard the implication of that question."

Neufeld asked a clearly improper question to put the idea of perjury and conspiracy into the jurors' minds, knowing that Judge Ito's admonition could not entirely unring the bell.

Sleazy? The constant, improper personal attacks on opposing counsel were highly unusual. If a prosecutor made similar comments suggesting to the jury that the defense attorney engaged in misconduct, the judge could declare a mistrial. So when Neufeld called me sleazy, I blew what I hoped was my usual lawyerlike composure. "Sleazy? What are you talking about?"

"That question when you asked Matheson whether, if there was no EDTA [preservative] in the blood on the rear gate, it would prove it wasn't planted," Neufeld responded.

"Weren't you paying attention?" I asked. "Blasier asked that exact same question. Only he asked, if there *was* EDTA in the blood would that prove that it *was* planted. Then Judge Ito ruled that I could ask the question I asked. You have a lot of nerve talking about sleaze."

By now Woody had maneuvered the cart past Neufeld. We were walking out the door when Neufeld fired another round by making some insulting comment that I cannot remember. But it was enough for me to turn and face him. In a normal tone of voice, I said, "Peter, I have worked with all kinds of attorneys over the years, with every type of different personality. You and Barry are the only ones I've ever worked with that I actually hate." Scheck, who was standing at counsel table next to Neufeld, turned upon hearing this and looked at me perplexed, as if to say, "What did I do?"

I continued, "You're just mad that you blew the cross-examination of Dennis by going too far and that Greg blew you away." Neufeld, like a schoolboy, retorted, "Oh, yeah? Then why did Rock say that the entire month of April was ours and that you were going to have to wait till May to strike back?"

"Because we're going to kick your ass in May," I said.

By now Woody was ushering me out of the courtroom as Neufeld continued his tirade. As we walked into the hallway, I turned to Woody. "What a fucking asshole."

Woody said, "We told you. Didn't Uncle Rock and I tell you. And you wouldn't believe it."

"Now I do."

In the elevator, we were silent for a few moments. "That was really unpleasant," I said.

"*Unpleasant?* It was *unpleasant?*" Woody exclaimed.

"I don't think I've had an argument like that in the last twenty years. It's unprofessional." I paused. "Woody, do you think I should apologize? I mean, it would be the gentlemanly thing to do."

"Hank, are you nuts? No way I'd let you."

Coming from Woody, that was about the strongest statement of support I could have gotten.

As I pushed our cart across the floor of the elevator lobby on the eighteenth floor, I passed Gil Garcetti. Laughing, Gil approached and put both hands on my shoulders. "Hank, you restored the reputation of the LAPD."

Not knowing what to say, I forced a laugh. But privately I thought, I'm not so sure about that.

22

The Answer Is in the DNA

Up to this point in the trial, I viewed my chief role in presenting the evidence as that of an unglamorous bulldozer clearing the ground on which our DNA case would be built. The DNA was the most significant evidence connecting Simpson to the murders. This phase of the case began on May 8, almost four months after Marcia Clark, in her opening statement, promised the jurors that test result after test result "matches the defendant." Woody Clarke called forensic DNA expert Dr. Robin Cotton.

Dr. Cotton is an attractive woman in her forties who conveys the image of a teacher with total confidence in her subject. In court, she spoke in a modulated, soothing tone as she guided the jurors through the technical evidence. She is the director of Cellmark Diagnostics, the nation's largest private DNA laboratory. She had been with Cellmark for seven years and has a Ph.D. in biochemistry and molecular biology.

Prior to calling Dr. Cotton to the stand, we had a number of conversations about how best to present the DNA evidence. One conversation took place in the War Room and involved Marcia, Woody, and myself.

I summarized the three options that Woody, Rock, Marcia, and I had previously discussed on several occasions. "There are basically three ways to present the DNA evidence. First, we could present it on the most simple level. We did these tests, the tests are reliable, and

167

here are the results, period. Or second, we could present a much more technical approach. We explain how the tests are conducted, why the tests are reliable, and why the results are valid. Or third, we can do a combination of both approaches."

Marcia said, "We can't use the first approach, just presenting the results without explaining how the tests are done and why they should be trusted. The jurors could use that as an excuse simply to ignore the DNA evidence: 'You didn't even try to explain it to me.'" Marcia's comment mirrored my own conclusion, reached long before I joined the prosecution team, that any jury would bend over backward to find excuses to discount any evidence.

Woody explained that no matter what we did, Scheck and Neufeld were going to approach the DNA evidence in a very technical way. We would have to counter their points in a like manner. Even if the jury didn't wholly understand what our answer was, they would at least see that we had one. When the defense raised technical issues, we couldn't just stand there mute.

Woody explained that our presentation of the DNA evidence would be on all three levels, ranging from the very simple to the relatively complex. Woody pointed out that on the simpliest level, "there's blood where there shouldn't be any blood. At Rockingham. In the Bronco. You don't have to understand anything about DNA to understand that." Getting just slightly more complex, Woody explained how we would show the jury that DNA tests are reliable because they are so widely used. "They're used for disease diagnosis, to identify war dead, and to save endangered animals. And finally, on the most complex level, we'll show the jury how the testing is done and why it works."

Under Woody Clarke's careful questioning, Dr. Cotton began her testimony with a scholarly but simple lecture—a beginner's course—on DNA testing. Her lecture was delivered succinctly, punctuated with many visuals meant to simplify her major points.

DNA is a molecule present in nearly all human cells, with the major exception of red blood cells. It is commonly referred to as a genetic blueprint. If you think of an architectural blueprint as containing all the information necessary to erect a building, the DNA contains all the information necessary to build *you*. People get their DNA from their parents. About 99 percent of the DNA molecule is common to most people. We all have hearts, livers, kidneys, etc. But it is the 1 percent difference between people that makes for the individuality of all humans, save identical twins. Dr. Cotton explained, "In order to distinguish people, expecially at the DNA level, you want to be looking at those sections of the DNA that are different from one person to the next, so you have to single out those sections."

DNA testing is carried out using two techniques. RFLP (restriction fragment length polymorphism) is the most discriminating of the two. That means that when a match is made through RFLP, the likelihood of another person's showing the same genetic match is usually extremely low, sometimes in the range of one in several billion. However, relatively large samples are required to conduct the RFLP test.

Like virtually all forensic tests, DNA tests compare something of unknown origin to something of known origin. In other words, the test compares the DNA in the blood from a crime scene, the unknown, to the DNA in a blood sample taken from the suspect, the known. In making the comparison, the forensic scientist is trying to determine whether the two samples match. The overall strategy in testing the evidence is to chop the lengthy DNA molecule up into little bits and sort them out by size. Because different people have different sizes, it is possible to distinguish between individuals.

The first step is to extract the DNA from the cell nucleus, where it is located. The cells are treated with chemicals to burst them and release the DNA.

The second step involves restriction digestion. After the DNA has been extracted, it is cut into fragments by mixing the DNA with restriction enzymes in a test tube. Restriction enzymes act as biological scissors. The end result is a large number of fragments that vary in length, called restriction fragments. A particular restriction enzyme cuts the DNA molecule every time a particular genetic sequence appears. The number and location of these sequences is different for different people. Thus, the fragments in the DNA specimen from one individual can be expected to differ in number and length from those of another. If we can sort these fragments out by size, we can compare one sample to another to see if they match.

The sorting is done by gel electrophoresis, the third step in the testing phase. This process is similar to several people holding poles parallel to the ground as they walk through a dense forest. The people with the longest poles will soon be stopped when their poles get stuck between two closely spaced trees. The people with the smaller poles will be able to walk much farther before they also get stuck. Essentially, the DNA fragments are sorted out by size using a similar principle.

The DNA fragments are placed at one end of a slab of agarose gel, which looks and feels like a small pan of Jell-O. An electric current is applied at the opposite end from where the DNA fragments are placed. Since DNA is a negatively charged molecule, the positively charged electric current attracts the DNA fragments, causing them to move toward it. The speed at which the DNA fragments move along the gel depends on their length.

The next series of steps involves creating a permanent copy of the DNA fragments with which to work. The end result of these steps is an "autorad," a picture of the results. This allows us to see how the testing process sorted the fragments out by size. Now we can compare two autorads to see if the patterns match. This completes the testing phase.

Once a "match" between the reference sample and the crime-scene sample has been "declared," one final question remains: What is the chance that someone *other than the defendant* deposited the biological sample? The laboratory uses a data base composed of numerous blood samples from unrelated individuals. This data base allows them to determine how often a particular DNA fragment is found in the population.

The RFLP testing process looks at a number of DNA fragments that differ from one person to the other. Therefore, the overall profile frequency is determined by multiplying the frequencies of the individual DNA fragments together. This is called the product rule. For example, under this rule, the probability of throwing a dice three times and having it come up 1 each time is calculated as follows: $1/6 \times 1/6 \times 1/6 = 1/216$. Each time you multiply this number, it gets dramatically smaller. For example, if you threw the dice a fourth time, the likelihood of it landing on 1 all four times is $1/216 \times 1/6 = 1/1,296$. Similarly, by looking at a number of DNA fragments and multiplying their individual frequencies together, it is possible to achieve astronomically low odds that someone else on this planet has the same profile.

PCR (polymerase chain reaction) is more sensitive than RFLP. This means that very small samples can be tested. Dr. Cotton told the jury that by using PCR it is possible to get a result from a blood sample containing as little as 2 nanograms (2 billionths of a gram) of DNA. Such a sample would be about the size of a pinprick. PCR works better than RFLP on relatively old and degraded samples. However, it is not as discriminating as RFLP. When a match is declared using PCR, the odds of someone else matching are often one in several thousand.

During her explanation of DNA, Dr. Cotton made one point very clear. Since people receive half their DNA from their father and half from their mother, a child's DNA does not match either of their parents. The child is "a blend of the mother and father, and the child will not be identical to either the mother or the father." This simple scientific explanation made it impossible for the blood at the crime scene to have come from Simpson's children.

Woody Clarke posed a series of questions to Dr. Cotton to address a point raised during Dennis Fung's cross. The defense alleged that putting the blood swatches into plastic bags before air-drying them back at the laboratory was a mistake. It is common knowledge that moisture tends to degrade biological evidence. For example, if you take all the water out of a piece of steak and turn it into beef jerky, you can preserve it for a long time. These same principles apply to blood found at a crime scene.

Woody used Dr. Cotton to corroborate a point I had made during my presentation with Greg Matheson. Degradation and/or contamination of samples could not have produced false results. Woody asked whether degradation of DNA could cause it to change from matching one person's DNA into matching another person's DNA.

"No . . . it will not," Dr. Cotton replied.

Later, she explained: "There is no environmental force, there is no environmental effect, that can work to simply change one type and make it become another. . . . Doesn't happen." Degradation may cause you to get no result, but it will not produce a false result.

Dr. Cotton also explained that the LAPD practice of using plastic bags to temporarily package the swatches before they were air-dried at the laboratory wouldn't result in significant degradation. She testified that the blood collected from the Bundy trail was significantly more degraded than the blood collected from Simpson's foyer. She explained that this is what one would expect, since Simpson's foyer is a better environment for preserving the blood than the outdoor, relatively dirtier, Bundy crime scene.

* * *

Woody was making a point we had discussed many times before. All the blood from the outdoor crime scene at Bundy and from Rockingham showed significant evidence of degradation from having been outside. Naturally, blood from Simpson's vial was not as degraded. So if someone had planted blood, they would have to have degraded it first by putting it outdoors overnight.

The defense's planting scenarios sometimes resulted in discussions that were probably even more bizarre than the defense theories floated in court. Once, at a downtown cafeteria-style deli, while watching the people behind the counter putting bowls of soup into the microwaves, I asked Woody, "I bet putting blood in a microwave for a short period of time would degrade it, don't you think?"

Woody shrugged his shoulders. "I don't think anyone's ever tested that. How soon would you have to take it out before the blood could no longer be tested? But why would someone plant degraded blood? Most of that blood on the Bundy trail was so degraded we couldn't do RFLP tests on it, we had to use PCR."

"Yeah." I said half jokingly. "Maybe I should ask Dr. Lee, 'How do you degrade blood so that you can do PCR but not RFLP? Is there a recipe?' Add one part water, a tad of garden soil, cook for twenty-eight seconds on medium in a microwave oven."

Woody, never a tough audience for even a bad joke, laughed.

As part of our continuing "cleanup" strategy to explain why Dennis and Andrea could not have contaminated the evidence, Dr. Cotton made it clear that "contamination" is not a precise word in the forensic-science context. All evidence from a crime scene is "contaminated" in the sense that it did not come from a sterile environment. However, the type of "contamination" forensic scientists are concerned with is that which might change the test results.

This testimony reminded me of my first interview with Dennis Fung. Early in the interview, he said, almost apologetically, "If they [the defense] ask me whether the crime scene was contaminated, I'll have to say 'yes.' " I almost fell out of my chair. This was when it first hit home that Dennis would have a hard time on the stand. 'What are you talking about, Dennis?"

He explained, "Well, other people were at that scene before I arrived. That contaminated the whole scene." After a few minutes, I concluded that Dennis was using the term contamination in the broadest, almost philosophical, sense, as Dr. Cotton later clarified. Under this broad definition everything in the world is contaminated. So I asked Dennis, "If you consider contamination to mean something that could affect the forensic results, was the crime scene contaminated?"

"Oh." He paused. "No. Of course not."

Woody Clarke's direct examination was a perfect illustration of something the commentators consistently missed. Woody was meticulously and quietly disposing of issues the defense had raised during their opening statement and continuing with Dennis Fung and Andrea Mazzola. Specifically, Dr. Cotton disposed of the notion that degraded samples, contamination, or Dennis's and Andrea's collection technique could have caused the test results to erroneously point to Simpson.

Trial strategy cannot properly be viewed as a series of individual days in which someone wins or loses. Nor is it a series of individual witnesses. Trial strategy often starts before the jury selection and ends after the jury's verdict. Woody's direct constituted a follow-through of themes that he, Rock, and I developed months before Dennis first hit the stand.

The trial commentators often overlooked these kinds of relatively subtle but extremely important connections. For example, when Dennis testified, the news was ablaze with the breaking story of the day, "Defense Says Criminalists Degraded Evidence by Putting It in Plastic Bags." However, over a month later, when Dr. Cotton showed that putting the evidence in plastic bags could not have affected the test result, that fact resided not in headlines but on back pages, if at all.

Neufeld pursued the defense's contamination theory during his cross-examination. Before hearing it in court, we were able to piece together their theory in stages. After my tour of the SID, I concluded that the defense would argue that cross-contamination occurred in the Evidence Processing Room, where all the evidence could be found after it was collected.

It became apparent to Rock, Woody, Lisa Kahn (our office's attorney–DNA expert), and me that the defense was going to link the concept of degradation with that of contamination. Rock, Woody, and I discussed this new twist one afternoon in the War Room.

"What's the relationship between contamination and degradation?" I asked.

Rock answered, "There isn't one. It's like apples and oranges. They are different processes."

Woody continued. "With degradation, the DNA molecule literally breaks down into smaller pieces until eventually you can't type it. The genetic material is lost. Contamination is when you introduce foreign DNA into a sample."

Sometimes these conversations with Rock and Woody were like a game of Ping-Pong between two experts keeping the ball in play. "But let's suppose," I said, "the Bundy swatches contain the real perpetrator's blood and they become totally degraded so the genetic information is lost. Then you cross-contaminate them with the Rockingham swatches, which contain Simpson's blood. Now when you test the Bundy swatches, all you would find is Simpson's blood, right?"

Rock said, "That's so theoretical. You have to believe that these fresh red blood drops from Bundy lost all their genetic activity to the point that they could no longer be typed, even with PCR. That's B.S."

"You can type soldiers' bodies that have been out in the desert for weeks," Woody added.

"So to believe the contamination theory, all of the Bundy swatches had to degrade to nothing," I said. "Then, in some bizarre way, you would have to somehow contaminate all of the swatches with Simpson's blood. You know what this defense theory reminds me of? It reminds me of that song—how does it go? 'Nothing plus something is something.' "

"Hank, I'm impressed, that's almost it," Rock said. "Billy Preston. I thought that was before your time." Rock started singing, "Nothing plus something is something so you got to have something if you want to be with me."

Rock Harmon is no Billy Preston.

*　*　*

Almost as if he were part of our strategy session, Neufeld advanced the defense's contamination theory while cross-examining Dr. Cotton. Because the hypothetical was so far-fetched and unsupported by any rational view of the evidence, it should have been disallowed. However, these kinds of hypotheticals peppered the defense cross-examination of scientific testimony throughout the case. Moreover, his hypothetical was equivalent to asking, "Dr. Cotton, if we assume, hypothetically, that the swatches were contaminated, would they be contaminated?"

Under the defense hypothesis, the contamination would have acted like a guided missile. It would have to magically contaminate *all* of the drops on the Bundy trail, yet somehow *skip over* the drops that contained the victim's blood and also *skip over* all of the substrate controls. As Dr. Cotton testified, "It would be a very specific contamination, not just sort of affecting everything." Wow!

During his redirect Woody asked whether the swatches from the Bundy trail could have been contaminated with fresh blood from Simpson's blood vial. This area of questioning also disposed of the claim that the swatches could have been been planted swatches made from Simpson's blood vial. Dr. Cotton explained that if the blood on the swatches came from Simpson's vial, the quality of the DNA on the swatches should all be the same, and it wasn't.

Dr. Cotton concluded that the idea that the blood on the Bundy trail swatches came from Simpson's vial was unreasonable. The blood on the five Bundy trail stains could not have come "from the same tube of blood."

To this day, however, the idea that the blood on the swatches came from Simpson's vial still resonates with many people, including some of the jurors.

During Woody's direct, Dr. Cotton presented the test results of the numerous bloodstains, just as Marcia had promised during her opening statement, in which she dramatically declared that bloodstain after bloodstain "matched the defendant."

Now, in much less dramatic fashion, Dr. Cotton, after teaching the jury some of the fundamentals of DNA, cut to the chase. Reviewing just one of the bloodstains found at Bundy, Dr. Cotton, looking directly at Simpson, flatly stated: "When you review the DNA bands that are visible . . . in each case they are consistent with the bands that are seen in Mr. Simpson's pattern.'' Later, commenting on this same drop, Dr. Cotton estimated that RFLP analysis revealed that only 1 in 170 million people would show the same genetic match.

The table on the following page summarizes the test results Dr. Cotton reported to the jury.

Trying to predict what would occur in Judge Ito's court was difficult. At times, I wondered whether some strange, mystical field force, akin to the Bermuda triangle, was operating in that space. Indeed, it was: the camera.

Before Woody went down to court for the first time, I said "Woody, you're going to be the only lawyer in this whole case who Judge Ito's not going to sanction or yell at.'' Woody is a prosecutor's prosecutor. I was sure his calm, professional, courteous approach to trial work would guarantee coming out of the force field unscathed. Again, I was wrong.

Before the Simpson case, Judge Ito had enjoyed an excellent reputation for possessing a "good judicial temperament.'' Normally, he was very polite and courteous to attorneys and did not lose his temper. However, by April 1995, about three months after opening statements, Judge Ito had been slammed in the press for allowing the lawyers to run roughshod over him. He was also unfairly criticized for having too many side bars. The latter criticism probably stemmed from the fact that most people did not know what side bars were before the Simpson case; they seemed to needlessly interrupt the entertainment value of the live courtroom action.

Throughout the trial, Judge Ito displayed a remarkable familiarity with the news coverage of the case, even the cartoons. By early May, a sudden, dramatic change took place literally overnight: Judge Ito now assumed a stern and strict visage. The press billed this demeanor as the "new Judge Ito'' and temporarily fell in love with it. When Woody marched down to court to present Dr. Cotton's testimony, he could not have known that the new Judge Ito was about to erupt.

Part of Neufeld's cross-examination consisted of an attack on the reliability of the statistics Dr. Cotton had offered. By the time of closing argument, this became a nonissue. But during Dr. Cotton's cross it was hotly debated. Neufeld implied that numerous experts took issue with the procedure used to calculate the estimates. During this line of questioning, Neufeld read a list of various experts

ITEM	TEST USED	CONSISTENT WITH	FREQUENCY (low end)
Bundy driveway, stain 52	RFLP	Simpson	1/170 million
	PCR	Simpson	
Rockingham foyer, stain 12	RFLP	Simpson	1/170 million
	PCR	Simpson	1/5,200
Blood drop from sole of Ron's boot, item 78	RFLP	Mixture of Nicole and Ron	
	PCR	Mixture of Nicole and Ron	
Socks, item 13, stain 13A (on ankle)	RFLP	Nicole	1/6.8 billion
	PCR	Nicole	1/2,500
Bundy trail, items, 47, 48, 49, 50, and 52	PCR	Simpson	1/5,200
Bloody shoeprint at Bundy trail	PCR	Nicole	1/48
Nicole's fingernail scrapings and clippings, item 84	PCR	Nicole	1/2,500
Bronco steering wheel, item 29	PCR	Mixture of Simpson and Nicole	
Rockingham driveway, item 7	PCR	Simpson	1/410

from around the country. He simply asked Dr. Cotton whether she knew who these people were. Then he marked a document (a letter), apparently the same one that the list of names came from, as an exhibit. The effect was to imply, without calling these people as witnesses, that they disagreed with Dr. Cotton's procedures. This tactic is objectionable because the letter was inadmissible hearsay. After Neufeld marked the letter, the following dialogue ensued *in front of the jury*:

JUDGE ITO: For the record, is this a letter in *Science* magazine?

NEUFELD: No.

JUDGE ITO: What is it?

Woody, upon hearing the court's question, obviously feared that Neufeld would give an answer that would allow the jury to hear about the inadmissible letter. Therefore, he strenuously asked for a side bar to discuss the matter. "May we approach, please, Your Honor?"

Judge Ito replied: "No. What is it? Just tell me what it is . . . ?"

Neufeld turned to Woody, who was examining the exhibit, and asked, "May I have my exhibit?"

Woody replied, "I would like to look at it first. . . . Your Honor, this is apparently a letter—

Neufeld interrupted. Previously, the judge had ordered the attorneys not to make "speaking objections," an improper form of objection that has the effect of offering an attorney's commentary, in front of the jury. Neufeld apparently felt that the ongoing dialogue in front of the jury constituted a speaking objection. So he queried, "Your Honor, now you want a speaking—"

The judge impatiently demanded, "Counsel, what is it?"

"It's a letter to *Nature* signed by twenty-five scientists," Neufeld replied.

Now the harm was done, the implication was that these twenty-five scientists disagreed with Dr. Cotton's procedures.

Woody clearly felt he had to correct this misimpression. "Well, Your Honor, that was rejected and never published."

Neufeld shot back. "Your Honor, it was rejected because—"

Judge Ito slammed his hands down on his bench. "Wait."

Neufeld continued, "That was—"

Judge Ito exclaimed, "Both of you. . . ." Judge Ito excused the jury. "All right, Dr. Cotton, you can step down. All right. The court's clear orders regarding objections were 'No speaking objections.'

Both counsel are sanctioned $250. Get your checkbooks out. Right now!''

There was a tense pause. Woody did not have his checkbook with him or $250 in cash. Chris Darden, seated at counsel table, dug into his pocket and calmly counted out $250 in cash and handed it to Woody. Neufeld and Woody marched up to the clerk, and each paid their $250 fine.

There were numerous occasions when the attorneys did improper things in front of the jury. This was not one of them. This was another example of Judge Ito improperly embarrassing attorneys publicly and in front of the jury. Woody clearly asked for a side bar, which was obviously necessary to discuss the issue. Peter clearly told Judge Ito that his questions were going to lead to improper speaking objections. Judge Ito ignored both attorneys.

He should have sanctioned himself.

Dr. Cotton's testimony was a high point for the members of the prosecution team. The day she presented the staggering DNA results to the jury, I asked Marcia, Chris, and Woody their reaction after they returned from court.

They felt that the jurors seemed visibly shaken. It looked as if some of them actually had tears in their eyes. It appeared that we had reached them.

"Thank God." I thought about my ordeal with Dennis and Andrea and my hope that we would be able to show that neither Dennis or Andrea could be used as an excuse to ignore the DNA evidence. At the moment, I knew what the people at mission control must have felt like when *Apollo 13* safely reentered earth's orbit. It was the one point in the trial when I thought we really had a shot at a guilty verdict. Excitedly, I asked, "They are really listening to the evidence? They're getting it?"

"Yes." All agreed.

It was not the "yes" Dennis shouted when we saw the video proving he received the blood vial, not the "yes" of Laker fans after a game-winning basket, just a quiet, simple, heartfelt "yes."

23

Dandruff in the Evidence

IN ADDITION TO PROVIDING THE JURORS with powerful DNA test results, DNA expert Gary Sims also destroyed what little remained of the contamination theory. Following Dr. Cotton, the prosecution called Sims, a forensic scientist who works for the California Department of Justice (DOJ) DNA laboratory in Berkeley, California.

I consulted with Gary many times about a variety of issues during the trial. Soft-spoken and precise, Gary is the model of a meticulous scientist.

Rock's direct examination of Sims squarely and effectively hit the defense's contamination issue. Sims also described my favorite study, the FBI cross-contamination study. During the study, the FBI tried to contaminate evidence samples in a variety of ways. The same pair of scissors that was used to cut some of the samples was reused on other samples without being cleaned. Doing so did not result in cross-contamination (transferring DNA from one sample to another). They found that perspiration from the analyst did not contaminate the samples. Coughing on the evidence for one minute did not contaminate it; nor did shaking dandruff on it.

Regarding the test results in our case, Rock relied heavily on the substrate controls—the little blank swatches that are placed close to a bloodstain—to explain why contamination could not have occurred undetected. Gary Sims, following up on the testimony of Dennis and Andrea, explained, "[I]f the substrate controls turn out to be negative, it shows to me that there is no cross-contamination from sample to sample." And the substrate controls he tested were all negative.

As to whether Dennis Fung's and Andrea Mazzola's collection procedures could have contaminated the Bundy swatches with Simpson's blood, Gary said, "No. I would say no."

Both Rock and I decided to judiciously use some humor and irony during our respective portions of the trial. We felt that this approach would colorfully illustrate the technical explanations as to why the defense's contamination theory was preposterous. Rock asked Gary how Simpson's DNA could have accidentally contaminated all the swatches from the Bundy trail. "Can DNA fly?"

Gary chuckled. "I don't think so."

Rock also asked whether the DNA of an athletic person has any special athletic prowess.

On his first day of cross, Barry Scheck seemed to make some inroads on the issue of contamination. Scheck started in with his hypotheticals. The problem was not what Gary was saying; it was what he was not saying. He was not following through on his answers, and he was allowing Scheck to create false impressions, just as Dennis Fung had.

For example, Scheck asked whether one should change gloves between handling the swatches from Rockingham and Bundy.

Gary answered, "I would say one should change gloves between those two sets, yes."

Then Scheck asked, "Let's say you didn't change gloves." This was an opportunity for Gary to give a concise, clear explanation of the relevant scientific principles involved. However, he responded, "Well, if you—I mean, the other thing about blood is, it's very visible, and one may look at the gloves and see whether or not there was any visible contamination that way." But this response did not squarely answer the issue of whether not changing gloves could cause all the results to erroneously point to Simpson. Therefore, the jury was left with the impression that the failure to change gloves was an error.

After Scheck's first day of cross-examination I was worried. Sims was falling into the trap of giving Scheck's hypothetical questions credence by answering them without explaining his answers. Rock's direct went so well, but Gary seemed to be caving in during cross.

At the end of the court day, I passed Chris Darden in the hallway. I was almost half afraid to ask him how things were going, but I
did. Chris, employing his usual economy of words, said, "This guy's
burying us."

However, Gary, an exceptionally intelligent man and experienced witness, was capable of objectively viewing his performance
under Scheck's cross. He obviously realized that he was giving
Scheck incomplete answers. The next day was different. For the
remainder of Gary's testimony Scheck gained no ground. For example, Scheck tried to goad Gary into testifying that Fung's and Mazzola's practice of using multiple swatches to collect a single stain was
not an additional safeguard against contamination.

Gary steadfastly refused to agree. "It would be unlikely that you
would get this uniform contamination across all the swatches."

On redirect, Rock disposed of each point Scheck tried to make.
Gary described the virtual impossibility of the contamination theory.
Under their theory "[t]he Bundy stains . . . , would have to have
totally degraded, and then somehow this contamination would have
to sort of play a game of hopscotch and miss the substrate controls
and just hit on the stain."

Anyone viewing Gary's testimony would have to conclude that
he had destroyed the defense's contamination theory.

The previous night, I had walked into Rock Harmon's cubicle
and had suggested to Rock that we bring in a microscope and let the
jurors examine the socks both with and without it. This would permit them to see for themselves that you can't see blood on those
socks with the naked eye.

Rock was tired and harried. "Bad idea. Don't like it. We've killed
this issue." However, Rock thought about it overnight, and the next
day we had a microscope set up in the court.

Rock concluded his redirect by allowing the jurors to make the
examination. In the courtroom, one simply could not see blood on
the socks without the aid of the microscope. This explained why the
LAPD criminalists did not see the blood until they closely inspected
the socks.

Gary convincingly disposed of what remained of the defense's conspiracy and contamination theories. But, naturally, the centerpiece of Gary's testimony was his compelling DNA test results. Nicole's blood was on the socks, as was Simpson's. Blood belonging to Ron Goldman, Nicole, and Simpson was on the Rockingham glove and in the Bronco. Selected results are summarized in the table on the following page.

Sheck got bad reviews for his cross. For example, as if commenting on a movie or play, *Los Angeles Times* pundit Prof. Laurie Levenson summed up Scheck's cross in these words: "Fascinating. Scintillating. Informative. Devastating. Dynamite. None of these words applied to Scheck's cross-examination of DNA expert Sims."

After his cross-examination of Gary was over, I talked to Scheck briefly in court. I cannot remember exactly how the conversation started, but I could see that Barry was somewhat upset about the harsh criticism he had received for his cross of Gary. I said, "Barry, I watched most of your cross. Technically, you did a very proficient job. Gary's just a great witness."

Barry said, "You really think so?"

"Yes."

Barry said, "Well, the press doesn't pick up on any of the subtleties of what's really happening in court. They didn't see how meticulously and painstakingly crafted your direct of Dennis was."

In reality, I thought that Barry's cross of Gary Sims, in any ordinary case, would have been much more effective than his cross of Dennis Fung. True, his cross was not "scintillating" or "dynamite," but a trial is not entertainment. More importantly, there was nothing in his treatment of Sims that might have offended a jury. Whereas in a normal trial a jury would have found the way he treated Fung highly offensive, in our case many people were anxious to believe, against all odds, that Simpson was innocent. With such an orientation, I suppose that no attack, criticism, accusation, or blow, no matter how low, would have seemed unfair.

In fact, during Scheck's cross of Gary, some members of the prosecution team felt that the jury appeared relieved. Almost as if they wanted someone to furnish them with reasons to discount Sims's test results.

ITEM	TEST USED	CONSISTENT WITH	FREQUENCY (low end)
13A, socks ankle	RFLP	Nicole Brown	1/7.7 billion
13A, socks toe	RFLP	Orenthal Simpson	1/5.7 billion
4, Rockingham driveway	PCR	Orenthal Simpson	1/520
14, master-bath floor	PCR	Orenthal Simpson	1/15
9, Rockingham glove inside ring finger	RFLP	Ron Goldman	1/12 billion
9, Rockingham glove inside middle finger	RFLP	Nicole Brown	1/6 million
9, Rockingham glove inside wrist notch	PCR	Orenthal Simpson	1/3,200
47, Bundy trail drop closest to victims	PCR	Orenthal Simpson	1/240,000
52, Bundy trail drop closest to alley	RFLP	Orenthal Simpson	1/170 million
117, rear-gate stain	RFLP	Orenthal Simpson	1/57 billion
303–305 Bronco console stains	RFLP RFLP PCR	Orenthal Simpson Ron Goldman Nicole Brown	

On May 22, 1995, during a CBS-TV interview, *Vanity Fair* correspondent Dominick Dunne said that he had focused on two jurors, who seemed shaken by the overwhelming DNA evidence pointing to Simpson's guilt. However, he said that the spirits of the two jurors visibly lightened when Barry Scheck trotted out the theories of contamination and conspiracy. He added that he could actually see the hint of a smile, a curl of the lips, a brightening of the eyes, as Mr. Scheck threw to them the lifeline of conspiracy and contamination.

24

Head-to-Head With Barry Scheck

AFTER JUST OVER TWO WEEKS OF DNA EVIDENCE, the prosecution called the witness who would either make or break the defense contamination theory. Concluding the prosecutions' DNA case, SID criminalist Collin Yamauchi took the stand.

Yamauchi was relatively new to the intricacies of PCR testing. He had been with the SID for five years. He was assigned to the Serology Unit, which conducts testing of biological evidence. He performed conventional testing until 1993, when he started performing PCR analysis. Collin is a compact young scientist who is very bright and committed to his work. However, he was inexperienced as a witness and sometimes halting in his answers. I was afraid he might fold under Berry Scheck's combative cross-examination style.

Immediately after discovering that the box and packages containing the evidence were unsealed, I started to try to figure out what we could introduce to show that someone could not have tampered with them.

At one time, we even questioned whether we would present the results of the LAPD testing at all. This issue was resolved in January 1995. I remember discussing the question with Marcia in her office shortly after my first tour of the SID.

As I munched on a fistful of pretzels, Marcia explained that the LAPD test results were duplicative. Cellmark and the Department of Justice lab had reanalyzed all the same evidence. "Hank, early into this case, I realized that the defense would focus their attack on the LAPD crime lab."

186

She lit a cigarette, looked at me, quickly turned on the smokeless ashtray, and put the cigarette down. "So I immediately tried to shift responsibility for testing to the outside labs. Since all the LAPD testing was reanalyzed, why put the LAPD testing on? Why not just bypass the initial LAPD tests?" She quickly picked up the cigarette and took a puff, waiting for my response.

"Marcia, that was an option had you asked me the question a week earlier. Not now." I told Marcia what I discovered when I toured the crime lab. I explained my theory that introducing the LAPD testing would shut down any argument that evidence was planted after the testing commenced. We had to let the jury know that Collin started sampling the evidence for testing at 10:00 A.M. the day after it was collected. "After that," I explained, "it was too late to plant evidence as to the items already tested. Therefore, whether at some later point the box was sealed or unsealed is no longer relevant."

Marcia, with a mouthful of pretzels, started to say something, smiled, and then made a hand gesture for me to continue.

"There's a second reason for calling Collin. On the morning of June 14, Collin worked with Simpson's blood vial in the same room where the evidence swatches were located. The defense will certainly bring out that fact and imply that somehow Simpson's vial contaminated the evidence. We've got to explain exactly what Collin did that morning to show the impossibility of contamination."

Marcia nodded. "Incidentally, you don't mind if I smoke?"

"Just as long as you keep supplying the pretzels," I said.

During my interviews with the SID witnesses, before Dennis Fung's testimony, I had a number of discussions with Collin Yamauchi. Over the course of these interviews Collin walked me through the PCR-DNA testing procedures he used in the case. The following represents a compilation of these discussions:

Collin and I were standing in the SID Evidence Processing Room one afternoon. Collin told me that on June 14, the day after the evidence was collected, he got to work at around 7:00 or 7:30 A.M. He told me that he went to the Evidence Processing Room shortly after arriving to access the evidence before he started testing it.

I wanted to know whether he could corroborate that Simpson's blood vial was already in the room, as opposed to having been delivered later by Detective Lange, as the defense had earlier implied as part of their theory that Detective Vannatter had kept the vial overnight. "Did you see Simpson's blood vial that morning after you arrived?"

"Yeah," Collin said. "Because immediately after seeing it, I pipetted some of the blood onto a Fitzco card." Collin showed me a Fitzco card, which is made of filter paper contained in a package. These cards are designed to be stained with blood samples for testing purposes.

Collin continued his narrative. "I had to wait for the card to dry before I could continue my work."

"Stop for a second, Collin," I said. This was the choke point of the contamination theory. "Collin, show me where in this room you were when you prepared the Fitzco card."

Collin stood at one of the tables in the Evidence Processing Room. "I was about here."

"Okay. Where was the evidence at that precise time?"

Collin pointed to another table in the same room about fifteen feet away from where he was standing.

Collin continued. "When I made this card, the rest of the evidence was there. The swatches were still in their bindles, in coin envelopes that were taped shut on that table over there, which is about fifteen feet away from this table, where I worked on the blood vial."

My next question went to the heart of the theory that Collin could have contaminated the evidence with blood from Simpson's vial. "Collin, is there any way that when you worked on the blood vial, it could have contaminated the evidence swatches, which were fifteen feet away and packaged in their coin envelopes?"

"No. This is blood we're talking about, not radiation. When I opened the blood vial, I wore gloves, and I also put a clean Chemwipe over the top to ensure that no blood would escape." After changing his gloves, Collin turned his attention to the evidence samples.

"I sampled the items in the Bundy trail between 10:00 A.M. and 11:00 A.M. on June 14, 1994." When Collin described to me how he worked on the evidence, we had a photographer take still shots of each step. Later, I turned this procedure into an exhibit that Rock used to illustrate Collin's sampling method.

Collin laid a clean sheet of paper down on the table near where the evidence would have been and sat down. "I worked on only one item at a time." He removed an individually packaged sterile scalpel from its foil package and he held it in his gloved hand. "I would first sample the substrate control by cutting it with a razor and place the cutting into a microcentrifuge tube, like this." He deftly cut a small section, about one-sixteenth by one-quarter of an inch, from a swatch he was using for demonstration purposes. He placed the cutting into a small plastic test tube with a cap attached and closed it. He then demonstrated how he used the same technique to sample the bloodstained swatch and put it into another microcentrifuge tube.

During Collin's demonstration, I noticed that he took a safe-guard against cross-contamination that is even more impressive than Gary Sims's practice of flaming his tools between working with different samples. Collin threw away the disposable scalpel blade after he used it to cut a swatch. When he moved to the next item, he took out a new blade. In this way he could not cross-contaminate the samples during the process.

"By the time I finished sampling the evidence, the Fitzco card was dry." Collin got up from his chair and walked over to the table where Simpson's Fitzco card and blood vial would have been on the morning of June 14. "Using the same procedures, I cut a sample out of the card and put it in its own microcentrifuge tube to test it, to determine Simpson's DNA results."

"Now what?" I asked.

"Now I take my rack of microcentrifuge tubes to the serology lab." We walked out of the room, down the corridor, and to the serology lab. Collin used his key card to buzz the door open. He walked into the lab with the assurance of someone entering his own domain. "Now, the testing process involves a three-step procedure. In this room we do the extraction." Collin walked over to a chemical venting hood toward the back of the room. "During extraction I add a chemical to the microcentrifuge tubes called chelex, which extracts the DNA from the cell so that it can be tested. Think of it as unpackaging the DNA."

Later that day, Collin and I drove the two miles to Parker Center, LAPD's headquarters, so that Collin could continue explaining his PCR-DNA testing procedures. Parker Center is a fifties-vintage mid-rise building, made famous in the *Dragnet* series. It has long since fallen into disrepair. As we approached the front entrance, I noticed that the large columns supporting the building were wrapped in masking tape. "I hope that's not supporting the entire building," I quipped.

"Wait until you see the lab," Collin said.

When we got upstairs, I noticed what I thought was an optical illusion. The floors seemed to be warped. Later, I read a newspaper article about the aging structure and learned that this was no illusion.

Collin let us into the "lab" with his own key. No one else was there. The lab consisted of four rooms that at one time were used for developing photographs. One of the rooms contained a large hood that must have been designed to vent the chemicals used to develop photographs. Large chunks of plaster had fallen off the walls. I could see that valiant efforts had been made to keep the room clean.

I said to Collin, "I hate to say it, but this actually looks like what Cochran was talking about when he used the phrase 'cesspool of contamination.' "

Collin replied matter-of-factly, "We definitely need a new space to do our DNA testing, and this looks pretty bad. But it's actually clean. We've done a bunch of tests here. The tests work. That's the bottom line."

Without missing a beat, Collin continued. "Anyway, this is where the cuttings I took were amplified. First, I added more chemicals to the microcentrifuge tubes. Then I placed them into the thermal cycler." Collin pointed to a sophisticated-looking instrument about the size and shape of a modern, computerized cash register. "The thermal cycler heats the tubes for a specified period of time. This causes the DNA to replicate thirty-two times. The process has been described as molecular Xeroxing. So were're turning a tiny little bit of DNA into a lot of DNA."

I jotted down some notes as Collin continued. "After that's done, the next step in the process is called hybridization. During this phase the amplified DNA is poured over a typing strip." Collin removed a typing strip and showed it to me. It was about five inches long and one inch wide. It had little circles on it and reminded me of a computerized multiple-choice test form on which one fills in the circles with a number 2 pencil. "The DNA binds to this strip. When it does that, some of these circles will light up; they turn a bluish color. The DNA type will determine to which circles on this strip the DNA will bind.''

"How?" I asked.

"See these circles." He pointed to the circles on the typing strip. "Each one of these contains a genetic probe. It's put on there by the manufacturer. That probe will only bind to DNA of a corresponding sequence. The circles that the DNA binds to tells you the DNA type. At this point the typing results can be read and photographed."

During Rock's direct examination, Collin used the demonstration boards I had created to explain to the jury exactly what he had previously explained to me about his handling and testing of the evidence. Before getting into the testing procedure itself, Rock elicited that when Collin performed his testing, far from being biased against Simpson, Collin believed that his test results would prove Simpson innocent. Rock wanted to show that if Collin was biased at all it was *in favor* of Simpson.

Rock asked Collin why he believed his testing would exonerate Simpson. Collin explained, "I heard on the news that, well, yeah, he's got an airtight alibi, he's—he's in Chicago . . . and I go, Oh, well, he's probably not related to the scene."

Then Judge Ito called a side bar. He said, "We've got a huge problem. We just brought in a statement [from the defendant]. I'm going to strike the answer." Ito was referring to the rule that if a party brings in part of a conversation, the other side can bring in any remaining parts of that conversation to put it into context. He had erroneously concluded that Collin had testified to part of the statement Simpson had given to Detectives Lange and Vannatter.

Scheck protested when Ito suggested he would strike Collin's testimony regarding why he believed the tests would prove Simpson innocent. Scheck said, "No, Your Honor. Your Honor, I'm not against it. It opens the door to [Simpson's] entire statement."

"It does," Judge Ito agreed.

Marcia jumped in, "Wait! Wait! Wait!"

"Proceed," Ito said.

Marcia explained that Collin had not referred to Simpson's statement to the police; rather, he had referred to a news report that claimed Simpson was in Chicago.

Judge Ito explained his theory, "You asked him a question that elicited, 'He's got an airtight alibi. He's in Chicago.' "

Marcia shot back, "That was this witness's opinion, Your Honor! What does that have to do with the defendant's statement, which, by the way, does not state that he had an airtight alibi because he was in Chicago. That was not [Simpson's] statement!"

Cochran softly and calmly stated, "We're certainly not going to yell at Your Honor and become hysterical. We would point out—

Marcia heatedly interrupted, "I object to that characterization, Your Honor. That kind of personal attack is very improper and inappropriate. . . . For Mr. Cochran to make that kind of sexist remark, 'hysterical,' I take great umbrage at it, and I think the court should not countenance that kind of behavior."

"I don't," Judge Ito replied.

When Marcia marched up from court, she came directly to the War Room, looking for me. "What the fuck is Ito thinking? No door has been opened. What's he talking about?"

I could not restrain myself from smiling. "It's like never-never-land down there."

"What's going on?" Marcia asked.

"Marcia, relax," I said. "Look, any reading of the transcript makes it clear that Rock's questions didn't open a window, much less a door. His questions didn't call for Collin to testify about any portion of Simpson's statement. So the defense doesn't get to put Simpson's statement in, period."

Marcia was moving side to side in a sort of nervous dance step. "I know, I know," she said, and then drew a breath as if coming up for air. "Look, would you look into this for me, Hank?"

That night, I reviewed, for the umpteenth time, Simpson's statement given to Vannatter and Lange the day after the murders. I looked at my detailed summary of the statement in my computer. Do we want to introduce this statement? I asked myself, as I had on many prior occasions. I made a mental list of what I liked and disliked about the statement.

First, when asked about his separation from Nicole, Simpson said, "For me it was, big problems, I loved her, I didn't want us to separate." Very interesting. But what does it mean? Unfortunately, Phil and Tom hadn't asked.

Second, when asked how he had gotten the injury on his hand, Simpson said, "I don't know. Not the first ti—I know I've had—when I was in Chicago I know how, but at the house I was just running around and the—"

Later, he was asked, "Do you—do you recall bleeding at all in the—in your truck, in the Bronco?"

"I recall bleeding at my house, and then I went to the—went to the Bronco. The last thing I did before I left, when I was rushing, was [I] went and got my phone out of the Bronco."

I liked this statement because it made it clear that the blood at Rockingham and in the Bronco was Simpson's. However, the defense didn't seem to be contesting this point.

The third item concerned Simpson's response when asked to take a polygraph test. He said, "I'm sure I'll do it. But it's like, hey, I've got some weird thoughts now. And I've had weird thoughts—you know, you've been with a person for seventeen years you think of everything." As with the similar statement made to Ron Shipp, the portion about the polygraph test would not be admissible in court. In the absence of the references to the polygraph, the phrase "weird thoughts" is rendered virtually meaningless.

As I carefully reviewed the interview, one of the things I actually liked about it was that it was one of the most innocuous police interrogations I had ever heard. They did not pin him down on any significant issue. They failed to establish what he was wearing after attending his daughter's dance recital. They did not get Simpson to give a detailed description of his whereabouts after the recital and before his departure for the airport. They did not specifically ask him about the McDonald's trip, and Simpson did not tell them about it except to say, "I ended up sitting with Kato."

The detectives never asked where? When? What happened right after you left Kato, etc.? It was about as hardball an interrogation as a celebrity interview with Larry King. They allowed Simpson to be so vague that virtually nothing he could testify to on the stand would have been inconsistent with what he told the detectives.

In any other case, such an interrogation would have annoyed me. However, in the Simpson case, along with the evidence of the LAPD's failure to properly investigate or even to document prior instances of domestic abuse involving Simpson, this demonstrated favoritism toward Simpson, not a conspiracy against him. Vannatter and Lange, who the defense claimed were evil co-conspirators, had treated Simpson with a level of deference I would hope would be denied the president of the United States, if he were to be questioned about a crime. Phil and Tom may have sensed that a sympathetic public might view an effort to press Simpson as police coercion.

Weighed against the very minor pro-prosecution points, there were two giant negative features of Simpson's statement. First, Simpson said that he had slept very little before the interview. The defense could attribute anything they disliked in the interview to exhaustion and grief. More importantly, it is a cardinal rule in a criminal prosecution that you do not introduce a defendant's self-serving statement unless you have no alternative. If the defendant wants to say he didn't do it, let him say it from the witness stand and subject himself to cross-examination. Evidence of a defendant's stating in his own words, "I didn't do it," can be very powerful for the defense.

I turned off my computer, leaned back in my chair, and rubbed my eyes. On balance, we shouldn't introduce this statement, I concluded.

That evening, when I got home, I made the mistake of turning on the TV. The commentators blared: Prosecution blunders by opening the door to Simpson's statement to the police.

Today I cannot help but think that we are seeing some revisionist history by some critics who contend that not introducing the statement was a blunder.

Finally, when Judge Ito next addressed the issue in court, he ruled that the prosecution did not open the door to Simpson's statement.

After Rock's direct, Collin Yamauchi seemed visibly upset. In fact, even under direct he seemed hesitant and unsure of himself on the stand. All of us were worried about what Barry Scheck might do to him in cross.

Surprisingly, the next day, a different Collin took the witness stand. Later, I asked Collin what accounted for the difference. He told me that he had made a promise to himself. He told me he would go head-to-head with Scheck. No faltering, no hesitancy. He was going to come off the stand feeling a sense of pride and dignity.

During his cross, Scheck finally hit a potentially probative area.

In regard to the fact that the vial containing Simpson's blood sample was not in a sealed envelope, Scheck asked whether blood vials are usually in sealed envelopes when Collin receives them. "Isn't that what you normally see?" Scheck demanded, pointing his finger accusingly, as he had when he asked Dennis Fung, "Where issss itttt, Misterrr Fung?"

Collin responded with great dignity: "Would you mind not pointing at me like that?"

Scheck backed off immediately, stating, "I was pointing—I'm sorry, Mr. Yamauchi. I was actually pointing at the [projector] screen. I wasn't pointing at you." Collin then calmly explained that it was not uncommon to receive evidence in an unsealed envelope.

On redirect, Collin also testified about a sock examination performed by defense expert Dr. Henry Lee. He testified that he did not see Dr. Lee change his gloves between examining the two socks. The point was that Dr. Lee had used the same type of forensic-examination procedures in handling this evidence that the LAPD had been criticized for using. Collin said that "basically [Dr. Lee] has a good reputation, and he handles evidence in the same fashion that we do."

For me, Collin's testimony ended on a high note. Down the line, Dr. Lee, an icon, was going to testify for the defense. We believed that the defense would use him to spearhead the contamination theory. But here we introduced into the record under oath: "[Dr. Lee] handles evidence in the same fashion that we do." On this note, the prosecution's DNA portion of the case came to a close.

25

Dear, Forgotten Dru

I WAS SITTING IN THE RECEPTION area of the War Room, watching the tail end of Collin's testimony. When he was excused from further testimony, I rested the notepad and pen I had been holding in my lap. I sat there quietly for about five minutes. Two months after I first called Dennis Fung to the witness stand, our DNA case was basically over. At the beginning of June, we would be moving into a new phase—the coroner, the gloves, the shoe-print evidence, and finally, the hair and trace evidence.

As I sat there, I reflected on the last two months: when Judge Ito dressed me down about showing the jury the form with the baggage claim and airline ticket; Dennis's faltering performance; the exhilaration of bashing the defense's staple-hole conspiracy; the videotape showing Dennis receiving the blood vial; the simple contentment of watching the solid, powerful testimony of Greg Matheson, Robin Cotton, and Gary Sims; the anxious waiting to see the outcome of Collin's testimony. I knew I should go back to my hovel to work on the shoe-print testimony, which I would have to present after the coroner and the glove evidence.

I slowly walked across the green carpet, which by now was stained with ten thousand drops from coffee mugs and five thousand drippings from Domino's pizza grease, Dem Bones barbecue sauce, Yang Chow's famous slippery shrimp sauce, and an assortment of miscellaneous weekend and late-night take-out food. It looked even filthier than it had on the day I first joined the prosecution team.

I sat down in my office and noticed a pile of unopened mail sitting accusingly in front of me.

I opened one envelope. The letter said that I had "fought the good fight." I had been in "Teddy Roosevelt's 'arena, marred with sweat and dust and blood.' " And so, it concluded, "I leave you, Hank Goldberg, with a warning that the Roman legions received when returning from victory in battle. When they were crowned, they were told, 'Glory is fleeting.' And so I whisper to you, Glory is fleeting. The road ahead is dusty, dry, rocky, and mountainous. Sometimes you will be without water, and the days will seem long."

I carefully folded the letter and replaced it in its envelope, putting it aside in a box. I glanced at the computer screen, which was filled with my endless notes summarizing Collin Yamauchi's testimony. Accidentally, I flicked off the computer and watched the screen go dead in a flash, like a magician who suddenly vanishes in a cloud of smoke.

I decided to go home early, around 5:30 P.M., and meet my parents and brothers for dinner. When I got to my parents' condo in Westwood, my mother and brothers were in the living room reading magazines and newspapers. My father was on the phone talking to my sister, Dru.

Dru! I thought, as I experienced the heart-dropping sensation when you realize you have forgotten something important. I hadn't talked to Dru since my part of the trial had started. "Dad, let me say hello to her after you're done." My father nodded and held up his hand.

Dru, six years older than I, began to exhibit symptoms of emotional disturbance, at the age of thirteen, which sent her into private therapy. In 1968, when she was ten, my father cowrote *Hang 'em High,* a Western starring Clint Eastwood. The *Hang 'em High* money enabled my parents to pay for my sister's private therapy, usually seventy-five dollars an hour, with stays in private hospitals at hundreds of dollars each day. Finally, when the money ran out, Dru went into the state hospital system.

For a period of time, my older brother, David, and I had to take time out from study and teenage play to help my mother and father watch over Dru. Dru, in her paranoia, conceived of my kid brother, Luke, who was little more than a baby, as her enemy.

Dru has been in a state mental health system for the past twenty-five years. I watched her grow from a lithe, beautiful, gifted athlete, dancer, talented artist, aspiring novelist and poet, into an over-weight woman, semicrippled by numerous aborted suicide attempts. Self-inflicted razor slashes now scar her arms, and her forehead bears the signs of her pounding her head against the floor. Her body is broken from throwing herself from twenty-foot heights.

I hadn't seen Dru since the trial started. But after occasional phone conversations, I would see her for days in my mind's eye, my mercurial, laughing older sister, who used to read to me, play Monopoly with me, and hold me soothingly in her arms when I fell off the swing and hurt myself.

When my father finished his phone conversation, never an easy task with Dru, he said, "Your brother Hank wants to talk to you." There was about a minute more of back-and-forth negotiation between my father and sister before I was handed the phone.

Dru was aware that I was involved in the Simpson case and had seen me on television. However, in her obsessive-compulsive mind, she was unable to relate to any member of my family except on the limited topic of what we could do for her. "Oh, hi, Hank. Hank, Dad said that when you come up to see me we're going to go to the Sizzler. Why can't we do something original? Maybe go to Tony Aroma's in the mall?"

"I don't know, Dru." I quickly changed the subject. "So are you doing any reading, Dru?"

"No. I lost my glasses. Anyway, can we go to Tony Aroma's?" I did not respond.

Dru seemed to be drifting off. "Hank?"

"What, Dru?"

"Hank?"

"Yes?"

"Why can't I come back and live at home?"

"Dru, did you see me on TV? Did you know I'm on the Simpson case?"

Dru readily disposed of the boring topic. "Yeah. Hank?"

"What, Dru?"

"Are you going to be rich?"

"No," I replied. "I work for the government. Do you know what I do?"

"Yeah. Ask Dad if instead of going out to eat when he visits, he can bring peanut-butter-and-jelly sandwiches, a large, no—*two* large Cokes, a bag of Lay's potato chips, and some Chips Ahoy cookies."

"Dru, I'm not in charge of those decisions."

"Oh," Dru replied. She seemed to drift off again for a few seconds. "But can you ask Dad. Can you just ask him?"

After a few more minutes of this conversation, Dru finally became terminally bored. "Put Dad back on the phone. I want to ask him something."

"Okay, Dru. I love you. Take care of yourself."

After the conversation with Dru, my family and I gathered around the table to eat dinner. My mother had prepared her famous breaded baked chicken. I have probably eaten this meal with my family a thousand times, and I have never grown tired of it. But as we sat around and ate, something was missing.

We were quiet.

26

The Murders, Blow by Blow

Dr. Lakshmanan Sathyavagiswaran, ["Dr. L"] the Los Angeles County coroner, took the stand on June 2. The display documented in full color and clinical detail the extent and ferocity of the attack. There were many ghastly close-ups of the wounds, some open and gaping.

Typically, the presentation of the coroner in a criminal case is not of great significance in terms of telling the jury who committed the murders. Unlike Quincy, the fictional coroner from television, coroners do not act as detectives who solve crimes.

Dr. Irwin Golden had performed the autopsies on Ron Goldman and Nicole Brown Simpson. Dr. Golden had testified for me in murder cases on several other occasions. He was a rail-thin man with thinning red hair, whose body is in almost constant movement with mannerisms I refer to as *shpilkes*. The rough English equivalent: ants in your pants. His appearance causes some to question his competence. However, he is one of the best medical examiners in the Los Angeles County coroner's office.

The coroner's office is abysmally underfunded. As a result of the ferocious pace, involving nineteen thousand cases a year, and poor facilities, the quality of the work is generally mediocre to poor. The primary cause is understaffing. There are only twelve full-time pathologists, including Dr. Lakshmanan. In Los Angeles County a pathologist handles 300–350 autopsies annually. As taxpayers, we must understand that we get what we pay for.

One problem Brian Kelberg, the brilliant, bearded prosecutor, had to confront were the numerous mistakes Golden had made during the autopsies on Ron's and Nicole's bodies. Prior to presenting this evidence, Brian outlined his strategy to Marcia, Chris, Bill, and me in the large press-conference room. He explained that he would call Dr. Lakshmanan, Golden's supervisor, who would testify that the approximately thirty mistakes Golden made during the autopsy were all relatively minor in that they could not have affected what Brian referred to as the "big-ticket items." Many of these mistakes were failures to properly document the wounds to the bodies. Under Brian's definition, "the big-ticket items" were the cause of death, the manner of death, the time of death, and the number of perpetrators.

For example, Brian made it clear that the defense allegation that important information was lost as a result of not calling the coroner for hours was without merit. Even if Dr. L had lived next door to the scene of the murder and had rushed over there immediately after the bodies were discovered and examined them, he could not have narrowed down the time of death except to say that it was between 9:30 P.M. and 12:10 A.M., when the bodies were found. Later, on the stand, Dr. L explained: "In no instance in my career have I seen a case where the range of death could be medically narrowed to less than a three-hour span."

Most of the coroner's testimony involved various theories as to how the murders could have been committed. These explanations were preceded with words of equivocation such as "could be" or "possibly." The reason is that it is impossible to reconstruct with any degree of certainty the exact order in which the killer inflicted the wounds.

Generally, this is the scenario I took from Dr. L's testimony. Nicole left her condominium and walked down the walk toward the stairs. At the base of the stairs, the killer probably confronted her. In an effort to ward off his knife, Nicole may have first received the cut to her left hand, a defensive injury. As she turned to flee, the killer inflicted several stab wounds to the back of her head. Then the killer, perhaps using the hilt of the knife, hit her on the back of the head, causing a scalp and brain contusion. This can cause a loss of consciousness. According to Dr. L, Nicole was "probably rapidly incapacitated and unable to offer much resistance."

Nicole collapsed at the base of the stairs on her left side. Approximately a minute elapsed before the killer inflicted the final wound.

During this approximately one minute period, the killer could have commenced or resumed an attack on Ron Goldman.

The last wound to Nicole severed her jugular. Dr. L saw a shoe mark on Nicole's back. This suggested that the killer planted his foot on her back, raised her head by grasping a handful of her hair and lifted her head back to expose her throat to the fatal knife wound, severing her jugular vein. Since she was on the pavement at the time, blood spurted directly onto the ground. Very little blood may have actually stained the killer's clothes.

Later, during the defense case, Dr. Michael Baden, a celebrity medical examiner from New York, disagreed with some of Dr. L's conclusions. Dr. Baden felt that the purplish area on Nicole's back was not caused by someone stepping on her. He also testified that Nicole was probably conscious when the killer inflicted the fatal neck wound. However, on cross, he admitted that she could have been unconscious at the time.

The following scenario is based on Dr. L's interpretations. Ron was probably caught by surprise near the front gate of Nicole's condominium, where Ron dropped the envelope containing the eyeglasses. Dr. L testified that two superficial, parallel incise wounds appeared to be "threatening cuts," as if the killer had held a knife to Ron's throat from behind while threatening or taunting him. Dr. Baden, on the other hand, said that this injury "could have happened" later in the struggle.

Early in the struggle Ron received stab wounds to the neck. He attempted to grab the knife, receiving numerous defensive wounds to the palm of his left hand, consistent with grabbing the knife. This may be when the killer's glove came off his left hand.

By now, Ron had received a number of fatal and nonfatal major injuries to the neck, the right chest, and the back of his head. He was bleeding profusely.

At some point, Ron fled or was moved into the caged-off area just to the right of the open gate as one faces Nicole's condominium. Here Ron may have been stabbed in the left thigh and behind the left ear.

By this point, Ron might have collapsed against the fence in the caged-off area. There are five small wounds to Ron's face, suggesting the killer poked Ron with the tip of the knife to check whether he was alive as he lay against the fence. Dr. Baden, on the other hand, testified that he had never heard of a killer poking his victim to check whether he was alive.

While Ron was lying helpless on the ground, the murderer could have plunged his knife six inches into the left side of Ron's abdomen.

Both the prosecution and defense versions are burdened with maybes, might have beens, and possibilities. However, inarguably, whichever version one chooses, a maniacal murderer carried out a savage attack that left his two victims dead within minutes. When motive, opportunity, and overwhelming physical and forensic evidence are factored in, what more did we need to know?

27

But the Gloves Did Fit

"IF WE CAN FIND THE RECEIPT showing that Simpson purchased a pair of Aris Leather Light gloves, it would be devastating," Marcia told me the evening when she gave me the overview of the case, shortly after I joined the prosecution team. "In some ways, it would be better than the DNA evidence."

When I became a member of the prosecution team in October 1994, we were still in the process of determining whether we could show that Simpson purchased Aris Leather Light gloves, of the type found at the crime scene. This effort involved contacting locations where those gloves were sold. The investigation focused on Bloomingdale's in New York. The records were not readily available or computerized. A herculean effort was under way to authenticate the glove purchase.

But well before Dr. Lakshmanan finished his testimony, Bloomingdale's found the receipt.

On June 15, 1995, Brenda Vemich and Richard Rubin testified. Vemich had been a buyer of men's gloves in 1990 for Bloomingdale's. She testified that the crime-scene gloves were Aris Leather Light cashmere-lined gloves. They were Bloomingdale's exclusives and retailed for fifty-five dollars.

Approximately three hundred such pairs of gloves were purchased in 1990. Of these, only two hundred pairs were sold to customers.

Chris Darden then showed Ms. Vemich a copy of a sales receipt dated December 18, 1990. The receipt reflected that Nicole Brown had purchased two pairs of these gloves.

During his cross-examination, Johnnie Cochran tried on one of the Bundy gloves and asked, "It is too small?"

Vemich responded, "It is too big."

On redirect, Chris asked how men's gloves are supposed to fit. Vemich explained, "They are supposed to fit like a glove. . . . They are supposed to fit tight and snug, and they stretch, and they are not supposed to be baggy."

Richard Rubin had worked for Aris Isotoner, the glove manufacturer, in 1990. He was the vice president and general manager. He started with the company in 1976 and had been responsible for the design, manufacturing, production, raw material, and sales and marketing of all men's gloves.

Rubin verified that the Rockingham and Bundy gloves were brown extra-large Aris Leather Lights. This model, over twice as expensive as the average men's gloves, had been exclusively sold to Bloomingdale's, the store where Nicole had purchased two pairs.

During the examination, Chris Darden asked that Simpson try on a new pair of gloves similar to the crime-scene gloves.

At a side bar, Chris explained to Judge Ito, "I would like to lay the foundation to show they are the exact same size, similar make and model, so that perhaps we can have Mr. Simpson try them on at some point to determine whether or not the gloves found at the scene and at his home will fit him."

Cochran responded, "We object to this, Your Honor. First of all, we've had no time to deal with this. At some point, if Mr. Simpson testifies and we want to have him try the gloves on in evidence, that is one thing."

The judge ruled, "I think it would be more appropriate for him to try the other gloves on." Judge Ito was referring to the crime-scene gloves.

Marcia interjected, "The only problem is, he has to wear latex gloves underneath because [the crime-scene gloves are] a biohazard." Marcia was referring to the fact that the crime-scene gloves were covered with blood, which constituted a biohazard, meaning the blood theoretically could contain infectious disease. She added that the problem with Simpson's wearing latex gloves during the demonstration is that "they're going to alter the fit."

Outside the jury's presence, Rubin was shown the pair of new gloves. He testified that they were not identical to the crime-scene gloves.

Judge Ito asked Chris, "I take it you're not going to use that in front of the jury?"

Chris said, "Probably not. . . . *Before the jury returns,* however, we would like to have Mr. Simpson try on the original evidence items." (emphasis added)

Cochran said, "I don't want him to have to do it without having latex gloves on. . . . I would ask this court insist that the camera be directed—*he doesn't want this to seem like he's giving some kind of performance."* (emphasis added)

Judge Ito refused to instruct the cameraman not to film the demonstration.

In retrospect, I find Cochran's request to use latex gloves and not to televise the glove demonstration very telling. In public appearances long after the trial, Bob Shapiro claims that he knew the gloves would not fit. Then why not have this televised to the world? Maybe the defense had seen Simpson act in the *Naked Gun* movies. He was not very good.

When the jury returned, Chris said, "At this time, the people would ask that Mr. Simpson step forward and try on the glove recovered at Bundy as well as the glove recovered at Rockingham."

Simpson attempted to don the gloves.

Chris stated, "Your Honor, apparently Mr. Simpson seems to be having a problem putting the glove on his hand."

In a barely audible voice, Simpson said that the gloves were "too small."

Chris asked the court, "Can we ask him to straighten his fingers and extend them into the glove, as one normally might put a glove on?"

Then Simpson appeared to have pulled the gloves on. Simpson was directed to grasp a marker with his gloved hand and was able to do so.

After the demonstration, Rubin testified: "His hands should be able to fit into that pair of gloves."

*   *   *

During the glove demonstration, I was at Bundy for the purpose of reconstructing the precise location of the shoe prints. When I returned to the office, I was surprised to see the flurry of activity, almost as if we had just experienced an earthquake.

One of the younger lawyers grabbed me. "Didn't you hear what happened in court today?" He started explaining that something went wrong during a glove demonstration. My mild reaction provoked this rebuke: "You're always so calm!"

Then some of the younger attorneys suggested, "Why don't you wander over to Chris's office to see if you can be of any help."

"Chris knows what he's doing," I said. "He doesn't need me to get in the way."

Nevertheless, I walked over to his office. His small eight-by-twelve-foot space was jammed with people. It looked like one of those acts from the 1960s where they used to see how many people could fit in a VW Bug. Most of the senior lawyers, not including Marcia, most of the junior lawyers, and many of the law clerks were there. I could not fit into the office, so I spoke to Chris from the hallway.

Someone popped in the tape of the glove demonstration. Since I had not heard any media stories, and the account of the event from the younger lawyers was very sketchy, I was viewing it fresh. During the demonstration I saw Simpson's face apparently mugging, his hands and arms broadly gesticulating, as he struggled to put on the gloves that were worn during the murder of his ex-wife and Ron Goldman.

Chris looked up at me dolefully, "Well?"

"I don't think this is a major problem. Looks like a grade-B acting job to me. Don't you think the gloves fit?" I asked.

"I know they fit," Chris replied. He pointed to Deputy D.A. Mike Stevens, who is about six-foot-four. "He just tried them on and they fit him, and his hands are as big as Simpson's. How do you think we should handle this?"

"Let me think." I paused for a few moments. I pointed to the TV. "Tomorrow I would mark this videotape of the demonstration as an exhibit."

"Are you crazy?" a voice from the back of the room shouted. There were so many people in the office, I could not identify the voice. "Do you want them playing that thing over and over?"

"Hold on. I'm not finished," I responded. "Mark it as an exhibit. Play it for the jury. Let them see it again and again and again. Remember the Rodney King tape? Everyone thought it was the greatest piece of evidence in the world for the prosecution. But the defense played it to the jury a hundred thousand times until they were bored with it. The defense microdissected it: 'You see his elbow cocking, like he's reaching for something. Look, look! See he's rising as if he's trying to get up.' Pretty soon the jury didn't see the cops viciously beating a helpless man anymore. But here it really is quite clear, in my mind, that Simpson is faking. So show it over and over. 'Stop the tape! Look at that grin! Watch that! Look how easily he popped the glove off.' "

The voice from the back of Chris's office repeated, "But do we want to continually remind the jury of this?"

"Yes," I replied. "Then call Mike Stevens as a witness. Establish that Mike's hands are bigger than Simpson's. Have Mike try to put the glove on. Have Mike pretend that it doesn't fit. Then pop on the glove. Then, in argument, we argue the hell out of it: 'Look at that tape, look what he tried to put over on you by not pulling those gloves on, blah, blah, blah.' Hell, ask Ito to give a consciousness-of-guilt instruction. The jury can infer that if Simpson was faking during the glove demonstration, they can consider it as evidence of a guilty conscience. Go on the attack. That's my opinion."

The crowded room grew silent, and everyone stared at me as if they had just heard the ravings of a madman. Chris, however, appeared to be listening intently. The best trial lawyers accept extensive input from others when possible, and Chris is an excellent trial lawyer. When I left that evening, I was under the impression that my proposal was going to be accepted.

When I got home that night, I couldn't resist turning on the TV to see how the story was being played. Because of its highly visual nature, the glove story was almost made for TV. Essentially, the media seemed to be trumpeting the defense position that would eventually be refined into the mantra "If the gloves don't fit, you must acquit."

The next day, June 16, Chris recalled Richard Rubin to begin the process of repairing the damage from the glove demonstration. Rubin testified that the gloves in their original condition "would easily go onto the hands of someone of Mr. Simpson's size." He went on to explain that "the gloves appeared to be shrunken in size from their original condition." He explained that when gloves are repeatedly wet, the "gloves could shrink approximately 15 percent from its original size."

Chris established through Richard Rubin that latex gloves would obviously have the effect of making it more difficult to put on the leather gloves.

Based on examining Simpson's hand and the gloves, Rubin repeated his conclusion: "They should fit him."

When Chris concluded with Richard Rubin, I was watching on TV from the War Room. What happened to our strategy of having Mike Stevens pop the gloves on in court? I wanted to jiggle the television set to see if more would come out.

Later, I asked Mike Stevens why Chris didn't use our planned strategy. Mike said that he had been waiting outside the court but that the plan was scrapped at the last moment. Perhaps the thought was that the proposed approach was a gimmick that could backfire if the jurors decided we had played some trick, such as stretching the gloves overnight. Recalling Rubin seemed like a more conservative and dignified approach.

Months later, I was told of an alleged incident that may belie Chris's perception of the glove demonstration in his book, in which he assumes full responsibility for the debacle. Apparently, on the day of the glove demonstration, a number of members of the prosecution team, all highly capable lawyers, were discussing the issue of whether Simpson should try on the gloves, even as Chris was in court. They believed that Chris had already determined that the gloves would fit Simpson, since Chris had asked Phil Vannatter, whose hands are as large as Simpson's, to try on the gloves. These prosecutors unanimously concluded that Chris should proceed with the glove demonstration. They sent a note to Chris in court, while Richard Rubin was on the stand, suggesting that he go forward.

To evaluate whether the glove demonstration was a "mistake," one should consider the duty imposed on prosecutors. A prosecutor has an ethical obligation to disclose information that could legitimately show someone is innocent. The U.S. Supreme Court has held that prosecutors "have the obligation to convict the guilty and to make sure they do not convict the innocent. They must be dedicated to making the criminal trial a procedure for the ascertainment of the true facts surrounding the commission of the crime. . . . But defense counsel has no comparable obligation to ascertain or present the truth. . . . [We] insist that he defend his client where he is innocent or guilty." So if a prosecutor actually believed that the gloves did not fit and proved Simpson's innocence, he would have to bring that fact forward. He could not hide it. In this event, the glove demonstration would not be a "mistake." If, on the other hand, a prosecutor believed the gloves did fit but that Simpson could easily deceive the jury into believing they did not, then the glove demonstration could be viewed as a "mistake."

Chris clearly believed the gloves fit. We had shown that Nicole had purchased a pair of Aris Leather Lights, we had photographs of Simpson wearing such gloves, and we had DNA evidence showing Simpson's blood on the Rockingham glove. The evidence showed to a virtual certainty that Simpson had worn those gloves when he murdered Ron and Nicole.

If the gloves were too tight, certainly the defense would not rest before bringing that fact to the jury's attention, anyway. Therefore, I cannot necessarily conclude that the glove demonstration was a mistake. What may have been a mistake was the lack of a preformed contingency plan to deal with any effort Simpson might make to feign difficulty during the demonstration and the failure to explain the shrinkage issue before the demonstration ever took place.

After Richard Rubin's testimony, photographs of Simpson continued to pour into our offices. Typically, they were photos of a glove-wearing Simpson commenting at a football game. He was wearing gloves in the rain and in the snow. Simpson team prosecutor Alan Yochelson would notify me every time we got a new photograph. As Alan studied the gloves, I would study Simpson's shoes, my area of the case. Once, Scott Gordon observed this routine and commented, "Alan handles the glove department, Hank handles the shoes, all other accessories are on a different floor."

On September 12, 1994, almost three months after the glove demonstration, Richard Rubin was recalled to the stand during the people's rebuttal case. He testified that he had examined a number of photographs of Simpson wearing gloves at several NFL football games. Rubin testified that they were Aris Leather Lights, the exact same type as the crime-scene gloves. Chris addressed the shrinkage issue by showing that at some of these games it was raining. The implication was that the gloves were subject to repeated wetting and rewetting. This could cause them to shrink.

Rubin was shown footage from the Bengals-versus-Bills game on January 6, 1991. Chris Darden directed his attention to one particular frame. Rubin said that the gloves seen in that frame were the exact same type as the crime-scene gloves.

"How certain are you of that?" Chris asked.

"I'm a hundred percent certain," Mr. Rubin replied.

28

Put Your Left Foot In

"WHAT IF THE SHOES DON'T FIT?" I jokingly asked shoe-print expert William Bodziak as we walked down to court to present his testimony on the heels of the glove demonstration.

Bill smiled. "They fit, Hank. They fit."

Over a month earlier, in May, I had been assigned the task of presenting the shoe-print evidence. Prior to the Simpson case, I knew very little about this type of forensic evidence and found it very interesting.

In the early-morning hours of June 13, 1994, when officers first arrived at the Bundy crime scene, one of the most obvious items of physical evidence was a set of bloody shoe prints. These prints led from the bodies about sixty feet toward the alley before the blood wore off the murderer's shoes and the shoe prints faded out.

From the standpoint of a forensic scientist or a prosecutor, shoe prints, like all evidence at a crime scene, constitute potential sources of information from which the suspect's identity can be extracted. For me, the phenomenon of viewing a crime-scene photograph only in terms of its informational content happened early in my career. I have prosecuted a number of homicides, most of which involved excessively gruesome crime scenes. It is possible to spend, literally, hours looking at a single photograph over and over again throughout such a trial. Such was the case in preparing for the shoe-print evidence.

About three years ago, during the prosecution of a particularly brutal murder in which a nurse had been stabbed to death with a

212

butcher knife, I noticed that a strange, somewhat troubling phenomenon occurs during the prolonged study of crime-scene photographs. Almost magically, the victims disappear. Suddenly, all one sees is evidence: shoe prints, blood splatters, hairs, fibers, and objects. The victim's body itself becomes mere evidence. I suppose this is a psychological defense mechanism; it allows us to do our job. But every so often, just as suddenly as the bodies disappear, they reappear again. And you realize—my God—I'm looking at human beings. The photographs become fuzzy as your eyes mist over.

When this happens, it is necessary to stop looking at the photographs for a moment. But it's only a moment before you pick up the photos and again see shoe prints.

William Bodziak was the FBI shoe-print expert assigned to the case. The FBI has a world-renowned crime lab that provides expert assistance to local law enforcement. Bill is a man who appears to be about forty-five and looks and talks like an engineer. He is a world-class witness and inarguably one of the leading experts in his field. He literally wrote the book on footwear examination.

One evening in May, about a month before he would testify, I spoke to Bill in detail in my cubicle. I typed notes in the computer while he spoke. He related to me the story of how he tracked down the manufacturer of the shoes that made the prints at Bundy.

"The FBI has a sophisticated, computerized shoe-print library, as do several other leading law enforcement agencies throughout the world. However, I couldn't find the prints at Bundy in our library."

"So what did you do?"

"Based upon looking at photographs of the prints, I determined it was a rubber-soled shoe with a pointed toe. The tread was a distinctive S-like waffle design. Probably a high-end Italian shoe. So I contacted seventy-five to eighty manufacturers and importers of high-end Italian shoes plus some South American shoe companies. I sent them sketches of the impression. I also contacted other countries that have computerized shoe-print libraries."

"Hold on," I said as I continued typing into my computer. "Okay."

He continued, "On August 17, 1994, I hit pay dirt. The Bruno Magli shoe store in New Jersey phoned and informed me that the shoe print was theirs. The soles of the shoe were manufactured for them by a company in Italy called Silga. Interestingly, of the eight countries that I contacted, only the National Police Agency in Tokyo had the shoe design in their library."

Bill paused and looked around. "Is it always this noisy in here?"

"I didn't notice. Sorry. This is county government here, Bill."

"Anyway," Bill continued, "I learned that the shoes sold for $160 and were distributed between 1991 and 1992."

I asked, "So after you determine it's a Bruno Magli, how do you figure out it's a size twelve?"

Bill replied, "Simply measuring the prints, one can only determine the approximate size of the shoes. However, once you know the type of shoe that made the print, the precise size can be determined."

"Okay," I said as I continued typing.

Bill continued, "Often shoes are manufactured using hand-milled shoe molds. Such molds, which kind of resemble a waffle iron, are used to make rubber soles. In such molds, the machinist cuts the pattern of the shoe tread into the mold using a template. Still with me?"

"Yeah," I said, "And since the molds are routed by hand, every mold is unique, right?"

Bill smiled. "You've been reading my book."

"Isn't it on the bestseller list, Bill?"

"Not yet," Bill said. "So, as you said, because it's by hand, each mold is slightly unique. These differences can be obvious to a shoe-print expert. Sometimes it's possible to find the precise mold that made the shoes that caused the prints at a crime scene."

This statement intrigued me. "Bill, are you saying that it's possible to find the exact mold that made the shoes that left the prints at Bundy?"

"Precisely," Bill said.

"And did you find it?" I asked excitedly.

"Yes. I traveled to the Silga factory in Italy on January 23, 1995. Silga had one mold for each size they made. These molds were hand-milled."

Stressing each word, I asked, "So can you say that the mold you found was the exact mold, to the exclusion of every other shoe mold on the face of the planet, that made the shoes worn by Nicole and Ron's killer?"

Bill looked directly at me. "Yes. I found the mold that made those shoes. And it was a European size forty-six. American size twelve. Simpson's size."

"Okay, okay, Bill. Now, what's the best way to demonstrate to the jury that Simpson would fit into the Bruno Magli shoes that made the prints?"

Bill said, "You can't have him try the shoe on in court." Bill pointed to the shoes he was wearing, which, as I recall, were dress lace-ups. "I could easily take this shoe off and put it back on in such a way as to make it look like it didn't fit."

Of course during this interview, about a month before the infamous glove demonstration, I had no idea how prophetic Bill's words would become. "Well, what do you think would be the most effective way to illustrate your opinion regarding fit to the jury?"

Bill answered, "I would suggest that I simply hold up a pair of Simpson's Reeboks and actually size them, tread to tread, to the Bruno Maglis.

"And the fit is perfect?" I asked, hoping Bill would not qualify with an "almost perfect," which might open a can of worms.

"The fit is perfect," Bill said. "It's very obvious."

One night, about a week before I presented Bill Bodziak's testimony, I arrived home from work at around 10:00 P.M. I went upstairs and opened the door to my exercise room, a door I had not opened in the last several months of the trial. I should do a little exercise, I thought. I had lost fifteen pounds. I stared at the dusty exercise equipment, debating the pros and cons. If I exercise, maybe I won't be able to sleep. Maybe I'll be sore tomorrow. As I stood there, the phone rang.

It was Marcia. She wanted to discuss my strategy in presenting the shoe-print evidence. After a quick "I hope I'm not disturbing you," she said, "I get the feeling you're wondering whether we should present the shoe-print evidence."

I said, "I'm not sure. I mean, we still can't say that Simpson owned the type of shoes that left the shoe prints. On the other hand, we can show that the shoe prints are size twelve."

"Hank, didn't you tell me that Bodziak would also be able to say only ten percent of the population is size twelve?"

"Yes," I replied. "And if this were any other type of case, I would want to put that on. Marcia, as we both know, in many cases, such as in rape cases, we have evidence of semen testing that matches the defendant and also matches ten percent of the population. Sometimes it matches twenty-five percent or more and we still present that evidence. The idea is that if only ten percent of the population have that blood type it would be a coincidence that the defendant just happens to match. It's a good piece of corroborating evidence. But in our case, we have so much better evidence. If the jury can discount the DNA statistics, which are billions to one, how much does the shoe-print testimony add?''

There was a long pause on the other end of the line. ''Hank, this is really good evidence. I mean, I like just the fact that the shoes cost $160 dollars. Just that alone. It tells you something about who committed this crime. It wasn't your average street robber.''

I agreed. By this point in the trial, perhaps we were all beginning to second-guess even the simplest tactical decisions, mostly because of the bombardment of ''media experts,'' with widely divergent opinions, second-guessing every tactical decision: Put on Simpson's statement: don't put it on. Hide Fuhrman: don't hide him. Marcia's words reassured me that the evidence should definitely be presented. ''Thanks, Marcia, I'll talk—''

Marcia interrupted, ''Hank, let me ask you something. What do you think about the Bronco-chase evidence?''

At the time, this was the furthest thing from my mind. But I quickly shifted gears. ''Well, of course, Chris knows more about that than anyone. How would I analyze it?'' I paused. I related to Marcia in detail my reactions when I viewed the Bronco chase, particularly to the sight of the cheering spectators. ''The events of June seventeenth evoked a level of sympathy for someone that just hours earlier everyone assumed had committed a brutal double murder.''

I knew that Marcia would immediately appreciate what I was saying, but I continued. ''In looking at this evidence we can't simply look at the reasonable inference: we have to assess its emotional content. That's what worries me. I mean, the facts are there. Shortly after he becomes aware that his arrest is imminent, he flees—the money in the Bronco, the passport, and the disguise.''

''The gun,'' Marcia added.

''Yes,'' I said. ''Ask Chris how well he thinks we can prove that Simpson had knowledge of the items in the Bronco.''

"They were in a bag," Marcia interjected. "We can't necessarily show that he knew about the money."

I asked, "What's the explanation for the evidence going to be?"

In a slightly ironic, rapid-fire tone of voice, Marcia replied, "Simpson was not trying to escape. He was trying to visit his mother or Nicole's grave or going to commit suicide, depending on which version they want to go with. The false beard in the makeup kit was because he wanted to disguise himself to take the kids to Disneyland. Like this guy ever shied away from the public: he loved the attention, and I think they let you go to the front of the lines at Disneyland if you're a celebrity. Anyway, they can say that he didn't know about the money or passport or that he wanted Cowlings to give money to his kids for immediate needs if he committed suicide."

"And I guess they can make these arguments without putting Simpson on," I responded. "I'm not trying to dodge your question, Marcia. On the facts, I'm leaning toward introducing it. But there's something else to consider. This concerns me even more. If Simpson made any statements around or during the time of the Bronco chase, I think we'd be opening the door to them."

"They are hearsay," Marcia said.

"Yes. But think about it. Why are we introducing evidence of the Bronco chase? We want to prove a consciousness of guilt. We want to show what his state of mind was—that he ran because he believed he was guilty. If we do that, his state of mind at and around the time of the chase is placed squarely in issue. If he said, for example, 'I am so devastated that Nicole was murdered, I would have given my own life to save her, now I want to kill myself, blah, blah, blah,' I think that would become admissible. Can you imagine the type of emotional garbage the defense may try to introduce to show what he was really feeling at the time of the chase?"

"Believe me, I can imagine it," Marcia said.

I continued: "As Brian [Kelberg] keeps reminding us: If the jury can find a way to explain away the DNA evidence, nothing will convince them. Do we dilute clear-cut evidence by giving the jury more stuff they can argue about?"

"What's your bottom line?" Marcia asked.

"On one side of the balance we have evidence which on its face seems to persuasively show he's fleeing from justice because he knows he's guilty. The counterbalance is the emotional content of the chase itself and emotional evidence the defense will undoubtedly introduce. That's how I would approach making this decision. I'm sorry, Marcia, for not giving you a more direct answer. I hope that's helpful."

"It was. Thanks, Hankster. Talk to you tomorrow."

I looked at the clock. It was around 11:00 P.M. Oh, well, I'll have to exercise tomorrow—or maybe the next day.

In the middle of June, just days before I presented the shoe-print evidence, I spoke to F. Lee Bailey in the hall outside Judge Ito's court to make sure he had all the discovery relating to this evidence. Mr. Bailey asked, "Are you going to present evidence showing that Simpson purchased a pair of Bruno Magli shoes?"

I said with a straight face, "Lee, didn't you get that in discovery? Didn't we give you the witnesses who will testify that your client owned a pair of the shoes?"

"Seriously," Bailey persisted.

"You know that if I had that evidence I'd have to give it over to you in discovery. I can't just put a witness on the stand out of the blue to say your client owned a pair of Bruno Magli shoes."

"So do you have any evidence of that?" he asked again.

"No."

The next day, Johnnie Cochran asked me the same set of questions, and we had virtually the same conversation. The day after that, Cochran, Bailey, and I revisited the issue. On the morning of June 19, 1995, when I entered Judge Ito's court, they asked yet again. "I've answered that question a million times. Why are you guys so worried about this?"

"We're not worried," Johnnie shot back. Then he smiled broadly. "You're never going to find anyone who can connect those shoes to O.J."

"Okay. Then you don't have anything to worry about."

On June 19, I called FBI shoe-print expert Bill Bodziak to the stand. The examination clipped along at a fast pace. It was punctuated with numerous demonstration boards that Bill had created to illustrate his testimony and the science of footwear examination.

Bill recounted the story he had related to me earlier about how he determined the make, and eventually the size, of the shoes that left the shoe prints at Bundy.

Bill told the jury that he compared Simpson's Reeboks to the Bruno Magli shoes. As he testified, Bill held the sole of the Reebok and the Bruno Magli together to dramatize that they were the identical size.

He testified that only 9 percent of the U.S. population wears a size-12 shoe.

In the middle of the Bundy walk there was a strange configuration of the shoe prints that was consistent with the killer having stopped, made a quarter turn to his left, stepped backward, and then forward. However, we could never reconstruct the precise movement. Some imaginative members of our office had suggested it could have been a football maneuver.

One night, in the War Room, I was trying to reconstruct the possible movements with some younger members of the office. To the untrained eye, it would have appeared that we were all playing the game Twister. Later, I quipped, "You put your left foot in, you put you're right foot out, standing on one leg you shake it all about, you hop to the left with both feet down, now you're doing the O.J. shuffle."

Since any reconstruction of what happened was both irrelevant and speculative, Bill and I agreed not to explore the question in detail during my direct. I thought it would be more effective if any speculative testimony was "forced out" of him on cross-examination.

I asked just enough questions on direct examination about the strange configuration of the shoe prints to pique the defense's curiosity and provoke cross-examination on the point. My questions implied that the prints could be explained if the killer was maneuvering to hide himself, perhaps because he heard a noise from the sidewalk in front of Bundy.

Another point of interest in Bill's testimony dealt with the blood pattern on the Bronco carpet on the driver's side, in "the part that you would step up into if you were getting into the car." He looked for a print that would come from blood in the grooves of the shoe.

Bill pointed to the print and identified "squiggles or little 'S' shapes that might represent the curved areas between the design elements" of the Bruno Magli shoe.

This was some of the most interesting forensic evidence in the trial. I later explained to Marcia that "showing that the shoe prints on the Bundy walk are consistent with the partial shoe print in the Bronco makes the fact that we didn't find the shoes almost irrelevant."

"Why?" she asked.

"Because the prints at Bundy are connected to the print in the Bronco, and the Bronco is connected to Simpson. So there's a chain of inferences linking the bloody Bundy shoe prints to the Bronco and to Simpson himself."

On the stand, Bill Bodziak testified that there were only forty locations in the United States and Puerto Rico that sold the Bruno Magli shoes that made the prints. He explained that we were not able to directly connect Simpson to that type of shoe "because every store had a problem searching their records back that far." However, Bill explained that in cases involving bloody shoe prints, perpetrators commonly dispose of their shoes and clothing because "it is obvious to the person who committed the crime that the clothing and the shoes are well covered with blood and that would be incriminating and they usually discard them."

Bill Bodziak testified that he "found three areas of a heel print on the front of [Nicole's] dress. . . . I cannot say that it was made by a Silga sole, but I can say that there was an impression which did share those three features."

Bill also examined an autopsy photo of Nicole's back. He testified that he "would interpret that as being either a toe or a heel impression and the beginning of a contusion as a result of contact with the shoe and the skin." In short, the killer placed his shoe on Nicole's back and ground her body into the bloody ground.

I concluded my direct by hammering home the key conclusions from Bill's analysis. While looking over at the jurors, I asked, "Mr. Bodziak, based upon your analysis of all of the items that we've discussed today, was there any indication that more than one pair of shoes was involved in this crime?"

"No, there was not."

I asked, "And based upon your comparison of the Bruno Magli shoe with the defendant's Reeboks, can you include him as a candidate who could have worn the shoes that created the impressions in this case?"

"Yes, I could include him as a candidate for possibly having worn those shoes."

"Okay. Thank you. I have nothing further."

In my interviews with Bill prior to his testimony he had told me that he felt the LAPD SID did a tremendous job in documenting the footwear-impression evidence in our case. He had said it was much better than what he is used to seeing. He also told me that the defense's contentions about officers tramping through possible footwear evidence were fallacious. This testimony would prove helpful in both boosting the image of the SID and illustrating to the jury the unfairness of the defense's attacks.

However, I decided not to elicit the evidence during direct. I felt that it would appear defensive and self-serving. I wanted Bailey to elicit the information first on cross-examination. My plan was to make a motion to preclude the defense from asking questions about crime-scene processing, which I knew Judge Ito would deny. I thought making the motion might lure the defense into questioning Bill about crime-scene issues.

Around the time I completed my direct, Robert Shapiro approached Bill during a court recess. Bob, as usual, was affable and friendly. He was also very complimentary to Bill. Bob said something to the effect of "you guys at the FBI do such an excellent job. Your work is so far beyond LAPD's. Their capabilities don't come anywhere close. It's really a shame."

I thought Shapiro was fishing. I figured he wanted Bill to say something that would indicate his opinion of how well the LAPD had investigated the crime scene regarding the shoe prints. This opinion would reveal whether it was safe to cross-examine Bill about the LAPD's performance. So before Bill could respond, I piped in with a truthful but ambiguous comment, "Bob, Bill doesn't think the LAPD did such a horrible job."

Bill Bodziak did not say much of anything during this exchange. However, I was now convinced that the defense would cross-examine Bill about the SID's performance. Seemingly, the fish had swallowed the bait.

On cross, Bailey opened by attempting to get Bodziak to criticize the LAPD's handling of the crime scene. Bailey asked, "What happens when officers . . . trample up the sidewalk before the technicians get there . . . ?"

Bill responded, "They could have marched a hundred people over them [the bloody footprints]. It wouldn't make any difference."

Bailey picked himself off the floor with another line of attack. He tried to imply that the LAPD may have destroyed valuable footwear-impression evidence in the leafy, narrow south pathway where the Rockingham glove was found. Bill explained: "With regard to leaves . . . I've never had a case where I had a footwear impression on leaves. . . . I've never seen one in over twenty years."

After Bailey's attempt to attack the LAPD was foiled, he posed a ludicrous hypothetical designed to imply that maybe the real killer stole a pair of Bruno Magli shoes from Simpson to commit the crime.

Bill explained, "You can always get into the hypotheticals . . . [that someone] could . . . have borrowed someone's shoes to commit a crime."

"Or steal?" Bailey asked.

"Or steal them or whatever, sure. There's always those possibilities," Bill admitted.

Bailey seemed stymied. So he tried another tack. "What are most bank robberies committed with by way of vehicles?"

"The perpetrator's vehicle," Bill retorted.

Bailey implied that Bill was wrong. "They usually steal a car."

Bailey had made two points. If people steal cars to commit bank robberies, maybe murderers steal shoes to commit murders. Moreover, Bodziak was wrong when he said that most bank robbers use their own vehicles. Bailey made another important point: If you want to rob a bank, don't take Bill Bodziak along.

Next, Bailey asked about the strange pattern of the shoe prints indicating that the killer had apparently stopped and made a quarter turn to his left. "And do you have any explanation as to how those were made?"

"[I]t appears likely that the person may have been standing over in that bush area where the tree was to get out of the line of sight."

Then Bailey zeroed in for the kill. He asked Bill about the fact that two of the prints seemed odd because a right shoe print was to the left of a left shoe print, as if someone were standing there with their legs crossed. Bailey thought he had Bill trapped. However, Bill deftly explained that the person could have stepped back out of the line of sight and stepped forward with his right foot. Then he stepped back out of the line of sight a second time and stepped forward with his left foot. "So there's a very logical explanation for that."

I looked over at Bailey. He was literally turning red. He quickly turned to an even more unsuccessful line of cross-examination. The two-killer theory. "Supposing you had two people with the same brand and size of shoe?" When I heard this question, I leaned over to Marcia, who was sitting next to me, and said, "Watch this. This is going to be good."

During my first lengthy interview with Bill, I had asked, "What would you say if they asked you whether two killers could have both been wearing size-twelve Bruno Magli shoes?"

Bill looked at me as if I were stupid. "That's preposterous."

"Yeah," I agreed. "But what will you say?"

"I'm not going to get asked that question," Bill snapped. "A first-year public defender wouldn't ask me that question."

"But what would you say?"

"Don't worry about it. They won't ask, and if they do, they'll appear ridiculous."

Bill never did tell me what his answer would be, but I knew it would be good.

So when Bailey posed the question, I thought Bill would bite his head off. However, at first Bill responded very mildly. "In my opinion, that would not occur in this case." It was as if Bill were trying to let Bailey off the hook.

But Bailey persisted, "Why not?"

"Because in all of the cases I've worked I can count on one hand the number of cases where a common shoe, like this Reebok, that's sold in many, many stores, both in size and design, was shared by two persons simultaneously at the crime scene. It has occurred, but only on a couple of occasions and only with common shoes."

Bill continued: "These [Magli] shoes were very uncommon, and most of the shoe stores around the country only carried at one time one size twelve. To conjecture . . . that two people independently bought size-twelve Bruno Magli shoes . . . from the same store or at different stores—and they were only sold by forty stores—and just happened to come to this crime together is impossible for me to believe."

Bailey didn't give up. "Would it be possible for two people to arrange . . . to arrive at a crime scene in the same footwear, make and model . . . ?"

"As I stated in my opinion, no. . . . And the reason I'm saying 'no' is because most people, even fairly knowledgeable people about evidence, would not have the degree of knowledge necessary to know where to find some kind of a rare shoe. . . . They would not be searching for a $160 to $180 Bruno Magli. . . . [I]n my opinion, it wouldn't happen. It's—it's uncanny. . . . I don't believe it happens intentionally or otherwise."

I was thinking, Give up, Lee, give up.

But he didn't. "But it's possible?"

Bill responded, "In my opinion, it's not even possible because it's so ridiculous!"

Stymied at every turn, Bailey, one of American's premier trial lawyers, a brilliant courtroom tactician, kept looking for a big finish. He addressed the testimony I elicited on direct that the vast majority of people with size-12 shoes tend to be between five-eleven and six-two. Simpson is six-two. Defense attorney Carl Douglas, who is about five-ten, was standing next to Bailey. Bailey asked Bill to estimate Carl Douglas's height.

Bill asked Bailey, "How tall are you?"

Bailey answered, "Five-nine."

Bill couldn't help but observe, "You've got raised heels on."

After Bill's testimony, I approached Cochran and Shapiro, shaking my head and smiling. Johnnie asked, "Did you know what he was going to say in explaining the pattern of the shoe prints?"

"Of course," I responded.

Then Shapiro, grinning from ear to ear, said, "Hank, you always get so lucky on [our] cross-examination."

29

No Splitting Hairs

"[T]HE MICROSCOPIC DEBRIS that cover our clothes and bodies are the mute witnesses, sure and faithful, of all of our movements and all of our encounters." This was the philosophy of famous early-twentieth-century forensic scientist Edmond Locard, who pioneered the field of trace analysis. The forensic science of trace analysis, which involves the microscopic comparison of hairs and fibers left at a crime scene, was first widely publicized during the infamous Atlanta Child Murders case. There the prosecution used a complex web of fiber evidence to connect the defendant to the brutal killings.

In *Simpson* such evidence was a small but important aspect of the case. The hair and fiber evidence was not subject to the defense's conspiracy and contamination arguments, which made it important enough for Marcia to decide to end our case with this evidence.

Douglas Deedrick is a special agent with the FBI. Doug bears no relationship to the stereotypical image of an FBI agent. He appears to be in his forties, with graying hair and wire-rimmed glasses that give him a scholarly look. He has a science background in biology. He was assigned to the FBI laboratory seventeen years ago. For the past two years he has been chief of the Hairs and Fibers Unit and is a world-class expert in his field.

As Doug explained on the stand, it is often possible to determine the race of a suspect from his or her hair. Moreover, because people are unique, there is great variation between one person's hair and another's when viewed under the microscope. During his direct Doug showed a chart with photomicrographs of hair from different

African Americans to illustrate the great variation from one person to the next.

He also explained that it is possible to examine fibers that come from fabrics. A microscopic examination will reveal whether they have the same characteristics. The fiber can be examined with a microspectrophotometer, which allows the examiner to determine small color differences between different fibers. Then fluorescent microscopy can be used. This procedure allows the examiner to determine the degree to which the fiber fluoresces under various lighting conditions. If the fiber is man-made, it can be examined through infrared spectroscopy, which measures the reaction infrared light produces as it passes through the fiber. Finally, a scanning electron microscope can be used to look at the cross section of the fiber. Different fibers, particularly man-made fibers, have very different looking cross sections.

The day before Doug's testimony, a dispute arose about a discovery issue. The defense claimed that they were not given adequate notice that Doug Deedrick would be using photomicrographs illustrating his opinion regarding Bronco carpet fibers found on the knit cap and Rockingham glove. Doug wanted to show that this particular carpet was relatively rare and was only used in Broncos for a short period of time.

At first, Judge Ito found no discovery violation. He said, "An obvious area of inquiry would be to the Ford Motor Company to ask them about the types of fibers that are installed in the Broncos. . . . [B]ecause this information was available to either side, anybody could have picked up the phone and called Dearborn [Ford headquarters] and gotten this information. I don't find a violation there."

Thus, Judge Ito ruled in our favor and would not preclude any evidence. However, the next day, the arguments continued. Doug gave the defense his notes from the various carpet manufacturers he contacted to determine the uniqueness of the Bronco carpet-fiber evidence. Through an oversight, Doug did not tell Marcia about the existence of the notes until the last minute. Cochran, with the bombast that characterized so many of the legal arguments in the case, called the late production of the notes "perhaps the most egregious, outrageous thing that has happened in this trial thus far."

In the course of arguing the motion to preclude the information, Cochran tried to use me as an example of how discovery was supposed to be properly conducted. He said, "Mr. Goldberg, who I think had Mr. Bodziak, he understood what the [discovery] obligation was, he works under Marcia Clark, so certainly she understood. They complied with it with Bodziak and the FBI. Things went smoothly. There was no attempt to deceive, and we went right through it, Your Honor."

I found those comments quite amusing. Now that it served their interests, the defense was trying to hold me up as a shining example of a prosecutor properly fulfilling his discovery obligations. This argument was made after the defense had the judge rake me over the coals for introducing evidence regarding the irrelevant airline ticket and baggage claim.

After the arguments were over, Judge Ito, in an apparent reversal of his ruling the previous day, ruled that "the prosecution will be precluded from presenting any evidence that is contained in then report [by Deedrick regarding the rarity of the Bronco fiber]."

Why did Judge Ito reverse himself? I have no idea. Had this evidence been admitted, it would have shown that Doug traced the carpet fibers found on the Rockingham glove and the knit cap to one particular company, Midland, which manufactured the carpet for General Motors. The particular carpet was only used in Broncos made between June 1993 and June 1994, including Simpson's Bronco.

Marcia, in her direct, began intricately weaving a web connecting together the key pieces of physical evidence, the crime scene, and Simpson.

Doug found hairs consistent with Nicole "on the [Rockingham] glove . . . a glove found at the Bundy location . . . as well as from the knit hat that was recovered at the Bundy location. Hairs that exhibited the same characteristics as those of Nicole Brown Simpson were also found on the pants and shirt of Ronald Goldman."

Doug testified that the hair consistent with Nicole on the Rockingham glove "did appear to be forcibly removed. It's approximately twelve inches long and was broken at the proximal end or at the end nearest the point of attachment near the skin." He continued: On Ron's shirt "[t]here were about thirty-five forcibly removed hairs" consistent with Nicole.

Marcia elicited this evidence to corroborate the prosecution's theory that Simpson probably attacked Nicole first. In the process of moving between Nicole and Ron, he unknowingly transported thirty-five of Nicole's hairs to Ron's shirt.

Marcia asked, "If you were to assume the following events, sir. That the killer pulled back Nicole's head with his hand, with his left hand, in order to slit her throat with his right hand and then went over to Ron Goldman for [the] final attack, touching him in the process with the hand that held Nicole's hair by the head, could that account for the hairs that you found on Ron Goldman's shirt . . . ?"

Deedrick replied, "Yes. That could account for the presence of those hairs."

However, Doug's most significant testimony related African-American head hairs consistent with Simpson's "coming from . . . a knit cap that was recovered from the crime scene [and] Ronald Goldman's shirt." On and inside the knit cap there were twelve hairs consistent with those taken from Simpson. At least nine of them were inside the cap. The defendant's hair was distinctive because "it had very light pigmentation."

He added that African-American limb hair (such as from arms, legs, or hands) was also found on "the Rockingham glove and Ronald Goldman's shirt."

Doug also testified that carpet fibers consistent with the Bronco were found on the knit cap at Bundy and on the Rockingham glove. This fiber was unique. Doug testified, "I have worked for many years with carpet fibers and I had not seen this particular cross section before."

Doug found a number of blue-black cotton fibers on the Rockingham glove, Ron's shirt, and one of the socks found in Simpson's bedroom. Doug explained that this evidence linked all three items together, since all three came into recent contact with a fabric that contained blue-black cotton. Thus, the Rockingham glove, Ron's shirt, and Simpson's socks were all linked to a fabric that contained blue-black cotton, and Simpson was last seen wearing a blue-black cotton jumpsuit.

The table below summarizes the hair and trace evidence presented in the case. (An *X* indicates that the particular hair or fiber was found on the item.)

ITEM	DEFEN-DANT'S HAIR	BLUE-BLACK COTTON FIBER	KATO (DOG)	BRONCO CARPET	RON'S HAIR	NICOLE'S HAIR
Rockingham glove	African-American limb hair	X	X	X	X	X
Ron's shirt	X	X	X		X	X
Socks		X				
Bundy cap	X			X		X

On cross, Bailey did not try to explain away this evidence by either a conspiracy or planting theory. He did get into a strange dialogue about what the words *same, similar,* and *random* mean.

The only thing in Bailey's cross that seemed to be an attempt to explain some of the hair and fiber evidence was very cryptic. "Were you informed that a defense investigator in the company of a lead detective in this case discovered in a closet on the second floor of the Bundy residence a knit cap similar in appearance to the one found near the body of Ronald Goldman?" It turned out that this knit cap was probably a child's knit cap. But Bailey seemed to be suggesting that if Simpson left a knit cap in a closet at Bundy, he also could have dropped a knit cap, perhaps weeks before the murders, in the garden next to where Ron's body was later discovered. Maybe it was just an unlucky coincidence that Ron was murdered within inches of this cap.

The hair and fiber evidence alone would have convicted any defendant in any other case. Unlike the DNA evidence, the hair and trace evidence is easily understood. Moreover, there was no serious effort by the defense to even explain this compelling evidence. Bailey did not try to conjure up the far-fetched hypotheticals he used during his cross of Bill Bodziak, the shoe-print expert. Bailey did not suggest that maybe the police had some of Simpson's hair on file and planted it in the knit cap or sprinkled blue-black cotton fibers on the Rockingham glove, Ron's shirt, and Simpson's socks. At most, he seemed to explain the evidence by using a third defense. The evidence resulted from an unfortunate set of coincidences, of almost cosmic proportions, which unjustly pointed to Orenthal James Simpson.

The hair and fiber evidence did not fit under the umbrella of the contamination and conspiracy theories. It was a powerful note upon which to rest a powerful case.

After 58 witnesses and 488 exhibits, the people rested.

30

The Brentwood Gang

THE DEFENSE OPENED their case on July 10, with their "demeanor witnesses." Most people have probably heard of character witnesses, but never demeanor witnesses. Neither had I. Trying to predict what type of a demeanor would be inconsistent with having murdered someone is something even expert psychologists would not hazard to attempt.

For example, Arnelle Simpson, the defendant's attractive daughter, was the first witness in the defense case. She described her father, upon learning of Nicole's murders, as "distraught." When Cochran pressed her to describe what she meant, she described Simpson as "numb, he was quiet, just sitting on the couch."

Does that mean emotionless? I wondered. Simpson's behavior was equally consistent with that of a person who knows he just murdered someone and is afraid of getting caught.

Marcia, apparently concluding that this testimony was subjective and equivocal, barely asked any questions during her exceptionally mild cross-examination.

Carmelita Simpson-Durio, Simpson's sister, and Simpson's mother, Eunice, offered similar testimony regarding his demeanor. There was no arguing with the love they felt for Simpson. However, in criminal cases, a defendant is permitted to call character witnesses to testify that he or she could not have committed the crime. Such testimony was conspicuously absent. Never did any of these witnesses testify that Simpson would have been incapable of having committed these murders.

The reason, undoubtedly, is if a defendant "opens the door" by presenting character evidence, then the prosecution can counter that evidence. The prosecution is allowed to cross-examine the character witnesses as to whether they had heard reports and even rumors concerning the defendant's character that were inconsistent with their testimony. For example, we might have been able to ask, "Had you heard that Nicole told friends that she thought Simpson was going to kill her?" Normally, such hearsay evidence would be inadmissible. But when the defense places character in issue, the door is thrown open—a risk Simpson could not afford to take.

To counter the overwhelming forensic evidence pointing to Simpson, the defense produced witness Carol Connors. She testified that Simpson had enjoyed an "exquisite romantic moment" with his girlfriend, Paula Barbieri, at a benefit the day before the murders. An even more probative witness, Mary Collins, an interior designer, testified that Simpson and Barbieri were preparing to redecorate Simpson's home.

By the close of this phase of the defense case, it was apparent that the prosecution's character evidence, all of which involved domestic abuse, went unanswered.

Next, the defense called a bevy of time-line witnesses, whom I called, collectively, the Brentwood Gang. A couple on a blind date, Ellen Aaronson and Dan Mandel, had dinner at the Mezzaluna on the night of the murders. They agreed that they were strolling past Bundy between 10:15 and 10:30 P.M. and did not hear barking dogs. Nor did they see Nicole's body. Marcia established that both witnesses gave prior conflicting statements about the time they left Mezzaluna. Earlier, through Detective Lange, Marcia had established that Nicole's body was not visible to a person on the sidewalk outside her condominium unless one made a special effort to look. Did Ms. Aaronson or Mr. Mandel look up Nicole's walkway? No.

Denise Pilnak testified that she was a stickler for time. In fact, she often wore two watches, which she happily demonstrated to the jury. She did not hear barking dogs before 10:30 P.M. On cross, Marcia portrayed Pilnak as a Simpson-case groupie: for one thing, she had appeared in news footage taped outside the Bundy crime scene the day after the murders. Ms. Pilnak assured the jury that the next day she just happened to be captured on news footage, this time in front of Rockingham. Moreover, the times to which she was testifying were at variance with what she had previously told the police. This was very embarrassing for a witness who prides herself on wearing two watches.

Another witness was Robert Heidstra, a fiftyish gentleman of French descent, who has lived for many years in the area of Nicole's condo. He testified to hearing voices at 10:45 P.M. near Nicole's condo. He admitted under cross his desire to make a buck from the Simpson case. Chris painted him as a man who wanted to testify regardless of which side called him. Chris elicited from Heidstra that he had earlier said to a friend, a Ms. Patricia Baret, that he had heard two voices near Nicole's condo. One of the voices belonged to a younger man, and the angry voice appeared to be that of an older black man.

Taking another opportunity to interject race into the case, Cochran claimed that Chris's suggestion—that it is possible to tell whether a voice sounded black—was "a racist statement." It did not seem to matter to Cochran that Chris had not made the statement; Heidstra had.

Heidstra may have done the defense more harm than good when he claimed to have seen a white vehicle, possibly a Bronco, drive away from the area of Nicole's condominium after the incident.

Of course, the real problem with the defense time-line witnesses was that even if the jury accepted the defense position that the murders occurred between 10:30 and 10:40 P.M., this gave Simpson ample time, between fourteen and twenty-four minutes, to make it back to Rockingham in time for Allan Park to have seen him at 10:54 P.M. The drive takes about six minutes. Chris drove this point home with Heidstra himself when he asked whether a person leaving Bundy at 10:35 to 10:40 P.M. could arrive at Rockingham at 10:52 P.M. "Yes," Heidstra admitted.

Following Heidstra were a series of defense witnesses who testified to seeing Simpson the night of the murders—more "demeanor witnesses." Collectively, their testimony was susceptible to any inference one wanted to draw.

For example, Capt. Wayne Stanfield, an American Airlines pilot who flew the plane that night to Chicago, testified that Simpson's behavior appeared to be normal. Then he offered that he got up at 2:45 A.M. to stretch his legs. He noticed that Simpson was looking out the window pensively, lost in thought, while the rest of the passengers were apparently sleeping. The point is that none of the witnesses knew, of course, how a murderer acts after committing a crime: perhaps one would remain awake at 2:45 A.M. and stare off into space while the other passengers are sleeping.

Two other witnesses at the airport described their brief encounter with Simpson after his limo arrived. The defense elicited that neither witness noticed any cuts on Simpson's hands. This defense tactic was strange, since they were conceding that Simpson had been, in fact, cut and had bled all over Rockingham that night.

Jim Merrill, a Hertz employee who had picked up Simpson at the Chicago airport, told the jury that later, when Simpson was leaving Chicago, Merrill rushed to the airport trying to put Simpson's golf clubs on the flight back to Los Angeles but missed the plane. Defense attorney Carl Douglas asked whether there was a time when Simpson called about the bags.

"Yes," Merrill responded. Simpson called the next day.

Think about it. The defense had spent several days with a gaggle of witnesses to paint Simpson as calm, relaxed, and affable before he learned of the murders and bereaved afterward. Now they elicited that in his grief, the day after learning of Nicole's murder, he was able to take the time to check on his golf bags.

After a week of watching the demeanor testimony and time-line witnesses torn to shreds, the defense brought forward a distinguished doctor, Robert Huizanga. He testified as to Simpson's medical condition at the time of the murders. On direct he said that Simpson looked like Tarzan but was walking like Tarzan's grandfather. On cross-examination, Brian forced the doctor to admit that a patient often lies about his medical condition. The doctor added that an athlete would often hide the full extent of his condition to get a fat pro-contract. The point was that if a man would lie about his injuries to get a football contract, wouldn't he lie to save himself from going to jail.

After Brian Kelberg's withering cross-examination, Huizanga was forced to admit that nothing would have prevented Simpson from having committed the murders, and little was left standing of the good doctor's testimony.

The testimony of exercise instructor Richard Walsh was not any more helpful to the defense. He had appeared with Simpson in a now-famous exercise video. Walsh corroborated the prosecution's position that Simpson was physically capable of committing the murders. Moreover, the videotape captured Simpson making an offhanded comment, while shadowboxing: "If you hit your wife you can blame it on the video."

After two weeks of blunders and missteps and presenting testimony that often helped us more than it did Simpson, the defense was ready to turn to a new phase of their case, their attack on the scientific evidence.

31

Hiding the Test Results

THE DEFENSE LAUNCHED its attack on the forensic evidence by calling Fredric Rieders to testify as to whether the blood on the rear gate and the socks had EDTA in it. EDTA is an anticoagulant that is in blood vials such as the one containing Simpson's blood sample. It is also commonly used as a preservative in processed foods. Therefore, people naturally have a small amount of EDTA in their blood. However, we could determine whether the blood on the rear gate came from Simpson's blood vial by knowing how much EDTA was in it.

By now, I had learned that toxicology, the science of testing body fluids to determine the presence of chemical substances, such as drugs, did not provide clear-cut answers. Testing does not always produce definitive results. There is a gray area. The tests are so sensitive that it is possible to detect extremely minute amounts of a substance, quantities so small that it may be difficult to determine with certainty what the substance is.

For example, early in the case, there were persistent rumors that Simpson and Kato Kaelin did not go to McDonald's on the night of the murders and instead went to a Burger King parking lot, where they purchased methamphetamine. Interestingly, none of the McDonald's employees remembered seeing O. J. Simpson or his Bentley. However, no *credible* witnesses could substantiate the methamphetamine purchase.

The LAPD toxicology report of Simpson's blood concluded that it was "negative" for methamphetamine. However, the test had detected very minute particles consistent with methamphetamine in his blood. Thus, the result fell into a "gray" area where it could not be determined with certainty whether he ingested methamphetamine shortly before the murders.

The same kinds of issues were involved regarding EDTA. The amounts of particles consistent with EDTA on the rear gate and on the sock samples were so minute that the FBI laboratory report concluded that no EDTA was present.

However, the test results fell sufficiently into the "gray" area and allowed defense expert Fredric Rieders to offer a different interpretation of the FBI results. He testified that EDTA was present in samples taken from the rear gate and stains of Nicole's blood on one of the socks. However, he never conducted his own testing.

Roger Martz, the FBI scientist who actually tested the samples, also drew a sample of his own blood. He testified that the levels of particles consistent with EDTA in his own blood were comparable to samples from the rear gate and the sock. However, the amount of EDTA in Simpson's blood vial was significantly greater. Marcia dramatically illustrated this point by showing the jury two graphs that were generated during the EDTA testing, which compared the molecular composition of the blood from the rear gate to the blood from Simpson's vial. The graph representing the rear-gate blood looked nothing like the one representing the blood vial. Roger Martz concluded that the blood on the rear gate and socks could not have come from Simpson's vial. "Those stains did not come from preserved blood."

Defense attorney Blasier, while questioning Roger Martz, attempted to explain the absence of EDTA in the rear-gate blood by suggesting it could have bleached out in the sunlight. Martz said this would not occur with EDTA, a stable compound.

Although the defense continued to argue that EDTA was present in the blood and that evidence was planted, they never did introduce any evidence of their own testing. Nor did they introduce test results on items which we did not test for EDTA, such as the Bundy blood trail or blood in the Bronco. During the trial, Rock Harmon discovered that the defense did conduct EDTA testing on one of the blood drops from the Bundy trail. Legally, the jury was not entitled to learn of this. But why would the defense not present their own test results? Maybe they did not like them.

32

Moving a Pawn to Check a King

As I sat in my cubicle one afternoon reviewing the reports we had received from the defense's forensic-science witnesses, I came across something that floored me. A report from Dr. John Gerdes, a defense microbiologist, claimed that his review of LAPD's DNA testing program showed outrageously high contamination levels. I immediately went over to Woody's cubicle to ask a few questions.

Pointing to the report, I asked Woody, "What's this?"

Woody responded matter-of-factly. "It's a report from—"

I interrupted, "I know. I mean, what accounts for all this alleged contamination Gerdes is talking about?"

By this time I was well aware that some contamination occurs in all DNA PCR testing in any lab, including Gerdes's. However, the test has numerous controls and safeguards that are built in to detect it.

Woody said, "What Gerdes's report really shows is that the safeguards and controls worked. They did what they are supposed to do. They detected the contaminant."

"What are you supposed to do when you detect it?"

Woody replied, "You junk the particular test and you do it again. It's that simple. That's what Gerdes's lab does, and that's what LAPD does."

"But what about the levels of contamination Gerdes is claiming?" I asked.

Woody changed his voice as if he were breaking the news to me of the death of a loved one. He knew that in the Simpson case the

SID was my bailiwick. "Hank, the fact is that the levels of contamination showing up in LAPD's testing are significantly higher than they should be in this type of testing. That's what Gerdes is basically going to testify about—what happened in other cases, not what happened in our case."

"What happened in other cases? But in our case the tests were great." I said.

"That's right," Woody replied. "The LAPD tests in our case are clean as a whistle." Woody waved his hands with his palms facing me to emphasize the point. "In fact, they are better than Cellmark's."

"So what gives credibility to Gerdes's claim that LAPD's test results can't be trusted," I asked.

Woody laughed. "Seven months into the trial and you're talking about credibility. How credible is it that Vannatter and Fuhrman invaded the Bronco and planted blood in it at five A.M.?"

The defense called John Gerdes, clinical director of Clinical Associates of Denver, a DNA laboratory that conducts testing for medical purposes. Gerdes had both strengths and weaknesses. Whatever may be his competence as a medical DNA expert, in forensic DNA testing he is an inexperienced scientific lightweight. His strength is that he has substantial experience as a professional witness and has mastered the image of a dispassionate, calm scientist.

During his direct examination, Gerdes laid out the defense's contamination theory, basically that the SID was a dirty lab. However, the most striking part of this theory was that he conceded that the most important pieces of evidence were not contaminated. For example, regarding the test results showing the victims' blood on the Rockingham glove, Gerdes said, "In that particular case, there is an adequate amount of DNA; it could not have been explained by cross-contamination."

When I heard Gerdes's testimony conceding the Rockingham glove, Bronco console, socks, and rear gate, I was astonished. When Woody returned from court that day, I observed, "How unbelievably convenient. Every single piece of evidence that the defense claims was planted the testing worked fine on. The only criticism he has is as to the one piece they can't claim was planted, the Bundy trail. Since the Bundy trail was collected before they ever had Simpson's blood, they can't argue planting. So they argue contamination."

Woody, smiling, agreed.

I continued: "It's so pat, so convenient. It's ludicrous. The jury's got to see through this."

On cross-examination, Woody launched several lines of attack which related to the overall strategy Rock, Woody, and I had developed for our section of the case.

First, Woody attacked Gerdes's embarrassing lack of qualifications in forensic DNA testing. This strategy would prove important because it was a component of our overall plan as to how to deal with the defense attack on our forensic evidence. The only other defense witness to offer testimony about the SID's performance would be Larry Ragle, the retired director of the Orange County Sheriff's Department Crime Laboratory. If I could successfully show that Ragle was unqualified, then the only qualified defense witness left who could attack the SID would be Dr. Henry Lee. If Dr. Lee did not testify about the SID's handling of the evidence and contamination issues, we could ask the jury, "Why did the only qualified witness, Dr. Lee, remain silent on the issue of SID and contamination?"

On cross, Woody asked Gerdes, "How many times have you conducted a PCR analysis on evidentiary materials, such as in this case?"

"We don't do PCR on evidentiary material."

Woody then asked Gerdes how many of his publications were "about forensic stain analysis?"

"None of them."

Woody posed two more questions about Gerdes's dearth of published writings. "Do you have any publication that deals with the area of PCR contamination in forensics . . . ? How many publications have you written, Dr. Gerdes, describing why PCR shouldn't be used in forensics?"

The answer to both questions was "None."

"Are you a member of the American Academy of Forensic Sciences . . . ? The American Society of Crime Laboratory Directors . . . ? Did you attend, for instance, the last annual meeting of the American Academy of Forensic Scientists . . . ? Or the one before that . . . ? Or any that have ever occurred . . . ?"

"No."

"You have no specific forensic training; isn't that correct . . . ? You have never taken a class in forensic science . . . ? You have never taught a class in forensic science . . . ? You have no training whatsoever in police evidence-gathering techniques, correct?"

"No formal training."

Woody pressed on. "It is true, isn't it, that you have conducted no experiments in the forensic area . . . ? You have done no studies to determine the effects of sunlight, rain, moisture, et cetera, on crime-scene samples; isn't that correct . . . ? You have never tested evidence in a criminal case, correct . . . ? Do you believe you are an expert in physically—and I'm sorry—analyzing evidence using DNA typing . . . ?"

Gerdes answered no to these questions.

Woody elicited significant information to prove that Gerdes was a "hired gun." He regularly earns money on the side inspecting forensic laboratories. He had inspected six labs as of the date he testified and had testified twenty-three times in forensic cases against DNA testing. His laboratory receives $100 an hour when he testifies. His lab would be paid approximately $30,000 for his testimony in the trial. Gerdes admitted that in every case in which he testified he always testified *against* PCR testing.

During Woody's cross-examination, he subtly elicited information that probably went unnoticed to most observers, but when I heard it, it went off like a bomb in the hold of a ship and should have sunk the entire contamination theory.

Barry Scheck's cross-examination style of telegraphing every point in clear, unmistakable terms is not always the preferred approach. Sometimes it is better to make one's points quietly so that the witness and hopefully the opposing counsel fail to realize what has happened until it's too late to correct it. This was almost impossible to accomplish with perceptive attorneys like Scheck and Neufeld. However, in this particular line of questioning neither Scheck nor Neufeld picked up what Woody was doing.

On direct, Scheck had Gerdes testify that the Bundy PCR trail results could have resulted from contamination. Woody, however, knew that Greg Matheson had used conventional testing on one of the drops from the Bundy trail that implicated Simpson. Woody had proved that the conventional testing could not be explained under a contamination theory. He asked, "If conventional serological techniques were used in this case . . . don't those constitute additional cross-checks of results?"

"Yes."

Woody asked, "*Is it your testimony that such cross-contamination would necessarily never be detected by serological techniques?"* (emphasis added)

"I think it is highly unlikely because PCR is the most sensitive method possible . . . ." (emphasis added)

This seemingly mundane testimony was critical. Gerdes was saying that it would be "highly unlikely" that cross-contamination could account for the fact that Greg Matheson's conventional test result pointed to Simpson. Greg's conventional serological typing, which showed that the blood on the Bundy trail matched Simpson's and that only 0.5 percent of the population has that blood, could not be explained through the contamination theory.

Another major component of Woody's strategy was to show that Gerdes was, in effect, biased against ever using PCR under any circumstances in criminal cases. Woody and I knew that Dr. Lee was a strong supporter of PCR technology in criminal cases. Therefore, if Woody set up Gerdes properly, I could use Dr. Lee to knock him down. On cross-examination Woody Clarke wanted to make Gerdes's position on PCR unequivocally clear. Gerdes testified that PCR was not ready to be used in criminal cases.

Woody showed that calling Gerdes to comment on the propriety of the SID's DNA testing would be like calling a member of the Flat Earth Society to comment on Christopher Columbus's efforts to seek a new route to India. Gerdes simply does not believe in using PCR under any circumstances in criminal cases. More importantly, Woody's cross-examination set up Gerdes perfectly for a fall when Dr. Lee testified. Just as Rock and Woody had used their witnesses to help clean up after Dennis Fung and Andrea Mazzola, I would use Dr. Lee to clean up what little remained of Gerdes. I had once looked toward cross-examining Dr. Lee with trepidation. Now I couldn't wait.

When I heard, just days before his expected testimony, that I was supposed to cross-examine former Orange County Crime Laboratory director Larry Ragle, I marched directly over to Marcia's office. Goddamnit, I thought, he's been on the defense's witness list for months.

I knocked loudly on Marcia's office door. When I opened it, she was talking to Chris Darden and Bill Hodgman. "Ragle has been on the witness list for months. I'm really pissed that no one told me

A. Mark Fuhrman is pointing to the Bundy glove. The knit cap, which contained numerous hairs both inside and out consistent with Simpson, is just above. To the right of Fuhrman's hand is a bloody Bruno Magli heel impression. In the upper-lefthand corner, a portion of Ron Goldman's shoe is visible.

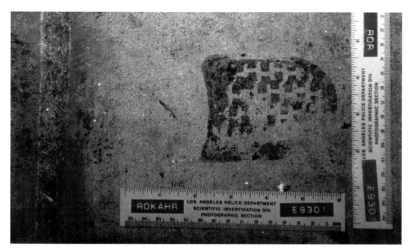

B. A close-up of one of the bloody size-12 Bruno Magli shoe prints left on the Bundy walkway. Note the distinctive squigglelike pattern of the tread. All of the distinct footwear impressions were consistent with a size-12 Bruno Magli shoe, a casual shoe retailing for $160 and sold at only forty locations in the United States. Simpson regularly purchased size-12 men's shoes at one of these locations.

C. The cards in this picture indicate the locations of two of the blood drops in the Bundy trail leading back to the alley. Conventional and DNA testing on this blood showed they were consistent with Simpson.

D. A blood drop on the Bundy trail that matched Simpson.

E. The location of one of the blood drops leading up the Rockingham driveway. The entrance to Simpson's home is to the right of the potted plants. The defense conceded this blood was Simpson's.

F. A close-up of one of the drops of Simpson's blood on the Rockingham blood trail.

G. The Rockingham glove was found on the south service pathway behind Kato's room. Testing on the glove showed blood consistent with Simpson, Ron, and Nicole. The glove contained African-American limb hairs, and hairs consistent with Ron and Nicole. It also contained fiber consistent with Simpson's Bronco carpet and blue-black cotton fiber consistent with the clothes Kato testified he saw Simpson wearing the night of the murders.

H. After the console was removed from the Bronco, blood was readily observed in the four numbered areas. The console contained mixtures of blood from Simpson, Goldman, and Nicole. The defense claimed that hours after Simpson bled on the Bronco console, Fuhrman broke in and rubbed the Rockingham glove on this portion of the console, thereby depositing Goldman's and Nicole's blood from the glove. To vote not guilty, the jury would have to have accepted this scenario as reasonable.

about this sooner!" Everyone in the room looked at me quizzically, as if I were speaking a foreign language. This was the only time that even a slightly angry word had ever passed between us.

"I'm sorry, Hankster," Marcia said. "You understand the crime-scene and evidence-collection issues better than anyone, so I figured you can do this easily."

I took a long look around Marcia's office. Marcia, Chris, and Bill were buried in paperwork. I realized that they had to be preoccupied with the mushrooming Fuhrman issues. The Fuhrman-McKinny tapes had just surfaced. Maybe I had no reason to complain. After all, I had a couple of days to prepare. Often lawyers in our office do not have that long to prepare entire jury trials. Someone may give them the case file only hours before the trial begins. It's called a "handoff."

Marcia, Chris, and Bill were still looking at me. I cleared my throat and backed out the door. "Sorry, guys. Back to work. I'll handle it."

As it turned out, the defense postponed calling Ragle for a day or two, giving me extra time.

I wanted to closely model my handling of Ragle after Woody's cross of Gerdes. If I could show that Ragle was as unqualified as Gerdes, my cross would neatly dovetail with Woody's. This would support our strategy of making Dr. Lee the only defense witness qualified to talk about crime-scene investigation, evidence collection, and testing.

On August 21, 1995, Ragle hit the stand. On direct, he criticized the SID's work in handling the crime scene. However, his criticisms did not relate to the reliability of the evidence that had been collected or the tests that had been performed. For example, he heavily criticized the paperwork Dennis Fung and Andrea Mazzola had filled out as being incomplete.

I started my cross by showing that Ragle did not have any recent hands-on experience at crime scenes. "And, sir, is it a correct statement of the record and your testimony in this case that it has been nineteen years since you've actually been in the field as a criminalist and processed a crime scene?"

"Yes," he admitted.

I asked Ragle about the leading forensic textbooks that I had read in preparation for my part of the case. I asked him about Richard Saferstein's leading text, *Criminalistics*. Ragle testified that he recognized it was a leading text. "And you've relied on this in forming your opinions about crime-scene investigation; is that correct?"

"No."

"You haven't?" I asked incredulously.

"No."

"Is there some reason for that?" I asked.

"I don't have it," he said sheepishly.

I then went through a similar litany of questions about other leading forensic-science testbooks on crime-scene investigation. Ragle admitted he had not read any of them.

After establishing that he was not familiar with the standard literature on crime scenes, I asked, "Now, in the area of serology, conventional serology, do you consider yourself to be an expert?"

"In doing the tests, no."

I continued. "Would you say that someone who is an expert in both . . . DNA testing and/or conventional serology would be in a better position to answer those kinds of questions?"

"About the [test] results, yes."

Toward the end of Ragle's cross-examination, we had a side-bar conference in which I was seeking permission to show pictures of Ragle leaning into the Bronco and pointing out a stain. He was not wearing a hair net, lab coat, or gloves. This was to impeach Ragle's testimony that when close to evidence one should wear such items. Judge Ito allowed the photos. During this side bar, Judge Ito said to me, "You're devastating him."

After Ragle's cross, I felt that our strategy of showing that Dr. Lee was the only qualified defense expert on crime scenes was a success.

Even the media experts seemed to understand this. *L.A. Times* critic Prof. Laurie Levenson said: "Hank Goldberg did what he had to do with Ragle. He showed him to be an 'expert' who had not touched a crime scene for years and is unfamiliar with leading textbooks on crime scene investigation. More important, Goldberg used Ragle to confirm that it is 'meshuga' to think that the Rockingham glove contaminated the evidence at Bundy."

The use of the word "meshuga" refers to the most lighthearted dispute in the trial. Before Ragle was called, I told Judge Ito that I should have been given discovery relating to Ragle's inspection of the Bronco. The defense countered by saying that since I was present during the inspection, I had seen what happened. I told Judge Ito that being present meant little, since the defense often predicated conspiracy theories on staple holes and microscopic specks. Therefore, I couldn't tell what Ragle and the defense were looking at when they were examining the Bronco. They were crawling around and looking in cracks between the door and the doorjamb, and they just looked as if they were "meshuga."

Barry objected. "He's got to pronounce that word better. . . . It's meshugana."

I jokingly countered, "This is Los Angeles. It's an L.A. pronunciation."

That evening, the biggest *Simpson* news was the "meshuga" dispute. Incidentally, the only thing that the critics ever unanimously agreed on in the trial was that I was right. Yiddish experts were summoned. In Los Angeles, NBC sportscaster Fred Roggin affirmed my proper use of the word but conceded that Scheck was not entirely wrong. Had I known that my use of this Yiddish word would attract so much attention, I would have recited an entire Shakespearean sonnet in Yiddish shortly before Dennis Fung's testimony, just to distract the critics.

33

Preparing for Dr. Charisma

DEFENSE ATTORNEY ROBERT SHAPIRO summoned Dr. Henry Lee to assist in Simpson's defense almost before the victim's blood had dried on the Bundy walkway.

Among the forensic-science witnesses, Dr. Lee arguably won the award for charm and charisma. After the verdict, one attractive young juror on *Nightline* rhapsodized over Dr. Lee as though he were a combination of Mickey Mantle, Tom Cruise, and Mother Teresa. The juror explained to Ted Koppel that when Dr. Lee used charts and his pointer, he taught the jury. He told them, "Something is wrong." Koppel did not probe by asking, What did he teach you? What was wrong?

Robert Shapiro now implies that the defense case against the forensic evidence was won when Henry Lee came aboard. If Dr. Lee really did play such an important role in the jurors' minds, we must carefully examine his testimony, particularly what he meant when he said, "Something wrong." The jury should have as well.

Dr. Lee, director of the Connecticut State Crime Laboratory, is a formidable witness. He has compiled a resumé that stretches over thirty-eight pages. He is considered one of the foremost forensic-science experts in the country and is known internationally. A *New York Times* article quoted a prominent New Haven defense attorney as saying, " 'If I were Marcia Clark, and I had heard that Henry Lee was coming on, I would not have slept that night. He's not the kind of adversary you'd want in any case.' " Hearing that I would be assigned the task of cross-examining Dr. Lee was akin to being informed that I would have to spar a few rounds with Mike Tyson (and, at the time, I didn't know that *this* "Mike Tyson" had a glass jaw).

For me, the task of preparing to cross-examine an expert witness involves several steps. First, I get general background information about the expert. A young attorney assigned to assist me, Diana Martinez, searched through computer data bases for newspaper articles about Dr. Lee. Diana is an attractive young attorney in her early thirties who worked doggedly to help me put together the thousand-piece puzzle that constituted my end of the case.

One Friday evening, Diana came into my office and handed me a three-inch stack of newspaper articles, neatly arranged in one of the six green notebooks I used to organize my materials on Henry Lee. "Some light reading for the weekend," she said, laughing.

Among the articles was one in the *Connecticut Law Tribune* entitled "The Redoubtable Dr. Lee." I wasn't encouraged. The caption read: "Prosecutors exult, defense lawyers quake and jurors swoon when Connecticut's chief criminalist takes the stand." Prominent Connecticut attorneys offered some sage advice on dealing with Lee. "Rearrange your defense so you don't have to go against him." Not an option. "[L]ong-winded attempts to discredit him only serve to make him look more credible. . . . Get him off the stand as quickly as possible."

I also had several conversations with Dr. Lee over the phone. My dialogue with him had a quality similar to a game of cat-and-mouse. I was trying to find out to what, specifically, he would testify. Dr. Lee seemed to be trying to determine specifically what questions I would ask him. There were certain things that he didn't tell me. For example, he didn't tell me he was going to say, "Something wrong," which turned out to be, to the jury, one of the most important "forensic" opinions offered during the trial. I didn't tell him certain things. For example, I didn't tell him that the imprints at the crime scene that he thought could have been caused by shoes were probably bloody fabric impressions of Ron's jeans.

During these conversations, Dr. Lee always turned to one topic: his examination of the socks at the LAPD lab in February 1995. He loudly proclaimed, "I change my gloves between handling each sock. Collin Yamauchi doesn't know what he's talking about when he say I didn't change gloves!"

I would answer, "Henry, from a scientific standpoint it doesn't matter whether or not you changed gloves. There's no reason to change them. Who cares?''

He would reply, "I know there is no reason to change them. But I changed the gloves!"

It seemed to be a point of honor with him, as if his standing in the forensic community turned on this topic. I then would try to change the subject. But throughout, it remained a personal sore point with Henry. In fact, I was present during Henry's sock examination, and I did not see him change gloves. Neither did the D.A. investigator Mike Stevens, who was present. Neither did the LAPD criminalist who monitored the sock examination.

However, I never brought this up with Dr. Lee because I didn't want him to be unnecessarily angry at me. I felt that he was more likely to be helpful to the prosecution if we were on friendly terms. But the glove-changing conversations did give me some insight into him: he obviously felt he had to be right. This character trait could be used during his cross-examination. Otherwise, our conversations were friendly and professional. Henry is a very affable person.

It became apparent to me that aside from his expertise Dr. Lee is a canny witness who knows how to use a jury. He establishes an immediate rapport with jurors and understands how to employ humor to lighten some of the cumbersome technical evidence.

My problem: How aggressively and extensively should I cross-examine Dr. Lee? One weekend afternoon prior to my cross, I spoke to Marcia and Chris about the various options. I also asked Marcia about the mystery package that the defense turned over to the court during the preliminary hearing, which turned out to have a stiletto in it. "Did that ever come into evidence?"

"No," Marcia responded.

At the preliminary hearing, before I had joined the prosecution team, Marcia called some witnesses who said that Simpson had purchased a stiletto at Ross Cutlery just prior to the murders. The implication was that he could have used the knife in the murders. So the defense handed over a sealed package to the court that subsequently turned out to contain a stiletto.

Marcia explained, "They say that they found the knife in a medicine cabinet at Rockingham. Interesting thing is that when LAPD did the second search at his house, they checked that cabinet, and guess what? No knife. But the whole issue is a red herring, so we kept it out."

"You know, Henry Lee did a presumptive blood test on that knife," I said. "Down by the handle, he got a weak positive reaction for blood."

"Are you fucking kidding?" Marcia exclaimed.

Upon hearing this, Chris, who had been slouching in his chair, sat up and looked at me.

"So," I continued, "I asked Gary Sims about it. He said that it very well could be a false positive in this situation. The trouble is that Judge Ito ruled that presumptive testing is inadmissible." (Such tests presume to show a substance is blood, but they are not conclusive.) "So even if the test results meant something, we can't introduce them."

"Then it really doesn't change anything regarding whether to introduce the knife," Marcia observed. "Interesting, but distracting."

I thought about it for a moment. "You guys are the ones who have to argue this case to the jury, so you have to make the final calls. There are certain things I can elicit which I'd only bring out if you intend to use them in your closing argument."

"For example?" Marcia asked.

"In reading Lee's books I came across this theory he has about four-way linkage. Here, I'll show you the diagram he uses to describe this." I showed Marcia and Chris the diagram.

"You see, what he says is that a successful crime-scene investigation will result in four-way linkage of the physical evidence to the suspect, the crime scene, and the victim. For example, take one piece of physical evidence—the knit cap at Bundy. The cap is found at the crime scene, so it's linked to the crime scene. It contains the defendant's hair, so it's linked to Simpson. It's near the victims' bodies, so it's linked to them. Four-way linkage: That piece of evidence ties together the cap with the crime scene, the victims, and the suspect, Simpson."

"Uh-huh," Marcia said as she reached into her large desk drawer where she kept the pretzel cache. She opened a bag, took a handful, and put the bag down on the table within easy reach.

I ate a few before continuing. "We can go through each piece of evidence and show the same four-way linkage. Obviously, Ron's shirt is linked to Ron, it's linked to the crime scene because Ron is at the crime scene, and it's linked to Simpson because his hair is on it. For each piece of evidence we can use a different color and show the linkages on Lee's diagram. Then the last chart would show all of the pieces of evidence together. You end up with so many linkages tying the physical evidence, the crime scene, the victims, and Simpson together, you have something resembling an airline flight chart of the United States! I mean, we use Lee's own theory to show how much evidence we have and the power of that evidence."

Marcia observed, "Easier said than done."

"Granted," I conceded. "If I try to get Lee to testify to this on cross, he'll fight me by giving evasive, equivocal, or ambiguous answers. That will give Scheck the ability, in redirect, to undo everything I accomplished. I propose to just ask Lee about the theory, mark a copy of his diagram as an exhibit, have him describe it in general. I won't ask him about it specifically in the context of our case. No one will even know exactly what I'm getting at in asking the questions until it's too late. Then, in closing, you can use Lee's chart and jam it up their ass. You can say, 'Under Lee's own theory the evidence is overwhelming. Just look at this.' "

Marcia interjected: "We use Lee as our witness and Lee's own theory to show that the crime scene was properly investigated because—"

I picked up her train of thought. "Because the crime-scene investigation resulted in a shitload of evidence which produces linkages tying the evidence, Simpson, the crime scene, and the victims together."

"I like it," Marcia said. "But do it quickly."

Chris, who said little during this conversation, was shaking his head in agreement.

"Okay," I continued. "Now here's some more questionable stuff. I've done a lot of research on this guy. You remember how, when Bailey was questioning Doug Deedrick, he was suggesting Doug was lying or exaggerating about having done four thousand hair and trace examinations during his career? Bailey seemed to be implying that it was too many?"

"What are you getting at?" Marcia asked.

"Well, you should look at the stuff Lee claims to have done since he joined the crime lab in 1979. In a 1989 case, he testified that he had investigated four thousand to five thousand homicide scenes. In the William Kennedy Smith case he said he investigated over a thousand rapes."

"Busy guy," Chris muttered.

I went on: "He says he's an expert in everything under the sun. I found a case where Lee testified that he's one of the world's leading experts in fingerprint examination, in hair examination, crime-scene reconstruction, and serology. It's a lifetime achievement to become a top expert in any one of those, let alone all four. On his CV [curriculum vitae] he claims to be an expert in handwriting comparison. He's an expert in ballistics. Those are virtually all of the major science categories within the traditional disciplines of criminalistics. But there's more."

Marcia smiled. "There's more?"

"He holds himself out as an expert in accident reconstruction, arson and fire investigations, and criminal profiling, which is an area of forensic psychology."

Marcia chuckled, and Chris permitted himself a smile.

"But there's more," I said. "In Connecticut they must think he's some kind of a god. One night there was this bridge that collapsed— the Hyannis River Bridge incident. It was a big deal there. Who do they call out to the scene? Henry Lee. I mean, now this guy's an expert in forensic engineering. No engineering background. But he's an expert. He's an expert in investigating airline crashes. On his CV he says he's an expert on home and industrial security. He is a black belt in judo, karate, and kung fu."

"Now you *are* kidding," Marcia said.

"No, I'm not. And in addition to this, as of 1991, he says he has conducted five hundred to a thousand workshops, two hundred to three hundred presentations at professional meetings. In addition to forensics workshops, he also gives numerous lectures at Rotary Clubs, high schools, social clubs, etc. He's flying all over the nation and world to do this. In one case, he testified he published two hundred papers. His CV says he wrote about twenty books."

Marcia and Chris shook their heads and exchanged smiling glances as I continued. "All of this stuff he accomplished is on top of his duties as the lab director, which include training, research, and significant administrative duties. Unless this guy's five hundred years old or has a half-dozen Henry Lee clones, how did he do all this stuff?"

By now we were all chuckling. I took a deep breath and ate some pretzels before continuing. "Then there is what I call the publicity-seeking, egomaniacal line of cross-examination. For example, Lee testified in the William Kennedy Smith rape case in Palm Beach,

Florida. There his testimony amounted to almost nothing—his observations of the relative lack of tearing or damage to the victim's clothing and the lack of grass stains on her skirt. Wasn't there any other criminalist in the entire state of Florida who was qualified to render such an *expert* analysis? Why did Lee have to do it? Well, there were cameras, and the media was going crazy, right?"

I added, "The defense retained him in the Robert Chambers murder case, the so-called Preppie Murder Case. The defense was that he killed the victim during 'rough sex.' Remember that one? Another major media event. He was also involved in the 1980 murder case of Scarsdale diet doctor Herman Tarnower. Now he's testifying in the Simpson case.

"In Connecticut he's become a celebrity criminalist. He makes himself readily available for interviews and puff pieces for the media. He has sold his autograph on 'blood spatter' coffee mugs for five dollars."

Marcia smiled at this. "How did you find out about that?"

I explained to Marcia how Diana Martinez did a computer search. "The one about the autographed mugs was in the *Hartford Courant*, December 21, 1994."

Marcia asked, "How long would this line of cross-examination take, and how effective will it be?"

"Well, it's risky. I have to get him, item per item, to say what he claims to have done. Each claim he made comes from a different case where he testified. You have to puzzle everything together and then hope this jury gets the idea that he's puffing his credentials. This will drive him crazy. He'll go through the roof, and he may then try to sink us. Right now he's being very careful about what he says because he does not want to alienate law enforcement. He hasn't said anything was planted or contaminated, and he won't. He hasn't attacked the LAPD head on, and he won't. But if he thinks we're attacking him, he may then declare all-out war."

Marcia observed, "When you look at what he's really saying, it adds up to nothing: maybe this, possibly that. He really hasn't hurt us. Not really. I think it's too risky."

"I'm just telling you everything I can do. This is kind of like informed consent," I said half jokingly. "I want you to know what the options are. But I want to say something else along these lines. There's this Crafts case. It's Lee's most famous case.

"Anyway," I continued, "in *Crafts*, he's asked about some presumptive blood testing. Lee swears under oath that he developed two-stage presumptive blood tests." I quickly paged to the place in my notes of the *Crafts* transcript. "He testified, 'I developed a procedure called two-step tests, to eliminate a false positive.' He said he did it, he developed it. Those tests were developed long before Lee became a forensic scientist. At worst, the jury could see it as a lie. At best, like Dennis, he said 'I' when he should have said 'we.' "

Both Marcia and Chris looked at me curiously. I wondered whether they both thought my excitement at having found this material was misplaced, that the question of Lee was beside the point, in light of the discovery of the Fuhrman tapes.

Marcia said, "I don't like it. And I don't want to try to use this guy to elicit favorable testimony for us. It's too risky. How do we know we can trust him?"

"I just want you to know about everything I have. Then there is another case where Lee testified. The defendant, Radamus Ortiz, shoots the victim to death. The New York crime lab looks at the victim's shirt and misses a bullet hole in it. Lee testifies for the prosecution and absolutely refuses to criticize the New York crime lab, even though they made an obvious mistake. He says he can't criticize the New York crime lab because he's not from New York. So the defense attorney asks him, 'You mean it changes in Connecticut? You have different rules?'

"Lee says, 'Of course we have different rules.'

"The defense attorney asks, 'Doesn't the science of criminalistics cross over from New York into Connecticut?'

"Lee says, 'No. . . . Each laboratory have different procedure, different standards, different way to do things. I only can respond for Connecticut laboratory. I cannot speak for New York City at all.' Later, he says he can't criticize any other criminalist without talking to them. Lee testified, 'I cannot judge somebody unless I talk to him, why is that, what's the circumstance. I cannot sit here judge like a Monday football coach. . . .' "

Marcia said, "Other than criticizing the way the socks were packaged together—which does not affect the outcome of the testing on the socks—Lee has not criticized LAPD. I don't think we want to push him into doing so."

"I agree," I said. "There's another case in 1984 called *State of*

Connecticut v. Hoeplinger. There Hoeplinger killed his wife by beating her to death with a brick while she was sitting on the couch. Then he drags her body outside the house to a fishpond. He tries to wash himself off in the fishpond. He claims that someone else broke into the house and killed her. The crime scene is a bloody mess. Interesting thing is that Hoeplinger only has two small drops of blood on his jeans. However, Lee doesn't find anything unusual about that at all. We could use this case to show that we wouldn't necessarily expect Simpson to have much blood on himself after the murder."

Marcia, in an exasperated tone of voice, said, "The things that I would do if I were cross-examining him is ask about the sock, the bindle with the blood transfers, the footprints, and that's it. Get in and get out. This jury is tired. They are shutting down. They have had it up to here. I'm just telling you what I would do."

Through all the trials and tribulations we had all been through together over the last months, this was the only time I sensed a note of impatience in Marcia's voice. "Marcia, don't get impatient with me."

Tenderly, Marcia reassured me, "Hankster, I'm never impatient with you."

"Marcia, I just want you to know every option available to us. You guys have to argue this thing. I just want to give you the ammunition you feel you need. If you don't need it, fine. If it's not going to help, fine."

Chris interjected. "Hank's my lawyer. We don't want to piss off my lawyer."

Chris's comments brought a smile to my face.

Marcia said, "Hank, you're doing the cross-examination. Handle it the way you feel is best. You have talked to Lee several times over the phone, so use your best judgment as to how much you think he can help us and where he can hurt."

I appreciated Marcia's confidence. "I'm going to think about it more and work out all the exact details of my strategy. But in a broad sense what I propose to do is divide my cross-examination into two parts. The first part is what I call the nice cross. It's what you're suggesting. I will very nicely, politely, try to elicit favorable testimony from Lee while minimizing the risk to us. Do nothing to upset him. Draw out everything I can to help our case and minimize anything he said on direct. Then phase two, the mean cross. Only if we feel we need to, only if the nice cross does not work, we will ask him questions in some of these riskier areas. In other words, we will play it by ear. If things go well, we won't have a mean cross."

Marcia nodded approvingly, "What do you think, Chris?"

Chris seemed somewhat distracted. "Sounds good."

But would it work? I wondered.

34

"Something Wrong," But What?

IN A LENGTHY DIRECT EXAMINATION spanning three court days, Dr. Henry Lee, arguably one of the case's most important witnesses, contributed little. It took defense attorney Barry Scheck about an hour to document some of Dr. Lee's achievements in the field of forensic science. A significant amount of time was spent detailing findings that didn't add up to anything. Most of them related to how various bloodstains could have been deposited at the crime scene: Some stains were smears; others were smudges; some were drops. Large poster boards with photographic blowups were used, and Dr. Lee, as expected, was charming and humorous. The ostensible purpose of this testimony was to convey the impression that the length of time for the murders was "not a short struggle," whatever that means.

Dr. Lee also conducted a demonstration, for which he is famous, in which he used red ink to illustrate blood splatter. According to Judge Ito, it resembled a Gallagher routine. Gallagher is a comedian who, near the end of every show, smashes various objects, such as watermelons, which squirt on the audience. Similarly, Dr. Lee's demonstrations had red ink literally flying through the air and splattering on white paper. Fun, but proving absolutely nothing.

Around the time of Lee's direct, before court commenced, Barry said to me accusingly, "You interviewed Dr. Lee without my being part of the conversation. You said you wouldn't do that."

"I said no such thing. I wrote you a letter informing you of my intent to talk to Dr. Lee. I called Dr. Lee. He told me he would check with you first before talking to me. When I spoke to him the next time, he told me he informed you that I wanted to talk to him and you said it was okay."

"That's not true. You told me I would be involved in the conversation," Barry said.

"Barry, you're hallucinating. I never even talked to you about this topic."

"I can't stand you," Barry said.

I didn't reply.

Later, before my cross of Dr. Lee, I approached Barry in the hall. I was holding hot coffee purchased at the concession stand. I said, "I've worked with a lot of attorneys with a variety of personalities over the years. Barry, I've never had such an unpleasant relationship with opposing counsel. It just makes things so unnecessarily difficult. This case is tough enough without—"

Barry interrupted, but in as gentle a tone of voice as he could muster. "What you're really saying is, let's bury the hatchet?"

We shook hands. After that incident, all further dealings with Barry were more civil, even friendly.

Barry Scheck has one major saving grace: He genuinely wants people to like him. Few watching his tenacious, in-your-face style will believe my assessment. But off-camera Barry occasionally manifests a genuine sweetness that makes it impossible for me to dislike him no matter what our disputes in court. I would not say the same of Peter Neufeld.

Before my cross, Judge Ito had some advice for me. A judge giving advice to an attorney is somewhat unusual. Perhaps Ito thought that by advising the attorneys to be brief, he might shorten the trial. From the bench in open court, out of the jury's presence but before the cameras, in front of millions, he said, "If I were in your shoes, I would cross-examine Dr. Lee for about half an hour, accentuating the positives of my case, doing it in a very professional, friendly manner with him, given his reputation, and get out."

I forced a polite smile. "Thank you, Your Honor." Judge Ito had no problem with Scheck's taking seven days with Dennis Fung on cross and Neufeld spending four days with Andrea Mazzola. However, with Lee, whose ambiguous testimony covered a wide range of the key forensic and physical evidence in the case, I was supposed to finish in half an hour. Judge Ito's comment also set me up for a fall. If I didn't follow his advice and my cross of Lee backfired, I could see the headlines and media sound bites: "Why didn't Hank Goldberg listen?"

From reviewing his notes and listening to his testimony, it appeared that Dr. Lee had examined virtually all of the physical evidence in the case. But nothing in his notes or testimony added up to much. Was I missing something? Nothing leaped out as being even remotely relevant. Nothing, that is, except findings that the defense might use to support its two-assailant theory.

The dubious two-assailant theory could not help Simpson, anyway. If Simpson had committed the murder with an accomplice, he would be just as guilty.

When Dr. Lee visited the crime scene on June 25, 1994, almost two weeks after the murder, he observed a second set of bloody shoe prints on the walkway leading to the rear alleyway, away from where Nicole's body was found. Specifically, Dr. Lee saw two imprints that exhibited a parallel-line design. One of these parallel-line imprints was definitely a shoe print. The design was different from the tread design of the bloody Bruno Magli shoe prints. This finding seemingly supported the defense's two-killer theory.

During the June 25 crime-scene visit, Dr. Lee documented these bloody parallel-line imprints. When I had first seen the photographs, months before Dr. Lee's testimony, they had struck me as being of very poor quality. As a result of my work preparing for the testimony of the criminalists, I had acquired a fair degree of knowledge necessary for a forensic scientist to investigate a crime scene. I knew that photographs of footwear impressions must be taken with a camera mounted on a tripod. The camera must be at a ninety-degree angle to the surface containing the print.

Dr. Lee's camera had obviously been handheld. Photographs of footwear impressions must contain a ruler. Metal retractable rulers are unacceptable because they do not lie flush with the ground and can cause problems when the photograph is being enlarged to natural size. Dr. Lee used a metal retractable ruler. I was surprised. These may seem like minor matters. But to me they indicated one thing about Dr. Lee's footprint examination: *something wrong.* I needed to take a closer look.

Long before my cross of Lee, I had wanted to find a photograph that could prove the bloody footprints Lee saw on June 25 were not present on June 13, the day after the murders. I wanted to show that the June 25 footprints were left *after* the crime scene was processed. I spent hours combing through the LAPD crime-scene photographs with the help of a young attorney, Jonathan Fairtlough, our computer-graphics whiz. Finally, we found close-up photographs, taken on June 13, 1994, that depicted the exact same spot on the tiles where Dr. Lee found the bloody parallel-line imprints almost two weeks later. The June 13, 1994 photography clearly showed that the parallel-line imprints Dr. Lee identified on June 25 *were not there* on June 13, 1994.

There were numerous LAPD photographs taken on June 13, 1994, of Bruno Magli shoe prints. Dr. Lee believed that one of them depicted a parallel-line imprint in addition to the Bruno Magli shoe print. We were able to locate the precise tiles that were depicted in this LAPD photograph. *The parallel lines Dr. Lee identified in the June 13 photograph were imbedded in the concrete tiles!*

Therefore, my strategy for cross on Lee's footprint testimony was simply to sit back and watch the defense present their evidence. Since I believed we would easily dismantle the second-killer theory, I would pin Dr. Lee down about the alleged second set of shoe prints in order to bolster this point. Then, when we tore that testimony apart later, with shoe-print expert William Bodziak, we would undermine the defense in general and Dr. Lee in particular. Most important, I wanted to use Dr. Lee essentially as a prosecution witness. If properly questioned, he would dismantle the defense position that PCR testing is unreliable and that DNA evidence is easily contaminated. With Dr. Lee, the defense avoided the subject of the DNA evidence like the plague.

But all this would take much longer than a half hour. It might take a few hours. But a few hours, or even a few days, to elicit evidence that might aid in convicting a man who, on the evidence, committed two brutal murders was well worth it.

As to the shoe-print testimony, the defense had taken the bait. When Dr. Lee had completed his first day of direct testimony, the defense clearly wanted to leave the jury with the unmistakable impression that a second set of shoe prints, with a parallel-line design, was found at the crime scene. He testified to seeing parallel-line imprints in a number of different locations.

First, he identified one on the eyeglass envelope dropped near Ron's feet. Before Lee testified, Bill Bodziak told me that the prints on the envelope were probably fabric impressions from Ron's jeans, a fact Doug Deedrick subsequently confirmed.

Second, Dr. Lee identified another set of parallel-line imprints on Ron's jeans. Doug Deedrick later testified that these impressions were probably a fabric impression from Ron's shirt.

Third, Dr. Lee identified the two bloody parallel-line imprints in photos he took on June 25. Unbeknownst to Dr. Lee, we had photographic proof that these prints were not present on June 13.

Finally, he identified the parallel-line imprint in the June thirteenth LAPD photograph. Dr. Lee did not know that *this imprint had been imbedded in the concrete* when it was wet. Later, he did admit that it wasn't necessarily a shoe print. In short, Lee was seeing parallel-line imprints everywhere.

The next day, the defense began by driving home the parallel-line-imprint theory. Dr. Lee admitted that, with the exception of one imprint on the Bundy walk in his June 25 photograph, he could not be positive that the various parallel-line imprints were, in fact, shoe prints. Scheck then asked a series of questions to convey the idea that the parallel-line imprints could have come only from a shoe.

"However, are these parallel-line-imprint patterns consistent with coming from the Bruno Magli? Mr. Goldman's boot? Mr. Goldman's jeans? Mr. Goldman's shirt? All right. Could it come from a lip print? An ear print?

Dr Lee answered no to all these questions.

"All right. I'm loath to say it, nose print?" Scheck asked.

Dr. Lee replied, "No . . . this is inconsistent with a nose print, either."

Scheck zeroed in on the two-killer theory. "However, these parallel-line-imprint patterns are consistent with having come from a shoe?"

"Could have," Dr Lee answered.

"Now, Dr. Lee, if we assume that these parallel-line-imprint patterns come from a shoe, I think you've told us they are not consistent with the Bruno Magli or Mr. Goldman's shoe, correct?"

"Yes."

Scheck asked two more questions to nail the door shut on the two-killer theory: "Would that mean that it—assuming it is a shoe print, it came from another person . . . ? Dr. Lee, in your experience at crime scenes have you ever seen a single assailant wear two pairs of shoes?"

"No."

This testimony clearly implied that Dr. Lee's conclusions could only be reconciled with one rational conclusion—a second killer wearing parallel-line-design shoes was involved in the murder. Scheck had unwittingly set the trap for his own witness.

During my cross-examination on the footwear-impression evidence, I had Dr. Lee identify more imprints, which I knew were imbedded in concrete. Dr. Lee testified about a wiggly- or wavy-line imprint on one of the photographs. I asked him whether this wiggly-line imprint could have been made by blood. Dr. Lee implied that the print could have been, saying, "I don't recall exactly . . . so long ago." Thus, Dr. Lee clearly identified a wavy-line imprint and even suggested that it may have been made by blood. I knew that this imprint was in fact a shoe print. But it was made many years ago, when the concrete walk was freshly poured and the concrete was still wet. It was imbedded in the concrete! During cross-examination I showed Dr. Lee more photographs from June 13. He identified an entire series of "imprints" on the walkway, which turned out to have been imbedded in the concrete.

During a recess, Cochran approached me, gloating. "Thanks, Hank, for eliciting that testimony about a set of additional shoe prints. Thank you very much." I had to bite my tongue. I wanted to say, "Johnnie, guess what? Your second killer's shoe prints Lee just identified are imbedded in concrete." I couldn't tip my hand.

Another area of Dr. Lee's testimony I wanted to deflate related to the length of the attack. I asked Dr. Lee whether he could tell "blow by blow" how the attack occurred. "No, I cannot," he replied.

"And, Doctor, would it be fair to say that if we cannot tell blow by blow what happened, then it's difficult to give any kind of a scientific estimation of time?"

"That's correct," he replied.

In short, after spending hours on direct examination eliciting evidence about various findings at the crime scene, Dr. Lee could provide us with no meaningful testimony as to how much time the attack took.

I also wanted to dispel the defense canard that, had Simpson committed the murders, he would have been drenched in blood and there should have been more blood in the Bronco and at Rockingham. I wanted to establish that if the murders occurred in the manner described by Dr. Lakshmanan, Simpson would not have been covered in blood. "Sir, if a person were to wrap their arm around someone's throat and slit that person's throat . . . and the blood spurted forward, would you expect the assailant to be covered in blood?"

"Probably not."

I also had Dr. Lee explain what would happen if only Simpson's front side were drenched in blood when he entered the Bronco. Lee said, "You don't have transfer." In other words, there would not be significant amounts of blood transferred from Simpson's clothes to the Bronco. So much for the defense contention that there was too little blood in the Bronco.

During my cross-examination, I also needed to puncture the defense contention that Nicole's blood had been planted on the socks found in Simpson's bedroom. The defense contended that no one was wearing the socks when Nicole's blood was splashed on them.

This theory had been expounded by Dr. Herbert MacDonell. He had testified that Nicole's bloodstain had penetrated one side of Simpson's sock and had transferred to the other side. The defense theorized that this could not have happened if someone had been wearing the socks at the time because blood cannot go through someone's ankle. They claimed that the idea that no one was wearing the socks when the blood was deposited on them supported their planting theory. The implication was that someone deposited Nicole's blood while the socks were lying flat on a table. Interestingly, the stain that would have traveled through the wearer's ankle was only a microscopic speck.

I easily dispatched this issue with Dr. Lee. I asked him whether the microscopic stain could have been caused if the socks were inside out and the toe of the sock was touching the ankle. I knew from my photographs that this was, indeed, how the socks were recovered. However, the defense only provided Dr. Lee with second-generation photographs. From his photographs of the socks, he would not have been able to see that the socks were recovered in this condition. I asked Dr. Lee whether this could account for the questioned microscopic stain.

"*I cannot rule out,*" he replied. (emphasis added)

"The scenario that I just gave you?" I asked.

"Yes," he replied.

After Dr. Lee admitted that my scenario could account for the questioned stain, I produced my photograph. It clearly showed that the scenario I outlined to Dr. Lee was, in fact, what had happened. The socks were collected inside out, with the toe touching the ankle, showing how blood got from one side of the sock to the other.

I also elicited evidence from the forensic-science literature that a single drop of blood on nylon material could take from seventy-five minutes to nine hours to dry. The socks were nylon. Therefore, the blood could also have transferred from one side to the other after Simpson returned to Rockingham and took his socks off.

In short, *Dr. Lee's testimony showed logical, rational explanations for how blood got from one side of the sock to the other.*

Clearly, to the casual observer of the trial, the most intriguing portion of Dr. Lee's testimony occurred on direct: "Something wrong." What did Dr. Lee mean when he said, "Something wrong"? To what was he referring? What was the basis for this conclusion? What was the effect of the "something," whatever it was, that was "wrong" with the evidence in our case?

I would be willing to bet that few observers could answer even one of these questions. In fact, I cannot answer most of them. Because there are no answers. This "forensic science" conclusion—"something wrong"—was one of the most ambiguous, unclear, utterly meaningless statements that I have ever heard any forensic scientist utter in a court of law. Although Dr. Lee may never have intended this to happen, the defense turned the phrase into a sound bite that could mean anything the listener wished. "Something wrong" became a rallying cry, part of the vernacular, like "I'm mad as hell, and I'm not going to take it anymore."

In reality, the famous phrase was uttered in reference to a very mundane phenomenon. As Dennis Fung and Andrea Mazzola had testified, they used cloth swatches to collect the blood. Often multiple swatches were used to soak up a single stain. After the swatches were dry, they were packaged in a small bindle.

Bloodstain number 47 was the first drop of blood along the escape route the killer took at Bundy as he headed toward the alley. Eight cloth swatches were used to collect that stain. When Gary Sims at the Department of Justice laboratory in Sacramento opened bindle 47, he noticed that there were some bloodstains on the inside of the paper bindle. Apparently, four of the eight cloth swatches were not entirely dry when they were packaged, and they left four stains inside the bindle. When we became aware of this, none of us—not Gary Sims or the other prosecutors involved with the DNA evidence, not Rock Harmon, not Woody Clark, and not I—thought it presented any problem at all.

During Dr. Lee's testimony, on direct, the defense had asked him why there were only four stains in the bindle if there were eight swatches. Obviously, Dr. Lee did not feel comfortable testifying that this discrepancy indicated planting. Perhaps his way of coping with this dilemma was to simply testify: "Only opinion I can give under this circumstance, something wrong."

The defense wasn't satisfied. At this point the defense asked for a brief opportunity to consult with Dr. Lee. I didn't hear what they were saying, but from all appearances, it was spirited. During the break, at an unreported side-bar conference in which Dr. Lee was present, he explained to the judge that he couldn't say anything more than "something wrong."

After the break, Scheck again asked about Dr. Lee's opinion. "Dr. Lee, the last answer that you gave this jury with respect to this board [showing the stains on the bindle] is 'Something is wrong.' Could you please explain what you mean?"

"What I mean, there are . . . eight swatches, four imprints, wet transfer on the paper. If [eight] swatches all dry, I shouldn't see any wet transfer. If [eight] swatches all wet, I should see [eight] transfers. I only see four. *The number did not add up.* There may be reason to explain. I don't know." (emphasis added)

So, according to the trial transcript, *all Dr. Lee meant was that the number of stains did not match the number of swatches.*

That evening, I reread this part of Dr. Lee's testimony. What did he say? Careful reflection led to the conclusion that his testimony really didn't mean much of anything. All he was saying was that he couldn't explain specifically why some swatches dried faster than others. It doesn't take a forensic scientist to figure out that some swatches could be wetter than others.

During cross, I wanted to defuse the implication that his inability to explain the transfers was an ominous sign. I had Dr. Lee testify that it was common for him to see phenomena that he couldn't explain. He said, "I spend my life in this. Still a lot of phenomena I still cannot explain and report to you."

I asked, "Just in general, Dr. Lee, are there many occasions where . . . as a forensic scientist, where you look at a case or a piece of evidence and you just don't have all the answers?"

"That's correct."

Later, in cross-examining Dr. Lee about the questioned stain on the sock, I returned to this theme. "And this is another one of those examples of something where a leading forensic scientist or a number of forensic scientists can look at an item and they just can't provide us with all of the answers; is that correct?"

"Yes, sir."

"That doesn't mean something is wrong, does it?" I asked. (emphasis added)

"No."

Then I had Dr. Lee testify that packaging swatches when they were still wet could not adversely affect the test result.

I also wanted to get him to make it clear that the four stains on the bindle could not have resulted from contamination with blood from Simpson's vial. "It would be very difficult to imagine that happening, correct?"

"Very, very difficult," Dr. Lee admitted.

I brought out certain references in the forensic-science literature that show it is very difficult to predict how long it will take blood to dry on a cotton swatch even under laboratory conditions. This literature included experiments that supported the very real possibility that if swatches were lying on top of each other while drying in test tubes, the swatches on the outside of the pile would dry but the ones within the pile would remain wet. This would account for why four swatches remained wet, whereas the other four dried.

Finally, I brought out that Dr. Lee had also observed the same type of transfers on another bindle that he did not testify to on direct. That bindle contained swatches from a pool of Nicole's blood at the crime scene. This logically proved that the transfers were not evidence of planting. After all, why would anyone want to plant Nicole's blood in a bindle containing swatches taken from a pool of her blood? What good does it do to, in effect, plant the victim's blood at the crime scene underneath the victim?

I felt that these points sufficiently refuted any suggestion that the "something wrong" sound bite supported the defense case. It supported neither contamination nor planting.

On direct, Dr. Lee had stayed clear of any specifics regarding the collection or testing of the blood evidence in our case. On cross, I wanted to use Lee to support our case on these points. I started out this line of questioning by using Dr. Lee to deflate defense expert Dr. Gerdes. Gerdes had said that unlike medical samples, forensic samples come from crime scenes and are dirty and degraded. On cross, Dr. Lee disagreed. According to Dr. Lee, PCR DNA testing was proper to use in criminal cases.

I also elicited from Dr. Lee that molecular biologists and other nonforensic scientists, like Gerdes, were not qualified to evaluate whether PCR could be used in criminal cases. Lee explained that as "forensic scientists, we should have a choice *not dictated by molecular biologists or other scientists* tell us what to do." (emphasis added) In a few minutes of cross-examination, Dr. Lee substantially undercut his fellow defense witness Dr. Gerdes.

I brought out the fact that Dr. Lee had previously used PCR technology in many cases. He had used it to identify war dead. He had used it on degraded and contaminated biological samples, *successfully.*

He had used it in the infamous Crafts case. Crafts murdered his wife and disposed of her body by passing it through a wood-chipping machine, which spread her remains over twenty-five hundred square feet, including some in a nearby river. Dr. Lee processed the crime scene with the Connecticut State Police. They melted the snow in buckets to collect the evidence. In the process the biological evidence sank to the bottom and was collected. Dr. Lee was still able to help convict the defendant with this biological evidence.

First, I established the basic facts of the Crafts case. In a friendly tone I asked about how he had collected the biological evidence by melting the snow in buckets. "And, Dr. Lee, when that occurred, when the various items would fall to the bottom of the bucket, various different biological samples could get mixed together or were mixed together; is that correct?"

Dr. Lee responded almost gleefully, "Yes. Yes!" Then Dr. Lee cheerfully admitted that the biological evidence was mixed with other biological material, like deer bones.

"And despite that, sir, it was proper, and you did decide to attempt DNA technology on this evidence. . . . And you were able to get results that identified the human remains in that case even though all the biological evidence was mixed together at the time that it was collected?"

"Yes, sir," he replied.

In fact, the police even collected the evidence in the Crafts case in sealed plastic containers to bring to the laboratory for drying. This was the practice the LAPD had been assailed for using.

Dr. Lee, who was clearly more qualified than Gerdes to talk about contamination, degradation, and biological-evidence issues, gave important testimony about the realities of forensic science. "Do you agree, sir, that one of the practical realities that criminalists face who are working for law enforcement is budgetary problems and monetary shortfalls?"

"Yes."

"So would you agree, sir, that generally speaking, forensic resources are scarce in the sense that we can't do all the testing and all the study in every case that we would like to do?"

"That is absolute correct," Lee admitted. "Of course, impossible to do every possible test in this earth for a certain case."

I had Lee admit that in his laboratory, until quite recently, the air-conditioning would shut down when they ran the machines that do conventional blood testing and that they used paper towels as blotters instead of blotter paper in their DNA testing. Lee offered that until recently "my laboratory is a men's room, literally a men's room, so you have to do the best you can."

"Yeah," I said.

Dr. Lee continued. "You can't just say, I'm in a men's room, I don't do any tests."

"Right," I agreed. "And the drying facilities, up until quite recently, for biological evidence [were] in the yard of the laboratory. Is that correct?"

Dr. Lee responded, "That is about fifteen years ago. We don't have a drying room, so everything have to dry in the yard. Even now sometimes dry my clothes in the yard. Nothing wrong dry in the yard."

> GOLDBERG: I'm not saying there is anything wrong with it, no, not at all. And that was particularly true in the summer months, some of the biological evidence you would try to dry in the yard because it was smelly?
>
> DR. LEE: Yes. the odor really terrible, you don't want to have the whole laboratory evacuate. Sometime the odor the young and normal person can take.
>
> GOLDBERG: And was the practice of drying the biological evidence in the yard discontinued once when a dog absconded with a rape victim's panties?
>
> DR. LEE: Not really. There are numerous clothing. One of my analysts was assigned to guard those clothing. Somehow a wild dog took a piece of garment and run away and luckily that just one piece of an undergarment.

Then I had Lee testify that despite these kinds of problems and issues, he and his laboratory were still performing good work in the area of DNA and conventional blood testing.

Lee said with some pride, "We try our best."

The defense called LAPD a cesspool of contamination. Gerdes said it was the dirtiest lab he had ever seen. But it was not in a men's room, as Dr. Lee's lab had been. The defense had spent considerable time criticizing the laboratory's evidence-drying room. But LAPD doesn't have wild dogs running around in there!

Even more importantly, Dr. Lee provided additional, powerful testimony on how difficult it is to contaminate biological evidence. I asked Lee a hypothetical: What would happen if a police officer accidentally stepped in blood. I asked whether he would still be able to analyze the blood on the shoe.

"If the shoe bring to me, yes."

So Dr. Lee testified that you could literally collect blood evidence on the bottom of your shoe. Then I asked him about what would happen if someone touched the blood evidence with their bare hands. "Let's say our same police officer, our police officer who is new [said], 'Oh, my heavens, not only did I do all those other things, I also touched the swatches with my hands.' "

Dr. Lee testified that he could still get valid test results.

This testimony came long after the eight days that Dennis Fung and the four days that Andrea Mazzola were cross-examined about the evidence-collection procedures. It followed the microdissection of every move that was made in physically collecting the bloodstains, the painstaking cross-examination about "textbook" collection procedures, as well as the defense cross-examination using videotape showing when the criminalists wore gloves and when they did not. After all this, here was a man, reputed to be one of the world's leading experts in forensic blood testing, saying you could have collected the blood on the bottom of your shoe, you could have touched it with your bare hands, and the tests would still have been valid.

I did not finish my cross in Judge Ito's suggested "half an hour." But I believed, and believe to this day, that in just under an hour of cross-examination of Dr. Lee about the contamination issues, the prosecution dismantled whatever little remained of the defense's contamination theory. This is perhaps one of the great underreported stories of the Simpson trial. A careful review of the defense's strategy after Dr. Lee, particularly during their closing argument, reveals a not-so-subtle shift—a virtual abandonment—of the contamination theory in favor of the planting theory.

When Dr. Henry Lee finished his testimony and passed me at counsel table, he whispered something to me. "See, gave you a little and gave them a little." I thought to myself: Wrong, Henry. You gave them nothing, and you gave us everything.

After the jurors filed out of the room, Henry wanted to take his photograph with Marcia. Then Barry said, "Hank should be in the photo, too." Henry waved me over. We put our arms around each other's shoulders and genuinely smiled as the photograph was taken.

Marcia, commenting on Henry's trademark magnifying glass, said, "That's really cool." A few moments later, after Marcia left the court, Henry insisted on giving me the magnifying glass. "Tell Marcia it's for her." Then, perhaps thinking I had been slighted, he added, "Well, you and Marcia can fight over it."

We were genuinely elated at the outcome of Dr. Lee's cross. Based in large measure on his testimony, Marcia and Woody decided that calling a witness to rebut Gerdes was unnecessary. The highly technical testimony Gerdes's counterpart could have provided would never have disposed of the contamination issue as convincingly as Henry had.

Something else was established during Dr. Lee's testimony: The defense claimed that someone could not have been wearing the socks when they were stained with blood. They were wrong. The defense claimed that the evidence collection had been botched and that blood could be easily contaminated. They were wrong. Gerdes said that PCR was unreliable for criminal cases. He was wrong. Dr. Lee's testimony implied that a second assailant left parallel-line imprints at the crime scene. He was wrong. Unfortunately, the jury either did not consider this testimony or misinterpreted it.

Yes, something was wrong here.

35

Should Have Gone to Siskel and Ebert

THE CROWN JEWEL IN THE DEFENSE'S ATTACK against the forensic evidence was not Larry Ragle. Nor was it John Gerdes or even Henry Lee. The defense's star witness for this phase of their case was a nurse, Thano Peratis, a bespectacled, pudgy, balding man in his fifties with the obscure job of drawing blood from drunk drivers, rape suspects, and miscellaneous others at the jail dispensary in Parker Center.

At around the time Denise Brown was testifying, I learned from Patti Jo Fairbanks, our senior legal office assistant, that the nurse who had drawn Simpson's blood, Thano Peratis, wanted to talk to Marcia. I phoned him, and he told me, "There's something I want to tell Marcia or whoever is the appropriate person."

I explained to him that I was the person assigned to handle the portion of the case in question. I asked him, "What do you want to tell us?"

Thano cleared his throat. "I—I don't think I should talk about it over the phone."

His jittery tone probably reflected his fear that a simple task, of the type he had probably performed ten thousand times before, could land him smack in the center of Simpson's conspiracy defense. "Okay. Why don't I come over and talk to you at the dispensary today,"

"That's fine," Thano said.

I walked over to Parker Center, and the officer at the informa-

271

tion booth directed me to the dispensary, which is in the lockup on the first floor. The dispensary consists of a room I thought looked like a school nurse's office except that it contained what appeared to be an operating table. It reminded me of the room in which they gave Jack Nicholson's character in the movie *One Flew Over the Cuckoo's Nest* electric shock treatment. Thano and I greeted each other, and he directed me into the office. I sat down.

"What did you want to tell me?" I asked.

"That testimony I gave about drawing eight mililiters of blood from O.J. was mistaken."

Thano was referring to the testimony he had given at the preliminary hearing months before I joined the prosecution team. Under Shapiro's cross, he had testified that there was approximately 8 milliliters of blood in Simpson's vial when he drew the blood.

When Thano told me that this testimony was mistaken, I asked, simply, "Oh? How so?"

"Well, I heard from a friend that Johnnie Cochran had claimed, during opening statements, that I drew precisely eight milliliters of blood and that blood was missing." He added haltingly, "I—I thought to myself, Thano—Thano, you screwed up. So I came to work the next day, and I did a little experiment."

"Could you show me what you did?" I interrupted.

"Um, sure," Thano replied. He then left the office and gathered several items in the adjacent room that housed the operating table. From my vantage point, he appeared to be filling something with water and doing something with a syringe. He then returned to the office. "Okay, Mr. Goldberg, how should I do this?"

"It's Hank," I said. "Just repeat exactly what you did when you performed the experiment you were telling me about."

With a syringe in one hand and a blood vial in the other, Thano illustrated. "Okay. I took this syringe, and I filled it with water, one milliliter at a time." As he spoke, he drew 1 milliliter of water into the syringe from a paper cup and injected it through the stopper of a blood vial, repeating the process several times. "I kept doing this until I got to how full the blood vial was of Simpson's blood."

"How did you know what point that was?"

"By looking," he said.

By looking, I thought. I was pretty sure I knew what he was talking about, but I wanted to be certain. "Thano, the blood vials aren't calibrated, are they?"

"No. Well, when the blood that I did the experiment with looked to be about as full as Simpson's vial, I stopped injecting water into it."

"Uh-huh, and how much was in it?"

"Approximately 6.5 milliliters," he stated.

"Approximately," I repeated. "Could it have been more?"

"Yes," he replied.

"Or less?"

"It could have been less," he admitted.

"How much more or less? I mean, could it have been as high as seven milliliters, or as low as only six milliliters?"

"Yes."

I thought, This guy doesn't really have any clear idea of how much he drew. "Thano, let me ask you something. Have you ever measured how much blood you drew before?"

"No. We don't measure it," he said.

"Did you write down anywhere how much you drew from Simpson, on a form, maybe? Or maybe even on some personal notes somewhere?"

"No."

Then I asked Thano about the testimony he had given Shapiro at the preliminary hearing. "So why, when Shapiro asked you how much you drew, did you say approximately eight milliliters, and then you said it was between 7.9 and 8.1 milliliters?"

He replied, "I thought, Here I am being cross-examined by Robert Shapiro. I mean, I thought he's a modern-day Clarence Darrow. And it was just a stupid answer. Eight milliliters is what we assume we normally draw. But we never measure it. There's no reason to. In all my years, no one has ever told me that I didn't draw enough blood."

Or accused you of being part of a conspiracy to frame a defendant by planting blood, I thought.

Thano continued: "A vacutainer is supposed to draw eight milliliters." He explained that a vacutainer is a device that utilizes a blood vial with a vacuum seal that, when injected into a person's arm, sucks the blood into the vial.

"Did you use a vacutainer?" I inquired.

"No. With big people, like O.J.—who has big arms—I have found that it's easier to use a syringe. I used the syringe on O.J. and at a certain point the needle hit the wall of the vein and the blood stopped. I could have turned the syringe to get the blood to continue to flow, but if I did that, there would be the slightest danger that I could damage the wall. So I looked at the syringe, and it looked like enough. So I stopped."

"When you looked at the syringe, did you look at the calibrations?"

"No. They were on the other side. I just looked at the syringe, and it looked like enough. And that was it. Bing, bang, boom."

After asking some follow-up questions, I thanked him for his time and walked, almost jogged, back to my office. During the walk, I thought, I found the so-called missing blood. I immediately began the process of mentally calculating the impact of this discovery. Let's see. The entire defense contention that there's blood missing from Simpson's vial presupposes that we know precisely how much blood was in the vial to begin with. If it were only 6.5 milliliters rather than 8 milliliters, there would be no missing blood.

But what's the defense going to do with Thano on the stand? He's kind of a character—undulating cadence, the funny remarks. Robert Shapiro a modern-day Clarence Darrow? Bing, bang, boom?

But now the defense will have to add him, this unlikely candidate, to their top-ten list of most evil conspirators. They've got to say he's lying about having made a mistake when he testified at the prelim. Otherwise, 'bye, 'bye, conspiracy.

As we saw with Dennis Fung, it is an extremely common phenomenon for witnesses to give testimony that is more precise than is reasonable. For example, suppose in a robbery case a witness testifies, "I was thirty feet away from where the robber was pointing the gun at the teller." Then the witness is asked, "Was it exactly thirty feet?" The witness replies, "It was within twenty-five to thirty-five feet." Later, it turns out that the witness was, in fact, sixty feet away. This problem could have been averted if the witness had simply said, "My best estimate is that I was thirty feet away; I didn't measure it." This is precisely what Thano failed to do when he answered Shapiro's questions about the blood vial.

Without remembering any portion of my three-block walk from Parker Center, I suddenly found myself back inside the CCB. As soon as Marcia returned from court and entered the War Room, I reported my findings. Smiling and in somewhat of a singsong voice, I said, "Marcia, I found the missing blood."

I was hoping for a positive reaction, but instead she looked at me for a moment and said, "Oh, really?" Having been brought down a peg, I then related to her my conversation with Thano. For a few seconds she appeared to be performing a quick mental calculation.

"I believe it, but will the jury?"

"Well, they should believe it," I said. "I believe it, too. I don't know whether they will," I answered. "When they see Thano, they shouldn't see the face of a coconspirator. Also, his testimony at the prelim's got to be wrong. He said there was between 7.9 and 8.1 milliliters. It implied that he knew how much blood he drew to within two-tenths of a milliliter, an amount so small that it can't even be measured with the calibrations on his syringe. If the jury doesn't believe his prior testimony was accurate, then the entire basis for the defense conspiracy—the allegedly missing blood—fails."

At around the end of Greg Matheson's testimony, Rock, Marcia, and I discussed whether we should call Thano as a witness at all.

"His testimony is going to be a mess," Marcia said. "There is no way around that."

Rock agreed.

"And if we don't call him," I said, "then he's a defense witness, not a prosecution witness. We get to argue, 'He's not our witness, he's their witness. And their whole case rests on him. If you think he's not that reliable on the issue of how much blood he initially drew, if you think he really doesn't know, then their entire conspiracy theory fails. Their entire conspiracy theory rests on the shoulders of their star witness, Thano Peratis.' "

Our decision was unanimous: that it was better for Thano Peratis to be a defense witness than a prosecution witness and that we shouldn't call him during our case.

By mid-July, well into the defense case, the defense informed us that they wanted to call Peratis. However, I learned that Thano was at home recuperating from heart surgery. His doctor would not allow him to testify. This made him legally unavailable as a witness.

One afternoon, I discussed the issue with Marcia and Brian Kelberg in Marcia's office. This was at around the time the defense was presenting the EDTA evidence. After I explained the situation, I said, "This isn't a problem. Since Thano is legally unavailable, the defense will be able to introduce his prior testimony from the preliminary hearing. All we need to do is go out and reinterview Thano about what happened. We can then introduce this interview as an inconsistent statement to impeach Thano's preliminary-hearing testimony."

"Are you sure?" Marcia asked.

"Positive," I answered. "This issue has come up with me before."

Brian said, "I don't know if we can do that. Let's look." Brian took a copy of the Evidence Code from Marcia's bookcase and quickly turned to section 1202, entitled "Credibility of Hearsay Declarant." This is the code section that tells lawyers what they can do to attack the credibility of a witness who is not present in court but whose prior testimony is read to the jury from a transcript.

After reading the code section, Brian said, "Hank's right. This means that if we reinterview Thano and he says things which contradict what he previously testified to during the preliminary hearing, it's admissible."

Marcia seemed distracted. "I'm not following."

"Okay," I said. "Thano previously testified at the prelim that he drew approximately eight milliliters. Right? But he made an inconsistent statement to me. He told me he drew approximately 6.5 milliliters. So if the defense puts in the prior testimony about drawing eight milliliters, we get to put in the contradictory statement that he only drew 6.5 milliliters."

"Right, right," Marcia said.

Brian added, "But it's only admissible to prove that his prior testimony about drawing eight milliliters should be distrusted."

"But that would be good for us," I added. "Because we aren't asking the jury to believe that Thano really did draw only 6.5 milliliters. The real point is that this guy doesn't know how much he drew because he didn't measure it and he never does." We agreed that I would go to Thano's home to reinterview him with a defense investigator and that I would videotape the interview.

Later that afternoon, I spoke to Bill Hodgman in his spacious corner office, one of the few nice offices, with a hypnotic southeast view of the downtown skyline. I wanted to ask Bill for his take on the Thano Peratis interview. Bill said, "You can take any investigator you want to with you." I wanted someone whose credibility would be beyond reproach and who could stand up to the unfair cross-examinations that were routine in this trial.

"How about Steve Oppler. He impresses me as being very sharp, very credible."

"Sharp and credible," Bill agreed.

As I stood up to leave, Bill said, "Hank, going to join us for some push-ups?" As part of Bill's recovery and to reduce stress, we had formed a push-up club that included about half of the prosecutors on the *Simpson* team and a few others.

"I don't know, Bill," I replied.

"Oh, come on," Bill said. "Hank, you're in second place, maybe you can overtake Kuriyama."

"Are you kidding, Bill. Kuriyama's a former gymnast. He's doing what? About 150? I don't think so. I'll stick with second place."

Bill looked at me and grinned. "Maybe."

I was pleased that after the earlier heart-attack scare Bill was back doing push-ups again.

About a week before John Gerdes's testimony and while I was preparing for Henry Lee, Neufeld asked me to stipulate that Thano was unavailable. This would make his transcript admissible. In court that day, I stated that the prosecution would be willing to agree that Thano was unavailable as a witness if Judge Ito would allow us to introduce an interview with Thano in which he contradicted his previous testimony. I said that Evidence Code section 1202 allowed this. Neufeld apparently didn't know what I was talking about. "Well, it's this unique little thing we have in California called the Evidence Code," Judge Ito said sarcastically.

Interestingly, weeks earlier Gerald Uelmen had conceded that the prosecution could introduce an interview with Thano. He said, If the prosecution wanted to introduce an interview of Peratis "to rebut or impeach [Peratis's prior testimony], they can do that during their rebuttal case." Apparently, Uelmen and Neufeld disagreed on this point. The media experts, who were shocked that the judge allowed the videotaped interview, also must have missed Uelmen's concession.

Although still preparing for Dr. Lee's testimony, I went to Thano's house with Steve Oppler and Teresa Ramirez, a video-camera operator with our office. Thano lived in a modest 1970s-vintage development of town house–style homes in a guarded, gated community, somewhere in that vast, uncharted area between Santa Monica and Culver City. We determined where he would feel most comfortable and where there was light for the camera. We went upstairs to a den that contained a television set and some VCRs.

After Teresa set up her video camera, I began the interview. Thano repeated the same statement he had given me months earlier, in early February. We concluded the interview and turned off the camera.

As Teresa was packing up, I remembered that I also wanted to ask Thano one more question about how much a standard blood vial actually holds. He previously had testified that it held 10 milliliters, though it actually held 12 milliliters. Teresa set up the camera again, and I asked him about this one issue.

Later, when I saw the videotape, my last question had not been recorded, only Thano's answer. However, Investigator Steve Oppler, had made a simultaneous audiotape just in case there was any problem with the videotape. Steve had tape-recorded everything. Since everything was recorded meticulously with both videotape and audiotape and since I had two very credible witnesses to the entire interview, I thought this should place a damper on any possible defense claim that I beat and intimidated Thano into saying that his earlier preliminary-hearing testimony was false.

When I viewed the video, I thought it had a homespun quality. It was very obviously not rehearsed or polished. It showed Thano getting up twice to get items he needed to replicate the experiment he showed me when I first interviewed him. I felt that this quality was antithetical to any possible charge that Thano was rehearsed or somehow pressured during the interview. But it seems that ordinary principles of common sense were in a state of temporary suspension in the Simpson case, so I wanted several independent opinions. Without saying anything as to my assessment of the tape, I showed it to Rock.

"I like it. It is what it is. And it shows Thano for what he is."

I did the same thing with Bill Hodgman. Bill's assessment: "A polished, rehearsed look is exactly what we don't want. This is very spontaneous. Even somewhat funny—the way Thano comes across. But I'll show it to Marcia and ask her what she thinks."

I appreciated this because around this time Marcia was so bogged down with the pending Mark Fuhrman issues that it was impossible for me to talk to her without a scheduled appointment. Apparently Marcia gave the tape a thumbs-up.

One afternoon, when Chris was walking through the War Room, I cornered him. I knew he had previously watched the Thano video. However, when I asked Chris about it, I got the typical Darden response.

"Don't like it," Chris said.

"Why?" I asked.

Chris shrugged his shoulders.

"Okay, Chris. Both sides are going to have their own spins on the tape. The tape is what you can make of it in argument. Look, I'm not the one who's going to have to stand before the jury and argue this thing. So the tape either helps, hurts, or it's neutral. You either want to have it for your argument, or you don't. What do you say?"

"Okay," Chris said as he turned and walked away.

"Okay? Okay what?"

Chris shrugged his shoulders as he continued walking.

I murmured to myself, "Should have gone to Siskel and Ebert instead."

In mid-September, during our rebuttal case, Marcia showed the videotape to the jury. That day, I went back to the Bundy crime scene with criminalists and a photographer to take some additional photographs of some of the imprints imbedded in the Bundy concrete that Dr. Lee identified as possible shoe prints. While I was driving back, I heard on the radio that the defense was arguing that I interviewed Thano before the tape was turned on for the interview. They also alleged that the fact that I ended the interview and then restarted the videotape to ask an additional question was evidence of a "gap."

Of course, by now we were always anticipating groundless defense attacks predicated on staple holes, initials on bindles, and microscopic specks of blood on a sock. After a "gap," could a "grassy knoll" across the street from Bundy be far behind? But the slightly more logical defense attack would have been to suggest that I, some other member of the prosecution, or perhaps one of the mysterious, unknown evidence planters got to Thano *before* I ever did the taping. There would be no way for us to categorically prove that didn't happen.

But we could prove that the defense's allegations were false. We had two highly credible witnesses. The one thing the tape didn't appear to be was polished or rehearsed. The allegations as to the question of the "gap" were equally nonsensical. The tape clearly showed that we concluded the interview and turned the camera off. Then the camera was turned back on to ask a follow-up question on an issue that neither the defense nor the prosecution felt was relevant to the case—the size of the blood vials. Everything was done in an above-board manner and turned over to the defense. Finally, why would I coach Thano after the interview concluded. If you are going to coach someone, you would do it before the interview, not afterward.

Despite this, Neufeld attempted to imply that Steve Oppler, Teresa Ramirez, and I were part of a cover-up relating to Thano's videotape statement. Marcia asked Teresa what happened during the supposedly sinister stopping and restarting of the tape.

Neatly closing the gap, Teresa answered, "I noticed that Mr. Peratis has a very nice television set and I asked him if we could check the tape on his set . . . and he agreed." She continued: "Then we played the tape . . . and then Hank said that he had another question. So I had to cue the tape . . . and start again."

After I returned from Bundy, I went to Judge Ito's court. Teresa Ramirez was still on the stand.

After court recessed, I had a chance to talk to Marcia and Chris. "I think this is good. The line of attack they chose to make is the easiest one to disprove. The more people they accuse of being involved in a conspiracy, the better for us. Now, I guess, Steven Oppler, Teresa Ramiriz, Thano Peratis, and I are all involved under the defense conspiracy theory. The conspiracy is growing."

Later that evening, after I listened to the backup audiotape-recording of the Thano interview, I went to Chris's office. The last time I had broached the tape issue, Chris had responded equivocally. This time he listened intently. I said to Chris, "I think you should introduce the audiotape recording because it clearly shows that we ended the interview and turned off the video- and audiotape. Then the audiotape is turned back on, and Steve Oppler says the date and time, then I ask Thano about the volume of a blood vial. Thano answers. And then Steve Oppler says the interview is over and shuts off the tape recorder. No gap."

Chris said, "No, we have put this one to rest. We're going to move on." I thought that Chris was probably right. To any reasonable jury the defense allegations were thoroughly disproved, through two eyewitnesses and a videotape. Perhaps I was being hypersensitive, for now I was being accused of being a conspirator.

Days after the Thano tape was played in court, Peter Neufeld, Robert Shapiro, and I were in the jury room looking at some exhibits William Bodziak intended to use during his testimony to impeach Lee regarding the alleged second set of footprints. Peter was, in effect, trying to justify his implication that the Peratis tape was evidence of a conspiracy.

"Look, Peter, I have always considered it to be unethical to accuse a colleague of misconduct in open court unless you have some actual evidence that he engaged in misconduct."

Neufeld responded, "I didn't accuse you of any misconduct. If you think about what I said, I just said that you talked to him before the tape was turned on. You are allowed to do that. That's not improper."

"I know that would not have been improper," I said. "But that's not what I did. Two witnesses testified to that. If I allowed them to testify and I knew they were lying, that would be sub—subordinating perjury." My annoyance caused me to stumble over the word suborning.

Mockingly, Peter asked, "Subordinating perjury?"

Shapiro remained silent throughout this entire exchange. He listened intently with a funny, closed-mouth smile, vigorously nodding his head in agreement with my comments. I didn't respond. We continued looking at the Bodziak exhibits.

After we went back into the courtroom, while court was not in session, I said, "Bob, Judge Ito is involved in the conspiracy, now I'm involved in the conspiracy. Is there anyone you guys are not going to accuse of being in the conspiracy?"

Bob smiled. "Nope."

I said, "Now they need someone from the defense to be involved in the conspiracy. They need a mole within the defense team conspiring to convict Simpson. Do you know who the most likely candidate is?"

Bob laughed. "Yes. Me."

36

Who *Is* Mark Fuhrman?

THE TIME BOMB HAD BEEN LIT four and a half months earlier, when Fuhrman denied having used the "N" word in the last ten years. It was now growing ever more precarious as we scrambled to defuse it. At the tail end of August, after the defense had concluded their attack on the forensic and physical evidence, they were ready to move on to a new and infinitely more promising phase of their case.

After Fuhrman's testimony in March, more defense witnesses continued to come forward with stories of Mark Fuhrman and the "N" word. The most important of these was a woman named Laura Hart McKinny, an aspiring screenwriter who created a series of tapes with Mark Fuhrman starting in 1985.

In the wake of the publicity of the Simpson trial, Laura McKinny's attorneys contacted a television news organization in an apparent attempt to sell the tapes. Later, she stated that they were simply attempting to "determine the value" of the tapes. In relatively short order, the word was out that potentially explosive tapes existed involving Fuhrman's racist attitudes. The prosecution first heard reports of the existence of the McKinny tapes on July 14, 1995. Immediately after learning of them, Chris Darden informed the court of their existence.

At this time, I was devoting most of my efforts preparing to cross-examine Dr. Henry Lee. I probably became aware of the tapes sometime during the third week of July. We didn't know their exact content, but we were generally aware that they recorded Mark Fuhrman using racist language. I recall asking Cheri Lewis what the tapes were about. She replied, "We don't know yet. It's very possible that they're just Mark spouting off in an effort to create a work of fiction."

Defense efforts to secure the tapes began immediately. In the United States one state does not have authority to subpoena a witness in another state. Since McKinny lived in North Carolina, the defense had to use a procedure in which Judge Ito signed papers recommending that a North Carolina court issue a subpoena for Laura McKinny and her tapes.

On July 28, 1994, the North Carolina court in the county of Forsyth heard the matter. Under Johnnie Cochran's questioning, Laura McKinny testified that she first met Fuhrman in February 1985 in a cafe in Westwood. She was using a laptop computer, and he asked about it because they were not that common at the time. She was working on a story on women in the police force. In April 1985 she began interviewing Mark Fuhrman, on tape, to create a screenplay.

She testified in North Carolina that Mark's comments were only in the context of creating a work of fiction. He only talked about implicating or fabricating evidence "in the context of developing a story."

Johnnie Cochran asked her, "You don't recall him referring to himself as the Grand Dragon?"

She replied, "That was in the context of the story we were developing. There was a character in the story who was the Grand Dragon."

She continued: "It wasn't a biography of Mr. Fuhrman's life. He was helping me develop characters for a particular story."

Later, she said, "I think that the transcripts indicate that he gave me information about ideas and feelings that some people might have about African Americans. *I don't know that it reflects his feelings about African Americans.*" (emphasis added)

The North Carolina judge ruled that the tapes revealed that Fuhrman "was helping [McKinny] write a work of fiction. He was a technical adviser. He was helping her with dialogue. He was helping her with character development. . . . This material is collateral [not directly relevant to the main issues in the case]. And I will deny the subpoena." Strangely enough, we were far from elated at hearing this ruling. Somehow, with the media blitz surrounding these tapes, we knew that they weren't going away and that no North Carolina court was going to rule them out.

The defense battle to get the tapes was waged largely in the media. However, the battleground was actually inside Judge Ito's courtroom. On July 31, 1995, around the time defense expert John Gerdes was testifying, Cochran gave a lengthy harangue decrying the North Carolina court's decision and stressed the importance of the tapes: "Now, this is a bombshell!"

In my view, Cochran's diatribe was patently designed for media consumption, since he clearly knew that Judge Ito had no authority over a North Carolina court. However, Cochran's "bombshell" reverberated around the world and in North Carolina.

About a week later, the North Carolina Court of Appeals reversed the decision. Laura McKinny would have to testify.

The next day, some of the pundits commented on the effect of the tapes on the trial. "It's going to be devastating," said veteran defense lawyer Harland Braun. "It does more than eliminate Fuhrman as a witness. It really tars the whole prosecution. He's part of their team, and if they didn't know about this, how can [jurors] believe anything."

Barry Scheck and Johnnie Cochran joined the ranks of the media commentators in pronouncing doom. Scheck was quoted as saying that the North Carolina court's decision was "huge, huge. It could be the case." Cochran called it "the key most important ruling in the case so far, from the standpoint of Mr. Simpson."

Mark Fuhrman himself had made a seeming prognostication of the tapes' eventual impact in a tape-recorded conversation with McKinny shortly after the defense allegations of evidence planting first surfaced. In explaining why the LAPD initially came to his defense, he said, "I'm the key witness in the biggest case of the century. If I go down, they lose the case. The glove is everything. Without the glove—'bye, 'bye."

A few days after the North Carolina court ordered McKinny to testify in the Simpson case, her attorneys turned over the tapes. Then the process of reviewing the tapes began. There is no question that the tapes are replete with vile racist language and descriptions of graphic violence. However, a careful examination of the transcripts reveals at least several instances that support Laura McKinny's testimony in North Carolina that Mark was not relating his personal views but was attempting to help create a work of fiction.

For example, in the April 5, 1985, interview, Mark relates this graphic story. Mark described an incident where supposedly two of his police buddies were shot and ambushed. "Both down when I arrived. I was the first at the scene. Four suspects ran into a second-story apartment and we kicked the door down, grabbed the girl, one of their girlfriends, by the hair, stuck a gun to her head, and used her as a barricade. . . . 'I'm going to blow her fucking brains out if you have a gun.' They all were like this—threw the bitch down the stairs—dead-bolted the door—next play, boys."

McKinny asked, "Can we use that in the story?"

"It hasn't been seven years. Statute of limitations. . . . Anyway, we basically tortured them. . . . [T]here was blood everywhere. All the walls, all the furniture, all the floor. It was just everywhere. These guys, they had to shave so much hair off, one guy they shaved had like seventy stitches in his head. Knees cracked. We had 'em begging that they would never be gang members again. So there were sixty-six allegations. [There was] a demonstration [against me] outside Hollenbeck Station chanting my name."

Certainly, this is a chilling, horrendous narration. However, in an April 23, 1985, conversation with McKinny, Fuhrman, apparently describing the same incident, embellishes it even more. This time, he said that one of the suspects actually died. An even more significant clue that the story is false can be found in Mark's psychiatric report relating to his disability claim. He apparently described the same story. However, as we saw, the experts concluded that he was not telling the truth in relating stories about violence. Finally, there is no record documenting the alleged incident, and based on Fuhrman's own description, one would suspect that it would have been extensively documented.

In another passage, Mark seems to be telling Laura McKinny about the importance of using authentic dialogue for the purposes of creating fictional police characters. "All the *cocksuckers*, everything, that is important. That is policemen's talk." (emphasis added)

McKinny responded. "It is life talk. It is not just policemen's talk."

"But we have mastered it," Fuhrman said. "No, the Marine Corps mastered it."

What he appears to be saying here is that words like "cocksuckers" and other vile, derogatory terms are authentic policemen's talk. One inference is that he was using such language to re-create dialogue for fictional purposes.

When I first heard these tapes, I found their content to be repellent. However, they did not surprise me for several reasons. First, I have been involved in law enforcement and have dealt with police officers for over ten years. Racism is a significant problem in society and law enforcement. The language used on the tapes is an authentic reflection of how a significant minority of police officers talk. I was not shocked that Mark knows this language or from time to time used it.

I can truthfully say that I have never used the "N" word in a derogatory manner. However, I think that I could have re-created the dialogue Mark used during the McKinny interviews, and so could any other prosecutor or criminal defense attorney, including Cochran and the other members of the defense team.

What did upset me was when the defense, the commentators, and others treated the tapes as evincing a shocking, aberrant view of an extreme zealot. To view them in this way ignores the fact that the tapes may illustrate a more widespread, institutionalized racism within our society as a whole. I witnessed an "emperor's new clothes" type of phenomenon. Everyone seemed to be pretending that they had no idea that such language was currently part of our society and law enforcement.

The second reason I was not shocked is that Mark's last use of a racial epithet on the tapes occurred in 1987. This is around the time I first met him. The person I knew in 1987 was the type of rigid individual that I could imagine holding racist beliefs. However, as I previously described, the individual I knew after 1990 was a different person. Therefore, nothing on the tapes caused me to reevaluate my theory that Mark may be a "recovered racist."

The New York Times conducted an extensive investigation of Mark Fuhrman entitled "A Portrait of the Elusive Police Detective in the 'O. J. Whirlpool,' " published in March 1996. It suggested that "the lurid stories the detective recounted on the tapes were simply braggadocio by an egotistical but troubled man." In January 1996 the Los Angeles County Public Defender's Office conducted a review of cases in which Mark Fuhrman had been the investigating officer. The defendants in those cases offered no complaints of planting evidence or racial animus. In fact, many complimented Mark, including some minority defendants.

Moreover, LAPD internal affairs has launched a massive investigation based on the Fuhrman tapes. They have gone to great lengths to substantiate the stories contained in the tapes. However, they have not been able to verify Fuhrman's claims. For instance, in the tapes, Fuhrman claimed that his partner, Tom Vettraino, ripped up the driver's license of an African-American motorist before issuing him a ticket. Internal affairs collected every ticket book of Vettraino's going many years back. They then tracked down every African-American motorist Vettraino had stopped, including some who had moved to other parts of the country. Not one of them could confirm that such an incident involving Vettraino ever occurred. They also asked each motorist whether Vettraino used any racial epithets. All stated he had not.

Tom Vettraino recently told me he felt that many of Mark's stories contained in the tapes were taken from plots of television cop shows.

But whatever the truth might be about Mark Fuhrman, the real issue was whether it was relevant to the Simpson case.

37

Fuhrman and the Judge's Wife

By MID-AUGUST, while I was deeply involved in preparing for my cross-examination of Henry Lee, the complexities the Fuhrman tapes raised were seemingly mushrooming out of control. During a conference in chambers on August 14, Marcia brought to Judge Ito's attention a new issue. On the tape, Mark Fuhrman was heard making certain extremely disparaging remarks about LAPD captain Peggy York, Judge Ito's wife. Captain York had been assigned to the West Los Angeles Division in a supervisory capacity. In the tapes Mark vividly related an argument that he allegedly had with Captain York. The argument supposedly occurred in the mid-1980s. However, Captain York signed a declaration denying that the incident Mark described ever took place.

The possibility that his wife could become a witness posed a major legal dilemma for Judge Ito. Generally, a judge must recuse himself if his spouse might become a witness.

At around this time, Marcia told me that Mark had related an incident about Captain York that could become very relevant. She theorized that if Mark had concocted the story about Captain York, maybe he could also make up hyperbolic stories about beating up people and about his racism.

On the morning of August 15, 1995, Judge Ito called both sides into his chambers. He stated that there was a potential that one side might want to call his wife as a witness on the Mark Fuhrman issue. He said, "If my wife is a material witness, then under this code section, I'm required to disqualify myself and perhaps declare a mistrial at this point. The alternate is to solicit a waiver from the parties." Judge Ito gave both sides an hour to evaluate how to handle the issue.

When the lawyers for both sides reconvened, Marcia explained that it was logically impossible to determine whether Captain York could be called as a witness without first determining how much of the Fuhrman tapes, if any, would be admitted. Captain York would only become relevant if the tapes were played and the prosecution needed to show that Mark fabricated certain incidents on the tapes. Judge Ito asked Marcia whether she was saying that another judge would have to step in to handle the entire issue regarding the Mark Fuhrman tapes.

This prompted Cochran to make an impassioned plea for Judge Ito to remain on the case and decide the issues regarding the Fuhrman tapes. Cochran argued that the incidents on the tape were not made up, they were true. "These are real people! These are real incidents!"

Marcia shot back, "[A]ll of this stuff with the tapes has no relevance to this case whatsoever! It is a very shrewd, cynical, and cold-eyed effort to make sure that the jury never looks at the case. That's all this is!"

Finally, Scheck piped in: "We think this is a deliberate effort to create a mistrial."

Marcia snapped, "I don't think Mr. Scheck should be allowed to be heard. One lawyer."

Barry complained: "You know, Your Honor, you heard her the other day, when she was opposing these tapes before you, tell me to shut up when I pointed out that she should just stop. She has quoted from my bar card. She has called me without a brain. I have been completely civil to her, and she should just stop it."

As I look back on this in-chambers conference today, I am struck by Cochran's assurance "These are real people. These are real incidents." To this date neither the defense nor the Los Angeles County Public Defender's Office have found any corroboration that the incidents related on the tapes were true.

After the meeting in chambers, the lawyers moved to open court. Cochran continued his bombast outside the jury's presence but before the cameras. "This is a blockbuster. This is a bombshell. This is perhaps the biggest thing that has happened in any case in this country in this decade. . . . They can run, but they can't hide." However, Cochran did not address the legal issue at hand—whether Judge Ito could remain on the case.

By now, one of the younger lawyers had torn me away from my efforts to prepare for Henry Lee's cross-examination, and I was standing in front of the TV set in the War Room lobby, watching the proceedings. After the arguments were concluded, Judge Ito summarized the issue before him. Since Fuhrman had made remarks disparaging Judge Ito's wife, the judge might have difficulty being fair in evaluating the admissibility of the Fuhrman tapes. Judge Ito explained that a reasonable person might conclude that he would admit the tapes to punish Fuhrman. Judge Ito also observed that one could argue that he might rule the tapes inadmissible to prevent his wife from becoming involved in the case.

Judge Ito said, "I love my wife dearly." His voice quavered and he continued haltingly, fighting back tears. "I am wounded by criticism of her, as any spouse would be, and I think it is reasonable to assume that could have some impact."

He ruled that he would have to recuse himself from deciding the admissibility of the Fuhrman tapes and whether his wife could be called as a witness.

When I heard Judge Ito utter the words "I am wounded by criticism of her . . . and I think it is reasonable to assume that could have some impact," I sat down in a chair facing the TV set. I had personally believed that Judge Ito could be perfectly fair in ruling on the Fuhrman issue. When he takes matters under submission, he has strong legal reasoning skills. I had thought he could set aside any emotions occasioned by criticism of his wife. However, Judge Ito was clearly saying that the emotional impact of Fuhrman's comments about his wife "could have some impact." Does he realize what he's saying? I wondered. The logical extension of his comments was to remove himself from the entire case! There would be no practical way another judge could replace Ito, since it would take months for a new judge to study the case. With a sequestered jury, such a delay was unthinkable.

After a few moments, I tried to go back to working on preparing the Henry Lee cross-examination. Although the War Room was unusually quiet, I couldn't concentrate. The case is over, I thought. I wouldn't have to worry about cross-examining Henry Lee.

Later that evening, Bill Hodgman came into the War Room. We spoke in my cubicle. "Bill, why can't we just waive the recusal issue, allow another judge to decide the issue regarding the Fuhrman tapes, and then send the matter back to Ito?"

Bill replied, "We've thought about it, and it just wouldn't be workable." He explained that if we had another judge decide the issue of the admissibility of the Fuhrman tapes, then that judge would have to rule on objections during the trial when the tapes were played. During closing argument, that judge would also have to rule on the propriety of arguments made about the Fuhrman tapes. We would basically have one case and two judges for the rest of the trial. "And it would look so strange to the jury," Bill continued. "Like the Fuhrman issue was so explosive it required its own judge. What do you think?"

I probably should not have answered this question, since Cheri Lewis was primarily responsible for the legal issues related to Fuhrman and I was buried in my preparation for Henry Lee. In fact, Cheri was already well under way with the recusal brief. But I said, "Notwithstanding what Ito said in court today, I still think he can be fair. Let's face it, Bill, the problems we have with Judge Ito do not stem from the fact that his wife could be a potential witness. If there is a perception that we used this issue as an excuse to force a mistrial in order to get a second shot at this case, it could present a real problem. I have talked to numerous people who strongly support the prosecution and believe in Simpson's guilt but have complained bitterly about the cost and length of this trial.

"So have I," Bill interjected.

I continued: "If people think we manipulated this issue to start over, with a new judge and jury we could be poisoning the well. Even otherwise proprosecution potential jurors could be angry with us. We could get a worse jury the second go-around than we have now. The second thing to consider is that we have to be absolutely certain that we have an airtight legal case justifying recusal. Because if we force a mistrial and we're wrong, double jeopardy attaches, and that's the end of the case. I just haven't researched the legal issue enough to express an opinion on that."

Bill gave me the funny little thoughtful look he gets when he's pondering a difficult issue. He cocked his jaw to one side and raised his eyebrows.

I was not involved in any of the conversations that undoubtedly took place later that night regarding how to best handle the issue.

*   *   *

The next day, I drove to work believing that the Simpson case would probably come to an end. I supposed the decision to end the case was the right one. After all, what kind of a chance did we stand with this jury, anyway? I started thinking about the landscaping project I had postponed back in October. It was August now, the middle of summer. Not the best time for planting, I thought.

As I walked into the War Room, I saw Cheri. "What's the news?" I asked.

"We're not going to proceed with the recusal. I'm kind of pissed because I worked all last night on the motion."

"Why?" I asked.

"I don't know," Cheri said.

I shrugged my shoulders. Looks like I'm going to have to cross-examine Dr. Lee, after all, I thought. I made a beeline for my cubicle and resumed work.

The day that Henry Lee first hit the stand, the last of the Fuhrman-McKinny transcripts of the tapes were completed. The preparation for arguments on the admissibility of the tapes was conducted primarily by Cheri Lewis, Marcia Clark, and Bill Hodgman. There was a considerable range of views within the prosecution as to how to handle the issue.

Shortly before the Fuhrman-McKinny tape issue was argued before Judge Ito, I went into Marcia's office to ask her a quick question about Henry Lee. Marcia was typing into her computer and had several open notebooks on her desk containing the McKinny-Fuhrman transcripts. There was a burning cigarette in the ashtray.

"I'll come back later," I said.

"No, it's okay. Come in," Marcia said. "I want to ask you something about the tapes." Marcia shoved an open bag of pretzels in my direction as if to entice me to enter.

I entered but didn't sit down. She told me that some members of the prosecution team felt that we should agree that the entire tape should be played to the jury.

"What's their argument for doing that?" I asked.

Marcia explained, "They feel the prosecution should take the public position that we have nothing to hide and want the jury to know everything. Playing the tapes unedited would allow for a public airing of the tapes."

"And you think?" I inquired.

Marcia paused and then said, "I think these tapes are totally irrelevant. They are introducing a completely irrelevant, explosive red herring into the trial. Personally, I think not to oppose their admission would be incompetent. We have to do what's right for this case, not what's right for public opinion."

I said, "We should do what we would do if there were no cameras in the courtroom. But the problem, as I see it, is that I think we can't totally block the admission of these tapes. These tapes show that Fuhrman lied about the 'N' word. Ito's going to allow them in for that purpose. Since he already ruled that they were allowed to ask about the 'N' word to begin with, he's going to allow them to show that Fuhrman lied when he answered those questions."

As I spoke, I sensed that Marcia had basically arrived at the same conclusion. I told Marcia that our best bet was to offer a stipulation (an agreement between both sides about a certain fact) that Fuhrman did, in fact, lie about never using the "N" word. "The stipulation gives something substantial to both sides," I said. "For us, it makes the tapes irrelevant, since the defense will no longer need them to prove Fuhrman lied; therefore, the tapes would be inadmissible. However, it also gives something substantial to the defense. We are admitting, without question, that one of our witnesses lied. That's a big deal. It's going to hurt."

"Uh-huh," Marcia said as she puffed on her cigarette and squinted at me.

I continued to explain that if the defense wouldn't stipulate, they should only get to use a small portion of the tape to show Fuhrman did, in fact, use the "N" word. But they shouldn't be allowed to actually play the full context in which all the statements were made. "I think that's the best we can hope for. If Ito goes along with this position, I think it would be our definition of success."

Marcia, still looking at me intently, said resignedly, "Yes, that's the best we can hope for from Lance [Ito]."

On August 29, 1995, the hearing on the admissibility of the tapes commenced. Playing the excerpts of the Fuhrman tapes the defense wanted to introduce would take up a significant part of the court day. The prosecution objected to this procedure. Judge Ito had already reviewed the tapes and transcripts at length. Hence, reviewing them again in open court was a waste of time. However, Judge Ito said that he did not want to "be in a position where there is any indication that this court would participate in suppressing information that is of vital public interest." He decided to allow the defense to play the tapes in open court in front of the cameras. "I will hear it again, and *that will be for the purpose of public dissemination* of this information." (emphasis added)

Anyone who has wondered whether cameras in the courtroom influenced the proceedings need only read this passage. I had always suspected that the cameras were influencing Judge Ito's actions. Here was the proof. Here Judge Ito was clearly admitting that he was engaging in the procedure of playing the tapes solely for the purpose of "public dissemination" via the cameras. This is not the purpose of a court proceeding.

After the tapes were played, the arguments commenced. The defense arguments were characterized by the usual hyperbolic rhetoric. Uelmen argued to the court: "We've . . . come to the sickening realization of who Mark Fuhrman really is, Los Angeles's worst nightmare."

Marcia responded with quiet anguish. "Let me begin by saying that the content of these tapes is so repugnant and so offensive that this may well be the most difficult thing I've ever had to do as a prosecutor. I don't think that there is anyone in this courtroom or in this country that could possibly envy me."

She continued: "But I cannot afford the luxury of being Marcia Clark the citizen. I am Marcia Clark the prosecutor, and I stand before you today, Your Honor, not in defense of Mark Fuhrman but in defense of a case, a case of such overwhelming magnitude in terms of the strength of the proof of the defendant's guilt that it would be a travesty to allow such a case to be derailed with a very serious and important but very inflammatory social issue. . . ."

"And I wanted to share with Your Honor something I saw. . . . [O]ccasionally these cartoonists come up with something that's edifying. It's a little child speaking to his mother watching television who says, 'What's the forbidden 'N' word they keep talking about, Mommy?' She said, 'Nicole.' "

Then Marcia summarized the facts showing why Mark Fuhrman could not have planted the glove. Fact: A number of police officers arrived at Bundy before Mark Fuhrman and saw only one glove. Fact: Detective Fuhrman was never alone outside around that evidence where he could have gotten the glove to take to Rockingham. Fact: There were thumps against Kato's wall right where the glove was found. Fact: Fuhrman didn't know if there were eyewitnesses, earwitnesses, if Mr. Simpson had an alibi. "I just can go on and on with that," Marcia said. "Ridiculous comes to mind."

Judge Ito interjected, "Bronco fibers on the glove."

"Right," Marcia said. "Bronco fibers on the glove, on the Rockingham glove and on the knit cap."

Then Marcia used the tactic we had discussed earlier: she offered to stipulate that Fuhrman had used the "N" word.

A couple of days later, Judge Ito ruled that the defense should be allowed to show that Fuhrman lied about not using the "N" word. However, the judge rejected the theory that the tape was relevant to show that Fuhrman planted any evidence. Therefore, he excluded the entire McKinny tape except for two relatively less inflammatory instances where Fuhrman had used the "N" word.

That evening, on national television, Johnnie Cochran expressed outrage over Judge Ito's ruling: "This inexplicable, indefensible ruling lends credence to all those who say the criminal-justice system is corrupt. . . . The cover-up continues."

The next day, before I left work, I stopped to say good night to Marcia. I knocked on the door and poked my head in.

"Oh, Hank. In case I forgot to mention, I just wanted to thank you for handling the Lee cross; it went beautifully," Marcia said.

"Thanks, you told me," I said.

"Hank, what do you think of the ruling?"

I took a deep breath. "Marcia, this is about the best we could hope for." I paused, thinking about what else to say. "We have to define this as a victory."

Marcia glanced out the window of her office. "I agree."

We both really thought it was a victory. Clearly, however, neither of us felt that way.

Marcia then asked, "Did you hear that they're accusing Lance [Ito] of being a part of a cover-up. So now he's part of the conspiracy?"

"Unbelievable. It's totally unfair. It may even be unethical. But, Marcia, they know exactly what they're doing. They have figured out that Ito can actually be influenced by being criticized in public. It makes him actually more likely to rule in their favor in the future.

They're hoping he'll allow in more inflammatory evidence in other areas.''

"Incredible, isn't it?'' Marcia said rhetorically. "I think he's going to allow the defense to call more witnesses to testify to the 'N' word.''

Later, my brother David, an avid sports fan, told me it was like a coach who screams at a referee's bad call, hoping he will get a makeup call later. Now we had to wait to see what that makeup call was going to be.

38

One Pointless Lie

AFTER DR. LEE LEFT THE STAND, the remainder of the defense case was devoted to proving what by now had become the single most important issue in the trial: whether Mark Fuhrman had used the "N" word within the last ten years.

The defense's next witness was Kathleen Bell. She testified that in 1985 and 1986 she had worked at a Century 21 office located over a marine recruiting station and had become friendly with the marines working there. Between 1985 and 1986 she saw Fuhrman there. She noticed that Mark was "handsome." A few weeks later, the next time she saw him there, she went inside and introduced herself.

She testified that she "thought that he would be interested in meeting my girlfriend Andrea Terry." She claimed that during the conversation Fuhrman's demeanor suddenly changed and he said that "when he sees a black man with a white woman driving in a car he pulls them over." According to Bell, he also said, "If I had my way . . . all the niggers would be gathered together and burned." She testified that she was shocked and became tearful.

Bell testified that about a month later, probably in 1986, she saw Fuhrman again at Hennessey's bar in Redondo Beach. She was there with Andrea Terry. As Terry and Bell were leaving, Terry "started kind of veering off towards his table. . . . She kind of had—kind of a grin on her face, like she was going to go get his goat or something like that." She saw Terry conversing with Mark but did not hear what they said to each other.

Upon seeing Mark on TV testifying at the preliminary hearing, she immediately contacted Channel 9 in Los Angeles. She talked to a reporter before she wrote the letter to Johnnie Cochran. About a month after talking to Channel 9, she contacted an attorney to represent her in the matter.

On cross, Chris asked, "Despite the horror and the trauma Detective Fuhrman's use of this word caused, isn't it true that you still introduced Andrea Terry to Mark Fuhrman?"

"I did not."

Chris also brought out that Bell had appeared on *Larry King Live* and *Dateline NBC.*

As Chris's cross-examination implies, Andrea Terry's version of the Hennessey's bar incident contradicted Bell's. Terry claimed Bell had introduced her to Fuhrman. He also had information from the marine witnesses to contradict the recruiting-station incident, as detailed earlier. Chris also possessed an August 31, 1994, defense memorandum stating that Kathleen Bell's attorney, Taylor Daigneault, said that "Ms. Bell has talked to the tabloids but no deal has been struck. . . . She is a credible and truthful person. However, she is 'not a wealthy woman,' and if a large sum of money was offered, she would consider it."

However, Chris had to be restrained in his cross-examination of Bell. If he attacked her credibility, the judge would be more likely to allow the defense to bolster the "N" word part of their case by introducing additional evidence. The defense could argue to Ito that they should be allowed to introduce more "N" word evidence, since the prosecution was suggesting that Bell could not be believed.

Next, witness Natalie Singer testified to another instance when Mark used the "N" word. In 1986 she lived in an apartment in Beverly Hills with her roommate, Karel Hannak. Singer met two police officers, Mark Fuhrman and Tom Vettraino. They were invited to visit the apartment. In explaining his work with gangs, Mark Fuhrman used the "N" word. Mark Fuhrman described how he would mistreat black people and said, "Oh, it really relieves your tension. . . . It hits you here." He said, "The only good nigger is a dead nigger."

On another occasion, Singer testified that she saw Mark Fuhrman and his partner leaving their car and walking to the apartment. She said, "Hi, Tom. Hi, you guys." Then, for no apparent reason, Mark called her "a fucking bitch." This comment was made when she heard them chatting outside her bathroom window. Through the window, she called Mark an "asshole" and said, " 'I do not want you in this house anymore; nobody does. Don't come up here. You are not welcome." She said to Officer Vettraino, "You are welcome to come up here."

Interestingly, when Singer came forward as a witness, she retained counsel. One can only speculate as to the reason. Ordinarily there is absolutely no reason for a witness in a case to retain counsel. Also, according to an interview with Vettraino, Fuhrman did not use the "N" word in Singer's presence.

When I look back on this testimony, it is utterly amazing that Mark Fuhrman's use of the word *bitch* almost ten years earlier was deemed relevant evidence in a trial to determine whether Simpson murdered Nicole and Ron. However, Judge Ito's rulings regarding this evidence were growing even more inexplicable. Over Chris's objection, Ito allowed the witness to testify why she was hurt by Mark's use of the "N" word. "It is bolstered and held up and pushed out of his mouth with hatred and arrogance and despicability and that is what hurts. That is what hurts."

Judge Ito should not have permitted such testimony. The witness's reaction to hearing the "N" word is totally irrelevant under any possible legal theory. Mark Fuhrman's state of mind when he used the word has some arguable relevance. However, her state of mind when she heard it was inadmissible.

After this testimony, Chris argued that more evidence regarding Mark Fuhrman's use of the "N" word was cumulative (more than the judge deems reasonably necessary to prove the point). "We have sat here and we have taken it on the chin with regard to these witnesses and their testimony as it relates to Mark Fuhrman's racial animus. . . . We have heard it, and we have not disputed it. It is done. Okay? Everything that they wanted to accomplish today I think is done." Judge Ito seemed to think Chris's argument was well taken and stated that if they called Roderic Hodge, another witness to testify about the "N" word, he might have to rule Ms. McKinny's testimony cumulative.

There was time to reargue yet another issue before calling the next witness. Uelmen was allowed to reargue the issue of the McKinny-Fuhrman tapes. He said nothing new.

Judge Ito slightly modified his earlier ruling on the McKinny tapes by agreeing to allow the defense to substitute one of the passages in the tapes involving the use of the "N" word with an excerpt about women police officers not being able to wrestle a six-foot "nigger." The reason for the substitution was that the passage it replaced was barely audible.

When Laura Hart McKinny finally took the stand, she testified that in 1985 she was a UCLA learning-skills counselor, a home instructor for the Santa Monica Malibu Unified School District, and a freelance writer. She was writing a story about women police officers working in areas of high crime and had engaged Mark as a consultant. She testified that in the course of their interviews he used the "N" word forty-two times. As with the other witnesses, Judge Ito inexplicably allowed Ms. McKinny to testify to how hearing the word made her feel. Her state of mind was, of course, irrelevant. Yet over Chris's repeated objections, Ms. McKinny was permitted to testify "It is a base epithet. There is no way of doctoring it up and making it sound better. It is offensive, and I didn't feel good about it, hearing it. However, I was very much in the journalistic mode. . . . I would need to not react, not to be judgmental about hearing some of the very base, offensive kinds of things that I would be hearing."

Then the first passage where the "N" word was used was played: "We have no niggers where I grew up."

Remarkably, Johnnie Cochran was permitted to expand the court's ruling that the only specific usages of the "N" word on the tapes would be limited to two instances. Referring to the quote just played, Cochran asked, "Can you compare that with the other forty-two times or so that he used this in the course of your interviews, if there is any difference between how he used the term there and the other forty-two times or so?"

Chris promptly objected. This question called for McKinny to testify about the uses of the "N" word that were excluded. But Judge Ito overruled the objection.

McKinny answered, "Yes, there is a significant difference here. This particular example is the least offensive and inflammatory in comparison to the others."

Now Judge Ito seemed to realize the impropriety of the question and responded, "All right. I'm going to strike that answer. . . . Next question."

Cochran then asked another question that flagrantly informed the jury that Judge Ito was keeping sections of the tape from them. When a judge excludes evidence, an attorney is not allowed to in-form the jury that the evidence was ruled inadmissible. For example, if in a drug case the judge excluded all but two of forty-two bags of marijuana and if the prosecutor asked, "How would you compare the two bags of marijuana to the other forty bags the judge wouldn't let me introduce," there would be a mistrial.

When Cochran asked McKinny to testify about another instance where Fuhrman used the "N" word, he said, "[L]et's move down to the second incident *we have been allowed to use* for Fuhrman [using the 'N" word]."(emphasis added) This question informed the jury that there was other evidence the defense was not allowed to use. Judge Ito said nothing about this impropriety.

McKinny's testimony about her personal reactions to the use of the "N" word was perplexing. It seemed contradictory to her prior testimony in North Carolina that during the tape-recorded interviews, Fuhrman was giving her examples of authentic police dialogue and that she *didn't "know that [the tapes] reflected his feelings about African Americans."* (emphasis added)

However, Chris was in an untenable position as a cross-examiner. He knew that her previous take on the tapes was contradictory to her current testimony. He also had love letters McKinny had written to Mark, contradicting her claim that they were not romantically involved. However, any false move on cross-examination could open the floodgates for the excluded portions of the tapes to come crashing down on our heads. If Chris impeached McKinny with the quote from North Carolina or otherwise suggested that Fuhrman was attempting to create a work of fiction, the judge might rule that the defense should be able to put in other uses of the "N" word so that the jury could determine whether they reflected Mark's true feelings. Similarly, any effort to rehabilitate Fuhrman by calling character witnesses would have opened the floodgates to the tapes. Nor would it have been wise for Chris to have been seen as rushing to the defense of Fuhrman.

I could understand and feel the frustration Chris must have been experiencing. The best illustration of his dilemma was when he asked, "When Mark Fuhrman used these words in your presence, why didn't you just tell him to stop?" This question allowed McKinny to bring in otherwise inadmissible material from the tape. She answered, "For the same reason I didn't tell him to stop when he told me of police procedures, cover-ups, [and] other information."

The statement about "cover-ups" had been excluded. Chris

tried to repair the damage by showing that Fuhrman's comment about "cover-ups" referred to the LAPD's refusal to acknowledge that female officers did not perform well in violent situations. In other words, it was a sexist comment.

On redirect, Johnnie Cochran apparently thought that the "cover-up" testimony possibly opened the floodgates on the issue of Fuhrman's sexism. There was a side-bar conference to determine how far he could go. Judge Ito wanted to know specifically what question Cochran proposed to ask. Cochran said, "I have the right, it seems to me, to ask the question."

Judge Ito said pointedly, "That is not what I asked. I asked you what [questions] are you going to ask?"

Cochran snapped back, "Your Honor, I resent that tone. I'm a man just like you are, Your Honor. I resent that tone, Your Honor. I resent that tone, Your Honor."

Judge Ito immediately asked the lawyers to step into chambers. "Mr. Cochran, let me just express to you some concern that I have regarding our personal relationship at this point in time."

"Yes, Your Honor," Cochran said.

For the first and only time, Judge Ito complained about Cochran's accusing him, in a press conference, of trying to cover up the McKinny tapes. "I have chosen up to this point to ignore your press conference last Thursday and what I consider to be in direct contempt of this court. I have chosen to ignore that."

Judge Ito continued: "And I think the record will reflect that I asked you a direct question and you started talking about something else. And I redirected your attention back to the question that I asked, and apparently you have taken umbrage at that. Well, Mr. Cochran, let me tell you something. I take umbrage at your response and your reaction. And I want you to know that I have chosen to ignore it thus far and that is because of our long relationship and what I will hope will be our continuing friendship."

Cochran said, "Perhaps my reaction was that I felt that I was a man, you are a man, we have been friends and I thought the tone—"

Judge Ito interrupted: "Counsel, when you say something, 'I am a man, you are a man,' that is—that is a challenge of sorts, wouldn't you say?"

"Well, no. I was just saying I didn't want to be talked to like a schoolkid."

The judge said, "I need to take a deep breath, too, Mr. Cochran. . . . Let's take a recess."

I had no idea that this incident took place until researching the transcript for this book. It is strange that the only time Judge Ito treated Cochran harshly was in chambers, out of the jury's and camera's view. Not so for any of the other lawyers in this trial. Personally, I do not interpret this incident as an accidental, emotional flare-up on Cochran's part. He is the consummate professional. I never saw Cochran lose control or display any genuine human emotion at any time in the trial. I believe his seeming loss of temper was a shrewdly calculated trial tactic. He must have believed, on the basis of his friendship with Ito, that his harsh criticism was likely to lead to some favorable rulings down the line.

Immediately after this incident, Judge Ito gave a favorable ruling to the defense, finding that Cochran could establish, through McKinny, that Fuhrman was also a sexist.

After McKinny's testimony, Chris observed, at a side-bar conference, "If Mr. Simpson is acquitted just because Mark Fuhrman uttered an epithet, well, then there is no justice, Judge."

Next, the defense announced that they would call Roderic Hodge. Another makeup call: Judge Ito decided to allow Hodge's testimony even though earlier that day he had indicated that he had serious questions as to what, if anything, Hodge would add.

Hodge, an African-American man, testified that sometime in January 1987, Mark Fuhrman took him into custody. It was on a charge of narcotics possession and battery of a police officer. While transporting Hodge in the police car, Mark turned around and said, "I told you we would get you, nigger." According to Mr. Hodge, Fuhrman said it with "anger, hatred, just something from deep inside, if you would, just—just very ugly." Over an objection, Judge Ito permitted him to testify that he felt "belittled, scared, very angry."

During cross-examination, Chris attempted to ask him specific questions about the actual date that he was arrested by Fuhrman. At a side bar, Chris explained that he was trying to establish that "there were many, many, many, many contacts by LAPD, from the narcotics and gang units, of Mr. Hodge. Mr. Hodge was a crack dealer over on Corning Avenue, an area where crack was sold by him and members of the Playboy Gangster Crips."

Ito responded by again giving Chris advice on how to handle the cross. "Why wouldn't you at this point say, Mr. Hodge, you were offended, that was a horrible thing? Thank you very much. Good-bye?"

Here Judge Ito was telling Chris not to cross-examine Mr. Hodge. This is the same stunt Judge Ito pulled earlier with me when he told me I should roll over on my cross-examination of Henry Lee by only taking thirty minutes to question him. From personal experience, I knew exactly what Chris was feeling when he heard Judge Ito's comments about Hodge.

Chris contained his anger. He calmly explained to Judge Ito that when "Mr. Hodge lodged complaints to [the Internal Affairs Division]. . . . he complained about everything else under the sun, but he didn't complain about" the incident with Fuhrman in the car. Chris forcefully explained why he wanted to cross-examine Mr. Hodge. "I feel no need to lay down or roll over and die just because the jury has been polluted with these epithets."

On cross, after showing Hodge the Internal Affairs complaint, Chris asked, "Did you see the epithet indicated here in these documents?"

"No, sir."

On redirect, Hodge claimed that he did make a complaint to Internal Affairs about the alleged epithet. In fact, the report does state that terms like "shut the fuck up" and "fat ass" were used; however, it says nothing about the statement "I told you we would get you, nigger," or any other use of the "N" word.

At around the time Hodge was testifying, I was preparing the evidence we would use to rebut Henry Lee's foot-print testimony. Phil Vannatter stopped by my cubicle. "They're going to call Fuhrman to the stand." Phil and I walked to the reception area to watch television. While we were waiting for the Fuhrman spectacle, he told me a story. "You know, when we went to the crime scene the other day with the defense, Carl Douglas said something kind of interesting to me. We were joking around a little, and I said to him, 'Carl, how can you represent someone who could commit such a horrible crime?' And Carl said to me, 'Phil, if you murdered your wife, I would represent you, too.'"

"Did he really say that?" I asked.

"Yeah," Phil said.

"Phil, let me ask you something. Now you know that the defense is going after you tooth and nail, saying you kept the blood vial and planted evidence. Didn't it ever occur to you that the press would be real interested if you repeated the story you just told me?''

"Yeah, I realize that," Phil said. "But I've been in this business for twenty-seven years. And I think there's kind of a gentlemen's agreement that those off-the-record type of comments are not going to be used against the other side."

I had to admire Phil's attitude. It proved to me that he's a real stand-up guy. However, I wish I had said to Phil, "Don't you think that after the way they have treated you, any unwritten, unspoken gentlemen's agreements are off?"

Weeks later, Phil told me that Shapiro apologized to him for the defense's unfair attacks on his character. According to Phil, Shapiro said, " 'Phil, we've hit a new low.' "

After Phil and I watched the tail end of Hodge's testimony, Judge Ito allowed the defense to recall Mark Fuhrman to the stand outside the jury's presence. They argued that they were entitled to reopen the motion made months before I joined the case to suppress the evidence. Before deciding whether they were entitled to a rehearing, Judge Ito allowed Fuhrman to be recalled as a witness.

Gerald Uelmen asked Fuhrman a number of questions, and Fuhrman invoked his right to remain silent. Then Uelmen asked, "Is it your intention to assert your Fifth Amendment privilege with respect to all questions that I ask you?"

"Yes," Fuhrman answered.

Dean Uelmen asked for a moment to confer with fellow counsel.

At this point, Mark's attorney, Darryl Mounger, stated, "Your Honor, further questions don't serve any purpose, since my client has already answered that he will not answer any question and will assert his Fifth Amendment privilege. Anything further can only be a show."

Uelmen said, "I only have one more question, Your Honor."

Ito asked, "What was that, Mr. Uelmen?"

Uelmen took Judge Ito's question as a green light, and Judge Ito didn't stop him. "Detective Fuhrman, did you plant or manufacture any evidence in this case?"

"I assert my Fifth Amendment privilege."

As a lawyer, I understood why Mark took the Fifth. Since he lied on the witness stand about the "N" word, he theoretically could have faced perjury charges. His attorney probably advised him that to answer any questions about anything could result in a waiver of his Fifth Amendment rights. So he couldn't answer the question about planting evidence or any other.

However, legalities aside, on a human level I was bitterly disappointed. Fuhrman's taking the Fifth made it sound as though he might have planted evidence; which constituted an indictment not only of Mark Fuhrman but of our entire case and everyone on it.

When Det. Phil Vannatter heard Fuhrman take the Fifth, his face turned a deep red, and he rose out of his chair. Trembling, Phil said, "In my twenty-seven years—in twenty-seven years of being a police officer—I never thought I'd hear the day when a cop would get up on that witness stand and take the Fifth."

Speechless, I nodded my agreement.

"I just don't understand it," Phil continued. "It's—it's dishonorable. I mean, if he lied—if he lied about not using the 'N' word, be a man about it. Be a man! Just say you lied—take—take what's coming to you."

This is devastating, I thought. The jury will undoubtedly learn of Mark's taking the Fifth when asked whether he had planted the glove. This could free a man who we had proved committed two brutal murders.

I said to Phil, "You know, I've known Mark for years. You would think he might feel he owed it to those of us whom he knew—who put so much into this case. Owed it to the Browns and the Goldmans—to tell the truth. If he would have told us the truth from the beginning, all of this could have been avoided."

Later that evening, I saw Ron's sister, Kim, in the corridor outside the War Room. She was sobbing uncontrollably as Chris was consoling her. Through her tears, she said, "I want to go and tell him what he's done! Why did he do this? I want to tell that son of a bitch off."

Now that the defense had concluded their case, they needed just one more crowning achievement. They requested Judge Ito to instruct the jury that Fuhrman was unavailable to testify. We witnessed the biggest makeup call of all. Judge Ito agreed to give the following instruction: "Detective Mark Fuhrman is not available for further testimony as a witness in this case. His unavailability for further testimony on cross-examination is a factor which you may consider in evaluating his credibility as a witness."

Marcia decided we should appeal this decision by filing a writ with the appellate court. Judge Ito's instruction was totally contrary to a basic principle of law. It is fundamental that a jury is not allowed to draw an inference about a witness's credibility based on his or her invocation of the right to remain silent. In fact, the standard jury instruction to be given in such situations provides that when a witness invokes his or her right to remain silent, "you must not draw from the exercise of such privilege any inference as to the believability of the witness." This law is clear and well known.

Nevertheless, that night, the legal pundits were unanimous that there was no chance of the writ being granted. They confidently predicted that Judge Ito's ruling on the instruction would stand.

The next day, the prosecution team went to lunch at the Los Angeles City Mall, down the street from the courthouse. After lunch, while in the mall's courtyard, someone told us the news. "The writ was granted!" Judge Ito's instruction was held to be improper. Most of the members on the team were jubilant. They were literally jumping for joy. The granting of this writ was extraordinary. Someone offered the opinion that maybe this was the court of appeal's way of slapping Judge Ito on the wrist.

I did not share in the jubilation. The damage that Fuhrman had inflicted on our case was not reversible. The genie was out of the bottle. Enough of the Fuhrman-McKinny tapes was admitted to make race a central issue in the trial.

Together the team walked back from the mall, the same one where months earlier Woody Clarke and I had discussed whether blood could be degraded in a microwave. Surrounded by the giggles, whoops, and cheers of my fellow prosecutors, I walked up Temple Street to the courthouse—the same route I had taken seven months earlier when I first interviewed Nurse Peratis and discovered the "missing blood," the same one I took the day I returned from touring the Parker Center DNA lab with Collin. When we reached the building, I could smell the smoke from the buses and the smog, which always seemed so much worse on these hot summer days.

As we rode up the elevators to our offices to continue our work, I looked at Marcia, who was smiling and joking with the younger lawyers and law clerks. I wondered what Mark felt. I wondered whether he realized that the endless hours of work, the pain and heartache that so many had invested in this case, had been more than canceled out by one pointless lie.

Much later, after the defense rested but before the verdict, I asked Fuhrman's partner, Ron Phillips, also a longtime friend and colleague of mine, "Ron, didn't *you* know anything?"

Ron swore that he didn't.

I asked Ron about the Fuhrman tapes recorded by Laura Mc-Kinny.

Ron said, "I knew Mark was a sexist, but I didn't think he was a racist. I was absolutely amazed by the McKinny tapes. Recently, I called him and asked, 'Mark, why did you make those tapes? You hate women. And you placed your whole life in the hands of a woman you didn't even know?' And Mark said, 'Yeah, I know. I wasn't even thinking of those tapes during this case. I thought they were so long ago.'"

Ron summed it up to me. "Mark said he feels terrible about what happened, that he is devastated by what he did to the case."

I didn't have to ask what "devastated" Fuhrman. By spilling his guts to a would-be screenwriter in the hopes of getting a credit, he turned the O. J. Simpson case into a sideshow about Mark Fuhrman.

39

Fifty-five Guilty Coincidences

"IF WE'RE GOING TO HAVE ANY CHANCE of winning this thing, we've got to give the best closing argument in history" was my constant refrain to Marcia, Bill, and Chris when the defense was ready to conclude their case. I used every spare moment to begin the arduous task of assembling the arguments.

Our case involved six prosecutors presenting evidence over a nine-month trial, generating over forty-five thousand pages of trial transcript, centering around "key" issues involving such minutiae as staple holes, microscopic specks of blood on socks, and mind-bending technological jargon, all mixed in a stew of racial epithets and allegations of a massive police conspiracy. Coordination was challenging. An attorney who puts the evidence on at trial knows how to present it best during argument. We needed to bring all the lawyers together to assemble their respective sections into a single argument. That was my function.

Scott Gordon was primarily responsible for writing Chris's argument. I was primarily responsible for assisting Marcia. Scott and I worked closely together. I also worked closely with Rock, Woody, and DNA prosecutor Lisa Kahn, on the forensic side of the case. When attorneys work together in a brainstorming session, it is necessary for the discussion to be flexible and free enough to encourage creativity and at the same time structured enough so that you are actually getting something accomplished.

To arrive at this balance, I created a large chart on butcher paper, divided into columns for each of the major issues in the case,

309

with headings across the top: Domestic Violence, Racism, Contamination, Planting, etc. The columns were subdivided. For example, within Planting, we had a section for the Bronco, the rear gate, the glove, and the socks. I used this chart during our various discussions. I might ask, "How do we know the glove wasn't planted?" As we all came up with different arguments, I would write them down in the appropriate spot. But if someone suddenly changed the topic because they had a good idea about why the rear-gate blood was not planted, I would simply write that argument down in the rear-gate section and then refocus on the glove. By the time we were finished with our meetings, the chart outlined all of our arguments in a fairly organized way.

About two weeks before the closing argument Scott and I met in Garcetti's conference room with the large granite table. We took the arguments on the chart and organized them into a closing argument. Our task at that meeting was to assemble the ideas from all the attorneys into final form. For the opening argument we came up with a list of over fifty items that pointed to Simpson's guilt. The factors were broken up into fifteen major categories: (1) motive to kill, (2) opportunity to kill, (3) evidence showing Simpson planned to commit murder, (4) Simpson's hand injuries, (5) Simpson's strange activities at Rockingham, (6) the glove, (7) the Bundy trail, (8) the Bronco, (9) shoe prints, (10) knit cap, (11) manner of the killing, (12) Ron's shirt, (13) the socks, (14) the Rockingham trail, (15) Simpson's conduct after the murders.

After arriving at our fifteen categories, we proceeded to discuss each one to make sure we had all the best arguments for each item. The following represents my best effort to reconstruct a condensed version of our discussion based on the outline we prepared.

"Let's take it from the top," I said. "Motive to kill: *One,* we have the history of domestic violence. *Two,* we have the estrangement, the events of June 12, 1994, which communicate to him it's finally over."

Scott added, "We also have his comments to Kato on the evening of June 12 in which Simpson disapproves of the dress Nicole was wearing. The rebuff at the recital. His strange demeanor that night at the recital."

"Those aren't independent factors that point to his guilt," I reasoned. "They are all part of the estrangement factor. All showing that this triggering event occurred on the evening of June 12."

Scott chewed on his pencil for a moment. "True."

"Okay," I continued. "Number *three*: Simpson told Ron Shipp he had dreams of killing Nicole. Next major category, opportunity to kill. Item *four*: His whereabouts were unaccounted for during the murders. Kato last sees him at 9:35, and he's not seen again until he appears at 10:54, when the limo gets there."

Scott, in a Socratic fashion, asked a question for which he knew the answer. "How incriminating is it that his whereabouts are unknown during the murders?"

I thought about Scott's question and the best way of articulating this point for a jury. "This is an extremely public man. He has people waiting on him hand and foot. So it's just another unlucky coincidence that at the very time of the murders no one knows where he is?"

Scott took the pencil out of his mouth and muttered something that sounded like "Good." He quickly jotted down some notes to include that argument. "Factor *five*: We can put the defendant in the Bronco at 10:03 through the cell-phone records. Just another really unlucky coincidence? He's in the Bronco only minutes before the probable time of the murders."

I added, "We know the person who murdered Ron and Nicole used that Bronco because Ron and Nicole's blood is in it. So we have Simpson in the murder vehicle just before the murders. Pretty compelling evidence."

Next I discussed factor *six*, the thumps Kato heard between 10:50 and 10:51 P.M., near where the glove was found. "Scott, I've always found this such powerful evidence. Think about it. How many times last night did you hear mysterious thumping outside your house?"

"None," Scott said. "And this is Brentwood, guarded by private security services, in a compound surrounded by gates."

I continued: "Yet on the very night his wife is murdered, at the very hour of her murder, there are mysterious thumping sounds. And the defense wants us to believe they're not related?"

Scott nodded his head. "I think that does it for opportunity to kill. The next major category deals with evidence indicating that Simpson planned to murder."

I said, "This would be factor *seven*. Marcia points out the fact that Simpson's maid was not at Rockingham suggests that there was an arrangement for him to be alone."

Scott said, "There seems to be evidence of an alibi set up with

Kato. This would be factor *eight*. In other words, Simpson asks Kato for some change to go get something to eat. How often do you think Simpson asks Kato for money? Unexpectedly, Kato invites himself along. This raises another question. What vehicle did they take? They're going to McDonald's, but they take the Bentley, not the Bronco."

"So?" I asked.

"So he doesn't want to use what you just dubbed the 'murder vehicle' "

"Very good, I didn't think of that," I said. "That would be factor *nine*."

Scott said, "This brings us to the next major category, hand injuries."

"My favorite." I smiled. "Number *ten*: the fact that he gets a hand injury on the very same day his wife is murdered. Number *eleven*: Both the defense and prosecution agree that it's at the very same hour his wife is murdered."

"Number *twelve*," Scott added. "Not only does he get this cut, but it's on the very same side of his body, the left side, that the murderer was cut. Because the blood drops are to the left of the shoe prints."

I continued: "So Simpson admittedly gets cut on the *same* night during the *same* hour as the murderer was leaving the Bundy trail, on the *same* side of his body as the murderer. Amazing coincidence!"

Scott picked up. "Number *thirteen*: His cut is on his left hand, and the glove, lost at Bundy, is a left-handed glove. To accept the defense explanation just of the factors in the hand-injury section, we have to believe—"

"In a constellation of coincidences, large enough to fill a galaxy," I interrupted.

The next category we discussed was Simpson's activities at Rockingham after the murders, before he left for Chicago. Number *fourteen*: His reappearance at Rockingham just happened to be within a couple of minutes of when Kato heard the strange thumping noises. *Fifteen*: He was seen outside at night, without an explanation, entering the house. *Sixteen*: He lied to Allan Park, saying that he was late because he had overslept. *Seventeen*: He also claimed that he had just showered, which is what one would expect someone to do immediately after a bloody murder. *Eighteen*: The mysterious black bag, which Simpson would not let Kato or Allan Park touch, disappeared, and we knew that the murderer had to get rid of a number of things.

"Speaking of bags," I asked, "wasn't there also evidence from news footage that Robert Kardashian [Simpson's friend and one of his attorneys] received a Louis Vuitton bag from Rockingham the day after the murders, which appeared to be full? And wasn't that bag produced in court months later empty?"

"Yeah," Scott said.

I recalled that Cheri had unsuccessfully attempted to determine from Kardashian what was in the bag by filing a motion that Kardashian could not hide behind the attorney-client privilege (which generally makes conversations a client has with his attorney privileged). It was another dead end.

Next, we ran through number *nineteen*: Simpson left the socks in the middle of the carpet, but there were no other clothes there. This was consistent with Simpson's having stripped down to his stocking feet in the foyer to avoid getting blood in the house and then taking the clothes upstairs. Finally, number *twenty*: He complained to Allan Park about being overheated even though it was a cold night.

"Sounds like a lot of strange stuff happening at Rockingham on the same night at the same time," I observed. "This brings us to our next major category, the gloves. These gloves tell us a lot about the profile of the murderer. Number *twenty-one*: The gloves are twice as expensive as average men's gloves. *Twenty-two*: They're cashmere lined. Your average criminal doesn't wear this to the crime scene. *Twenty-three*: They're extra large, the defendant's size. But the most striking thing is that we know Simpson owned a pair of those gloves and there were only about one thousand of that size and style sold."

Scott offered, "Another huge coincidence. The real killer just happened to own a pair, and so did Simpson. This is number *twenty-four*.

I smiled. "Now my math's not that good. But if we assume that there are 125 million adult men in the United States, and only a thousand of them have a pair of those gloves, that means that only one out of every 125,000 men owns a pair. That's eight ten-thousandths of one percent of the male population owns a pair. That means that if we assume someone else killed Ron and Nicole, the percentage likelihood that that person just coincidentally happened to own extra large Aris Leather Lights is eight ten-thousandths of one percent. That's better, in my opinion, than the DNA evidence, and it's not subject to any contamination or planting defense. That's proof beyond a reasonable doubt right there.''

We then discussed the remaining factors related to evidence found on the Rockingham glove: number *twenty-five*, an African-American limb hair; *twenty-six*, a blue-black cotton fiber consistent with what Kato said Simpson had been wearing; *twenty-seven*, Simpson's blood; and *twenty-eight*, Bronco carper fiber.

''Maybe the real killer is a rich African American with extra large hands,'' Scott said ironically. ''Who likes expensive gloves and is one of the eight ten-thousandths of one percent of the population that owned those gloves and just happened to be wearing blue-black cotton on June twelfth. Just like Simpson. But it's not Simpson.''

We both chuckled for a moment before I continued. ''Another factor is that the glove was found outside, near the air conditioning, and that's where Kato heard the thumps, and Kato heard the thumps shortly before Simpson reappears at Rockingham. So everything ties together—the thumps, the location of the gloves, and Simpson's reappearance.''

Scott nodded his head. ''That's number *twenty-nine*.''

''Our next major category is the Bundy trail,'' I said. ''Number *thirty*: we have the PCR results. And number *thirty-one*: we have the conventional results.''

Scott asked, ''Why are you counting the conventional results separately from the PCR results? They're just two separate tests of the same item, so isn't it all really one item?''

''No,'' I responded. ''The PCR results on the five Bundy trail drops point to Simpson. However, the defense, through Gerdes, claims those results could be explained through contamination. So this is another unfortunate coincidence the jury has to accept to find Simpson not guilty. The only evidence they claim wasn't planted—the Bundy trail drops—gets contaminated in such a way as to erroneously point to Simpson. So if we're counting coincidences you have to accept to vote not guilty, that's number thirty.''

Scott nodded his head and scribbled down some notes as I continued.

''Number thirty-one is the conventional testing on the Bundy trail. Gerdes admitted that contamination cannot explain the conventional test results. Conventional testing shows that only one-half of one percent of the population would match the Bundy blood drops. Simpson is within that one-half of one percent. So to vote not guilty, you have to believe that it's just a coincidence that the person who murdered Ron and Nicole just happened to match Simpson's conventional blood type. The conventional testing, almost standing alone, proves guilt beyond a reasonable doubt. Now, on to the rear gate, item *thirty-two*. The RFLP testing on the rear gate matches Simpson. The defense is claiming that the blood was planted.''

"So you have to use three different explanations to account for this one piece of evidence," Scott observed. "First, the blood got contaminated to cause the PCR results to match Simpson. Second, Simpson was unlucky that the real killer's conventional blood type just happened to be the same as his. Third, Mark Fuhrman and his evil minions came along and planted the blood on the rear gate."

"Right. That brings us to our next major category, the Bronco. Let's start with Woody Clarke's argument: 'Forget the DNA testing. There's blood where there shouldn't be blood.' "

Scott picked up. "According to Simpson's statement to Dr. Baden, which came out during Brian's cross of Baden, Simpson said he cut himself when going into the Bronco to get the cell phone around the time the limo arrived at Bundy."

I added, "So the defense must admit that on the very night that Simpson's ex-wife is murdered, within the very hour that she was murdered, Simpson just happens to bleed in the Bronco. That's coincidence number *thirty-three*. *Thirty-four*, Ron's and Nicole's blood is also in the Bronco. *Thirty-five*, there's a possible shoe print on the Bronco carpet which is consistent with the Bruno Magli design."

"Number *thirty-six*," Scott continued. "Defense witness Heidstra, who claims that he heard noises at the Bundy location, says he saw a white Bronco-like vehicle at the Bundy location at the approximate time of the murders."

"I'm not sure that we want to argue that one," I observed. "Heidstra isn't a very credible witness, but let's write it down for now.

"That brings us to the next major category, and one dear to my heart, the shoe prints. Number *thirty-seven*: The shoe prints are size twelve, Simpson's size. Only ten percent of the male population has that size."

I continued: "The next fact, number *thirty-eight*, is that they are expensive casual shoes, one-hundred and sixty dollars. That tells you something about the profile of the person who committed this murder. It excludes your average murderer."

"It excludes your average deputy D.A." Scott grinned. "How many people spend one-hundred and sixty dollars on casual shoes? Not many people spend that much on dress shoes. Between the cashmere-lined gloves and the Bruno Magli shoes, sounds like the killer went to a fashion consultant. 'Excuse me, what would be the best outfit to wear to a murder?' "

"The most striking fact relating to the shoes," I continued, "is that only forty stores sold them. This is number *thirty-nine*. If you're a detective and you're trying to figure out who killed Ron and Nicole, you know the killer purchased men's shoes at one of those only forty locations. Guess what? So did Simpson. He regularly purchased men's shoes at Bloomingdale's, New York. If we figure that there are at least ten thousand locations around the country that sell men's shoes, what's the likelihood that Simpson just coincidentally regularly shopped at one of the same forty locations where the real killer purchased the shoes? Its 0.4 percent. The likelihood that the real killer and Simpson also just happen to be size twelve is 0.4 times .10, which is the percentage of all men who wear size-twelve shoes. That comes out to .04 percent, or four hundredths of one percent. That evidence is even better than the conventional testing on the Bundy blood drops."

I leaned back in my chair and rubbed my eyes. "Scott, we've been at it for several hours. I could use some coffee."

"So could I," Scott said. "I still have a relatively fresh pot in my office."

As we walked toward Scott's office, I said, "You know, people can't believe it when I tell them the D.A.'s office doesn't provide free coffee. You have to join the 'coffee club.' "

"Coffee?" Scott asked. "What about the water club? Aren't you also a member of the water club? I think I've seen you sneaking a cup of water every now and then," Scott said in a mock-accusatorial tone.

"I've been paying my dues. I'm not taking water without paying."

Supplied with fresh cups of coffee, we returned to the conference room to continue work. "The next major category is the knit cap," Scott said. "There's hair consistent with Simpson inside the knit cap. That's number *forty*. Number *forty-one*: There's a fiber on it consistent with Simpson's Bronco carpet. What's the defense explanation for the knit-cap evidence?"

"They're not claiming it's planted," I replied. "They can't claim it's contaminated because there were numerous hairs inside the cap. The claim has to be it's just another coincidence. The murderer's hair just happens to match Simpson's, and he just happened to have a carpet matching Simpson's Bronco carpet. What I think would be very effective is for Marcia to quote from the material I read into evidence during Lee's cross-examination. The quote was that although hair comparisons are not conclusive, they can be done 'to a high degree of certainty and can often establish partial individuality of a specimen with confidence based on experience and analytical results.' Translation: According to Henry Lee's testimony, you can figure out whether the hair was Simpson's to a 'high degree of certainty'; you can't be a hundred percent sure it's him, but you're pretty darn close. Close enough to be convinced on this evidence alone, beyond a reasonable doubt."

Next we discussed the category of items related to the manner of the killing. *Forty-two*: As Detective Lange testified, the evidence showed that the motive for the killing was rage. And *forty-three*: There was no evidence of theft or burglary or any motive for anyone other than Simpson to kill Ron and Nicole. Scott continued: "*Forty-four*: The victims did not scream. *Forty-five*: little evidence that Nicole resisted."

"Hold on there," I said. "How do those last two facts, no screaming and little resistance, point to Simpson?"

"Victims of domestic violence may suffer from learned helplessness," Scott said. Scott was referring to a psychological phenomenon—that women who are traumatized by abuse may become incapable of defending themselves. Scott continued: "She recognizes it's Simpson, so she can't fight back or even scream."

"That's an interesting point," I noted as I wrote it down in my notes.

The next category we discussed was Ron's shirt, on which was found a hair consistent with Simpson, number *forty-six*; and a blue-black cotton fiber matching the one on the Rockingham glove and the socks, *forty-seven*. The socks, the next category, contained Nicole's blood, *forty-eight*; and Simpson's blood, *forty-nine*.

"That brings us to the Rockingham trail," I said. "My favorite category. Now the defense explanation for this is that Simpson cut himself on the cell phone when he went into the Bronco around the time the limo driver was there. He left a trail of blood from the

Bronco to the front door, into the foyer, and left a drop in the master bathroom.

"We should ask the jurors, 'How many of you left a trail of blood from the jury room to the jury box today or anytime this week or anytime during this nine-month trial?' People just don't leave trails of blood around. It's not a daily occurrence. It's not a yearly occurrence. When you cut yourself, you hold your hand and stop the bleeding. You don't drip a trail of blood around unless you're not in your right frame of mind."

I concluded, "So the jury has to believe that it's just a coincidence that on the *very* day, on the *very* night, and at the *very* hour his ex-wife is murdered, Simpson just coincidentally happens to leave a blood trail at Rockingham that just coincidentally has blood drops of the *same* size and configuration and spaced at the *same* intervals as the trail the killer left at Bundy. That's quite a coincidence. That's number *fifty*."

"Simmer down, guy," Scott said. "No more coffee for you. I'm starved; let's see if there's anything to eat."

Scott wandered out of the conference room to the snack bar. While he was gone, I examined the pictures on the conference-room wall for probably the sixth time during the trial. The pictures portrayed L.A.'s old Victorian courthouse, a magnificent, massive stone structure that was demolished. When Scott returned to the room, I mused aloud, "Isn't it incredible that they could destroy something like that?"

Scott examined the pictures, open bag of chips in hand. "No one will ever build another building like it."

I contemplated the "state of the art" building that replaced the old courthouse, the elegant Beaux-Arts–style Hall of Justice, which now lies deserted. In those days, they built courthouses to reflect the majesty and dignity of the law. Today courtrooms are often run out of trailers. "It's remarkable how we paper over history in this city, isn't it?"

"We better get back to work," Scott said.

"Like changing a street in Boyle Heights to Cesar Chavez," I continued. "Not that Cesar Chavez shouldn't have a street named after him. But there was a whole history and life on that street. It was L.A.'s historic Jewish neighborhood: synagogues, kosher butcher shops, delicatessens, old Jewish men wearing yarmulkes on their way to shul. How can they just sweep that all away like yesterday's garbage?"

Scott said seriously, "You're right, you're right." He paused for a moment. Then he smiled. "But what does this have to do with the Simpson case?"

"Where are we, fifty, fifty-one?" I asked. "If the jury just looks at a tenth of these facts, they'll have to convict."

"Our last major category," Scott said. "Simpson's posthomicide conduct. A number of things here tell us, as Henry Lee would say, 'Something wrong.' "

We reviewed number *fifty-one*, that Simpson forgot to set the security alarm and had to call Kato and ask him to do it; and *fifty-two*, his strange demeanor on the flight to Chicago when the pilot saw him staring out the window when others were sleeping. *Fifty-three*: Simpson did not ask appropriate questions when Ron Phillips notified him of Nicole's murder. Scott said, *"Fifty-four*: the strange circumstances in Chicago regarding his cut. There's broken glass on the counter near the sink, but there's no blood on it or on the paper covering the glass. It seems like he's trying to create an alibi for the cut on the finger of his left hand."

"What are the chances of getting a cut on the same finger of the same hand twice in the same day?" I asked rhetorically.

"Fifty-five," Scott continued. "On June 13, one of the first people he calls is Kato Kaelin. His ex-wife's just been murdered. What's the urgency to speak to Kato? It's a great opportunity to get his story straight and make sure Kato will go along with it."

We paused and examined our notes. "I guess we're done," I said. "When's Marcia going to get here?"

"Right now," Scott replied as Marcia poked her head into the room.

She looked refreshed and ready to work. "I'll be with you in a second, guys." Then she disappeared.

"I need some more coffee," I said.

After Marcia arrived, we quickly presented our laundry list of factors that pointed to Simpson's guilt. Then we proceeded to discuss the overall strategy for the argument. We discussed ways of recapping the impact of all of the evidence.

I said, "In order to believe he's innocent, you would have to believe that a lot of things just happened, by coincidence, to point to his guilt. You would have to accept that there was a massive convergence of coincidences of almost cosmic proportions. We must tell the jury that. But what devices can be used to get that concept across?"

Marcia suggested, "I like the 'just because' argument. The defense tells you that 'just because he cut himself doesn't mean he's the murderer. Just because he left a trail of blood at Rockingham doesn't mean he's guilty. Just because he was behaving strangely at the recital the night of the murder doesn't mean he's guilty. And continue with a list of each of the fifty-five 'coincidences.'"

"We could perhaps use that at the end to summarize everything. This is our case. I think you go through all the evidence that says he's guilty. After you get to the end of your detailed discussion of all the evidence, you could do a final recap."

I said, "By now, you've given them a mind-boggling array of evidence. I think we should have one large board that lists everything you just covered. To impress the jury with the magnitude of the evidence, the overwhelming evidence, against this man. Maybe you use the 'just like the defendant' argument here as you simply read down the list. The effect should be staggering."

Marcia said, "Let's do that. Let's get a graphic that summarizes the fifty-five items we have all on one board."

Later, I said to Marcia, "One of the problems you're actually facing is that we have too many pieces of evidence. We don't want the jury to get lost. I think it's good to show the absolutely overwhelming nature of our case—the fifty-five items. But in addition, we need to pare it down so the jury appreciates what our key pieces of evidence are."

Marcia asked, "What do you see as the key pieces."

"There are eight key pieces of evidence which say he's guilty: the socks, the Rockingham glove, the Rockingham trail, the Bronco, the knit cap, Ron's shirt, the shoe prints, and the Bundy blood trail."

"Why not the Bundy glove?" Marcia asked.

"Because there's no evidence on it. Its relevance is that it matches the Rockingham glove. But I don't think of it as being a piece of evidence which independently points to guilt. So we have eight key pieces, each one of which powerfully points to guilt."

"So the trick is to reinforce those eight key pieces," Marcia said.

"And hammer it home in so many different ways that all twelve of them would have to be brain-dead to avoid getting the message," I said. "We need to make sure that there is no key piece of evidence that they don't consider simply because they overlooked it."

Marcia suggested, "So in addition to the board with the fifty-five items, I want to have a series of exhibits that emphasize these eight key items. So that after I've gone through everything, I can go back and say, 'Okay, these are the key items. Let's look at them one more time.' "

Later, working with Jonathan Fairtlough, the young attorney who was in charge of coordinating our graphics, we created a series of very simple boards that focused on these items. All of the graphics were provided by a firm called Decision Quest, which donated its services to us for the trial. None of the prosecutors had ever tried a case using such sophisticated professional graphics. Typically, we make our own graphics using a T square and color markers. When we get fancy, we use a stencil.

The weekend before the closing arguments, as I was walking down the hallway in the relatively deserted building toward Marcia's office, I could hear Chris's and Marcia's raised voices. Before I reached her office, I bumped into Scott Gordon, who was walking away from Marcia's office. Like every other member of the team, including myself, Scott tried never to lose his sense of humor, even under fire. This probably accounts for why we were all able to work so well together as a team.

Scott, employing the voice of a police dispatcher, said, "Four-fifteen's in progress at Marcia's office. Four-fifteen in progress at Marcia's office." The number 415 refers to the Penal Code section for disturbing the peace and would cover a loud, raucous argument. "Well, whatever it is, let them hash it out themselves."

Later, after I thought it was safe, I returned to Marcia's office to continue working on the closing argument. Tentatively, I asked, "What happened between you and Chris?"

"He complained about me arriving later than expected today. I have worked my butt off in this case."

"Marcia, I know. Everyone knows. And particularly Chris knows how hard you have been working. You've had to deal with some of the personal stuff with your ex-husband, the media, all on top of this crazy trial. None of that ever got in the way of your commitment. Believe me, Chris knows that."

"Okay, Hankster, let's go through this closing argument."

By about seven I was exhausted. I called my older brother. "David, you want to see a movie tonight?"

"Sure. What do you want to see?" he asked.

"Something mindless. Something that requires absolutely no thought, intellect, or concentration." Before I left, however, I decided to stop in to say good night to Chris and Marcia.

Chris was sitting behind his desk, typing into the computer. I came in and sat down. Neither of us spoke for a long few moments. Chris turned from the computer, which was on a side table, and faced me, his eyes downcast. I could see he was still upset over the argument. Quietly, he asked, "Well?"

"Chris, this is a really bad time for you and Marcia to have any disagreements." It was clear from Chris's plaintive look that he already knew this.

"Chris, this argument is just stress and frayed nerves. It's not about any real disagreement, as I understand it." I decided to use a little politically incorrect persuasion for expediency's sake. "You're the man. You have to apologize whether you're right or wrong so we can get on with business."

Chris nodded. I thought to myself, The guy's a consummate pro. As I was leaving, Chris called out, "How's the closing going with Marcia?"

When I stopped by Marcia's office, she was still poring over the laundry list of fifty-five factors proving Simpson's guilt. I could tell that she had put the argument with Chris behind her.

"Marcia, I have an idea for an exhibit to use in closing. In about two minutes, it will powerfully present our case to the jury."

"I'm listening," Marcia said as she continued leafing through her notes.

"I want to splice together the 911 tapes from the 1989 and 1993 incidents, together with still photographs from the case. I want to create a video which will look like this. We'll see a picture of Nicole's battered face from 1989. In the background, faintly, we'll hear the 911 tape starting: '911 emergency.' We'll see the photograph from 1989 of Nicole covered with mud. We'll hear Nicole scream. As the soundtrack of the 911 tape from the 1993 incident gets louder, we'll see the sock, the Rockingham glove, the Rockingham trail, the Bronco. As we see the Bronco, we'll hear Nicole saying, 'He's O. J. Simpson, I think you know his record. He's fucking going nuts.' Then we'll see the Bundy trail, the knit cap, a picture of Ron at Bundy which shows his shirt. As we're looking at Ron, we'll hear Simpson raging in the background. As the tape reaches a crescendo, suddenly the audio will go off, almost like a needle being jerked off a record. In silence, we'll hold for thirty seconds on a picture of Nicole's body at Bundy.''

Marcia's eyes misted over. Quietly, she said, ''It's great. It's great. I love it.''

40

The Last Word

AFTER MARCIA AND CHRIS presented their powerful closing arguments, which outlined the fifty-five facts proving Simpson's guilt, the entire prosecution team was focused on one cause. We carefully monitored the defense's closing arguments in order to prepare our rebuttal.

The attorneys, including Rock, Woody, and me, watched the defense arguments on the TV set up in Rock and Woody's cubicle. As we did so, we prepared an extensive list of every outright misstatement, half-truth, or logical flaw. We sent the law clerks and younger lawyers scurrying back to the trial transcripts to search for testimony that would prove our position correct. I might write a note such as: "Henry Lee never said, 'Something is wrong with the prosecution's case.' Look up tail end of his direct and get me exact quote." I would tear the page off my legal notepad and hand it to the nearest clerk.

Of all of the misstatements, one troubled me the most. Barry Scheck made an argument to the jury that contained an extremely convoluted and highly misleading explanation of the concept of reasonable doubt. Scheck told the jury that if they had a reasonable doubt as to any single piece of evidence in the case, the jury had to vote not guilty. For example, he said that if the jury had a reasonable doubt as to whether the sock was planted, "that is reasonable doubt for this case, period, end of sentence, end of case." According to Scheck, the jury didn't have to look at any other evidence.

Under this twisted definition, in any case such as ours, in which we presented overwhelming evidence—fifty-five facts pointing to the defendant's guilt—a "not-guilty" verdict would be assured. The jury would be bound to find that they had a reasonable doubt regarding at least one of the facts. If we only presented ten facts, the jury would be less likely to find one. Five facts would be even less likely to raise a reasonable doubt. The less evidence, the stronger the case. The more evidence the jury had to choose from, the greater the likelihood of finding one piece of evidence about which they had a reasonable doubt. This is how the defense turned logic and law on its head during their argument.

In reality, the law is just the opposite of what Scheck said. If the jury believed that any single fact or group of facts proved guilt beyond a reasonable doubt, they would have to convict. For example, say a juror thought, I'm not sure about the socks, but the knit cap plus the fact that Simpson just happened to be cut on the left side of his body convinces me. They would be required to vote guilty.

Marcia needed to carefully explain this to the jury. Although the judge instructs the jury on the laws, the lawyers are allowed to explain the law during arguments, but they are not allowed to misstate the law. Judge Ito, however, did not stop Scheck from doing so. Therefore, Marcia needed to explain what the phrase "reasonable doubt" means. The instruction Judge Ito gave to the jury started by explaining what it is not. "It is not a mere possible doubt." The reason is that everything "is open to some possible or imaginary doubt." To vote not guilty, the doubt must be *reasonable*. For example, if a juror thought, It's *possible* Nicole's blood was planted on the socks, but it's not *reasonable* to believe it happened, they would have to vote guilty. A common illustration is that it is *possible* that when we get on a plane the plane will crash. Planes crash all the time. However, if it were *reasonable* to believe the plane would crash, we would not get aboard.

By the time the defense arguments concluded, we had prepared a three-inch notebook in reply to the misstatements, logical flaws, or outright contradictions contained in the defense argument. The evening the defense concluded, we had to sort through this material in order to use it in a coherent rebuttal argument. That evening, Marcia had a tooth abscess requiring emergency dentistry, painfully accomplished. When she returned, she found the prosecution team in the press-conference room discussing overall strategy for the rebuttal argument. Most of the time was spent going over the list of misstatements and misconceptions contained in the defense's closing argument. It was decided that Chris would handle these issues during his half of the rebuttal.

I was very impatient during that meeting. The plan was for us to break up into two small groups, a Marcia group and a Chris group, to refine and review both rebuttal arguments. This would be the last word the jury would hear from counsel. I kept looking at the clock. Periodically, I'd say, "Marcia, let's get out of here; let's get started on your end of the argument." Finally, at around 11:00 P.M., Marcia, Woody, Rock, and I left the conference room and met in Marcia's office. We decided that the best approach was to work our way, point by point, through what Marcia needed to address during rebuttal. Mostly, we discussed the rebuttal arguments to the defense contamination and planting theories, since the remaining portions of Marcia's rebuttal were already well mapped out.

Marcia looked tired and was in discomfort. "Marcia, maybe we should ask Ito for a one-day continuance. I think your emergency dentistry is good cause."

"I don't want the jury sitting there stewing any longer than necessary on the crap they just heard from Scheck and Cochran," Marcia said. "I want them to hear our response immediately. I think that's important. I don't want to wait. I'm fine. I want you to just go over all of the rebuttal arguments with me tonight. Hearing you repeat them will help get them in my head."

Marcia then said, "Okay. Let's talk about contamination. Hank?"

I showed Marcia a memo I had written with some of the other prosecutors that contained an argument for her to present to the jury. Marcia read quickly and half out loud, using a highlighter pen to mark key words and passages. Occasionally, she gestured slightly, as if addressing the jury.

" 'I bet you ladies and gentlemen think that I'm going to talk to you about substrate controls and swatches and reagent blanks and cross-hybridization, and amplicons. And I may mention some of those things very briefly.' "

Marcia continued reading: " 'During his argument Mr. Darden mentioned the old defense adage, When you have a weak case on the facts, argue the law; when you have a weak case on the law, argue the facts. And when you have a weak case on both the facts and the law, argue about the police prosecutors or the victim. Shift blame. And I suppose that this whole contamination nonissue is just a dressed-up, high-tech approach to that time-honored trial tactic. The culprits are not only the police, not only the prosecutors, not only the crime laboratory scientists, but flying amplicons, fragments of DNA.' "

Marcia looked up briefly. "This is good." She continued reading:

" 'But we start with the simple fact that flying amplicons don't account for the evidence which points to the defendant's guilt. Flying amplicons did not beat Nicole in 1989. Flying amplicons did not grab her by the throat so hard that a hand print was left on her neck. Flying amplicons did not break down her door in 1993. Flying amplicons did not put the defendant's hair in the cap at Bundy. Or the defendant's hair on Ron's shirt. Flying amplicons did not put the defendant's blood in the Bronco or create a trail of blood from the Bronco to the defendant's bathroom. And flying amplicons did not take a knife and butcher Ron and Nicole to death. The defendant did all those things. This high-tech attempt to lay it all off on flying amplicons just doesn't wash.

" 'Now you ladies and gentlemen have more expertise in forensic science than nearly all Americans. You now know that a murder scene is not a scientific palace. It's not a laboratory. It's a death scene. A place stained by violence, rage, and blood. The murderer does not carefully preserve the evidence for us. But, as you've learned, he leaves plenty of it behind. The issue of contamination is no stranger to the forensic scientist. It is no stranger to the Dr. Lees and Gregory Mathesons. It's not something to be feared. Not a new villain to shoulder the blame for crimes committed by this defendant. It's not something to be turned into a sound bite. Rather, it's something that is rather easily dealt with on a daily basis in thousands, if not tens of thousands, of cases involving biological evidence prosecuted every year in this county alone.' "

Marcia looked up and nodded. "Then I'll start out with what the defense conceded regarding the contamination issue. Why don't you run through that, Hank?"

I said, "We have to make it absolutely clear that the contamination issue is, basically, erased from the case. Gerdes conceded every item except the Bundy blood trail." I paused and looked at Woody. Woody nodded his affirmation.

"Now, why doesn't the defense just say those drops were planted?" I asked. "Certainly the defense isn't shy about offering totally implausible explanations to account for the evidence. Then why?" I paused and waited for Marcia to respond.

"Why?" Marcia asked thoughtfully. "Why? Because the blood drops were collected *before* the LAPD ever had the defendant's blood vial. So unless the defense wants to argue that maybe they had his blood on file somewhere just in case sometime in the future his wife was murdered and they wanted to sprinkle his blood around, they *can't* argue that it was planted. Therefore, they have to argue contamination." Marcia paused to drink some coffee and winced as the liquid contacted her tooth. "Let's run through the arguments as to why there wasn't contamination during the evidence collection," Marcia said.

"The most important point along this line," I continued, "is that Scheck conceded that contamination did not occur during the evidence-collection process. After that incredible marathon cross-examination of Dennis, Andrea, and microdissection of their work, he has conceded to the jury that nothing they did contaminated the evidence." (This concession was particularly important to me because it proved that I was successful in my goal of showing that Dennis and Andrea did not contaminate the evidence.)

"Do you have Scheck's quote making that concession?" Marcia asked.

"Yes." I riffled through my notes. "Scheck said, regarding their contamination theory, 'The contention is specific. It is in the Evidence Processing Room.' That's where Collin Yamauchi worked with samples of the evidence for testing the day after it was collected."

"Then you think I should explain why contamination didn't occur in the Evidence Processing Room during the evidence-testing phase at LAPD?" Marcia asked.

"Yes," I said. "I would actually act this out in court using coin envelopes and a vial as props. On June the fourteenth, Collin samples all the evidence in the Evidence Processing Room. Picture for the jury this setup. Collin's working with Simpson's blood vial. The rest of the evidence is sitting on another table in the same room, fifteen feet away. It's in sealed coin envelopes. The defense contamination theory is that blood from the vial got on the swatches in those envelopes. That's impossible. Illustrate this in court."

As I described this, I noticed that Marcia kept closing and rubbing her eyes. Two things were becoming obvious. Fortunately, Marcia was asking the right questions and meticulously annotating her outline. Unfortunately, it was clear that she was dead tired and in physical pain and we still had a long way to go. "Marcia, you need a break?"

"In a few minutes. Keep the coffee coming," Marcia said to one of the law clerks who kept drifting in and out of the room. "So the bottom line is that the contamination either happened inside the Evidence Processing Room when Collin opened Simpson's blood vial, or it didn't happen."

"Exactly," I said. Marcia was getting her second wind.

Marcia picked up one of the graphics we had created to show how impossible it would have been for Collin to have contaminated the swatches with blood from Simpson's vial. One graphic showed a picture that the graphics firm had previously created as part of our courtroom display. It showed DNA with wings flying through the air. Though exhausted, Marcia laughed. "I love this one. Contamination did not occur because DNA did not fly across the room fifteen feet when Collin opened the test tube. I love it."

"There was something real interesting that Scheck argued," I said. "Even though this is contrary to the evidence, he said that Collin spilled some of Simpson's blood on the table. If that were true, then there's no missing blood! Because Collin spilled some. You can drive this one home. Scheck's argument concedes that there's no missing blood from Simpson's vial!"

"The next contamination argument," I added, "relates to how Dr. Lee completely demolished Gerdes's testimony."

Marcia interrupted. "Yeah, I know this stuff cold. Lee says you can collect the stuff on the bottom of your shoe or with your bare hands and still do the testing. They say LAPD was a cesspool of contamination, and Lee's lab was in a men's room. Oh, and the shtick about the wild dog that stole the rape victim's panties is great." Marcia started laughing, which seemed to aggravate her pain. "Hank, can you run through the bridge between the contamination and conspiracy arguments?"

"Why conspiracy?" I asked as if arguing to the jury. "Because that's the power of DNA technology. The arguments and theories of Johnnie Cochran and Barry Scheck were not exclusively created in their minds. They were dictated by the power of DNA. How do you know DNA and PCR work? Because the only defense that was left in this case was a ludicrous one—a massive police conspiracy. And why, you may wonder, do we have this defense of a massive police conspiracy to frame a beloved former sports hero and grade-B movie star? Why do we have it? Because they can't argue contamination. Because they tried to pursue contamination and they just couldn't pull it off. Because DNA works.' "

"Hankster, simmer down. It's past midnight," Rock said.

Everyone chuckled. "Sorry," I said. "Anyway, that's the transition leading into the conspiracy arguments." I looked at Marcia, and she looked as if she were about to drop. "Let's take a quick break," I suggested. She must have felt as if there were a jackhammer operating in her mouth. "Just for a couple of minutes," Marcia said almost apologetically. She and Woody left the office.

Rock remained seated. I stood up and looked out the window, which had a great southern view of the downtown skyline at night. The city lay still. No pedestrians. No moving cars. The clock on the L.A. Times building read one-thirty. By now Marcia's pretzel stash had long since run out. What a wonderful old building, I thought. "Have you ever been to the L.A. Times building cafeteria, Rock?"

"Huh?" Rock muttered.

I stared fixedly at the building. I remembered reading somewhere that the previous L.A. Times building was supposed to have been an extraordinary structure, looking somewhat like a fortress. They say that publisher and owner Gen. Otis Chandler was supposed to have housed a massive gun collection in the building. I wondered what old General Otis was expecting. Then I remembered. The old building was destroyed in the twenties during a labor dispute. Clarence Darrow came to Los Angeles to defend the McNamara brothers, who were suspected of having blown it up.

Woody then returned. And Marcia soon thereafter. The short break had not refreshed her. I wondered how much more she could take before shorting out. I sensed that Marcia was asking the same question of herself. With a slight note of irritability, Marcia said, "Okay, let's go—let's go through the planting arguments, starting with the Bronco. Hank?"

"At one time, the defense suggested that Ron's and Nicole's blood was planted on the console after Dennis collected some samples from the console on June fourteenth."

Marcia asked, "Hank, didn't they abandon that argument? Isn't Scheck now claiming that Fuhrman planted the victim's blood on the morning of June thirteenth by rubbing the glove around in there?"

"Right," I replied. "Nail them for changing their theory."

Marcia looked at me. "Next, I want to run through what you would have to believe in order to accept the current defense planting scenario."

I replied, "Obvious problems with the idea that Fuhrman rubbed the glove around in the Bronco on the morning of June fourteenth. The biggest problem is the bloody shoe print. To explain that, Scheck comes up with this Rube Goldberg–type explanation. Marcia, try to get the jurors to picture this. Scheck says that Fuhrman must have left the bloody Bronco shoe print after he supposedly stepped in Nicole's blood at Bundy. However, there's a major problem with that fairy tale. Any blood on Fuhrman's shoes would have dried by the time he got to Rockingham. Anticipating this, Scheck argued that Fuhrman must have stepped on some wet grass, thereby rewetting the blood on his shoes. When he got into the Bronco, Fuhrman accidentally left the bloody shoe print in Nicole's blood on the carpet."

"Amazing, absolutely amazing," Marcia observed. "The chutzpa it takes to believe that any rational human being could accept that argument."

"I'd repeat that whole argument for the jury," I said. "Unless they buy it, Simpson's guilty. That's the best fantasy the dream team could come up with to explain this evidence. If it's not reasonable, you must convict."

"Here's what I'll tell the jury as to why it's totally unreasonable," Marcia said. Marcia quickly rattled off the reasons: The Bronco was locked, and they didn't have the key. Fuhrman could not have stepped in wet blood at Bundy; otherwise, he would have left a set of footprints there. And Bodziak said that Fuhrman's shoes didn't make any of the prints.

Marcia was in a zone, so we kept rolling. I suggested to Marcia that we should take an overlay of the Bruno Magli shoe and put it over the picture of the Bronco carpet to show the match. "Marcia, it's really impressive. In and of itself, the Bronco print proves guilt beyond a reasonable doubt or even an unreasonable doubt."

"Hank," Marcia said, "demonstrate that to the jury during my rebuttal. We had another argument as to why it's unreasonable to believe in planting blood in the Bronco, didn't we?" Marcia quizzed.

"Yes," I continued. "Remember, the explanation for Simpson's blood on the console is that he cut himself on the cell phone. Now

Simpson lives on an estate. Think of all the places on an estate you could plant blood. You could plant it on a shower door, front door, bathroom, anywhere. This is an estate! Of all the places on that estate to plant blood, Fuhrman comes along and plants blood in the very vehicle, on the very console, on the very same side of the console, and on the very same spot on the console where Simpson just happened to bleed only a few hours earlier. Think about what the defense is saying. Simpson bleeds in the Bronco console around ten-fifty P.M., then Fuhrman plants more evidence on that very same spot just six hours later. What are the odds of that? Poor Simpson, he's got to be the unluckiest man on earth." I paused and looked at Marcia. "Holding up okay, Marcia?"

Marcia replied, "I want to run quickly through the rear gate and the Bundy trail, then the socks, and we're home free."

It looked as if Marcia were running on adrenaline now, like a marathoner kicking the last half mile. "I know the arguments about the rear gate cold," Marcia said. She reviewed the facts refuting the concept that blood was planted on the rear gate, including that a half-dozen police officers saw the blood the night of the murders, and that there was a photograph taken on June 13 showing one of the blood drops.

"This brings us to the Bundy trail," Marcia said.

I then recapped Greg Matheson's testimony showing that the door-entry records proved that all the evidence was secure between the time Dennis and Andrea put it in the Evidence Processing Room until Collin started his testing the next morning. At first, it appeared that the defense theory explaining the Bundy trail was contamination, but later they apparently switched to planting. Marcia chimed in: "Consistency and logic don't present any problem to the defense. When they realize they can't show contamination of the Bundy trail blood drops, they switch to planting, the old standby."

I smiled at this. "Pretty darn good for two-forty A.M. Now, what's the alleged evidence of planting of the Bundy trail drops? It all rests on Lee's testimony 'Something wrong.' " We then reviewed the arguments explaining what Dr. Lee meant by this.

"This brings us to the socks," Marcia said. Rock summarized the defense planting theory regarding the socks. "The defense claimed that first someone took Simpson's socks out of the hamper and put them on the rug on June thirteenth. On that day, Dennis and Andrea collected them. However, the defense claimed there was no blood on the socks. Because the blood wasn't discovered until August fourth. But no one examined them for blood prior to that date." Rock also explained that many of the bloodstains on the socks were microscopic specks. "How do you plant microscopic spatter stains?"

I smiled. "Details, details. Illustrate what the defense theory requires the jury to believe. Here's the kicker. Under their theory the police planted blank socks! Wouldn't you just love to have been a fly on the wall listening to the conversation between the officers who did the planting under the defense scenario. Maybe Fuhrman's talking to Vannatter, the 'twin demons of evil,' as Cochran called them. Fuhrman says, 'Let's plant something. How about a fingerprint?'

"Vannatter says, 'Fingerprint? Too old-fashioned.'

" 'Okay, how about a murder weapon?' Fuhrman asks.

"Vannatter objects, 'Murder weapon? Too obvious. I got it. How about we plant some socks!' "

Everyone in the room laughed at this. "Wait, I haven't reached the punch line yet. Several months later, Fuhrman and Vannatter are yakking it up at a bar. They're bragging about how clever they were. Fuhrman laughs. 'Socks, what a brilliant idea! Bloody socks!'

"Vannatter looks like he's about to pass out. 'Bloody socks? I didn't put any blood on the socks. I just planted socks.' "

This drew another laugh. "So now they dress up in their ninja-style evidence-planting suits. They break into a secured LAPD crime lab where they plant blood on the socks. That's what you have to believe to accept the defense planting scenario. If it's not reasonable, you have to vote guilty."

Woody deadpanned: "If the socks are filthy, you have to vote guilty." We all glared at Woody, but it didn't faze him a bit.

I concluded our discussion of the socks, again as if addressing the jury. "So once we see our way through the ridiculous planting theories, the socks, in and of themselves, prove guilt. That's Nicole's blood on the socks. Ladies and gentlemen, there is no innocent explanation for that. There is no getting around that. Not even Gerdes, Henry Lee, Houdini, or Johnnie Cochran could figure a way out of that one."

"I think that covers it," Marcia said. "If I don't get some sleep, I'm going to be useless."

Rock, Woody, and I walked out together. It was after 3:00 A.M. The corridors were deserted. It was difficult to imagine that in less than five hours they would be bursting with sound and fury. Tomorrow would be Superbowl Sunday, the Kentucky Derby. We did not say much en route to the elevators. Rock broke the silence. "Don't worry, Hank. She's going to do great."

At about 3:20 A.M. I was on the freeway. I was surprised to find it virtually deserted. I exited at Santa Monica Boulevard in West Los Angeles at 3:40 A.M. I realized that I hadn't had anything to eat except coffee and pretzels. I wondered whether there was anything in the refrigerator. I hadn't looked inside it in over a week.

Los Angeles isn't New York. There are few places open at that hour. Norm's on Pico was open all night. I started south on Sepulveda toward Pico, decided it was too far out of my way, so I made a U-turn and headed home. I slowly walked up the thirty steps to my front door. I opened the door, walked to the kitchen, and stood there stunned. The kitchen was spotless. My beautiful, bright mother, world-class Olympian cleaner, must have been here. I opened the refrigerator and found three pieces of fresh home-made chicken inside. I poured myself a glass of milk and went upstairs.

I got ready for bed. I couldn't go to sleep. Did we miss anything? I thought of reviewing my voluminous notes for the closing argument on my home computer. But I had been doing that for weeks. So I checked my calls. There were three calls from my father and my brother David. I had promised to try to get them seats for the rebuttal arguments. I had forgotten. I'd call them in the morning, humbly apologize, and tell them they might be able to watch the closing on TV in the War Room.

About four hours after I had arrived home, I was back in my car heading downtown. On Friday morning, September 29, at about 7:00 A.M., crowds had already assembled outside the courthouse. They had signs: Free O.J. and Fry O.J. The Free O.J. signs seemed more numerous. I wondered whether a guilty verdict would cause a riot.

Los Angeles knows about riots. So did I. My mother was a peace activist from the 1960s to the 1980s. I recalled being at Century City, in West Los Angeles, when I was about six years old. Lyndon Johnson was giving a speech, still trying to sell the Vietnam War as a noble effort in behalf of humanity. But the massive crowd outside kept chanting "LBJ, LBJ, how many kids did you kill today?" My mother was pregnant with Luke at the time. My father, my brother David, my sister, Dru, and I were standing at the rear of the massed thousands. David shinnied up a tree to give us an eyewitness account of what was happening up front. He yelled, "Mom, Dad, the cops are beating people up." I vaguely remembered my mother and father grabbing me by the hand as a line of police officers advanced on the demonstrators. We frantically managed to scramble out of the area. My family knows about riots.

When I entered the War Room, it was packed. The reception area with the TV was presided over by Patti Jo Fairbanks, our senior legal office assistant, kind of a cross between a paralegal and a legal secretary. Patti was like a mother hen out of central casting. She knew everything about the case and everyone involved in it. I asked her whether my father and brother could get seats in the courtroom. "No way," Patti said. "But they can watch up here." I phoned my father, who picked up immediately, and told him he and David could watch the trial in the War Room.

Later that morning, Rock, Woody, and I went down to court. Rock said to me, "Sit up at counsel table. It will make Marcia feel more comfortable."

"No," I said. "I'll be in the way. Marcia and Chris are the leads. I'll sit in the back."

"Sit up there," Rock insisted as Marcia joined us. Before even saying hello, Marcia said, "Hank, sit up here at counsel table."

After court was called to order, Chris rose to give his rebuttal argument. I really did not know exactly what he was going to say because I had been working with Marcia. Chris spoke eloquently about the murders, about Ron and Nicole, and about the domestic-violence evidence. He was magnificent. I was moved.

When Marcia rose to speak, I had no idea how she would hold up with the tooth problem she had had the previous night. She began to slowly and methodically dissect each of the claims the defense made about their contamination and planting theories. As she continued, she found her rhythm and forcefully presented the arguments we had worked out over the past several weeks and had reviewed the night before. Just as Rock had predicted, she knew them all. By the time she finished going through a chart in the shape of a pyramid, which listed the uncontradicted evidence, I felt that the defense's case was in shreds. She concluded by speaking powerfully and emotionally about the murders of these two innocent people.

Finally, she played the montage. Even though I had seen the tape dozens of times, hearing it over the court's sound system was like seeing it for the first time. As we heard Simpson's voice raging in the background over the shot of Ron's body, quiet sobs began to rise from the spectators behind me. When the sound suddenly and brutally stopped, over a picture of Nicole lying in the pool of her own blood, the courtroom was filled with the sounds of anguish and tears.

I thought, She did it! Marcia did it! I looked at the jury. As usual, emotionless. Then I noticed one of the alternate jurors, an elderly African-American man, who I thought had looked at me and other prosecutors with daggers throughout the trial. Now he was staring at me as I sat at counsel table. We looked directly at each other for what seemed like a minute, during which it felt as though the courtroom had become dark and silent. Then the corner of his mouth began to rise as the creases deepened near his eyes, forehead, and cheeks, forming an expression I had thought his face incapable of producing. He smiled.

It was as if he were saying, "Okay, you got me. I understand. You got me."

41

The Verdict

AS I DROVE DOWNTOWN the day the Simpson jury returned with their verdict, I remembered that the following day would be the first anniversary of the jury's failing to reach a verdict in the Iversen case, which involved the police officer who shot the tow-truck driver. This wasn't a good sign. It was hard to believe that a year of my life had been devoted to the Simpson case.

On October 3 I arrived at work by 7:00 A.M. A few other people had already shown up, and the War Room was filled with a nervous quiet. Chris wandered through. I asked, "What do you think, Chris?"

In a deep whisper he said, "A two-hundred-pound turd is about to fall on someone." Then he walked away.

I interpreted that to mean that the jury's shockingly quick verdict, after only four hours of deliberation, represented a complete categorical rejection of one side's presentation. It was as if nothing that side had said or done in the last nine months meant anything. We were about to find out which side's labors had been ignored.

The "media experts" and many of the prosecutors were overwhelmingly predicting a guilty verdict. In fact, later that morning, all of the members of the prosecution team were called into Garcetti's conference room. Garcetti and the head of our media relations division briefed us as to how to deal with the media after the verdict. The assumption from everyone who spoke, including Gil Garcetti, was that the verdict would almost certainly be guilty. There was a feeling of restrained jubilation.

The primary reason so many felt the verdict would be guilty was that the only testimony the jury wanted reread was that of limousine driver Allan Park. In Marcia's closing, she had dramatically underscored the importance of this totally neutral and unrefuted witness. He established that Simpson returned to Rockingham at 10:52 P.M. and lied by claiming he did not answer the buzzer because he had overslept. Marcia had argued to the jury that this testimony was the defining moment of the trial. If Park's testimony was all the jury wanted to rehear, it was reasonable to expect a guilty verdict. In Garcetti's conference room that morning, the discussion focused on what to say about the fact that the jury convicted Simpson.

However, weeks earlier, I had dreamed that the verdict would be not guilty. It must have been my way of mentally preparing for that possibility. The feeling stemmed from my perceptions of the jurors during the trial and my long-held belief that a sizable segment of the public, including both African Americans and whites, did not want to believe O. J. Simpson was guilty.

By midmorning much of the prosecution team had filled Rock and Woody's cubicle, our eyes and hearts glued to the TV set. About fifteen seats covered almost every square inch of floor space. Each seat was occupied, and many people were standing as we watched the screen. We saw perhaps a first in journalism. One reporter from a local news station, hard up for an interview, was standing in an elevator lobby at the CCB, mike in hand, interviewing a fellow reporter from the same station. The room, perhaps because of the tension, burst out in laughter. Then came a commercial break.

After the break, the same two reporters were still on camera, except the mike had changed hands. Now the interviewer was questioning the interviewee. Again, the room burst out in thunderous laughter. The laughter and tension were getting to me. I had to walk out.

I returned shortly before the verdicts were read. The laughter in the room completely subsided as the judge inspected the verdict. Then the clerk began to read. "Not guilty."

Just as quickly as the room had previously filled with laughter, it was now filled with cries of anguish and tears. All I could see on TV was the odd expression of Robert Kardashian, Simpson's longtime friend and now an attorney on the defense team. His face was a model of disbelief and shock. Stranger still was Jason Simpson's face, reflecting an intense look of anger and rage. His father had just been found not guilty. I could not interpret this reaction. Prosecutor Lisa Kahn turned to me. She seemed on the verge of being almost physically sick. "Hank, let's get some air."

We stepped out onto the building's fire escape, which was opened to the outside. Lisa, hands trembling, lit a cigarette. We stood there without saying anything to each other as we gazed out at Los Angeles through the jail-like metal bars that separated the landing of the fire escape from the outside. We listened to the crowds below cheering the verdict. The smoke from Lisa's cigarette filled the air. The sound of the cheering crowd below strangely blended with the roar of the news helicopters overhead.

I have heard many people describing traumatic experiences say that they felt as if they were in a "dreamlike state." I never understood what they were talking about—until that day.

Since the verdict I have spent hours and days asking myself one question. Why did the jury vote to acquit Orenthal James Simpson?

In discussions of this verdict, numerous explanations have been offered, including LAPD mistakes, prosecution mistakes, a brilliant defense team, and the fact that Simpson's riches bought his way to an acquittal. None of these theories accounts for the jury's verdict.

Did the LAPD make mistakes? Yes. But these mistakes did not determine the jury's decision. Throughout the book I have shown how the serious underfunding of law enforcement adversely affected us. A clear example was the underfunding at the SID.

On March 15, 1996, Rock Harmon, Greg Matheson, and I gave two lectures to police property and evidence custodians. We candidly discussed some of the problems we had confronted. I outlined many of the issues discussed in this book. The press of business at the SID produced shortcuts which do not hurt the typical criminal prosecution. The evidence was left in the Evidence Processing Room without being stored in a locked cabinet or sealed envelope between the evening of June 13, when Dennis Fung and Andrea Mazzola left it there, and June 16, when it was booked. Later, when the box containing the evidence was brought into the serology lab, it was not maintained in a sealed condition. This required me to prove through the computerized door-entry security system that the evidence could not have been tampered with between the time it was brought to the lab and the time the testing commenced.

During my lecture to the police property and evidence custodians, I told them that in order to have avoided these issues, we would have to have known in advance that the defense was going to accuse us of conspiracy. Then the evidence-handling procedures could have been altered to address this accusation. I recommended that in handling evidence, special procedures should be used in any case that is likely to involve allegations of police wrongdoing. Such cases include crimes involving a celebrity, a political, religious, or controversial figure, or a popular or influential victim.

Although these issues made my job harder and more painful, they did not affect the verdict. When Greg Matheson spoke at this meeting, he told the audience about the overwhelming burdens facing the SID. These included 856 murders in Los Angeles in 1994, the year Ron and Nicole were murdered. He said that a double homicide is not considered an unusual case requiring special handling. "You need at least three bodies before it's special." He explained that if all the procedures the defense claimed we should have followed were implemented in every case, law enforcement would come to a grinding halt.

Moreover, Greg explained that following procedures cannot prevent allegations of wrongdoing. "Even if we sealed all the evidence immediately and every time I opened the evidence to test it I resealed it, even if the evidence had twelve seals, it wouldn't matter. What's to stop the defense from just saying that I put all those seals on there on one occasion and postdated them to make it look like the package was always sealed. It is always going to come down to trust."

When Greg said this, I thought about my interview with Thano Peratis, the nurse who drew Simpson's blood. I brought two credible witnesses to the interview, which we audiotaped and videotaped. Of course, I have never taken so many precautions to prove that an interview was properly conducted. Yet that did not prevent defense accusations. Maybe something happened when the video wasn't on, and maybe the credible witnesses were liars. In the Simpson case, there was no limit to the defense's willingness to add additional conspirators.

In the final analysis, it will ultimately come down to trust and a jury's willingness to determine whether the police and the prosecutors had any motive to frame an innocent man. If jurors do not carefully scrutinize accusations by the defense to determine whether they are reasonable, all the evidence seals in the world will not help.

The LAPD made fewer mistakes in the Simpson investigation than in the typical murder case. In most criminal investigations in Los Angeles, even routine techniques like dusting for fingerprints are not employed. Moreover, as Henry Lee made clear during cross-examination, there are very real limits regarding the extent of investigation and testing that can be performed in a case. If the public demanded a textbook investigation in order to convict, we would have to empty the prisons.

What about prosecution mistakes? Throughout this book I have explained in detail the prosecution's trial strategy regarding virtually every significant decision. I have also discussed the defense's tactics. Both sides made mistakes. One of the problems in judging lawyers is that what constitutes a mistake is often subject to fierce debate. After I returned to work in Santa Monica, respected colleagues gave me their opinions of the trial. One said that presenting any hair and trace evidence was a mistake, since it was not conclusive. Within an hour, an equally respected colleague told me that we had made a mistake by not presenting the hair and trace evidence first; he reasoned that it was the *best* evidence in the trial. Of the innumerable mistakes ascribed to the prosecution, I have yet to hear many that were inarguable or that could have affected the verdict.

The strongest support for the proposition that the prosecution skillfully presented a powerful case is found in the evidence we introduced and the arguments Chris and Marcia made during closing. This book amply demonstrates that any small portion of our case was sufficient to prove guilt beyond a reasonable doubt. The strength of a prosecutor's presentation should be measured by the strength of the case he or she presented.

Moreover, after it became known that the jury had reached a verdict, the overwhelming majority of commentators concluded that the verdict was guilty. These commentators included Simpson's appellate attorney, Alan Dershowitz. I recall seeing him on the news the evening before the verdicts were read. His new book—in which he argues that he knew all along that the prosecution made a number of mistakes that sealed our fate—is unquestionably revisionist history. He apparently did not feel that way on the eve of the verdict, when he was ruminating about the appeal.

There is one arguable exception to the observation that the

prosecution made no clear mistakes that could have affected the trial's outcome. The exception concerns the decision as to where the case should be filed. This decision is a matter left to the discretion of the prosecutor. In the American legal system, the prosecutor is vested with considerable discretionary powers. Many people have argued that the district attorney should have exercised his discretion by filing the Simpson case in the Santa Monica judicial district. This district includes the city of Santa Monica, the city of Malibu, Beverly Hills, West Los Angeles, Culver City, and the city of West Hollywood. On the typical Santa Monica jury panel the clear majority is white, while downtown the majority is often composed of minorities. The racial composition, however, changes from panel to panel. The Simpson jury pool was not typical of downtown jury pools. Downtown juries usually have a significantly greater percentage of whites than did the Simpson jury pool.

As I described in chapter 1, the Santa Monica courthouse was in disarray at the time and the case probably could not have been tried there. The decision to file the case in downtown Los Angeles was made months before I had any idea of my eventual involvement. Therefore, I have no personal knowledge about this decision.

With that disclaimer in mind, I will attempt to articulate the factors that would have gone into making this decision. There are several reasons for favoring a downtown filing. First, the facilities downtown are equipped to handle a case such as *Simpson.* The ninth floor of the CCB had recently been renovated to handle high-profile, high-security cases. Second, the D.A.'s office had available office space downtown to house a large prosecution team. There is no available office space in the Santa Monica branch office. Third, the D.A.'s office's trial support services, such as investigators, graphics, the video and photo unit, all of which we utilized extensively, are either located or better equipped downtown. Fourth, the unit to which the case would be assigned, the Special Trials Unit, is located downtown. When the Special Trials Unit of the D.A.'s office is assigned a case, it is often tried downtown even if the crime was committed elsewhere. Fifth, downtown is closer to the other law enforcement entities that played a major role in the case: the SID, LAPD Robbery/Homicide, and the coroner's office. Sixth, it could have been reasoned that a trial downtown would be likely to have more African-American members. Therefore, a guilty verdict would be less subject to criticism and have more widespread public acceptance. Personally, I would reject this argument, since the not guilty verdict in the Simpson case ultimately undermined public confidence in the criminal justice system.

By comparison, one factor favoring a Santa Monica filing—to put it bluntly—is that a Santa Monica jury pool would probably have had significantly fewer African Americans. For reasons that will become clear in the following chapter, I believe that we would not have convicted Simpson in Santa Monica or anywhere else in Los Angeles County.

If all other objective criteria indicate that a case should be filed downtown, can a prosecutor properly exercise his discretion by filing the case in Santa Monica for the sole purpose of having fewer African-American jurors? The answer is a resounding *no*. A prosecutor cannot exercise any of his discretionary decision-making authority in a racially biased manner. To do so would be both immoral and unethical. Therefore, the prosecution's filing decision cannot ethically, morally, or legally consider which jury pool would have the fewest African Americans.

The second argument favoring a Santa Monica filing is that a case should be tried in the judicial district where the crime occurred. In part, this argument is supported by the concept of "vicinage," our Founding Fathers' strong belief that the community where a crime occurs has the greatest stake in a case's resolution. A policy of filing a case in the jurisdiction where the crime occurs also avoids the appearance that a filing decision could have been gerrymandered for political reasons. In my view, cases should be filed in the judicial district where they occurred unless there is an overwhelming countervailing reason not to do so. Although this is a tough issue, I am not convinced that such a reason existed in the Simpson case.

We have also seen numerous instances of what I would label defense mistakes throughout this book. For example, Barry Scheck's staple-hole line of cross-examination or the presentation of Henry Lee's shoe-print testimony—which added little to the defense and gave the prosecution an opportunity to seriously damage Henry Lee. What must be kept in mind, however, is that even the most skilled lawyers cannot conduct an error-free trial. If Pete Sampras double faults several times during a tennis match, we do not assume he is an incompetent player.

Before the verdicts, California attorneys did not have such laudable comments about the defense team. The *California Bar Journal* reported, in June 1995, that California lawyers gave "strong backing for the prosecution's case," with more than two-thirds, 67 percent, believing that the prosecutors were doing an effective job.[1] A stark contradiction was revealed in assessments of the defense's presentation. "Just over one-third of those polled think defense attorneys' case alleging police mishandling of evidence and conspiracy has been effective, and 29 percent think their case has been ineffective."[2]

Furthermore, the state's official publication of the state bar found that "O. J. Simpson's so-called 'dream team' is embarrassing the defense bar by failing to focus on one theory of the case, according to some of the country's top criminal defense lawyers." Jerry Spence was quoted as saying, "You would think that with all the money that O. J. Simpson had, you would have really great trial lawyers. . . . [W]hat we are looking at is a large sum of money being spent for a very small service.[3] Before the verdicts, Vincent Bugliosi went so far as to say, "It's nothing short of remarkable that [Simpson] still doesn't have one lawyer representing him in court who has demonstrated any real competence in murder cases."[4] Although I do not share these views, the idea that a highly skilled team of defense lawyers presented an extremely effective case is, again, revisionist history.

Often people ask me whether the Simpson case is an example of a rich person's being able to buy his way out of a criminal conviction. This notion stems from the perception that wealthy clients are able to purchase exceptionally talented, high-priced lawyers who can win an acquittal or skillfully negotiate more lenient punishment.

It also stems from the misperception that public defenders, who represent the poor, are ineffective lawyers. This is far from the truth. Imagine that Simpson had lost all his money before the murders. I am absolutely certain that if he had been represented by the Los Angeles County Public Defender's Office, he would have been assigned a defense team with substantially more experience litigating homicides than Simpson's "dream team." They would probably have presented a more coherent, technically more proficient defense. Of course, the result would have been the same. The speed of the verdict indicated that the jurors not only ignored the prosecution's evidence and arguments but ignored those of the defense as well. For example, one juror still questioned whether Andrea Mazzola's collection procedures had contaminated the evidence even though Scheck had conceded they had not.

I believe that Simpson's status as a rich person, as distinct from a famous person, was not a factor in the case's outcome. Contrary to the widespread public perception, I do not see evidence that wealthy defendants get better dispositions in their criminal matters. The research confirms this view. One recent survey examined 127 studies of the relationship between socioeconomic status and case outcomes. The author concludes: "While the conventional criminological wisdom is that court outcomes are affected by the defendant's socioeconomic status, there is a sizable body of empirical evidence which seems to suggest otherwise."[5]

Therefore, the reasons for the verdict cannot be explained in terms of LAPD "mistakes," the evidence or courtroom tactics of the prosecution and defense, or Simpson's wealth. We must look outside the courtroom.

42

Why the Jury Found Simpson Not Guilty

THERE WERE FOUR POWERFUL social forces that, like the Four Horsemen of the Apocalypse, galloped into the Simpson case and spelled doom for the prosecution: sexism, the media, celebrity, and race. In other words, understanding the verdict requires that we examine the case in its larger social, political, and cultural context.

The prosecution's theory of the case was that the domestic-violence evidence proved Simpson's motive for murder. Chapter 3, "Presenting the Motive," and chapter 5, "Could We Tell the Jury About Domestic Violence?" explain why the evidence, the psychological studies, and common sense support this theory. As for the contention that the defense advanced in *Simpson* that there is no connection between domestic violence and murder, the statistics prove otherwise. In 1990, the American Medical Association reported that 50 percent of all female homicide victims are killed by a boyfriend or husband. Ninety to 95 percent of domestic-violence victims are women;[1] and domestic violence "may be the single most common source of serious injury to women, accounting for almost three times as many medical visits as traffic accidents."[2]

These statistics have led many people in the field of domestic violence to observe that women are safer walking the streets of our cities than they are in their own homes. I remember a conversation in which Scott Gordon summarized this statistic as follows: "It's as if a 747 filled with women slams into a mountain every month; and if that happened we would close the airports."

These are the facts. But the jurors in *Simpson* did not see it that way. One juror, Lionel Cryer, referring to the domestic-violence evidence, said he "never bought into it. I didn't see it." Brenda Moran, another juror, agreed. "This was a murder trial. If you want to get tried for domestic abuse, go in another courtroom."[3]

This is one of the difficulties that has always faced prosecutors in domestic-violence cases. People do not want to believe such cases. Why is this so? One reason has to do with the patriarchal nature of our society. When our nation was born over two hundred years ago, we inherited our legal system from the English. It is known as the common law. Under the so-called rule of thumb, a man was permitted to beat his wife with a stick as long as it was no thicker than his thumb. In one form or another, this rule was followed in all common-law jurisdictions. In early Los Angeles, a man was allowed to beat his wife with a leather strap less than two inches wide.

The evidence in *Simpson* amply reveals this historical attitude, which is still very much alive today. A number of Simpson's comments evinced his view that Nicole was merely an object of his use and enjoyment. Simpson grabbed Nicole's crotch and said, "This is where babies come from and this belongs to me." When Nicole would lose weight after having the children, Simpson would say, "Look at her . . . She is mine." During the 1989 incident Simpson told police, "I don't need her anymore. I have three women in my bed." These statements reflect attitudes that are still a part of our society.

Another reason we have difficulty accepting and understanding domestic-violence evidence has to do with an outdated notion of "family," documented in such television programs as *Ozzie and Harriet*. This notion of family has recently gained powerful political currency in this country. Under the traditional view, the family must consist of a father, mother, and children living together in peaceful harmony. Our almost fanatical desire to see all families as conforming to this mold distorts our ability to see reality. As a society, we want to view domestic violence as a private matter. In the Simpson case, the clearest evidence of this was in a 1989 incident when Simpson said, "This is a family matter."

The attitude that domestic violence is not a criminal matter exists today even among professionals within the criminal justice system. Almost a quarter of criminal justice professionals believe that domestic violence is better treated as a social problem than as a crime. Almost half of social service professionals hold this belief.[4]

These attitudes account for why the defense could minimize the importance of the domestic-violence evidence so successfully. Johnnie Cochran trivialized the evidence by telling the jurors that "none of us is perfect." This is also why the defense strategy of seeking to rename the prosecution's domestic-violence evidence "domestic discord" evidence proved so appealing. It permitted us to recast the evidence in a form that fits more harmoniously with our ideal preconception of family. Calling it domestic violence might force us to confront a reality that is too painful for many to accept. The defense's attempt to rename the evidence "domestic discord" did not merely involve semantics; rather, it made evident a culturally widespread worldview. The phrase "domestic discord" allowed us to view the events the way Simpson did: as a family matter.

A third factor making domestic-violence evidence very difficult to accept has to do with the way victims of such violence respond. Nicole returned to Simpson's home the day following the incident in which he physically threw her and Denise Brown out of the house. She desired to drop charges against him in the 1989 incident. At least one juror questioned this behavior. This juror suggested that she personally wouldn't have put up with such abuse; she would have fought back.

Nicole's decision to return to her abuser is typical. In January of this year, I was conducting a hearing at the Culver City court in which the defendant had beaten his girlfriend to a state of unconsciousness. The defendant claimed that he and the victim had gotten into an argument and she had stormed out of the apartment. He followed her. After he caught up to her, a stranger approached and asked for a cigarette. The stranger started attacking the victim. He defended her. In the process, she was accidentally beaten. The police, on the other hand, testified that after arriving at the scene the defendant claimed that the victim was a diabetic and had collapsed. The officer testified that when the victim regained consciousness, she informed him that her boyfriend "beat the shit out of me."

By the time I became involved in the case, months after the beating, both the victim and defendant presented the implausible story about the stranger and claimed the police were lying. Fortunately, there were so many holes and inconsistencies in this story that the judge did not believe it.

Later, I spoke to one of the officers on the case about how he felt. He told me that such cases "are a waste of time. If the victim doesn't want to prosecute, why do we have to make an arrest? Look at how much time this has wasted." I could certainly understand how he felt. It is difficult for a police officer to understand the human dynamic that explains why she recanted her statement that her boyfriend beat her. However, it was even harder for the officer to understand and accept being called a liar, according to the victim's new story. This case shows how easily the police and criminal justice system can, unwittingly, become coconspirators, joining with the victim and defendant to cover up the violence.

However, the Simpson case reveals an even more compelling tale of police and judicial complicity. There was clear evidence in *Simpson* of a police conspiracy: the conspiracy of silence that still surrounds domestic violence. Nicole told Officer Edwards during the 1989 incident that the police had been out to the house eight times and had never done anything. Reports were not filed, and the officers who responded to these incidents did not come forward. Even Mark Fuhrman, who was theoretically out to frame Simpson, walked away from the 1985 incident after Simpson characterized the dispute as a family matter.

The case also presents a tale of a judicial complicity. Simpson was sentenced to a fine and was allowed to complete a private counseling program. Some of the sessions were completed over the phone. Attitudes such as these make it clear that laws, in California and other states, that require police officers to arrest batterers are absolutely essential.

Health-care professionals, too, whether wittingly or not, play a role in the conspiracy. Nicole sought treatment for what she claimed was a "bicycle accident" in 1986. Despite the obviously suspicious circumstances, which made the event appear to be more consistent with a beating, the incident was not clearly diagnosed as domestic violence, and nothing happened as a result. In fact, only 4 to 5 percent of battered women who seek medical treatment are identified as battered.[5]

When we ask why the jury did not credit the domestic-violence evidence, we should look not only at the jurors but also at ourselves.

Changing traditional ways of thinking and behaving requires us to question our own belief systems and cherished myths.

A second major factor in the case was the media coverage. It had a distorting and prejudicial influence and contributed to a circuslike atmosphere that was detrimental to the prosecution. There are significant disadvantages to televising trials.

First, the credibility of witnesses may be adversely affected. The prosecution, and to some extent the defense, were both hampered in that potentially relevant witnesses became tainted because they sold their stories to the news media. Similarly, in the William Kennedy Smith case, the defense successfully challenged a prosecution witness's credibility because she had sold her story to a television show. One of Mike Tyson's grounds for appealing his conviction was that his accuser had hired an attorney to negotiate the rights to her story.

One of the *Simpson* jurors doubted Ron Shipp's testimony because she thought he was interested in profiting from the case. She believed this notwithstanding the fact that Ron never made any attempt to profit in any way. Interestingly, the defense witness Robert Heidstra, who claimed to have heard a struggle at Nicole's condo at 10:40 P.M., desired to profit from the case. Yet he was deemed credible. Thus, a possible desire to profit furnished another ground to selectively disbelieve witnesses.

Television is a distracting influence that alters the behavior and performance of the trial's participants. Throughout this book we have seen numerous instances where the camera coverage influenced counsel's arguments and even Judge Ito's trial procedures. For example, many of Cochran's arguments about the Mark Fuhrman issues were calculated exclusively for public consumption. Judge Ito stated that his sole reason for playing the Fuhrman-Mc-Kinny tapes in open court during the motion regarding their admissibility was for public dissemination.

Third, television coverage can affect the jury. Around the time of the opening statements, when Rock Harmon and I saw the jury for the first time, we were both concerned that the jury was unusually well dressed. Rock and I expressed the fear that when something happens to make the jurors believe that it is a special case or that they have to act differently, the prosecution is harmed. Others have expressed these sentiments. As former U.S. district judge Edward Harrington, of Boston, said, "I am disinclined to allow cameras into the courtroom because it lets jurors know this is an unusual, that is, a celebrated case. . . . When they are asked to make a judgment in a celebrated case, I think . . . it might distort the verdict."[6] Since jurors who admit to having been prejudiced as a result of media exposure are excluded from service, media coverage can have a distorting influence on the pool of potential jurors. The potential jurors remaining are either those who are least likely to be exposed to the media or least likely to admit the effects of prejudicial information.

Judge Ito ensured that there would be a jury with a low educational level when he decided during the jury selection process to automatically exclude prospective jurors who had read newspaper accounts of the upcoming trial. Only two of the jurors had graduated from college. Most received their information from tabloid TV. One read nothing except the racing forms.

Simpson is a case study of the evils of excessive media coverage of a criminal trial. The camera in the courtroom unleashed a power beyond Judge Ito's, or any judge's, control.

A related factor that explains the verdict is Simpson's celebrity status. Prosecutors I have talked to unanimously believe that it is very difficult to convict celebrities. To my knowledge, there is no broad-based scientific study of this phenomenon, perhaps because there are too few criminal cases involving celebrities for a statistical analysis.

The phenomenon of acquittals of celebrities is not new. Evidence of it can be found in cases from around the country: for example, the Mayor Marion Barry case, and the William Kennedy Smith case. However, the phenomenon is more likely to occur in California, usually in Los Angeles.

In the 1920s, a San Francisco jury acquitted Fatty Arbuckle of murder charges. In 1982, carmaker John De Lorean was acquitted of narcotics charges, notwithstanding the fact that the crime was captured on videotape. In 1994 a jury failed to convict the Menendez brothers, who became celebrities for the shotgun murders of their parents. The case was retried without television cameras and with comparatively little publicity. On March 20, 1996, the jury convicted both brothers of first-degree murder.

Actor Todd Bridges was acquitted of homicide charges. Bill Hodgman prosecuted the murder charges, and Johnnie Cochran represented Bridges. Shortly after joining the Simpson prosecution team I talked to Bill in his office about the Bridges case. Bill said that Bridges's celebrity status was the key ingredient in his acquittal. "If you're a celebrity," he added, "you can get away with murder."

In 1987, producer John Landis was acquitted of murder charges arising out of an explosion and helicopter crash on the set of *Twilight Zone.* The jury also acquitted him of relatively insignificant child-labor-law violations, which the defense conceded he had committed. After the verdict, the jury was invited to Landis's house to celebrate. Most recently, in 1996, a jury failed to convict rapper Snoop Doggy Dogg of murder charges arising out of an apparently gang-motivated shooting. A detailed analysis of each of these cases is beyond this book's scope. Later, I will discuss the De Lorean and Barry cases at greater length, since both are particularly instructive.

Simpson's celebrity status was probably the single most difficult hurdle that stood between the prosecution and a guilty verdict. His status made many people not want to face the evidence because the evidence so starkly contrasted with Simpson's public persona.

Before Nicole Brown and Ron Goldman were murdered, Simpson made a living in show business. We all knew an artificial "O. J. Simpson." But we were trying the man in court, the real Orenthal James Simpson. The best minds in the advertising industry had been employed and millions of dollars had been spent to show us he was a good guy. He was the affable fellow we saw happily running through an airport on TV commercials. It was difficult for us to imagine that the manufactured image was different from the real Simpson. As one of the male jurors asked shortly after the verdicts, "How could a man with everything commit murder?"

In this consumer society image making may contribute to our inability to hold the famous accountable for what they do. It may explain why we are willing to accept the fact that celebrities are entitled to special privileges. Although we can understand that a celebrity can get the best table in a restaurant without waiting in line, it is not tolerable to live in a society in which celebrity entitles one to commit a double murder.

* * *

The fourth major factor in understanding the verdict is race. One of the best-kept secrets of the justice system, the one that criminal-trial lawyers are not willing to publicly discuss, is that the race of the jurors significantly affects their attitudes and reactions to a case.

Having been reared in a liberal household, I did not believe that this could possibly be true. Yet after several personal and numerous vicarious experiences of verdicts that were predictably split down racial lines, I concluded that a person's race is likely to influence his or her view of the case.

In a recent *Yale Law Journal* article, George Washington University law professor Paul Butler wrote about similar discoveries he had made as a prosecutor in Washington, D.C., in 1990. He stated that among the discoveries that profoundly affected him as an African American and as a prosecutor was that "we would lose many of our cases, despite having persuaded a jury beyond a reasonable doubt that the defendant was guilty. We would lose because some black jurors would refuse to convict black defendants who they knew were guilty."[7]

In fact statistics support Butler's view. For example, in the Bronx, where juries are disproportionately black and Latino, acquittal rates of black defendants are close to three times the national average.[8]

The phenomenon of a jury's deciding to acquit a defendant even though the facts and evidence clearly show him to be guilty is called *jury nullification*. Butler calls the process of African-American jurors ignoring the law in order to acquit African-American defendants "racially based jury nullification."

When I tried the Iversen case, William Murray, a white journalist who viewed the entire trial, concluded: "The outcome reinforces the general impression that in cases involving police and race, it is now impossible for any twelve people of mixed heritage to agree on the guilt or innocence of anyone, no matter what the evidence or how serious the crime."[9] The jury was composed of eight whites, one Cambodian, and three African Americans. Three jurors concluded that Iversen was guilty of murder, and nine believed that he was guilty of involuntary manslaughter. Based on our interviews of the jurors after the mistrial, we determined that the split was along racial lines, with the white jurors favoring the lesser charge of involuntary manslaughter.

While I was on the Simpson case, *Iversen* was retried, resulting in another hung jury. Interviews of the jurors after the second trial revealed that the jurors were again divided along racial lines. One of the African Americans who voted guilty expressed bafflement that the white jurors appeared to make up their minds after only ten minutes of debate.[10] After the second trial, the judge dismissed the case.

Similarly, on April 29, 1992, a jury composed of ten whites, one Asian, and one Latino acquitted police officers of brutally beating Rodney King. Hours later, rioting erupted throughout parts of Los Angeles. The officers' retrial in federal court before a racially mixed jury resulted in convictions.

A number of studies also show that a juror's race is related to how he or she votes in a criminal case.

However, the extent to which this is a widespread phenomenon should not be exaggerated. It is well known that African-American jurors are willing to convict other African Americans and often do so. The evidence for this conclusion can be found in our office's overall 93 percent conviction rate.

Similarly, race alone probably does not explain the verdict in *Simpson.* In public statements made after the verdict, none of the jurors expressly admitted that race was a factor in their verdict. However, shortly after the verdicts were read in open court, one of the male African-American jurors gave a black power salute to Simpson.

In addition, there is indirect evidence that race played some role in the trial's outcome. Throughout the trial, and even before I joined the prosecution team, many polls demonstrated a racial disparity between white and African-American perceptions of Simpson's guilt. After the verdict, this disparity did not change. According to a *Newsweek* poll, 85 percent of African Americans agreed with the verdict. Only a third, 32 percent, of whites agreed with it.

What happens when the issue of race is combined with factors like celebrity, extensive media attention, and questions about the police? This combination presents the prosecution with a quadruple whammy that is probably impossible to overcome.

The John De Lorean and Mayor Barry cases provide insight as to what happens when race, celebrity status, and excessive media attention are combined with a defense which claims government wrongdoing. In 1982, John De Lorean, who is white, was desperate to save his failing car company. A government informant put him in contact with a drug dealer and with an FBI agent posing as a banker who was willing to finance a major cocaine deal. Although negotiations regarding the deal were captured on videotape, De Lorean was acquitted. Prof. Rita Simon, of the School of Public Affairs of the American University, said that the verdict may have represented the jurors' perception that following the law would have resulted in an injustice in that case.

After the verdict, one of the jurors summarized the jury's position. "We weren't trying to make policy or send messages, but there was a message here. . . . It's that our citizens will not let our government go too far. . . . [T]he government had gone too far in this case."[11] This verdict may have represented that jury's desire to "send a message" that alleged government overreaching in setting up a sting to capture this celebrity would not be tolerated. But the same sting to catch a notorious drug dealer would not only have been tolerated but would have been applauded.

Professor Simon conducted a detailed analysis of the trial of Washington, D.C., mayor Marion Barry. Barry was charged with, among other things, possession of cocaine. A former girlfriend, who, unbeknownst to him, was working as a government informant, invited Mayor Barry to a hotel room. There he was captured on videotape using crack cocaine. According to the trial judge, he had "never seen a stronger government case." The jury consisted of ten African-American jurors and two white jurors. Barry was convicted of only one of the fourteen counts, for perjury, but was acquitted of the possession charge, which was captured on videotape. Professor Simon concluded that a significant number of the jurors in that case "engaged in the time-honored tradition of 'jury nullification. . . . ' Marion Barry was perceived by these jurors as a black victim of the white establishment."[12]

These illustrations suggest that whenever celebrities are charged with crimes, there is tremendous media attention, and when a defense alleging government misconduct is offered, jury nullification is apt to occur. This is especially true when one of the trial's dimensions is race.

During his closing, Cochran expressly made a jury nullification argument. He told the jury to "police the police. You police them through your verdict. You are the ones to send a message. Nobody else is going to do it in this society." This argument is legally improper, and Judge Ito should have prevented it.

Juror research reveals that pro-nullification arguments like Cochran's, asking the jury to send a message, "influenced the jurors' decision-making."[13] Furthermore, such arguments lead "jurors to acquit a sympathetic defendant and convict an unsympathetic one by altering the direct weight that they assign to evidence in the decision-making process."[14] In other words, in cases where nullification is an issue and the defendant is sympathetic, jurors will assign less weight to the prosecution's evidence.

This means that evidence showing that the jurors in *Simpson* ignored or unreasonably devalued the prosecution's case would support the view that the verdict represents an instance of jury nullification. Virtually all of the jurors whom I have heard have stated that they would have convicted Simpson had they believed the evidence proved guilt beyond a reasonable doubt. I believe that these jurors are people of goodwill and that these statements were honestly made. However, what the research indicates is that in a case such as *Simpson*, many of the jurors would never have found any evidence sufficient.

The most persuasive argument that the jury did not consider the prosecution's evidence is that they took less than four hours to "deliberate." After the verdict, Jim Moret, substituting for Larry King, interviewed two Simpson jurors, David Aldana and Yolanda Crawford. Moret wanted to know how they arrived at the verdict so quickly. Aldana explained that since everyone agreed that Simpson was not guilty, it wasn't necessary to go over all the evidence. Crawford agreed. They had gone over it and listened for almost nine months: there was nothing left to discuss. Apparently, the jurors did not understand Judge Ito's clear admonitions not to form or express any conclusions regarding the case until after they had deliberated with an open mind. Moret questioned Aldana about whether, in the weeks following the verdict, Aldana had questioned the verdict. Aldana replied that certain things had come up and he had wished that he'd had someone to discuss those points with him in the jury room.

In the book *Madam Foreman*, Carrie Bess discounted the blood evidence in part "because they never tested to see what the kids' blood drops were. They never compared anybody else's blood."[15]

Presumably, she also discounted Robin Cotton's testimony that it could not have been the children's blood. The odds in the range of several million to one that someone else left the blood were not compelling to this juror.

Juror Armanda Cooley was troubled that Marcia and Chris seemed frustrated and nervous at times in court. It made her think, "If your case is so strong, why are you so frustrated?"[16] Marcia Jackson, another juror, was concerned that the Rockingham glove appeared *too wet* when it was discovered.[17] Conversely, Ms. Cooley apparently thought the glove was *too dry* when it was dropped.[18] She wanted to know why there wasn't more blood on the leaves under the glove. This opposing viewpoint might have made for an interesting topic of discussion between the two jurors, had they deliberated. They might have decided that how wet or dry the glove was or appeared to be really was not terribly relevant. The jurors' comments after the verdict provide ample support of the view that they simply ignored and unreasonably discounted the evidence and, in turn, indicate that the verdict was an example of jury nullification.

The verdict can best be understood in terms of the social forces that produced it. It has more to do with decisions made by men who died hundreds of years ago than with the tactical decisions of the prosecutors or defense lawyers. Many want to find simple explanations for the verdict. The jury was not educated enough. Clever lawyers used every trick in the book to let a guilty man go free. A bumbling prosecution botched the case. A rich man bought himself out of a murder rap. These explanations for the verdict are attractive in their simplicity. They do not require us to examine the larger social forces at work in this case. They give us permission not to look into the mirror and ask who we are. No doubt, these explanations are attractive. But they are not the truth.

Afterword: What We Can Learn From the Simpson Case

SEXISM, INFLUENCE OF THE MEDIA, AND RACISM represent some of the most challenging problems we face as a nation. Unfortunately, all three were centrally involved in the Simpson case.

We have seen that sexism makes it difficult to prosecute domestic-violence cases. This was not to deny that over the years considerable progress has been made within the criminal justice system regarding domestic violence. Over a thousand battered women's shelters are now operating in the United States. Most states, including California, make arrest of the batterer mandatory. In 1994 the federal government passed the Violence Against Women Act, which funds efforts to respond more effectively to domestic violence.

The media, too, has helped. Shows such as *Geraldo* and *Oprah* have devoted considerable time to discussing issues of domestic violence. In terms of educating the public about the subject, such programs have accomplished three things. First, they have shown that domestic violence is "bad." Second, they have made it clear that domestic violence is a widespread phenomenon. Third, they have demonstrated that it cuts across social and class barriers.[1] However, other than in these three significant but limited areas, the media have not sufficiently raised public consciousness regarding those domestic-violence issues that make such cases particularly difficult for jurors to understand.

To a lawyer, one of the most interesting developments in reforming the criminal justice system relates to the admissibility of expert testimony to explain domestic-violence issues to a jury. We need expert testimony to explain it and to help jurors place seemingly isolated instances of violence and abuse into the larger psychological and sociological context in which they occur.

In chapters 3 and 5, we saw the constraints that the current California Evidence Code placed on our efforts to introduce such testimony. The law is so sexist, it would be laughable if it were not so tragic. Its practical effect is to generally allow expert testimony to explain the behavior of the domestic-violence victim while disallowing such testimony to explain that of the defendant, the very person whose actions are presumably at issue.

Under current psychological paradigms, expert testimony about domestic violence emphasizes the victim's traumatization, generally described as battered woman's syndrome. The victim's deteriorating psychological state incapacitates her and makes her unable to respond rationally to her predicament. She wants to escape her situation, but she cannot. Logically, evidence of this condition would make her appear to be a less credible and rational individual. Meanwhile, absolutely no expert evidence can be admitted to similarly analyze her tormenter. The jury can hear absolutely no evidence of the psychological dynamic that accounts for his behavior—his desire for power and control. The lack of logic of this position is striking. Yet this irrational view represents current California law.

If admitted, expert testimony about the batterer might shift emphasis from the victim's pathology to the defendant's need to maintain power and control. Such evidence is very helpful to juries. Studies of how jurors make their decisions show that when social-science evidence is presented, jurors do consider and rely on it in rendering their verdict.[2] Specifically, introduction of evidence on battered woman's syndrome significantly improves the ability of jurors to understand the victim and influences jury verdicts.[3]

In addition to changing California law to allow expert testimony about the batterer, other evidentiary reforms may help make domestic violence more understandable to juries. The California Evidence Code should be amended to specify that in domestic violence cases, including homicides, evidence that the defendant abused the victim on prior occasions is admissible. Such a rule would have eliminated the need for the time-consuming domestic-violence hearing that occurred in the Simpson case.

Finally, the rules of hearsay should be amended to permit the victim's out-of-court statements expressing her fear of the defendant, such as Nicole's diaries, to be admitted when they are relevant to prove her mental state. Together, such amendments would express a clear legislative mandate to give juries the maximum amount of information to understand and correctly decide domestic-violence cases.

Moreover, a program should be funded to improve law enforcement's response to domestic-violence cases. We know that a major problem that invariably presents itself in such cases is a recanting victim. One solution is for police officers responding to a domestic-violence call to immediately turn on a microcassette recorder upon arrival. Imagine how much more compelling the 1989 incident would have been if Officer Edwards was able to play a tape of Nicole's frantic pleas and Simpson's angry rantings throughout his encounter. The LAPD does not purchase microcassette recorders for its officers. However, several officers have purchased them with their own money. I have asked some of these officers, "Why don't you record what happens from the time you arrive?" They invariably respond, "The department won't buy the tape for us. I use this recorder as sparingly as possible."

Similarly, victims should be asked to give videotaped statements to the police at the station as soon as possible. Such evidence would prove invaluable to prosecutors if the victim, fearing for her safety, later recants.

Hopefully, one simple lesson learned from the Simpson case is that televising high-profile trials will never happen again. The Simpson case illustrates the dangers of televised trials. Southwestern University School of Law professor Robert Lind cataloged the parade of horribles the media committed during the Simpson trial in the *Southwestern University Law Review*:

> Any semblance of journalistic ethics and responsibility has been left in the hallowed halls of journalism schools. The media has violated [Judge Ito's] court orders by broadcasting confidential conversations between Mr. Simpson and his attorney, interviewing attorneys in the hallway outside the courtroom, and televising the identity of an alternate juror.

In addition, the media had rushed to judgment by relying on single sources, used digitally distorted photographs on magazine covers, compromised witnesses by paying for interviews before they testified and hounded others.[4]

As Professor Lind intimated, the only restrictions Judge Ito placed on the media were that no interviews could be conducted outside his courtroom and that confidential conversations and the identity of jurors could not be revealed. Other than that, the press had free reign inside and outside the courthouse. Repeated breaches of the few rules Judge Ito had imposed did not lead to discontinuing the coverage. The only exception was that coverage was temporarily suspended for one brief period during the closing arguments because the camera took a close-up shot of the privileged notepads on defense counsel's table.

One might wonder whether there is anything positive about cameras in the courtroom. There are basically only two arguments supporters of cameras in the courtroom use to advance their position. The first argument assumes that televising courtroom proceedings advances public understanding of the third branch of government, the judicial branch. This argument is entirely inconsistent with the available evidence. As was amply illustrated throughout this book, the commentary on television, and by other media, promoted confusion and misunderstanding about what really occurred. For example, the observations of many "legal experts" sometimes amounted to commentary on which side was the most entertaining. Entertainment is not the purpose of any court proceeding. But this seemed to be the major reason for the coverage of the Simpson trial.

The reporting on the case tended to be fragmented, unanalytic, and often erroneous. After the trial, I discovered one reason for this. A journalist, who regularly appeared on a panel discussion of the case on evening TV, told me that many of his "expert" colleagues "didn't even watch the trial. One of them prepared for the discussion of the day's events by reading the *L.A. Times* summaries of the trial from the day before."

I asked another TV expert commentator about the issue of preparation. Several months after the trial, we had lunch and discussed various aspects of the case. I asked, "Didn't you have to watch the trial all day in order to comment on the events in the evening?"

"No," he replied. "After I realized they [the producers of the program] weren't interested in your being right, just in your being interesting, it was easy. It was lots of fun.''

Another explanation for the misinformation and shoddy analysis was the stunning lack of qualifications of many of the media "legal experts." Unknown to the viewing audience, some "experts," such as former district attorney Ira Reiner, had never prosecuted a felony case in their entire careers; others had little or no homicide experience. However, since much of the case was show business, it might have been more fitting to have Jerry Seinfeld and Jay Leno cover the trial. In many ways their shticks were just as illuminating, and certainly more entertaining, than the "expert" analysts' critiques.

Jeffrey Toobin, who regularly covered the case for the *New Yorker*, in an October 23, 1995, article, wrote some introspective assessments of his role as a member of the press in covering the case. He discussed the pressure reporters were under to present and entertain the implausible positions the defense advanced. "The case against Simpson was simply overwhelming. When we said otherwise we lied to the audience that trusted us." He also discussed the willingness of reporters to engage in the horse-race method of reporting. "[G]enerally, I did my duty in the sound bite culture into which I had willingly propelled myself: Braves in five; Jets with the points."[5]

Social-science research supports the view that media coverage distorts rather than illuminates the judicial process. A study conducted by two social scientists from the University of Delaware concluded: "Our analysis of the content and style of media coverage of legal issues leads to the conclusion that the media mirror presents a distorted view of law."[6]

The second argument advanced in support of televised trials is a legal one: The First Amendment gives the public a right to know, and the Sixth Amendment guarantees a public trial. However, these legal arguments are not supported by the case law. There is none to support this view. However, based on my reading of the case law, there appears to be a sliding scale in determining whether press coverage violates the right to a fair trial. Press coverage does not violate the right to a fair trial except possibly on those rare occasions when it creates a circuslike atmosphere. In such cases, the trial judge is required to take steps to mitigate the effects of the press coverage, which can include barring camera coverage in the courtroom, imposing gag orders on the attorneys, restricting cameras around the courthouse, regulating press access to the courthouse, and requiring jury sequestration and curative jury instructions (instructing the jury about disregarding media influences).

These steps can and should be used in any high-profile case. Court rules should be amended to prohibit cameras in high-profile cases and to specify what other curative steps a judge may take to remedy media abuses.

Clearly, the most challenging issues the case posed deal with race and racism. In the previous chapter I argued that the verdict represents an instance of "jury nullification" produced by powerful social forces. Following the Simpson case, there has been more public discussion about this concept.

Interestingly, not everyone believes "jury nullification" is wrong. In his lengthy and carefully reasoned article in the *Yale Law Journal*, discussed in chapter 41, Paul Butler, an African-American law professor, concludes that "the race of a black defendant is sometimes a legally and morally appropriate factor for jurors to consider in reaching a verdict of not guilty or for an individual juror to consider in refusing to vote for a conviction." According to Butler, too many African Americans are in prison, and African-American jurors decide whether their community will benefit from the defendant's being incarcerated. He argues that it is the "moral responsibility of black jurors to emancipate some guilty black outlaws."

Under the old common-law tradition, juries did have the authority to acquit a guilty defendant on the grounds that they believed that a conviction would work an injustice. Today, in California, as in almost every other state, there is no legally recognized doctrine called "jury nullification." Jurors must convict guilty defendants whether they agree with the law or not. However, as a practical matter, if jurors admittedly fail to convict, even though they believed the defendant to have been guilty, the concept of double jeopardy prevents the prosecution from appealing the not-guilty verdict or otherwise setting it aside. A not-guilty verdict is final. Hence, while a right to jury nullification is not legally recognized in California or most other states, in practice it does happen, and there is no legal remedy to correct it when it does.

Today many people who advocate jury nullification are right-wing extremists. Occasionally, I have seen these groups pass out pamphlets to jurors entering the courthouses informing them of

their "right to jury nullification." Professor Butler joins these advo-
cates of jury nullification. "African Americans should embrace the
anti-democratic nature of jury nullification because it provides them
with the power to determine justice in a way that majority rule does
not." Arguing that race-based juror nullification should be carried
out on some principled basis, Professor Butler proposes that African-
American jurors acquit guilty African-American defendants when it
is "in the best interests of the black community." To describe how to
make this determination, he gives this illustration. "A juror might
vote for acquittal, for example, when a poor woman steals from
Tiffany's, but not when the same woman steals from her next door
neighbor."

The fatal problem with Professor Butler's theory is that any form
of jury nullification leads to anarchy. It creates unpredictable, random results. It produces a system that is the antithesis of law. Consider the following hypothetical case: An African-American
defendant and his white accomplice break into a large electronics
store owned by a Korean American. They steal a large-screen TV for
their own personal enjoyment. The store is located in a mixed-race
neighborhood. Should the jury acquit the African-American defendant because the store is not owned by an African American? Or
should the jury convict because the store is contributing to the economic activity of a minority neighborhood? Suppose the prosecutor
discovers that the store owner is heavily involved in supporting the
African-American business community. Shouldn't the jurors be allowed to hear that evidence to better assess whether a conviction is
"in the interests of the black community?"

Should the rules of evidence be changed to allow such evidence
in cases where African Americans are tried? If the jury decides to
acquit the African-American defendant, does fairness dictate that
they must also acquit his white accomplice? Alternatively, if the jury
first deliberates and decides that the white accomplice is guilty, do
they now have to convict the African American even though doing
so would not otherwise be in "the interests of the black community"? What if another white defendant burglarized the same store
on a separate occasion under similar circumstances and was tried
before a different jury? Should he be convicted?

Those who subscribe to the racially based jury-nullification view
cannot offer any principled answers to these questions. However, I
must applaud Professor Butler for his willingness to both acknowl-

edge and discuss the phenomenon of racially based jury nullification by African-American jurors.

Steps can and should be taken to address the issue of jury nullification. We may now be witnessing the beginning of a frightening development in American history: people from the extreme right and other radicals openly espousing an un-American, anti-law-enforcement agenda. If we desire to prevent a new age of lawlessness, we must act. It is a simple fact that some people will refuse to uphold the law. It is often said that in our legal system, "where there is a wrong, there is a remedy." This means that the law always provides some means of redressing any injustice. The exception to this rule is that under the concept of double jeopardy, when a jury in a criminal case violates their oath to follow the law, there is no recourse.

Americans have an almost religious belief that the rules protecting a criminal accused were divinely inspired when our Founding Fathers wrote the Bill of Rights. Therefore, any proposed refinement of those rules made after 1780 constitutes heresy. It may be time to discuss reconsidering some of those rules. We might consider whether, in cases where there is clear and convincing evidence that jury misconduct resulted in an acquittal, the prosecution should be permitted to retry the defendant.

Less ambitious measures should also be implemented. California is heading in the right direction in attempting to change the law to permit less than a unanimous jury verdict, a verdict of 10–2. In lengthy cases, such as *Simpson*, a disproportionate number of government workers and retired people serve. Others claim "financial hardship." To draw a wider, more representative cross section of potential jurors, jury service should be made truly mandatory. Companies should be required to compensate employees for jury service, and/or juror fees should be increased.

Several years ago, California voters implemented a measure to restrict the ability of attorneys to conduct probing questioning during jury selection. Although this measure was intended to eliminate abusive and unduly time consuming questioning, overall it was a step in the wrong direction. Jury-selection procedures should be reexamined to *enhance* the ability of lawyers to identify people who may not follow the law. On the other hand, trial judges should maintain sufficient discretionary powers to limit the abuses that were possible before the law was changed. Perhaps a proper balance can be struck by permitting a panel of jury-selection experts and attorneys to design standardized jury questionnaires for a variety of typical cases. This would increase the amount of relevant information lawyers have about the jury, and make jury selection less of a guessing game, without increasing the amount of court time spent on jury selection.

One thing I find particularly interesting about my job is the exposure to sections of our community I would otherwise not have experienced. In 1989, I was assigned to a juvenile courthouse on Central Avenue in South Central Los Angeles. Until then, like many white residents of Los Angeles, I had never seen this neighborhood.

Sometimes I had the privilege of having lunch with Judge William Clay, an elderly, avuncular African-American man who grew up in the very neighborhood where he sat as a superior court judge. He would tell me stories about the vibrant life on Central Avenue that he knew as a young man. It was a neighborhood filled with nightclubs, restaurants, a world-class hotel, and jazz joints where one could hear Duke Ellington, Louis Armstrong, and Billie Holiday. His description bore little resemblance to the endless blight that characterizes the neighborhood today. In the Iversen case, I spent a significant amount of time in South Central interviewing African-American tow-truck drivers, body-shop owners, and community activists in search of witnesses who could testify against Iversen. Nowhere did I observe the kind of lively neighborhood Judge Clay described.

Through such experiences, I have seen for myself that our community is characterized by de facto apartheid. And, apparently, to the extent that it has changed since the passage of the 1964 Fair Housing Act, it has gotten worse. Some researchers have described the new state of affairs as "hypersegregation," where African Americans are not only segregated by race but also by class. This "hypersegregation" links high rates of African-American poverty with high rates of African-American segregation.

These neighborhoods are also characterized by spiraling crime rates. It is the public's widespread perception that crime rates, in general, are mushrooming out of control. That perception is wrong. In fact, the FBI's *Uniform Crime Report*, released in November 1995, indicates that crime rates are actually falling.[7] Between 1990 and 1994, murders were down 4.3 percent. During the same period, property crimes fell 8.5 percent. Burglaries fell 15.7 percent. There is one exception to this downward trend in crime rates. They are rising for African Americans.

According to Douglas Massey, professor of sociology at the University of Pennsylvania,

> blacks are now more likely to become victims of violence than at any point during the last two decades. Black teenagers are eleven times more likely to be shot to death and nine times more likely to be murdered than their white counterparts. Among black males, in particular, homicide rates have skyrocketed. . . . This alarming trend has prompted some observers to dub young black men "an endangered species."[8]

These findings simply confirm what those of us in the criminal justice system have known for a long time. Our system systematically devalues African-American life.

Former San Jose police chief Joseph McNamara, in a recent law-review article, tells a story about his experiences as a white New York police officer. As a rookie, he arrested an African-American suspect for murdering an African-American victim. He felt good about the arrest. However, his colleagues were indifferent because "both the perp and the victim were niggers."[9] Even today the phrase "no humans involved" (NHI) is one we in law enforcement have heard and know that some police officers use to describe such cases.

In December 1987, as the gang wars in South Central and East Los Angeles were turning neighborhoods into slaughterhouses, a south-side gang shooting mistakenly resulted in the death of a young Asian woman in fashionable Westwood Village. Merchants clamored for more police protection, which was immediately granted. The murder occurred within blocks of where I lived and had attended college, at UCLA. After the murder, I continued to frequent Westwood. I felt safer than ever. After all, there was literally a police officer on every block, and the streets into the village were barricaded and guarded by uniformed officers. A local politician offered a huge reward to apprehend the "urban terrorists."

Meanwhile, as I was benefiting from the increased security, the African-American community was justifiably outraged. The disproportionate law enforcement response in Westwood could not be justified when, in corners of South Central smaller than Westwood, multiple gang murders were a weekly occurrence.[10]

The devaluation of African-American life in our legal system can clearly be seen by studying the outcomes of death-penalty cases. The Congressional Accounting Office reviewed twenty-eight studies showing that killers of whites, regardless of their race, were more likely to be sentenced to death than were killers of African Americans. In the state of California, 2.6 percent of murderers of black victims were condemned compared to 6.3 percent of those who killed whites. In some jurisdictions outside of California studies show that "[a] homicide in which a white killed a white was more than five times more likely to be handled as a capital case than a homicide in which a black killed a black."[11]

Ironically, this form of racism actually works to the benefit of the typical African-American defendant. The reason is that crime in our country is overwhelmingly intraracial. That is, African-American defendants tend to victimize other African Americans. Whites tend to victimize other whites. According to the latest statistics from the FBI's *Uniform Crime Report*, 94 percent of the time an African-American murder victim was killed by an African-American assailant.[12] Because of the victim's race, his assailant is less likely to be sentenced to death.

This may be precisely why there is no convincing statistical evidence that African-American defendants are discriminated against within the criminal justice system. After reviewing the host of studies on the issue, even academicians—who seem predisposed to finding such evidence of discrimination—are forced to conclude that no persuasive evidence of such discrimination exists. Kathleen Daly, associate professor of sociology at the University of Michigan, reviewed the research on race and sentencing. "To summarize the body of statistical research on race and sentencing, overt or 'direct effects' of race may not be commonly found."[13] A study of the California judicial system found that when the defendant's criminal history and other legitimate factors are considered, race plays no role in determining his sentence.[14] In short, there is no convincing evidence that minority defendants are prosecuted, convicted, or sentenced disproportionately to the rates at which they commit crime.

Conversely, according to Professor Daly, the statistics show that

some violent crimes (murder and rape) with white victims receive a more active prosecutorial response and a more severe sentence than those with black victims. In the aggregate, this means that white defendants are subject to harsher punishment than black defendants since most violent crimes are intraracial. The problem then is how to redress the devaluation of black bodies. The answer, it appears, is to increase the punishment of black defendants.[15]

Living in a racist society does not necessarily result in discrimination against African-American defendants any more than living in a sexist society results in discrimination against female defendants. In fact, females constitute only 5 percent of the prison population and only 1 percent of those on death row.[16] If men have more power and control within our society and within the criminal justice system than women, why are women defendants so disproportionally underrepresented? The reason is that sexism, like racism, expresses itself within the criminal justice system in ways other than discrimination against those who are charged with crimes. Those of us who work in the criminal justice system almost never see any evidence that racism or sexism is directed against minority or female defendants.

Our criminal justice system has failed to take the necessary steps to reduce crime rates and improve public safety for African Americans. Both anecdotal and empirical evidence clearly demonstrates that herein lies the racism to be found within our criminal justice system. This racism results in ever-increasing numbers of African-American crime victims, not massive police conspiracies to frame beloved American sports stars.

The victims of this racism are not African-American defendants but African-American crime victims. This racism does not produce evidence-planting white police officers but, rather, some cops who are indifferent to the suffering of millions of African-American crime victims throughout this country.

For this reason, I found the allegations of racism in the Simpson case particularly painful. Suggesting that the problem of racism produced a conspiracy to frame O. J. Simpson diverts attention and public debate away from the real problem and focuses it on a fictitious one.

William Raspberry, a prominent African-American journalist for the *Washington Post*, in his book *Looking Backward at Us* discussed the willingness of African-American jurors in Washington, D.C., to accept the defense conspiracy theory in the Mayor Barry trial. "The trouble with laying the problems of black America at the feet of white conspirators is that it frustrates the search for solutions. Define the troubles of black officials in terms of conspiracy, and blacks find themselves coming to the defense of people they ought to be kicking out of office." (paragraphing omitted)

The criminal justice system must play a critical role in any strategy intended to reverse the growing problem facing African-American communities. Law and order within the inner cities must be restored. This is necessary in order to permit attempts to attract new businesses into these areas and provide people with the education and job skills they require.

There is no need for debate as to how best to accomplish this end. We know how. A growing body of evidence clearly demonstrates that community policing is highly effective in reducing crime. Even before the concept of "community policing" was part of the modern lexicon, we knew that massive increases in police presence have an impact on lowering violent crime. During the 1984 Olympics, hosted in Los Angeles, the maintenance of public order was briefly given almost the amount of attention it deserves. LAPD deployment was increased throughout the city, although mostly near Olympic venues. According to my calculations, Los Angeles experienced a 9 percent decline in homicides from 1983 to 1984. After the Olympics, the increased enforcement effort ended. However, rates did not instantly rise: They began to crawl forward toward today's staggering highs of about 850 homicides in the city each year.

It is now clear that scarce law enforcement dollars must be redirected to make community policing a priority.

Another issue the Simpson case clearly raises is whether Mark Fuhrman personifies a significant problem within the LAPD. In chapter 10, "The Mark Fuhrman We Thought We Knew," I described my own observations of Mark Fuhrman over a nine-year period and how the Fuhrman I knew in 1987, as a patrol officer, was a different person than the detective I knew in 1994. In my experience, this change is very common. After years of police work on the streets, by the time an officer makes detective, I have often noticed a higher level of growth, maturity, and greater tolerance. I have often wondered exactly what accounts for this change.

If we take the career of Mark Fuhrman, for example, we know that early in his career he worked in a minority community.

I met him in approximately 1987, after he had been assigned to the west side of Los Angeles, a predominantly white area. After nine years of law enforcement in a predominantly white area and as a homicide detective, Mark had undoubtedly learned that while minorities may be statistically more likely to become involved in violent crime, white Americans also commit their fair share. My own personal observations led me to believe that white police officers who are assigned to minority neighborhoods tend to develop prejudiced attitudes. However, these attitudes may be reversible when the officers are transferred out of such areas.

The psychological research supports this view. Some research has been conducted on police prejudice in multiracial countries throughout the world. Such studies have found that "police who regularly encounter members of a racial minority performing antisocial acts are provided with ample evidence to support the development of prejudice. Equally, one would expect police who do not have significant negative contact with racial minorities not to become as prejudiced as those police who do."[17] Furthermore, "[d]espite the apparent success of the Academy in containing prejudice, recruits quickly succumbed to environmental and occupational pressures once they were stationed in the community. As both motivational and cognitive theories suggest, prejudice developed as a function of intergroup contact."[18]

Publicly, prejudiced attitudes by police have been exposed by the Rodney King beating and the Fuhrman-McKinny tapes. The police attempt to explain such cases using what is termed the "rotten apple" theory. Under this theory, incidents of racism represent aberrations committed by a small minority of "rotten apples." It was upsetting to me that this theory was advanced during the various defense arguments on the Fuhrman issue. In fact, Cochran actually used the imagery of "rotten apples" during his closing argument.

My personal experience, as well as scholarly studies, supports the view that racism within the police department is not confined to a small number of "rotten apples." Rather, it is a significant phenomenon. It cannot be adequately addressed until it is acknowledged by us.

Currently, we do not know how best to tackle this issue. The LAPD now carries out cultural sensitivity training for its officers.

However, we do not know whether such training is effective. One study found that academy training programs designed to reduce prejudice have no significant long-term impact. The authors suggest that "it may be that the youth and inexperience of new recruits make them particularly susceptible to training decay, and more resilient changes could be obtained by delivering ongoing training to police throughout their careers."[19] Unfortunately, I found few recent psychological studies that track police prejudice in officers over time. More research is necessary to determine whether academy training, in-service training, and/or deployment changes are the best approach to combating this problem.

The LAPD and other major police departments should implement a broad-based, long-term study to determine how to reduce prejudiced attitudes of officers.

Finally, the Simpson case raises the issue of whether it was proper for the defense to have introduced race into the case. Just as I was less shocked than the average person about the revelations of Mark Fuhrman's racist ramblings on the Fuhrman-McKinny tapes, I was also less disappointed than the average person about the role that race played in Simpson's defense. Bob Shapiro decried the fact that the race card was dealt from the bottom of the deck. But it was not the first time it has happened in a criminal trial or in many other contexts.

In my childhood, I can remember the mayoral race between Mayor Yorty, a white, and Tom Bradley, an African American. Yorty's campaign used posters depicting a picture of Yorty and a picture of Bradley side by side. The caption read: "The difference is clear." More recently, George Bush's infamous Willie Horton ad is a graphic illustration of playing the race card from the bottom of the deck. Until we, as a nation, decide that the president of our country is prohibited from engaging in such tactics, how can we condemn Johnnie Cochran for his defense of Simpson?

On the day I finished this book, I decided to go to the Museum of Tolerance in Los Angeles. At the entrance to the exhibit, a visitor encounters two doors. One is for "prejudiced" people and the other for "unprejudiced." The "unprejudiced" door was locked.

Interestingly, inside the exhibit, I noticed that it was possible to exit through the "unprejudiced" door.

I saw images of the Rodney King beating, the L.A. riots, the Reginald Denny beating, and—in my mind's eye—the unrecorded image of Officer Iversen shooting John Daniels from behind. I wondered whether someday images from the Simpson trial would be added to this exhibit.

After finishing the tour, in a strange way I felt a sense of relief. The Simpson case was not a personal loss or a loss for our office but simply part of a long historical tradition in this community and in our society. As I walked to my car to return home, I wondered whether this experience would finally provide a sense of closure for me. I thought how fitting it would be if I should finally come to understand this case here in Los Angeles, in a museum of human cruelty and injustice.

Notes

Chapter 41: The Verdict

1. Nancy McCarthy, "California Attorneys See Hung Jury in Simpson Trial," *California Bar Journal* (June 1995): 1.
2. Ibid.
3. Ibid., 7
4. Vincent Bugliosi, "Bugliosi for the Prosecution," *Playboy* (November 1994): 193.
5. Roger Douglas, "Social Class and Court Outcomes: Making Sense of the Empirical Literature," *Law in Context* 12 (1994): 97.

Chapter 42: Why the Jury Found Simpson Not Guilty

1. Jennifer Robertson, "Domestic Violence and Health Care: An Ongoing Dilemma," Albany Law Review (1995): 1194.
2. Ibid., 1197; citing Mark Rosenberg, et al., "Interpersonal Violence: Homicide and Spousal Abuse, Public Health and Preventive Medicine" (1986): 1412.
3. *Los Angeles Times* staff, *In Pursuit of Justice* (1995): 92.
4. Ida Johnson and Robert Sigler, "Domestic Violence: A Comparative Study of Perceptions and Attitudes Toward Domestic Abuse Cases Among Social Service and Criminal Justice Professionals," *Journal of Criminal Justice* 22, no. 3 (1994): 247.
5. Robertson, "Domestic Violence," citing Wendy Goldberg and Michael Tomlanovich, "Domestic Violence Victims in the Emergency Department," *Journal of the American Medical Association* 251, (1984): 3263.
6. Cristo Lassiter, "Put the Lens Cap Back on Cameras in the Courtroom: A Fair Trial Is at Stake," *Trial Lawyers Guide* 38 (1994): 397.
7. Paul Butler, "Racially Based Jury Nullification: Black Power in the Criminal Justice System," *Yale Law Journal* 105 (1995): 678.
8. Editorial staff, "Unreasonable Doubt," *New Republic* (October 23, 1995): 8.
9. William Murray, "The Tow Truck Buster" *Buzz* (April 1995): 111.

10. Ibid., 111.

11. Rita Simon, "Jury Nullification, or Prejudice and Ignorance in the Marion Barry Trial," *Journal of Criminal Justice* 20 (1992): 266.

12. Ibid., 265.

13. Richard Wiener, et al., "The Social Psychology of Jury Nullification: Predicting When Jurors Disobey the Law," *Journal of Applied Social Psychology* 21 (1991): 1381.

14. Ibid.

15. Armanda Cooley, Carrie Bess, Marsha Rubin-Jackson, Tom Byrnes, and Mike Walker, *Madam Foreman*. Los Angeles: Dove Books, 1995, 202.

16. Ibid., 97.

17. Ibid., 122.

18. Ibid., 161.

Afterword: What We Can Learn From the Simpson Case

1. Sheryl McCarthy, "The Role of the Media in Domestic Violence Cases: A Journalist's Perspective," *Albany Law Review* 58 (1995): 1235.

2. Comment, "Social Science Research in Domestic Violence Law: A Proposal to Focus on Evidentiary Use," *Albany Law Review* 58 (1995): 1304.

3. Ibid.

4. Robert Lind, "Book Review: Defender of the Faith in the Midst of the Simpson Circus," *Southwestern University Law Review* (1995): 1215–16.

5. Jeffrey Toobin, "A Horrible Human Event," *New Yorker* (October 23, 1995), 48.

6. Valerie Hans and Juliet Dee, "Media Coverage of Law, Its Impact on Juries and the Public," *American Behavioral Scientist*, 35 (1991): 136.

7. U.S. Department of Justice, Federal Bureau of Investigation, "Crime in the United States 1994: Uniform Crime Reports" (1995): 15.

8. Douglas Massey, "Getting Away With Murder: Segregation and Violent Crime in Urban America," *University of Pennsylvania Law Review* 143 (1995): 1203.

9. Joseph McNamara, "The Police and Violent Crime," *Washington and Lee Law Review* 51 (1994), 500.

10. Mike Davis, *City of Quartz*. New York: Random House, 1990, 271.

11. Robert Bohm, "Capital Punishment in Two Judicial Circuits in Georgia," *Law and Human Behavior* 18 (1994): 326.

12. U.S. Department of Justice, infra, "Crime in the United States 1994," 14.

13. Kathleen Daly, "Criminal Justice System Practices as Racist, White, and Racialized," *Washington and Lee Law Review* 51 (1994): 444.

14. Stephen Klein, Joan Petersilia, and Susan Turner, "Race and Imprisonment Decisions in California," *Science* 247 (1990): 812.

15. Daly, "Criminal Justice System," 447.

16. Ibid., 432.

17. Richard Wortley and Ross Homel, "Police Prejudice as a Function of Training and Outgroup Contact," *Law and Human Behavior* 19 (1995): 307

18. Ibid., 314.

19. Ibid., 315.

Source Note

The portions of this book that discuss what happened in court during the trial are based on the approximately 45,000-page trial transcript. In order to present this information in the confines of this book, significant editing was required. This made it possible to use as much of the witnesses' actual words as possible rather than paraphrasing. The editing does not change the substance or flavor of the testimony. The following represents the techniques used.

Under Marcia Clark's questioning, Kato Kaelin testified as follows (emphasis added):

> Q. And he never said I don't like the idea of a man living under the same roof with Nicole? He never said that?
> A. That *it wasn't right for me to be in the same house, a man in that same house with Nicole and the children.*
> Q. And what did you take that to mean, Mr. Kaelin?
> A. I moved out. I wasn't—
> Q. What did you take that to mean, Mr. Kaelin?
> A. That *it could possibly have been that he was thinking that I might be with Nicole.*
> Q. *Sexually?*
> A. Possibly that he was thinking that, yes.

This exchange was edited as follows: Kato got the feeling that Simpson felt "it wasn't right for me to be in the same house, a man in that same house with Nicole and the children. . . . [I]t could possibly have been that he was thinking that I might be with Nicole [sexually]." I used ellipses (. . .) to show that material was excised between the beginning and end of the witness's statement. In this case, a number of Marcia's questions were edited out, converting Kato's statement into a narrative. The brackets [ ] indicate that I added a word to make the meaning more understandable. Here I added the word [sexually], since Kato agreed to the use of that word.

I believe this technique is more accurate than paraphrasing and allows readers to form their own opinions regarding the meaning and significance of the testimony. It has also allowed me to condense large sections of transcript.

Extensive sections of the book relate behind-the-scenes meetings between the attorneys and meetings with the witnesses. These scenes represent my best effort to re-create for the reader what actually happened and what it felt like to have been there. Obviously, I did not have a tape recorder during such events. I *reconstructed* the dialogue based on my memory of what occurred and my general knowledge regarding how the parties spoke and thought and their speech patterns and mannerisms. In the case of many such meetings, such as an interview I participated in with Kato Kaelin, and the two scenes in chapter 39, "Fifty-five Guilty Coincidences," and chapter 40, "The Last Word," relating our preparation for closing arguments, I was able to refresh my recollection with notes prepared for or during the meetings. I have done my best to accurately and faithfully dramatize these events.

The book relates a number of comments by Judge Ito and the defense lawyers that were not on the record. This dialogue I clearly remembered. These comments are close to what was actually said verbatim.

Index

Forms, crime-scene, page 4 of, 137–39,
141
Foss, Joseph, 74
Four-way linkage, 249–50
Fuhrman, Mark, 29, 61, 65, 66, 70–95,
80, 97, 104, 123, 282–308, 315,
333, 349, 370–71
Bailey's cross-examination of, 87,
90–94, 132
Fifth Amendment and, 305–6
planting evidence allegations and,
72–73, 77–78, 81–83, 87–88, 90–
94, 330–32
racism allegations and, 71–79, 82–
87, 91–94, 282–95, 297–308
tapes of, 78, 243, 253, 282–95, 299–
301, 307–8, 350, 371, 372
testimony of, 87–90, 95, 151, 305–7
Fung, Dennis, 44, 77, 85, 96–98, 113,
118–19, 120–24, 144–56, 160, 162,
172–73, 179, 181, 239, 243, 245,
330, 332, 339
Scheck's cross-examination of, 132–
34, 137–41, 145–46, 183, 195, 257
testimony of, 121–24, 126–29, 132–
42, 144–48, 159, 164, 171, 181,
183, 196, 242, 264, 274

Garcetti, Gil, 5, 24–25, 43, 84, 135,
166, 310, 337
Garvey, Candace, 57
Gate, rear, blood on, 61, 65, 68, 88,
95, 98, 120, 127–28, 146, 165, 184,
239, 315, 332
EDTA in, 236–37
General Motors, 227
Gerchas, Mary Anne, 43
Gerdes, John, 238–43, 266–71, 314,
329
Giss, Harvey, 117
Gloves, 67, 150–51, 204–11, 310, 313–
14
Bundy, 61, 65, 66, 87–88, 98, 120,
145, 206, 294–95, 312, 320
handling evidence and, 181, 247–48
Rockingham, 51, 61, 77–78, 81–83,
87–88, 90, 92–94, 104, 120, 145,
149, 150, 183, 184, 206, 210, 222,
228, 239, 284, 294–95, 314, 317,
320, 323, 357
hair and fiber evidence, 226–30
sales receipt for, 204–5

shrinkage of, 208–11
Goldberg, David, 21, 124–25, 132,
133–34, 197, 335
Goldberg, Dru, 21, 197–99, 335
Goldberg, Hank M.
assigned to Simpson trial, 6–7
chain of custody evidence and, 111–
96. *See also* DNA evidence; *and
specific topics*
cross-examination by, 242–45, 261–
69, 295
preparation, 246–55
father of, 21, 124–25, 132, 133, 197–
99, 335
Iversen case and, 353–66
legal background of, 20–22
mother of, 21, 124–25, 132, 133,
197, 334–35
sister Dru, 197–99
Goldberg, Luke, 21, 133, 197
Golden, Irwin, 200–201
Goldman, Fred, 11
Goldman, Kim, 11, 306
Goldman, Patti, 11
Goldman, Ron, 10–11, 34, 38, 133
DNA evidence, 177, 184
murder of, 2, 11, 59–61, 69, 200–
203
Good, Connie, 29–30, 40
Gordon, Scott, 16–18, 22, 24–26, 36–
38, 62, 72, 210, 309–19, 321, 346–
47
Guns, 3–4, 216

Hair and fiber evidence, 225–30, 295,
316–17, 341
Handshaking incident, 147
Hannak, Krel, 298
Harmon, Rock, 10, 41–42, 113, 118,
119, 126, 144, 173, 174, 180–82,
182, 188, 191, 192, 237, 242, 264,
275, 278, 309, 324, 326, 330, 333–
35, 339, 350
Harrington, Edward, 351
Harris, Jeanette, 82
Hartford Courant, 252
Hearsay, 39, 232, 276, 360
Heidstra, Robert, 233, 315, 350
Hodge, Roderic, 299, 303–5
Hodgman, Bill, 6–7, 9, 10, 12–13, 42,
68, 111, 113–14, 141, 242–43,
276–77, 309, 352